T0329769

U.S. INTERNATIONAL MONETARY POLICY

WRITTEN UNDER THE AUSPICES OF THE
CENTER FOR INTERNATIONAL AFFAIRS,
HARVARD UNIVERSITY

A LIST OF OTHER CENTER PUBLICATIONS
OF RELATED INTEREST APPEARS
AT THE BACK OF THIS BOOK

U.S. INTERNATIONAL MONETARY POLICY

Markets, Power, and Ideas as
Sources of Change

JOHN S. ODELL

Princeton University Press

FOR MARGARET

CONTENTS

LIST OF TABLES

LIST OF CHARTS

PREFACE AND ACKNOWLEDGMENTS

This book is concerned, at a general level, with the problem of explaining and anticipating states' foreign economic policies. None of our previous approaches to this problem has been fully satisfactory, and future work will no doubt proceed in multiple directions. This book selects one country and one family of policy issues and looks at them in detail. The validity of its arguments for other countries and other issues can be known only when those are investigated directly. I hope the book will prove useful to readers concerned with the same general problem in other settings.

Writing this book has been an education in itself. The following pages will show plainly which thinkers have taught me through their writings. I have also learned how supportive the communities of scholars and officials can be when approached by a new member. I am grateful for help of many kinds.

This book appeared in its first incarnation as a doctoral dissertation. My advisers at the University of Wisconsin, Charles Anderson and especially Bernard Cohen, gave me detailed, expert guidance and inspiration, and they managed to save me from some of my errors. A grant from the Carnegie Endowment for International Peace made interview trips possible and helped me in other ways. During that time the Brookings Institution allowed me to use its facilities as a guest scholar.

Joseph Nye, Raymond Vernon, and Samuel Huntington invited me to spend 1975-1976 at the Harvard University Center for International Affairs, where I completed the dissertation. A grant from the Rockefeller Foundation to this Center brought together a stimulating "cell" of scholars who were studying the politics of money and banking that year. In subsequent years, the CFIA has continued its generous sponsorship of my work, including the reanalysis and complete rewriting of this study. It is a pleasure to record my thanks to the Center and its leaders for this enriching experience.

Robert Art, Francis Bator, Fred Bergsten, John Conybeare, Jorge Domínguez, Michael Doyle, Janet Kelly, J. David Richardson, and Raymond Vernon each contributed specific suggestions or criticisms to parts of this study at one stage or another. Jonathan Aronson, Francis Bator, and Kent Calder shared documents or interview transcripts with me. I. M. Destler, Stephen Krasner, Joseph Nye, Kenneth Oye, Robert Paarlberg, Robert W. Russell, and my editors Sanford Thatcher and Robert A. Feldmesser each read the entire manuscript carefully and rewarded me with wise advice, which I was occasionally wise enough to follow. Jorge Domínguez and Robert Paarlberg have been far more than professional colleagues. In this book I am indebted most of all to Robert Keohane and Jonathan Aronson, for special, sustained attention and care going well beyond the call of duty. Not all these scholars and institutions will agree with what they find within these covers, and of course none of them should reap any of the blame for its shortcomings. But each has my deepest thanks.

I have been able to interview almost all the American officials involved in the international monetary decisions that are the subject of this book. Interviews with them and others provided me with some of my most interesting learning. The names of most of these interviewees are shown below. I found them, almost without exception, to be encouraging, generous with their scarce time, and willing to respond directly. I am grateful not only for specific information and hospitality but also for the general ideas they shared.

Most of them spoke freely on condition that the source of the information would not be identified. I have attempted to use this evidence in a way that meets scholarly standards while protecting these pledges of confidentiality.

In any case in which permission was granted, I cite an interview with a named individual. Whenever the supporting evidence is a confidential interview transcript, rather than published or other sources, I cite an interview with one of a class of individuals, such as "a participating U.S. official," with the class specified as narrowly as possible. Some text passages attribute viewpoints to persons interviewed. Some of those statements are based on interviews with those persons themselves; some, however, are based on other evidence, and they should not be attributed to the interviewees unless so indicated explicitly. No interviewee should be held responsible for my statements of fact or conclusions.

My first and last debt is to Margaret Gonder-Odell, my wife, for help of every kind.

Cambridge, Massachusetts
November 1981

NAMES OF PERSONS INTERVIEWED

The institutional affiliation shown for each person is the one most relevant to this study. All interviews were conducted during 1975 unless otherwise indicated.

U. S. GOVERNMENT OFFICIALS

Barr, Joseph. Under Secretary of the Treasury, 1965-1968 (Seminar at Harvard University, 1975)

Bator, Francis M. Deputy Special Assistant to the President for National Security Affairs, 1965-1967 (1975, 1981)

Beasley, W. Howard. Assistant to Secretary of the Treasury John Connally, 1971

Bennett, Jack F. Deputy Under Secretary of the Treasury for Monetary Affairs, 1971-1974

Bergsten, C. Fred. Senior Staff Economist, National Security Council, 1969-1971 (1975, 1981)

Bodner, David E. Vice-President, Foreign Department, Federal Reserve Bank of New York, 1970-1974

Brimmer, Andrew. Member, Board of Governors of the Federal Reserve System, 1967-1974 (Seminar, Harvard University, 1976)

Burns, Arthur F. Adviser to President Richard Nixon; Chairman, Board of Governors of the Federal Reserve System, 1970-1978 (1979)

Cohen, Stephen D. Office of International Affairs, Department of the Treasury, 1964-1967

Coombs, Charles A. Senior Vice-President in Charge of Foreign Function, Federal Reserve Bank of New York, 1959-1975

Cooper, Richard N. Deputy Assistant Secretary of State for International Monetary Affairs, 1965-1966

Daane, J. Dewey. Member, Board of Governors Federal Reserve System, 1963-1974

Dale, William B. Executive Director for the United States, International Monetary Fund, 1962-1974

Deming, Frederick L. Under Secretary of the Treasury for Monetary Affairs, 1965-1969

Erb, Richard D. Assistant Director, Council on International Economic Policy, 1971-1974

Feketekuty, Geza. Senior Staff Economist, Council of Economic Advisers, 1972-1974

Fowler, Henry H. Secretary of the Treasury, 1965-1968

Fried, Edward R. Senior Staff Economist, National Security Council, 1967-1968

Harley, Charles R. Director, Office of International Financial Policy Coordination and Operations, Department of the Treasury, 1964-1970

Hennessy, John M. Assistant Secretary of the Treasury for International Affairs, 1972-1974

Hormats, Robert. Staff Economist, National Security Council, 1969-1973

Houthakker, Hendrik S. Member, Council of Economic Advisers, 1969-1971 (1976)

Karlik, John R. Economist, Subcommittee on International Exchange and Payments, Joint Economic Committee, Congress, 1968-1975

Katz, Samuel I. Adviser to Director of International Finance, Federal Reserve Board, 1965-1974

Martin, William McChesney, Jr. Chairman, Board of Governors of Federal Reserve System, 1951-1970

Okun, Arthur M. Member, Council of Economic Advisers, 1964-1969; Chairman, 1968-1969

Petty, John R. Assistant Secretary of Treasury for International Affairs, 1968-1972

Samuels, Nathaniel. Deputy Under Secretary of State for Economic Affairs, 1969-1972

Shultz, George P. Director, Office of Management and Budget, 1970-1972; Secretary of the Treasury, 1972-1974

Solomon, Anthony M. Assistant Secretary of State for Economic Affairs, 1965-1969

Solomon, Robert. Adviser to the Board of Governors, Federal Reserve System, 1965-1975; Director of the Division of International Finance, 1966-1972

Stein, Herbert. Member, Council of Economic Advisers, 1969-1974; Chairman, 1972-1974

Trezise, Philip H. U.S. Ambassador to Organization for Economic Cooperation and Development, 1965-1969; Assistant Secretary of State for Economic Affairs, 1969-fall 1971

Volcker, Paul A. Under Secretary of the Treasury for Monetary Affairs, 1969-1974 (1975, 1976)

Weintraub, Sidney. Deputy Assistant Secretary of State for International Finance and Development, 1969-1973

Whitman, Marina von N. Senior Staff Economist, Council of Economic Advisers, 1970-1971; Member, Council of Economic Advisers, 1972-1973

Willis, George H. Deputy to Assistant Secretary of the Treasury for International Affairs, 1961-1975

OTHERS

Dale, Edwin L., Jr. *New York Times*

Dubin, Michael. Assistant Manager, Brown Brothers Harriman and Company

Jager, Elizabeth. Economist, American Federation of Labor-Congress of Industrial Organizations

Kirbyshire, John A. Bank of England

Krause, Lawrence B. Senior Fellow, Brookings Institution

Lanyi, Anthony M. J. Economist, International Monetary Fund

Milhaupt, Peter S. Assistant Vice President, Morgan Guaranty Trust Company

Schmitt, Hans O. Economist, International Monetary Fund

Peltier, Philippe. French Embassy at the European Community, 1968-1973 (1976)

Wakatsuki, Mikio. Bank of Japan, Alternate Executive Director for Japan, International Monetary Fund, 1973-1976

U.S. INTERNATIONAL MONETARY POLICY

In international relations, as in any other branch of learning, a knowledge of causation is important. . . . The real investigator . . . must acquire a factual background as to the conditions precedent. He must raise eternally the question: Why, in any emergency, do governmental officials act as they do? This is not a simple inquiry. National policies are seldom entered upon for single reasons. More frequently do they arise from a complex of motives. . . . The economic motive is frequently given less importance than is its due. . . . On the other hand, one should not become doctrinaire on the subject of economic determination of national policies. There are many different kinds of reasons for action. There are often powerful psychological forces, springing from other than economic causes, which bear down upon foreign offices and state departments and persuade or coerce them into their decisions.

BENJAMIN H. WILLIAMS, *Economic Foreign Policy of the United States*, 1929

I am sure that the power of vested interests is vastly exaggerated compared with the gradual encroachment of ideas. Not, indeed, immediately, but after a certain interval; for in the field of economic and political philosophy there are not many who are influenced by new theories after they are twenty-five or thirty years of age, so that the ideas which civil servants and politicians and even agitators apply to current events are not likely to be the newest. But, soon or late, it is ideas, not vested interests, which are dangerous for good or evil.

JOHN MAYNARD KEYNES, *The General Theory of Employment, Interest, and Money*, 1936

1

Introduction

THE international monetary system is to the world's broader political-economic structure what a foundation is to a tall building. When the monetary system performs its functions effectively, it remains unnoticed by most of the inhabitants. But when the foundation begins to crumble or shake, it sends reverberations throughout the structure. The analogy is imperfect, since the monetary foundations of the world may be shifted substantially without destroying the structure, at least in principle. But the connotations are apt, since any effort to deal with monetary problems is delicate, raising always the ultimate possibility of toppling the entire edifice.

The United States was largely the architect of the international monetary regime dating from the Bretton Woods Conference of 1944, and U.S. markets and the American dollar became central pillars. When difficulties appeared during the 1960s and 1970s, Washington altered its foreign monetary policy on three major occasions, attempting in a sense to shift the foundation. In each case the systemic consequences were profound. For this reason it is important to establish carefully why each of these American policy changes occurred as it did. That is the primary purpose of this book.

The first policy shift in 1965, surprised the financial world. In July of that year, Washington reversed several years of opposition to a reform of the gold-dollar standard, quickly becoming instead the foremost proponent of an effort to create a new international money through international organization. As a result of this collective effort, SDRs— Special Drawing Rights on the International Monetary

Fund—have been held by governments as primary reserve assets since 1969. After its first decade, the SDR's roles remained quite limited, compared with the hopes of its advocates. The IMF had hardly been converted into a world central bank. Even so, this limited change in that direction planted a new permanent feature of international monetary organization that has the potential for further development over the long term.

The second U.S. shift, in 1971, jarred the established monetary and trade foundations even more dramatically. On an August weekend, President Richard Nixon officially did the unthinkable, suspending the gold-convertibility of the U.S. dollar and attempting to force other major governments to depreciate the dollar on the foreign exchange markets. Acting unilaterally and coercively, Washington demanded unrequited monetary and trade concessions from its major economic and military partners, imposing a tariff surcharge on their exports to the U.S. until they yielded. The ensuing period of floating exchange rates and tough interstate bargaining was brought to an end in December 1971. The Group of Ten nations reached agreement on a set of exchange rate changes partly satisfying the Nixon administration. The United States agreed to devalue the dollar and removed the tariff surcharge.[1] Exchange rates

[1] The following definitions are taken largely from Walter Salant, "A Partial Glossary of International Finance," in *European Monetary Unification and Its Meaning for the United States*, ed. Lawrence Krause and Walter Salant (Washington, D.C.: Brookings Institution, 1973), pp. 310-314.

Exchange rate: The price of a specified unit of one currency measured in a specified unit of another, as indicated by actual trading. For example, US $1.00 = 4 DM or 1 DM = US $0.25. The weighted average of the exchange rates of one currency with each of a set of other currencies is called the average or "effective" exchange rate of that currency.

Par value: The value of a currency declared by a government or an intergovernmental organization as a specified number of units of a numéraire. To be distinguished from "parity."

Numéraire: A unit of measure or common denominator in terms of which the par values of currencies are defined—for example, gold, the SDR.

were pegged once again, but the U.S. did not restore asset convertibility. Thus the Bretton Woods regime was partly revived, amid hope that further negotiations would improve both monetary and trade practices. Many came to regard this 1971 shift in U.S. foreign monetary policy as the beginning of a more general and lasting turn away from U.S. policies of "responsibility" for the global order.

In late 1972, the U.S. shifted its monetary diplomacy a third time, returning to a policy of leading multilateral bargaining over new international monetary rules. The central feature of the U.S. proposal of that year was a scheme for insuring more prompt adjustment of payments imbalances—surpluses and deficits alike—by more frequent par value changes and other techniques. The plan also called for enhancing the role of the SDR as a reserve asset, at the expense of gold and perhaps reserve currencies. Before the ensuing discussions had proceeded far, however, they were sidetracked in January 1973 by an eruption of massive flows across the exchanges. In this crisis, in contrast to the 1971 case, Washington responded by initiating secret multilateral bargaining. The U.S. suggested that it could devalue the dollar a second time, or that the other states could instead accept a general floating of currencies. A second devaluation was agreed upon, again without any American commitment to act to defend pegged rates. After this second devaluation it was widely agreed that the dollar was no longer overvalued, in terms of conventional market analysis. Yet almost immediately speculative selling resumed with even greater force. By this time the Canadian dollar, the British pound, the Japanese yen, and other currencies had been set free, and in March 1973 the members of the European Community reached agree-

Parity: The ratio between the par values of two currencies, based on some common denominator.

Devaluation, revaluation: A change in a par value—for example, a change in the gold price of the dollar.

Depreciation, appreciation: Change in an exchange rate or effective exchange rate.

ment to float their currencies jointly against the dollar as well. The U.S. joined a conference in Paris which in effect pronounced an end to the Bretton Woods regime of internationally agreed par values and inaugurated a new mixed practice of flexible exchange rates.

At that time, many felt the collapse would again be temporary. But partly because of uncertainties caused by the explosion of international oil prices and the high and diverging inflation rates of the 1970s, subsequent negotiations did not produce agreement on a new set of international monetary rules having the degree of intergovernmental coordination of the previous era. At the close of the 1970s, the United States continued to pursue the basic foreign monetary policy direction developed during the disorders of 1971 and 1973.

These policy shifts represent both of the two major dimensions of international monetary policy. *Liquidity policy* is government behavior regarding the size, composition, and control of world monetary reserves. The U.S. policy change in 1965 involved this liquidity dimension. *Exchange-rate policy* is government behavior regarding the external value of its currency and the international rules and conventions controlling exchange rates. In 1971, the U.S. changed both liquidity and exchange-rate policies, while the third change pertained primarily to exchange rates. These three changes are explored in detail in Chapters 3, 4, and 5, respectively. Behavior includes actions such as devaluation, exchange market intervention, reserve conversions, and changes in controls on international transactions, as well as positions taken in international negotiations. Other areas of international monetary policy—e.g. regulation of Eurobanks—are not emphasized but are introduced as necessary for dealing with the main questions, as are issues of domestic monetary policy. Interest centers on international as opposed to domestic monetary policy, as conventionally differentiated, without denying the relationship between the two.

My second purpose here is to propose an improved comprehensive framework for explaining and anticipating foreign economic policy changes more generally. Theories of foreign policy remain notoriously fragmentary, indeterminate, and contradictory. Significant progress has nevertheless been made toward the goal of at least identifying variables that will help the observer make a discriminating "diagnosis" of why governments do what they do.[2] Five alternative perspectives for explaining foreign or economic policy shifts are presented in Chapter 2. Each of the five casts light on a different strand of the historical tapestry. None meets the more rigorous definitions of "theory." But each provides a set of questions, hypotheses, and expectations that can guide a search for the sources of American behavior in the international monetary system.

The most familiar perspective on foreign policy points to the *security and power* of the state relative to other states, and the struggle for influence among states, as the major determinants of policy content. What is the meaning of international power shifts in the monetary field? To what extent have interstate struggles been responsible for U.S. policy changes? A second analytical perspective emphasizes changes in *international market conditions*, putting pressure on the government to change its policy in the direction indicated by this pressure. The relevant markets are those in foreign exchange, reflecting the condition of a state's balance of payments. To what extent have market changes been responsible for policy changes?

In contrast, a *domestic politics* framework directs attention to changes in a political leader's domestic situation—perhaps a change in pressure from interest groups or a change in election results or opinion surveys. In what ways would policy have been different if domestic politics had been different? A fourth approach argues for the importance

[2] See Alexander George, David K. Hall, and William R. Simons, *The Limits of Coercive Diplomacy: Laos, Cuba, Vietnam* (Boston: Little, Brown, 1971), p. xiii.

of the internal *organizational structure* of the government, or of a process of bargaining within the government or, in some versions, bargaining between middle-level bureaucrats and their counterparts in foreign governments and international organizations. Finally, in a *cognitive* perspective, the critical variables are intellectual rather than objective, policy content and its change being explained by reference to the influence of ideas, ranging from widely shared ideologies to idiosyncratic perceptions or priorities of official leaders.

None of these five approaches is unheard of, yet before they can be used jointly for present purposes, significant refinements and clarifications will be necessary. Concepts developed especially for explaining features of an international system as a whole may be equally useful for analyzing the behavior of an individual state within that system, but this cannot be determined without direct consideration at the national level as well. Concepts developed in order to explain the behavior of markets rather than governments, or for prescribing policies, need to be recast if the purpose is to explain government behavior. Perspectives that have been stretched to the point of tautology must be trimmed to their essentials in order to conserve their strength. (This problem has afflicted the domestic politics, bureaucratic politics, and cognitive approaches.) These refinements are the tasks of Chapter 2. Each of the succeeding chapters then applies the alternative perspectives to a single case. An hypothesis that remains salient and persuasive after such consideration of rival ones is more persuasive than one used only in isolation.

Theories of foreign policy can be improved if we can integrate international monetary policy into the analysis of foreign policy generally, a task no previous work has accomplished. Various models or frameworks have been applied in a number of closely reasoned case studies, but with some exceptions these studies have dwelled on political-military issues, like the making of the Monroe Doctrine,

U.S. moves during World War II and the early Cold War, the Cuba missile crisis, deterrence theory and practice, and U.S. weapons-sharing policy in NATO.[3] Although there has been a flood of writing on international monetary problems, much of it has analyzed markets or prescribed policies, rather than offering empirically based explanations of policies.

Theories of foreign policy can be improved further if we can integrate the systemic level of analysis with the national level. Many of our previous efforts to explain international monetary policies have been cast at the system level of analysis.[4] That is, the focus is on explaining properties of the international order and international organizations, rather than the behavior of states. While such works invariably include claims about the causes of state behavior, their focus makes it difficult to investigate policy influences at the national and subnational levels that have been found to be important in military-political and trade issues. Systemic factors may well be important influences, but there

---

[3] Ernest R. May, *The Making of the Monroe Doctrine* (Cambridge, Mass.: Harvard University Press, 1975); Ernest R. May, *"Lessons" of the Past: The Use and Misuse of History in American Foreign Policy* (London: Oxford University Press, 1973); Graham T. Allison, *Essence of Decision: Explaining the Cuban Missile Crisis* (Boston: Little, Brown, 1971); Alexander L. George and Richard Smoke, *Deterrence in American Foreign Policy: Theory and Practice* (New York: Columbia University Press, 1974); and John D. Steinbruner, *The Cybernetic Theory of Decision: New Dimensions of Political Analysis* (Princeton: Princeton University Press, 1974). In several respects the present book can be read as a companion to the Steinbruner study.

[4] For example, Robert O. Keohane and Joseph S. Nye, *Power and Interdependence: World Politics in Transition* (Boston: Little, Brown, 1977); Stephen D. Cohen, *International Monetary Reform, 1964-69: The Political Dimension* (New York: Praeger, 1970); Susan Strange, *International Monetary Relations*, vol. 2 of *International Economic Relations of the Western World 1959-1971*, ed. Andrew Shonfield (London: Oxford University Press, 1976); Robert Solomon, *The International Monetary System, 1945-1976: An Insider's View* (New York: Harper and Row, 1977); Benjamin J. Cohen, *Organizing the World's Money: The Political Economy of International Monetary Relations* (New York: Basic Books, 1977); John Williamson, *The Failure of World Monetary Reform, 1971-74* (London: Thomas Nelson and Sons, 1977).

is no reason why questions about national policy should be neglected as a central focus.[5] On the other hand, many studies of the domestic sources of foreign policy are weakened by their neglect of the global context. Here, the influences of systemic and subsystemic factors are compared within a single study.

Theories most familiar to economists and political scientists are inadequate for explaining policy changes such as these. The general argument of this book is that an adequate explanation or forecast of U.S. international monetary policy requires a combination of three approaches: markets, power, and ideas. Conditions in international currency markets affect policy content, but the market perspective is ambiguous or misleading in two of these three cases. A second general source of change is the shifting international economic power structure, but this perspective also leaves crucial features of new policies unaccounted for. The third decisive influence on policy direction is the circulation of policy ideas, useful especially in explaining new policy content. In a nutshell, these experiences confirm Keynes' famous dictum, "the power of vested interests is vastly exaggerated compared with the

[5] For a related argument, see Peter J. Katzenstein, "International Relations and Domestic Structures: Foreign Economic Policies of Advanced Industrial States," *International Organization* 30 (1976): 1-46. Other recent national-level studies reflecting theoretical concerns include Susan Strange, *Sterling and British Policy: A Political Study of an International Currency in Decline* (New York: Oxford University Press, 1971); David P. Calleo and Benjamin M. Rowland, *America and the World Political Economy: Atlantic Dreams and National Realities* (Bloomington: Indiana University Press, 1973); Edward L. Morse, *Foreign Policy and Interdependence in Gaullist France* (Princeton: Princeton University Press, 1973); C. Fred Bergsten, *The Dilemmas of the Dollar: The Economics and Politics of United States International Monetary Policy* (New York: New York University Press, 1975); Fred L. Block, *The Origins of International Economic Disorder: A Study of United States International Monetary Policy from World War II to the Present* (Berkeley and Los Angeles: University of California Press, 1977); and Stephen D. Krasner, *Defending the National Interest: Raw Materials Investments and U.S. Foreign Policy* (Princeton: Princeton University Press, 1978).

gradual encroachment of ideas." The common assumption that attention can concentrate on "interests," that intellectual variables need not be conceptualized and investigated carefully, is called into serious question. A cognitive approach makes sense of actions that appear anomalous under market and power hypotheses. Domestic politics exercises some, though clearly weaker, influence, and government organization and internal bargaining, even less.

The primary reason for selecting the three cases is their substantive importance in the international monetary system and all that in turn depends on that system. They were not selected primarily to test or prove a theory. Therefore what follows cannot be assumed to be unbiased evidence regarding any theory. Each of the changes occasions a "disciplined configurative" case study.[6] Each case taken alone shows that theoretical perspectives used in the study of other foreign or economic policies can identify the most important influences on U.S. international monetary policy at a decisive turning point. They also show that the relative importance of causal variables can be ascertained, at least roughly. Each case, defined as a *change* of policy, points to possibilities of comparison, albeit longitudinal (before/after) rather than cross-sectional. (Of course, concentrating on turning points does not prevent one from recognizing continuities of behavior at the same time.) Taken together, the three cases also support a general argument for the importance of the intellectual sources of foreign economic policy content.

Finally, this book locates itself at the intersection of political science, economics, and history. It arrives there from the direction of political science most of all, but it participates in the unfinished collective project of building a discipline of international political economy. This discipline is concerned, at its broadest, with "the reciprocal and dy-

[6] Harry Eckstein, "Case Study and Theory in Political Science," in *Handbook of Political Science*, 8 vols., ed. Fred Greenstein and Nelson Polsby (Reading, Mass.: Addison-Wesley, 1975), vol. 7, pp. 79-137.

namic interaction in international relations of the pursuit of wealth and the pursuit of power."[7] This broad subject encompasses many components and approaches. The assumption here is that states are and will remain the preeminent players in the game, however much they vary and whatever nonstate actors may also affect them. Therefore, one of the chief analytical tasks is to explain why national governments adopt the foreign economic policies they do, and why states' economic relations manifest the forms of conflict and cooperation they do.

[7] Robert Gilpin, *U.S. Power and the Multinational Corporation: The Political Economy of Foreign Direct Investment* (New York: Basic Books, 1975), p. 43. Gilpin continues: "In the short run, the distribution of power and the nature of the political system are major determinants of the framework within which wealth is produced and distributed. In the long run, however, shifts in economic efficiency and in the location of economic activity tend to undermine and transform the existing political system. This political transformation in turn gives rise to changes in economic relations that reflect the interests of the politically ascendant state in the system."

2

Explaining Change in Foreign Economic Policy

THE facts of foreign economic policy will not organize themselves.[1] Commentators on them normally reach for one or two major conceptual tools for sifting through the evidence and identifying possible explanatory factors. Often, to no one's surprise, the commentator finds that his or her chosen tool provides the best explanation, even though significant rival explanations were not even considered.

For the serious observer, the challenge is to select and sharpen a few approaches that will identify key forces that

[1] The term "policy" is here understood to mean a course of action or inaction (e.g., laissez-faire) moving through time. A policy is identified by observing actual behavior of the national government as a whole according to the observer's criteria, which may differ from the policy makers'. Policies are not defined to include the intentions behind the behavior; intentions or the absence thereof are part of the explanation. A policy is not assumed to be internally "coherent" or consistent with other policies of the same government, but often a general direction and major changes of policy direction can be identified. For a similar view, see H. Hugh Heclo, "Review Article: Policy Analysis," *British Journal of Political Science* 2 (1972): 83-108. For contrasting approaches and other reviews, see Bernard C. Cohen and Scott A. Harris, "Foreign Policy," in *Handbook of Political Science*, 8 vols., ed. Fred Greenstein and Nelson Polsby (Reading, Mass.: Addison-Wesley, 1975), vol. 6, pp. 381-438; James N. Rosenau, *The Scientific Study of Foreign Policy* (New York: Free Press, 1971); *The Study of Policy Formation*, ed. Raymond A. Bauer and Kenneth J. Gergen (New York: Free Press, 1968); Richard Rose, "Comparing Public Policy: An Overview," *European Journal of Political Science* 1 (1973): 67-94; E. S. Kirschen et al., *Economic Policy in Our Time*, 3 vols. (Amsterdam: North-Holland, 1964); Charles W. Anderson, "System and Strategy in Comparative Policy Analysis: A Plea for Contextual and Experiential Knowledge," *Tulane Studies in Political Science* 15 (1975): 219-241; Sir Geoffrey Vickers, *The Art of Judgment: A Study of Policy-Making* (New York: Basic Books, 1965).

move policies, and to ascertain which are more and less useful in analyzing concrete cases. Here let us consider five perspectives on foreign economic policy. Each stresses a different general explanatory factor, and with varying degrees of precision each sets up expectations about the content of new policy. Versions of each approach have been used before, though often haphazardly and separately. Nonetheless, illustrations will show that certain historical events have been viewed from several contrasting angles. These five are selected for dealing with U.S. international monetary policies of the 1960s and 1970s. But none of the tools is limited in principle to the United States or to international monetary matters.

The five approaches are presented in such a way as to make each as powerful as seems reasonable and to highlight the contrasts among them, contrasts deriving from substantial intellectual traditions. Most of them have had strong or extreme advocates, but the purpose here is not to create straw men to be demolished in later chapters. A strong statement of the core ideas is valuable, in the first place, because there are cases for which such formulations turn out to be valid. Furthermore, if in analyzing other policies it is necessary to qualify the argument or to blend several approaches together, that particular modification or blending may not be the most persuasive application of the basic approaches when one turns to still other cases. Hence, an interest in developing analytical tools of wider relevance suggests the value of keeping in mind a sharp image of the core ideas of each perspective.

The five approaches are rivals in that they identify factors which can and do vary independently of each other. This does not mean that the respective explanatory factors do not influence each other at all, as will become clear. Nor does it mean that they are mutually exclusive. In explaining U.S. international monetary policy in the 1960s and 1970s, none of them is sufficient by itself and none can be rejected as entirely worthless. But the conclusion will not be that they are equally valuable or powerful. The cases to be analyzed indicate the relative strengths and weaknesses of each.

The most widely influential framework for viewing U.S. foreign policy, at least on political-military issues, is the traditional *realpolitik* perspective, which emphasizes the security and power of the state. But discussions of international monetary affairs, including American policy, are often couched in a quite different framework. Most commentators familiar with this arcane subject are educated and experienced not nearly as much in the language of world politics as in the language of markets. These two approaches are not contradictory or mutually exclusive in every application, but their roots and implications are markedly different in critical respects. Let us first consider in turn these approaches emphasizing international conditions. The market approach will be introduced first, because power thinking in the economic realm has often arisen as a reaction to it.

INTERNATIONAL MARKET CONDITIONS

Content of the Perspective

An international market approach for explaining policy change is found more often in the popular press and in other less formal writing than in scholarly literature. For example, one of the purest specimens is the *Economist*'s account of the 1967 devaluation of sterling:

> The devaluation of the pound sterling last weekend was not caused by any bankers' ramp, or wickedness by speculators, or even any sudden upsurge in either the incompetence or the revived common sense of the present British Government. It was the inexorable pressure of facts alone that caused Mr. Wilson and Mr. Callaghan to eat so many of their past words, and any dangers that now beset Britain or the international monetary system

arise mainly from the fact that their meal has been so unconscionably long delayed. It has been clear for some years that sterling has been overvalued in relation to the main trading currencies of continental Europe and Japan. . . .The truth is that the men responsible for managing Britain's affairs in the last three years honestly have not understood that the level of a currency, like the tide on King Canute's beach, really does not depend on what anybody, even a Chancellor of the Exchequer, says it is. It depends on a whole series of adamantine forces which can be readily analysed by the application of either ordinary common sense or scientific techniques.[2]

This approach identifies international market conditions as the chief, or a major, source of change in policy content. For present purposes, the conditions of greatest interest are supplies and demands for currencies in the markets for foreign exchange. Underlying the foreign exchange markets are the state of payments balances, which in turn depend on trends or cycles in relative prices, incomes, and national money stocks.

This approach focuses attention on these "underlying" international economic conditions and on the behavior of markets. In general, a market explanation for policy change claims that international market conditions changed so as to make it economically irrational for a government to continue prevailing policy, and it was for this reason that the government yielded and adopted a new policy more in conformity with market signals. Market conditions would have made such a change likely, regardless of other conditions also present.

This perspective has its roots in the classical liberal tradition of Hume, Smith, Ricardo, Cobden, and Mill and in the notion of the self-regulating market. In this well-known conception, a large set of small buyers and sellers engaging in unregulated exchange gives rise to natural forces press-

---

[2] *The Economist*, 25 November 1967, p. 825.

ing toward equilibrium and efficient allocation of resources. If an item demanded by buyers is in short supply, its price will rise, calling forth reallocation of resources and increased production and trade; conversely, surpluses lead to price declines. If prices are allowed to remain flexible, their movements will signal how resources should be shifted among different activities so as to reduce imbalances and produce the largest possible bundle of those goods and services currently demanded by families and firms. The strong implication is that government intervention in private exchange, beyond minimal policies necessary to enhance the self-regulation mechanism, is irrational. If governments interfere with the market, in many circumstances they will only make their people worse off. Policies departing further from laissez faire than minimal intervention are therefore always in danger of sinking under the weight of efficiency costs.

This core idea of the efficient, self-regulating market then becomes the basis for an explanation of policy change, and it sets up some expectations about the content of new policy. The analyst of government policy who uses this core idea monitors not interstate power structures, nor which party is in power, but monitors instead the relevant markets, through the lenses of neoclassical liberalism. A market imbalance is a clue to expect some shift in policy involving either a lesser degree of government intervention or a change in the form of intervention to perfect the market. One such change might be to make regulations less restrictive. Another would be to move a controlled price up or down as indicated by excess demand or supply, respectively. Another might be to organize greater interstate policy coordination, or to create supranational institutions, in order to widen the market. From the perspective of the market analyst, the efficiency incentives presented by changed market conditions are likely to make for such a policy shift, at least in the long run, regardless of domestic politics, or the ideology or skill of the rulers, or domination by foreign governments. Modern uses of this type of policy explanation all recognize that the institutional heritage in virtually every state establishes a backdrop of extensive government participation in and regulation of economic activity. Viewing such a world through the concepts of the liberal tradition then sets up a rationale for expecting and explaining policy changes in the direction of laissez faire.

What is here characterized as a market perspective on foreign economic policy is not the same as liberal economics. The central task of economics as a discipline is not to explain government behavior,[3] but rather to explain trade flows, the commodity composition of trade and production, financial flows, price movements, and so on. A liberal economist qua economist views an exchange rate as a price in a market, not as a feature of government behavior. For the classical political economists of the early nineteenth century, the political organization of the world recedes into a dim background. The convention of treating government as an exogenous variable has been carried into contemporary neoclassical economics, as economist Assar Lindbeck complains.[4]

Individual economists, however, do sometimes step outside the conventional boundaries of their discipline. They

[3] There are exceptions. Some economists have attempted to construct formal economic models to explain government behavior. For examples, see Anthony Downs, *An Economic Theory of Democracy* (New York: Harper and Row, 1957); *Economic Theories of International Politics*, ed. Bruce Russett (Chicago: Markham, 1968); Harry G. Johnson, "An Economic Theory of Protectionism, Tariff Bargaining, and the Formation of Customs Unions," in Harry G. Johnson, *Aspects of the Theory of Tariffs* (Cambridge, Mass.: Harvard University Press, 1972); and Anthony Lanyi, "Political Aspects of Exchange-Rate Systems," in *Communications in International Politics*, ed. Richard Merritt (Urbana: University of Illinois Press, 1972), pp. 423-446.

[4] Assar Lindbeck, "Endogenous Politicians and the Theory of Economic Policy," Seminar Paper No. 35 (Stockholm: Institute for International Economic Studies, University of Stockholm, 1973). Anthony Lanyi, an economist writing on exchange-rate regimes, observes: "The presentation of ideal methods of economic-policy-making notwithstanding, economists have advanced little in trying to predict how governments will generally behave" ("Political Aspects," pp. 443-444).

offer explanations of government policy, as well as pre-scriptions. On those occasions it is not surprising that, when asking themselves why a government acted as it did or how it is likely to act in the future, they reach for—among other things—the familiar concept of the self-regulating market. If the economics tradition as such has any implication for government behavior, the most obvious is that governments, if rational, will yield to market forces, at least "in the long run." The efficiency costs of defying the market are one force continuously tending to push policy in the direction indicated by market conditions.

Other Illustrations

The tradition of treating government as an exogenous variable, and relying on the simplifying assumption that governments will be dragged along by market conditions eventually, is what Harry Johnson has in mind when he distinguishes the "scientific economic approach" to international monetary relations from the "political-economic" one.

> The scientific economic approach to the international monetary system, which goes back to David Hume's elaboration of the price-specie-flow mechanism, involves the basic concept of an automatic self-adjusting international monetary mechanism based on gold, in which national governments (more properly, their central banks) were simply automatons reacting blindly to the market pressures communicated to them through the balance of payments. This orientation of theory changed during the 1930s. . . . However, the post-World War II development of the theory of economic policy for the open economy by Meade, Tinbergen and others restored the concept of an automatic system, on the basis of the assumption that once the theory had been clearly laid out governments could be relied on to apply it intelligently.[5]

[5] Harry G. Johnson, "Political Economy Aspects of International Monetary Reform," *Journal of International Economics* 2 (1972): 408-409. Cf.

The vision of governments yielding to market forces is also incorporated as an implicit causal assumption in prescriptions for freely flexible exchange rates and a reconstituted gold standard. To propose that governments adopt a set of rules prohibiting them from intervening in foreign exchange markets plainly involves the assumption or strong hope that governments would in fact obey such rules. Similarly, under an international gold standard governments would bind themselves to convert their currencies to gold on demand and allow the free export and import of gold by private parties. They would thus rule out fluctuations of exchange rates, and they might also engage in some monetary management by means of changes in discount rates. But the key element of this regime is that government otherwise be constrained to yield to the market, in the sense that it would allow outflows of gold to be felt as contractionary pressure on domestic income and employment, rather than imposing controls. Gold movements would serve as a "signaling system" for authorities, who would respond, if at all, with policies that reinforce rather than interfere with the effects of market pressures.[6] Once again, such a regime could not function unless governments yielded to markets. Precisely this implication is the sticking point for most observers. Advocates of free-floating currencies and proponents of a return to the gold standard remain minorities because the majority believes that the requisite assumptions are politically naive, as well as economically suboptimal.

Another example of a more explicit use of this perspective to explain concrete government actions refers to monetary policy in de Gaulle's France. That case, according to

Fred Hirsch and John H. Goldthorpe, "Prologue," in *The Political Economy of Inflation*, ed. Hirsch and Goldthorpe (Cambridge, Mass.: Harvard University Press, 1978), p. 2.

[6] Michael A. Heilperin, "The Case for Going Back to Gold," *Fortune*, September 1962, as reprinted in *World Monetary Reform: Plans and Issues*, ed. Herbert G. Grubel (Stanford, Cal.: Stanford University Press, 1963), p. 332.

political scientist Edward Morse, is perhaps the one most likely to show the weakness of international market forces or interdependence. De Gaulle pursued, with unusual determination, nationalist or statist policies intended to resist or control market forces. During the 1960s, de Gaulle and Finance Minister Debré opposed the American campaign for multilateral creation of a synthetic international reserve asset, demanded an end to unequal treatment of the dollar, and above all defended the franc. But what Morse calls "the increasing momentum of crises" in the international monetary system during 1967 and 1968 seemed to undermine France's stout denial of a shortage of international liquidity. Most important, the May 1968 uprising of students and workers in Paris and subsequent large wage increases set in motion a run on the franc in the foreign exchange markets. France's balance of payments went from surplus into deficit, and the changed international market conditions strongly indicated a franc depreciation against other currencies. In negotiations during November 1968, de Gaulle resolutely refused to submit to external state and market pressure to devalue. Nevertheless, Morse writes,

> De Gaulle's refusal to devalue, if it illustrated his emphasis on the morale of a nation in conducting foreign affairs, was economically irrational. In the end it did not stop a run on the franc and eventual devaluation.[7]

After de Gaulle's resignation the following summer, the French government devalued and accepted the scheme for a new reserve asset. Even France was forced eventually to yield to market conditions. Morse's account employs, among other things, a clear version of this type of explanation.

This perspective also appears occasionally in the form of

[7] Edward L. Morse, *Foreign Policy and Interdependence in Gaullist France* (Princeton: Princeton University Press, 1973), p. 249. Whether the French devaluation of 1969 was justified by economic conditions is questioned by Robert Solomon, *The International Monetary System, 1945-1976* (New York: Harper & Row), p. 163.

explicit expectations for future trends. In the realm of international investment, for example, Harry Johnson paints the following vision of government response to market incentives:

> In an important sense, the fundamental problem of the future is the conflict between the political forces of nationalism and the economic forces pressing for world economic integration. This conflict currently . . . [is] between the national government and the international corporation, in which the balance of power at least superficially appears to lie on the side of the national government. But in the longer run economic forces are likely to predominate over political, and may indeed come to do so before the end of this decade. Ultimately, a world federal government will appear as the only rational method for coping with the world's economic problems.[8]

Similarly, in the monetary realm Robert Triffin argues that "the thrust of history" is in the direction of replacing commodity moneys and national currencies as reserves with man-made moneys controlled at the international level—in short, in the direction of a world central bank.[9] Triffin represents those liberals for whom market conditions indicate not the retirement of government from efforts to regulate, but rather active government efforts to create interstate arrangements to widen the market and stabilize it. Morse also maintains that, over the long term, modernization and interdependence are drawing governments toward more cooperative foreign economic policies.[10]

[8] Harry Johnson, *International Economic Questions Facing Britain, the United States, and Canada in the Seventies* (London: British-North American Research Association, June 1970), p. 24, quoted in Robert Gilpin, *U.S. Power and the Multinational Corporation: The Political Economy of Foreign Direct Investment* (New York: Basic Books, 1975), p. 220.

[9] Robert Triffin, "The Thrust of History in International Monetary Reform," *Foreign Affairs* 47 (1969): 477-492.

[10] Edward L. Morse, "The Transformation of Foreign Policies: Modernization, Interdependence, and Externalization," *World Politics* 22 (1970): 371-392; Edward L. Morse, *Modernization and the Transformation of International Relations* (New York: Free Press, 1977).

This is a convenient point at which to note a key ambiguity or divergence within the market perspective. Does it expect a government behaving in accordance with market rationality to act unilaterally, or through bargaining and organization with other states? This perspective of itself does not offer a clear answer. Both types of policy are consistent with the imperatives of the self-regulating market.

This ambiguity has been associated historically with another: Is the government that is acting in accord with market rationality likely to allow a freely flexible exchange rate, or to maintain a fixed or pegged exchange rate? For decades, liberal doctors of the international monetary system have been divided on the meaning of minimal intervention in the foreign exchange market. On the one hand, some maintain that minimal intervention implies that the government declares an official parity and follows a policy of intervening in trading when necessary to maintain the currency at parity. One variant of the market hypothesis, then, would expect that if a country's international payments develop a persisting imbalance, its government is likely to respond sooner or later by moving the parity to a new level, as the British did in 1967. They will do so because defying this pressure would generate a number of avoidable economic costs for the society (unless the imbalance is caused by a transitory disturbance).

On the other hand, other liberals insist that minimal intervention is limited to much less management by governments. The school of flexible exchange rates asks why price controls should be considered rational for the foreign exchange market if they are thought to reduce efficiency and welfare in other markets. Milton Friedman's classic 1953 essay outlines the view that in the absence of distortions caused by central bank trading, private trading in the foreign exchange market would tend toward equilibrium.[11]

[11] Milton Friedman, "The Case for Flexible Exchange Rates," in Milton Friedman, *Essays in Positive Economics* (Chicago: University of Chicago Press, 1953), pp. 157-203. See also Harry G. Johnson, "The Case for

The equilibrium would be stable unless fundamental economic conditions were unstable in the first place. That is, if a temporary disturbance pushed a basically strong currency below its equilibrium value, then farsighted private traders would go against the tide, seeing an opportunity to buy low and then sell high later. They would govern their behavior according to the long-run market prospects for each currency. To act otherwise would be to lose money. Their buying would bid the currency back up to its equilibrium value, keeping exchange rates fairly stable without government intervention.

Friedman is arguing a case, not claiming to predict or explain actual government behavior. But his analysis does suggest a theoretical basis for expecting governments to yield to market forces when pressed. In fact, it takes the market perspective to its extreme. On this view, the policy analyst would expect the rational government facing a payments imbalance to respond by withdrawing from currency intervention altogether.

Despite their historical association, there is no logically necessary connection between unilateral versus multilateral policy on the one hand, and floating versus fixing on the other. It is logically possible for a group of states to negotiate and adhere to a multilateral set of rules prescribing floating exchange rates—that is, prohibiting all exchange intervention. This possibility is interesting in that it underlines how high a level of international political integration would be required to effectuate a true regime of floating exchange rates, at least among twentieth-century states.

Possible Objections

It might be objected that the analytical perspective summarized here is a distorted representation of what economists have to say about international monetary policy. For

Flexible Exchange Rates, 1969," in *International Trade and Finance: Readings*, ed. Robert E. Baldwin and J. David Richardson (Boston: Little, Brown, 1974), pp. 367-386.

instance, one might object that economists have often prescribed laissez-faire policies, but that this does not mean
they would have predicted that such policies would be
adopted. Yet explanations and predictions of this sort have
also been frequent. Probably most of them appear in less
formal writing and conversation, and not necessarily those
of scholars.

It is true that economic theory does not always imply that
governments will respond in a laissez-faire direction. Economic theory has developed immensely since Ricardo, of
course, and in this development many arguments for policy
interventions have emerged. A market perspective could
be made much more complex for some purposes—for example, by introducing various market imperfections and
their implications, or externalities in production that may
indicate interventions in the form of subsidies or taxes to
make private costs equal to social costs. If resources are
assumed to be immobile, policies to induce movement may
be anticipated, and so on. There are other possible responses to a payments imbalance than an exchange rate
change, particularly in the short run.

This presentation nevertheless centers on the core ideas
of the classical tradition for three reasons. First, despite the
many possible qualifications, the core idea of inexorable
natural market forces and the irrationality of more than
minimal government intervention has retained its strong
hold on the minds of laymen and specialists in many countries ever since the early nineteenth century. Second and
more important, this core idea turns out to be quite useful
analytically in its simpler, more powerful form later in this
study. Third, some of the possible qualifications are taken
up as parts of other perspectives. In particular, a number
of market imperfections pertain to market power, as for
example in the case for optimal tariffs and in the infant-
industry case for protection. "Market power" belongs by
definition to both the traditional market perspective and

the traditional power perspective, and it will be treated here as part of the latter.

This raises a final possible objection—namely, that in any concrete situation, market pressure against an existing policy is always itself partly a reflection of previous action by governments as well as the international distribution of power among states. The validity and importance of this general point are the reasons for introducing the security-and-power perspective next. For now, let it be said that an extreme *a priori* position holding that there is nothing to be gained by even considering market conditions as potential independent influences would be unreasonable. The difficult problem comes in disentangling the influences of interstate relations and international market processes, particularly when the two seem to point in the same direction. The disentangling, to the extent that it is possible, is best attempted in the context of concrete cases.

Transnational Relations and Transnational Actors

It has been suggested that international market analysis is inadequate without the addition of the more political concept of transnational relations. Transnational organizations, including certain banks and business firms, have become important actors in international relations in ways that make them comparable with state actors. Particularly in relation to weaker states and middle powers, a vertically integrated resource-extraction firm or a consortium of Eurobanks may have the capacity to deny or provide goods, services, or values of great concern to governments. If transnational organizations act in concert, they may be able to exercise veto power or positive influence over domestic or foreign policies. This capacity is easiest to see in reference to the weakest governments and in cases where firms or banks have an oligopoly or oligopsony position. Middle powers sometimes also discover both the ability of the transnational organization to contribute to or interfere with its activities and its tendency to act independently of home and host governments. Even the United States, until recently the spawning ground of most transnational commercial organizations, has watched while they have engaged in some activities whose contribution to U.S. national interests is debatable. To the extent that transnational enterprises are protected by barriers to entry, and to the extent that international transactions among the affiliates of a firm are conducted at less than arm's length, these enterprises become nonmarket actors. Dealing with them is significantly different from dealing with the markets of classical theory.[12] Thus there are phenomena for which the notion of international market forces becomes inadequate unless supplemented with the more political concept of the transnational actor.

This concept will be needed in an analysis of foreign monetary policies and outcomes during the period 1972-1974. On the other hand, the present study will suggest limitations on the importance of this theoretical innovation. Focusing first on international market conditions as traditionally understood reveals that in some circumstances transnational relations have only a spurious relation to policy and outcomes. The new concept adds little for the cases of 1965 and 1971.

The Case of the United States

Finally, among the industrial countries the United States is widely regarded as the one in which liberal laissez-faire ideology is held most widely and strongly. Therefore, evidence that the U.S. government responds to market forces as indicated in this perspective would be less compelling

[12] *Transnational Relations and World Politics*, ed. Robert O. Keohane and Joseph S. Nye, Jr. (Cambridge, Mass.: Harvard University Press, 1971); Susan Strange, "The Study of Transnational Relations," *International Affairs* 52 (1976): 333-345; Joseph S. Nye, Jr., "Multinational Corporations and World Politics," *Foreign Affairs* 53 (1974): 153-175; Gerald K. Helleiner, *World Market Imperfections and the Developing Countries*, Occasional Paper No. 11 (Washington, D.C.: Overseas Development Council, 1978).

support for the power of the perspective than would be evidence from a nation like France. Conversely, evidence showing that even the United States resists market pressures would constitute a telling limitation on the scope of the perspective.

INTERNATIONAL SECURITY AND POWER STRUCTURE

In contrast to the market perspective, and sometimes in reaction against it, the traditional *realpolitik* worldview sees a world not of markets but of states. The decisive fact about international relations since the seventeenth century, from this perspective, is that the world is essentially anarchic, consisting of sovereign states interacting under no higher authority. Each state must be the protector of its own integrity. In the modern period, no state, not even the most powerful, has ever eliminated all potential external threats to its security. This perspective explains the foreign policies of states according to the imperatives of such an international system. The fundamental objective of any state must be survival, and deriving from that is the urge to accumulate and preserve the state's power and to limit the power of its rivals. The state's relative position is more significant than its absolute strength. This traditional perspective emphasizes the zero-sum nature of international relations.[13]

For present purposes, the core idea of this approach is that shifts in the international distribution of power, and the behavior of rival states in the struggle for influence, are the dominant forces producing major changes in foreign economic policies. This perspective orients the analyst toward external political compulsion and competition arising in interstate relations, rather than international mar-

[13] See, for example, Kenneth Waltz, *Man, the State and War* (New York: Columbia University Press, 1959); Kenneth Waltz, "Theory of International Relations," in *Handbook of Political Science*, vol. 8; Hans Morgenthau, *Politics Among Nations*, 5th ed. (New York: Knopf, 1973); E. H. Carr, *The Twenty Years' Crisis, 1919-1939* (New York: Harper & Row, 1964).

kets, domestic politics, government organization, or leaders' beliefs.

Elements of Power

This approach includes several more specific propositions, which are discussed below. But since the meaning of power is often unclear, it may be helpful first to identify the national capabilities that are likely to make the greatest differences in the net influence a state has on the behavior of other states on monetary issues. Four elements are likely to account most for these differences. The four elements are listed here and then developed with examples below and in chapters 3, 4, and 5.

THE STATE'S SHARE OF WORLD MILITARY AND PRODUCTIVE CAPABILITIES

Some theorists regard the military or overall power structure as the key determinant of international relations. Others emphasize that behavior on some issues departs significantly from what would be expected from the distribution of military forces, productive capacity, and general spending power. International monetary relations are more affected by the general international power structure than some have claimed. There seems to be a significant fungibility of military and general resources into the monetary issue area. Even so, changes in the general structure need not be the most important source of policy change in a given case. Structures, by definition, tend not to change rapidly.

THE STATE'S SHARE OF INTERNATIONAL TRANSACTIONS

States accounting for relatively small shares of world exports, imports, or credit have lesser means with which to reward or punish other states, and therefore their wishes are less likely to be complied with. Similarly, we may suppose that a given state's international monetary policies will be more responsive to a second state that accounts for a large share of its national transactions than to a third that accounts for less. The large trader or large lender affects commercial conditions in other countries willy-nilly, whether or not its government deliberately manipulates transactions.

THE SELF-SUFFICIENCY OR OPENNESS OF THE ECONOMY

A more closed or self-sufficient economy is more immune to disturbances in the world economy and to other states' influence attempts. Conversely, the economy whose international transactions are large relative to total national activity finds it more costly to resist foreign influence attempts. Thus its net interstate influence is less.

ABILITY TO FINANCE OR ELIMINATE PAYMENTS DEFICITS

The strictly monetary elements of power may also be important. There are a variety of subdimensions here, having unknown weights. Large international reserves, relative to the state's international transactions, give a country in deficit the ability to postpone complying with foreign demands to change its policies. Larger reserves may also support larger lending to other countries (and greater ability to block credit flows). But reserves are not the only means of financing deficits. The greater the country's ability to raise loans abroad, the greater its financing ability. Countries operating international currencies derive some access to short-term credit by this means. Furthermore, as C. Fred Bergsten points out, countries differ in their ability to eliminate payments deficits at relatively low cost. The country for which adjustment through internal measures is less onerous thereby enjoys a way to escape from the need to borrow abroad and submit to foreign influence. Bergsten is referring to the country's ability to reduce inflation relative to the cost in terms of unemployment, and to the leverage of domestic income and price changes over changes in the external accounts.[14] Another monetary dimension is

[14] This section on elements of power is much indebted to C. Fred Bergs-

relevant for a reserve-currency country that seeks to maintain convertibility of its currency into its own reserves. Its ability to defend convertibility is greater to the extent that the ratio of its reserves to its liquid liabilities to foreign governments is higher. The more that foreign claims rise relative to the reserve backing, the more difficult it will be to deter foreign governments from converting, other things being equal.

Security, Balance, and Realignment

The most familiar hypothesis from this perspective directs attention to the distribution of military capabilities among states. It holds that the more balanced the power structure, the more stable it is likely to be, in the sense either of peace or the preservation of the sovereignty of the major actors. This is so because a state situated in a more balanced structure is presented with incentives to restrain its quest for gain at the expense of the others.

Shifts in the military power structure are expected to touch off shifts in state policy, sometimes producing realignments that establish a new equilibrium to constrain the newly strengthened state or alliance. Such realignments may involve foreign economic policies as well as other policies. Thus one hypothesis suggested by the power-structure perspective is that a fall in a state's relative military capabilities (or a rise in external security threat) leads that state to change its foreign economic policies so as to strengthen a military-political alliance or to weaken an adversary, at some point and to some degree. These policies can be quite surprising to an international market analyst.

This mode of explanation has been used often by historians. A classic example was France's policy of directing heavy loans to tsarist Russia, beginning in the 1890s, as well as to southern European countries that were hardly at-

ten, *The Dilemmas of the Dollar: The Economics and Politics of United States International Monetary Policy* (New York: New York University Press, 1975), chap. 2.

tractive credit risks. The French were responding to the rise of German power with the startling Dual Alliance, cemented with financial ties, and with links to lesser states for the same reasons.

One interpretation of changes in British international monetary policies during the 1930s is another clear example of this mode of explanation. In September 1936, the major financial powers—the United States, Britain, and France—announced the Tripartite Monetary Agreement, a modest step away from the ruins of the 1933 London Economic Conference and toward coordinated stabilization of exchange rates. As Benjamin Rowland reads the evidence, the lack of an agreement before 1936 was partly due to larger political rivalries between Washington and London. The British government refused to meet American demands to give up the empire as long as the isolationist United States was not prepared to make any reliable political commitments to stand behind Britain in a conflict. But in March 1936 came Hitler's bold remilitarization of the Rhineland. The German threat to the security of the Western democracies increased, and the Western governments responded with changes in foreign monetary policies, retreating toward the alliance they later formed. The U.S. Treasury had already been thinking of a monetary agreement to protect U.S. trade in the event of a French devaluation.

> Eagerness to take a strong stand against the Germans and fear that an economic crisis might drive France to embrace fascism were two potent political reasons which now joined Morgenthau's economic calculations. . . . In Britain, too, the overriding motive for stabilization was concern over the deteriorating political situation. The decision to cooperate was not one that Britain reached with any great enthusiasm. It sprang, instead, from a failure of alternatives. . . . Britain dropped her objections to a measure of stabilization as she would later cease to resist a degree of trade liberalization, less from the in-

trinsic economic merits of following such a policy than from a growing fear of alienating the United States.[15]

Hegemony

A power perspective leaves us with ambiguities, however, no less than a market perspective does. Power analysts have long been divided. A second, contrary hypothesis holds that imbalanced systems are more stable than balanced ones. Here, a shift toward a more equal structure is said to widen incentives for the state to engage in *de*stabilizing behavior. For the military-political realm, A.F.K. Organski presents evidence in support of such a "hegemony" theory of stability.[16]

In the realm of foreign economic polices, the most influential statement of a hegemony theory has come from Charles Kindleberger.[17] His thesis is that an international economic system is likely to remain open and stable only if it is structured around a single country able to lead and manage it. Openness and stability are international public goods, benefits that accrue to all members whether or not they pay their share of the costs of providing the goods. According to this theory, "leadership" is required for the provision of the collective goods. Kindleberger defines leadership as setting standards of conduct, seeking to get other states to observe them, and, especially, assuming a disproportionate share of the burden of defending the system itself in a crisis. These burdens include maintaining a relatively open market for distress goods during depressions (while others are raising tariffs), providing counter-

[15] Benjamin M. Rowland, "Preparing the American Ascendency: The Transfer of Economic Power from Britain to the United States, 1933-1944," in *Balance of Power or Hegemony: The Interwar Monetary System*, ed. Benjamin M. Rowland (New York: New York University Press, 1976), pp. 207-210.

[16] A.F.K. Organski, *World Politics*, 2d ed. (New York: Knopf, 1968).

[17] Charles P. Kindleberger, *The World in Depression 1929-1939* (Berkeley and Los Angeles: University of California Press, 1973).

cyclical long-term lending, and performing as lender of last resort during banking panics.

A single leader is necessary for maintaining such a system. A clearly dominant competitor will gain sufficiently from an open system to justify paying the short-range costs of acting on behalf of the system. But only such a dominant state will so act. In a large group most members will find it rational to take advantage of the "free ride." Most states are too small to undertake a stabilizing initiative that would have any effect, while some powers are nonetheless large enough for their actions to disrupt the system. In general, duopoly will be unstable, since with more than one possible leader "the buck has no place to stop."

By implication, a change in the economic power structure toward or away from single-state hegemony will lead to policy shifts, at least by the rising or declining leader. Decline causes the erstwhile leader, now unable to reap so disproportionate a share of the collective good, to cease providing the costly leadership services.

Kindleberger sees the late nineteenth-century structure as one with a single economic leader. Britain dominated industrially and financially.[18] Its relative position explains the leaderly behavior it exhibited during that period. But by the 1920s, Britain had lost the capacity for carrying these burdens, and it therefore abandoned the earlier policies. The United States by then had the capacity but not the will. "In 1929, the British couldn't and the United States wouldn't. When every country turned to protect its national private interest, the world public interest went down the drain, and with it the private interest of all."[19]

[18] For a contrary argument that Britain under the gold standard did not in fact exercise monetary hegemony outside her own empire, so that *balance* led to stability, see David P. Calleo, "The Historiography of the Interwar Period: Reconsiderations," in *Balance of Power or Hegemony*, pp. 225-260. To confuse matters further, Kenneth Waltz (*Man, the State and War*) sees the gold standard period as one of a balance of power and for that reason plagued with tariff wars.

[19] Kindleberger, *World in Depression*, p. 292. This hegemony theory is

A refinement of the economic hegemony hypothesis distinguishes between the general interstate power structure and the special power structures peculiar to particular international issues. Robert Keohane and Joseph Nye suggest that the distribution of power capabilities most relevant for a particular issue may vary independently of the distribution of general capabilities. In their formulation, incongruity between the overall power structure and the issue-specific one leads to change in the international regime for that issue. That is, the strong make the rules in their own interest, and they can be expected to change the rules when their interests change. But a state's power and interests are determined at two levels. Its general capabilities may be useful for influencing the creation of a set of issue rules, but once the rules are accepted, these general capabilities are not of much immediate use. Under a given set of rules, capabilities specific to the issue will determine relative influence and state interest. This issue-structure model suggests that it is only when a formerly hegemonic state loses its issue-specific relative power position, and hence its interest in supporting a given regime, that it will abandon its policies supporting that regime.[20]

This refinement is applied to international monetary issues by focusing on the maintenance or suspension of gold convertibility by reserve center countries. Keohane and Nye argue that the issue-structure model and structural incongruity are important for explaining Britain's suspension in 1931. In contrast to Kindleberger, they picture Britain's general capabilities as still substantial at that time. But her monetary capabilities, especially official reserves, were relatively weak. The monetary rules of the time called for

---

generalized for trade policy by Stephen D. Krasner, "State Power and the Structure of International Trade," *World Politics* 28 (1976): 317-347. The theory is ambiguous as to whether hegemony facilitates stability because of the sacrifices borne by the leader, or because of the coercion exercised by the leader.

[20] Robert O. Keohane and Joseph S. Nye, Jr., *Power and Interdependence: World Politics in Transition* (Boston: Little, Brown, 1977), chapters 3 and 6.

convertibility and fixed rates. But for Britain, maintaining prewar parity was difficult in the 1920s, and it

> became impossible once the banking collapse of 1931 occurred. Thus Britain found that she was helpless within the old rules (because she could not change the value of the pound in terms of gold, but also could not supply sufficient gold or foreign exchange to meet the demand at the current rate). Yet Britain was still a major financial power. Thus when she went off gold and allowed the pound to float (or intervened to manipulate the float), her position immediately strengthened.[21]

This policy change was predictable, they argue, from the issue-structure model. Britain had lost her interest in the old monetary regime, yet she still had sufficient general capabilities to force a monetary rule change that supposedly was in her larger interest.

Competitive Weakness and Interventionism

Other elements of this viewpoint suggest that an increase in economic power leads to policies of greater international openness, while relative decline makes policies of greater intervention more likely. The strong economy is naturally likely to favor policies of conforming to market forces, while a less competitive one is likely to prefer resisting them, in this traditional view. Critics since Alexander Hamilton and Friedrich List have insisted that what are called markets rarely feature equal competition, but rather reflect unequal market power. Pointing out that the English had an industrial head start, List poured sarcasm on the English ideology that all would gain from laissez faire, holding—as E. H. Carr did more than a century later—that "Laissez faire, in international relations as in those between capital and labour, is the paradise of the economically strong."[22] For a weak state to forego protectionism and other inter-

---

[21] Keohane and Nye, *Power and Interdependence*, pp. 139-140.
[22] Carr, *Twenty Years' Crisis*, p. 60.

ventionist policies would be to ensure permanent inferiority. Moreover, according to these critics, not only are some nations' industries more competitive than others', but what appear to be market forces are also actually shaped by government policies.

The power perspective begins with the premise that policies are most determined by the drive for gain relative to other states. The weaker competitor, seeking means for overcoming its relative weakness, is thus expected to intervene in markets more than the stronger competitor state. In the mid-nineteenth century, German and Japanese industry lagged behind British, and the German and Japanese governments followed clearly more interventionist trade and industrial policies than did the British. By implication, changes in competitive strength on the part of a single state can be expected to lead to corresponding changes in policy emphases. Broadly speaking, such patterns of change are illustrated by British decline and interventionist policies beginning in the 1930s, U.S. rise and policy liberalizations in the 1940s and 1950s, and Japanese rise and liberalization in the 1970s.

DOMESTIC POLITICS

Content of the Perspective

A third perspective for explaining changes in international economic policy content points not to the international military-political situation and not to international markets but to the domestic political scene. This perspective, like the others, has evolved into several variants, two of which are especially relevant here. First, policy content in a variety of fields may respond to shifts in the strengths of the major political parties or, between elections, to the strength of the governing party as measured by mass opinion surveys. Writing about domestic social policies, Hugh Heclo notes that "the most pervasive tradition identifies the electoral process and party competition as central to policy formation in democratic states."[23] Rarely is it argued even with regard to domestic policy that citizens' policy opinions are transmitted directly via the party system into policy. But this perspective does suggest that the electorate exercises indirect control by setting limits on the range of policies available for consideration and by voting out administrations that fail to solve important problems.

The starkest theoretical formulation, in a work by Anthony Downs, holds that parties in and out of office formulate policies and platforms exclusively for the purpose of winning elections, tailoring the elements of the platform carefully to maximize the size of the coalition.[24] In this perspective, a change in the policy preferences of the electorate or in the popularity of the incumbent government gives rise to a political party or coalition reflecting the growing policy view, which then ousts the incumbents and enacts policies according to the direction of the electorate's change. Alternatively, these changes in public opinion are monitored by the incumbents, who change their policies accordingly.

Alternations among political parties or factions might have a significant influence on policy content even with regard to an issue on which the mass electorate had no opinions, or one which had not been salient in a recent election campaign. If the different parties' leaders and their appointees hold systematically different policy views or ideologies, then a change of party could lead to a predictable change in policy direction, whatever the forces that produced the defeat of one and the victory of the other. In the United States, the leaders of the Democratic and Republican parties distinguish themselves clearly in their ideologies regarding government involvement in economic activity. According to data from 1956 and 1968, Republican

---

[23] H. Hugh Heclo, *Modern Social Politics in Britain and Sweden: From Relief to Income Maintenance* (New Haven, Conn.: Yale University Press, 1974), p. 6.
[24] Anthony Downs, *Economic Theory of Democracy.*

leaders' personal attitudes correspond to their popular image as the party of business, and Democratic leaders' attitudes are clearly more favorable to assertive government regulation.[25] In this important respect, the parties are not Tweedledum and Tweedledee, although the range of difference is certainly smaller than in other countries. This accounts in part for different responses to inflation, for example. Compared with the Democratic Truman administration's response to the inflation of 1950-1952, the Republican Eisenhower administration's response to the inflation of 1955-1958 involved much less use of direct controls over the economy. During the same period, an analogous difference in response was observed in nine other advanced industrial countries, in most of which conservative parties had gained control in the interim.[26]

With reference to U.S. exchange-rate policy, a political

[25] Herbert McClosky et al., "Issue Conflict and Consensus Among Party Leaders and Followers," *American Political Science Review* 54 (1960): 406-427; John W. Soule and James W. Clark, "Issue Conflict and Consensus," *Journal of Politics* 33 (1971): 72-92.

[26] In many countries parties of the Left and Right differ regularly on several other questions of economic policy. See E. S. Kirschen et al., *Economic Policy in Our Time* (Amsterdam: North-Holland, 1964). In the U.S., Democrats and Republicans in office have also differed clearly in the predispositions they have brought to the trade-off between fighting unemployment and fighting inflation. In the words of Arthur Okun, "When the chips were down, the Democrats have taken their chances on inflation and the Republicans on unemployment and recession." Quoted in Edward R. Tufte, *Political Control of the Economy* (Princeton: Princeton University Press, 1978), p. 83. For comparative data on these party ideologies in the 1960s and 1970s, see Tufte, *Political Control*, chap. 4. Regarding this trade-off, he finds that "political party ideology has shaped economic priorities—by our measures at any rate—far more than the objective economic conditions prevailing at the time of the [Presidents'] reports" (p. 83). He concludes: "The single most important determinant of variations in macroeconomic performance from one industrial democracy to another is the location on the left-right spectrum of the governing political party. Party platforms and political ideology set priorities and help decide policy" (p. 104). Related evidence is presented in Douglas A. Hibbs, Jr., "Political Parties and Macroeconomic Policy," *American Political Science Review* 71 (December 1977): 1467-1487.

party hypothesis would imply that Democrats will be more likely than Republicans to use controls and foreign-exchange market intervention to defend a declared parity or preferred rate. By this reasoning, Democrats would be somewhat less likely than Republicans to yield to market pressure and allow an exchange-rate change. This hypothesis has no clear implications for international liquidity policy.

A slightly different party comparison indicates the same sort of difference in exchange-rate behavior. Voters commonly believe Democrats to be freer spenders than Republicans, and have the image of Republicans as more orthodox financially, just as Democrats are often thought more likely to be "soft on Communism." On one view, these party reputations will affect policy makers. A Republican, faced with a serious payments deficit, and less vulnerable to partisan charges of financial irresponsibility, will be more likely to devalue than a Democrat, just as it was easier for Richard Nixon to go to Peking than it would have been for a Democratic President.

A second variant of the domestic-politics perspective emphasizes interest-group influence as the decisive source of policy change. Groups have more or less self-evident interests regarding a given policy issue, and group representatives articulate their respective positions. They urge policies aimed at maximizing their group's interests, and presumably the more a group would be affected by a given measure, the more intense would be its political pressure. Policy content is explained by pointing to the political coalition of groups that benefit from the mix of actual policies and by showing that these groups acted to promote those policies, either by placing sympathizers in positions of authority or by directing lobbying and publicity campaigns at officials. In general, the stronger its pressure, the more a group succeeds in bending policy in its preferred direction. A change in the policy mix is explained by a change in the mix of group interests and pressures converging on the government from the domestic political environment.

In theory, group politics could explain U.S. exchange-rate policy. A fundamental deficit in international payments and an overvalued currency hurt exporters and American producers competing with imports. In such an international financial situation, these groups have an interest in dollar depreciation, since U.S. exports would then be more competitive abroad and foreign products would be less competitive in the United States (assuming that sales are affected by relative prices). But at the same time, U.S. consumers of imported goods, tourists going abroad, and producers using imported inputs gain from an overvalued dollar; a depreciation would increase their costs. Therefore on one side U.S. farmers and producers of high-technology goods would be expected to press for a depreciation, and the textile, shoe, steel, and other industries would join in the campaign. On the other side, workers in service sectors and consumer organizations would be expected to oppose such a step, which would reduce their standard of living. The better organized forces would be expected to prevail. In the opposite situation—a payments surplus and an undervalued currency—we would expect to see the same two coalitions exerting pressure in the opposite directions.[27]

Interest groups, however, often do not in fact express the views attributed to them in this theory. Thinking through the implications of an interest-group explanation for policy

[27] As Anthony Lanyi points out, a policy of pegging the exchange rate, rather than letting it float, is equivalent to granting a subsidy to members of the society engaged in international transactions, by reducing one of the risks of this type of economic activity, while the costs of defending the currency may be borne by the society as a whole. One might speculate that different groups have different interests with respect to pegging. Lanyi, however, makes the case that the costs of pegging are more than offset by its benefits to the society as a whole, inasmuch as the practice encourages international trade and thereby increases productive and allocative efficiency. See Lanyi, *The Case for Floating Exchange Rates Reconsidered*, Essays in International Finance no. 72 (Princeton: International Finance Section, Princeton University, 1969).

forces recognition of the complexity of the causal linkages in economics and politics. If groups find that their interests actually are multiple or uncertain, then the analyst searching only for group interests is not likely to discover an adequate explanation for policy formation and may find it necessary to turn to other variables.

Illustrations

Many examples can be cited to show that American public opinion restrains, or sometimes drives, foreign policy on political-military issues. East European immigrant voters constrained the Roosevelt administration from concluding a sphere-of-influence deal with Stalin; McCarthyist fervor delayed U.S. reconciliation with the People's Republic of China; mass protests limited or ended the campaign in Vietnam; American liberal beliefs in representative institutions and human rights burst forth during the Wilson and Carter administrations.[28] But analysts often conclude that, even in America, public opinion is not a significant influence. Other factors would have accounted for the same policies; the public in the aggregate pays little attention to concrete issues, or is divided; the President can often shape the public opinion he hears.[29]

In the realm of foreign monetary policy, illustrations of

[28] See discussions by Gabriel A. Almond, *The American People and Foreign Policy* (New York: Harcourt, Brace, 1950); John Lewis Gaddis, *The United States and the Origins of the Cold War, 1941-1947* (New York: Columbia University Press, 1972), p. 139; and Stanley Hoffmann, *Gulliver's Troubles, Or the Setting of American Foreign Policy* (New York: McGraw-Hill, 1968), chap. 8.

[29] See, for example, Bernard C. Cohen, *The Political Process and Foreign Policy: The Making of the Japanese Peace Settlement* (Princeton: Princeton University Press, 1957); John E. Mueller, *War, Presidents and Public Opinion* (New York: Wiley, 1973), chap. 4; Milton Rosenberg, Sidney Verba, and Philip Converse, *Vietnam and the Silent Majority* (New York: Harper & Row, 1970); Bernard C. Cohen, *The Public's Impact on Foreign Policy* (Boston: Little, Brown, 1973); and Kenneth Waltz, "Electoral Punishments and Foreign Policy Crises," in *Domestic Sources of Foreign Policy*, ed. James Rosenau (New York: Free Press, 1967).

the first domestic political variant are scarce. In the West German election campaign of 1969, exchange-rate policy was perhaps the most salient issue dividing the main rivals. The balance of payments was in persistent surplus and the Social Democratic party campaigned for a currency appreciation to hold down inflation and cheapen imports; the incumbent government, led by the Christian Democrats, opposed it, in line with the interests of industrial exporters of the Ruhr region and farmers. The challengers were victorious, and they repegged the deutsche mark at a new higher value as their first major act.[30]

Most past interest-group explanations of foreign economic policy pertain to trade policy. England's turn in 1846 away from the protectionist Corn Laws of 1815 resulted not only from shifts in comparative advantage and from the intellectual arguments of Ricardo and his followers, but also from a long domestic campaign by middle-class manufacturers against the agrarian landowners and shipowners who dominated Parliament. The free-trade reform did not succeed until after the electoral reform of 1832 had increased representation of the manufacturing districts in the north of England.[31]

In the United States, the 1930 Smoot-Hawley tariff, which

[30] *New York Times*, 28 September, 30 September, and 25 October 1969; Charles P. Kindleberger, *Power and Money* (New York: Basic Books, 1970), p. 204; Susan Strange, *International Monetary Relations*, vol. 2 of *International Economic Relations of the Western World 1959-1971*, ed. Andrew Shonfield (London: Oxford University Press, 1976), pp. 328-330. An effort to explain variations in monetary reform proposals of the Group of Ten nations according to the party or class in power was unsuccessful; see (Robert W. Russell, "The Politics of International Monetary Reform," in *What Government Does*, ed. Matthew Holden, Jr., and Dennis L. Dresang, Sage Yearbook in Politics and Public Policy, vol. 1 (Beverly Hills, Cal.: Sage, 1975).

[31] J. B. Condliffe, *The Commerce of Nations* (New York: Norton, 1950), pp. 159-162. Peter Gourevitch, "International Trade, Domestic Coalitions, and Liberty: Comparative Responses to the Crisis of 1873-1896," *Journal of Interdisciplinary History* 8 (1977): 281-313, makes an interest-group argument for a later period.

raised high protection even higher and spread it to many industries, is often regarded as the extreme example of successful pressure upon Congress by interest groups.[32] A study of a different type of trade-legislation politics during the 1950s, however, questions the generality of the Smoot-Hawley case. In the later instance, much of the initiative was found to originate with members of Congress themselves rather than with lobbyists. In addition, businessmen's positions on protection depended not only on what products they sold, but also on their general ideas, such as attitudes of isolationism or internationalism. Political behavior sometimes departed from simple economic self-interest.[33]

Perhaps the clearest instance of interest-group influence on U.S. monetary policy is the successful pressure by silver-mining firms for a policy of buying and monetizing more silver, begun in 1933 and maintained despite objections from other domestic groups and despite the disorder it caused in China and Mexico.[34]

During the 1920s, American bankers played a direct role in international relations in the context of the isolationist and laissez-faire policies then dominant in Washington. J. P. Morgan, Jr., Thomas Lamont, Charles Dawes, and Owen Young negotiated currency stabilization loans with foreign governments and chaired international conferences dealing with reparations. The Depression and the New Deal then brought a sharp decline in bankers' influence on policy. During the diplomacy that created the International Monetary Fund and World Bank at the end of World War II, U.S. bankers played only a small part, though they

[32] E. E. Schattschneider, *Politics, Pressures and the Tariff* (New York: Prentice-Hall, 1935).

[33] Raymond A. Bauer, Ithiel de Sola Pool, and Lewis A. Dexter, *American Business and Public Policy: The Politics of Foreign Trade*, 2d ed. (Chicago: Aldine-Atherton, 1972).

[34] Arthur W. Crawford, *Monetary Management under the New Deal* (New York: Da Capo Press, 1940, 1972), chaps. 5, 7, and 14; Kindleberger, *World in Depression*, pp. 234-235.

nevertheless prospered under the subsequent operation of these institutions.[35]

Finally, according to some analysts the dominant groups in America are big banks and corporations and their Wall Street lawyers, who have little need to engage in active lobbying because they are so successful in placing their own members directly in high office.[36] In the monetary sphere, a familiar Washington generalization maintains that private bankers have a firm hold on the Treasury Department and the Federal Reserve system. Treasury Secretaries Andrew Mellon, Douglas Dillon, David Kennedy, and William Simon illustrate this maxim, which survives despite the long disconfirming case of Henry Morgenthau, as well as more recent exceptions like Henry Fowler, John Connally, and Michael Blumenthal.

Other Domestic Influences

This exposition of a domestic politics perspective has omitted several possible analytical tools, and the reasons can be identified in a few words. Some theories center on the effects of "domestic structure" for foreign policy. While the meaning of this concept is often fuzzy, it does clearly include the relatively permanent political institutions of a state as contrasted to those of other states.[37] However useful this may be in explaining policy differences *among* states,

[35] Jonathan David Aronson, *Money and Power: Banks and the World Monetary System* (Beverly Hills, Cal.: Sage, 1977), chap. 2; Fred L. Block, *The Origins of International Economic Disorder: A Study of United States International Monetary Policy from World War II to the Present* (Berkeley and Los Angeles: University of California Press, 1977), chaps. 3-5; Alfred E. Eckes, *A Search for Solvency: Bretton Woods and the International Monetary System, 1941-1971* (Austin: University of Texas Press, 1975); Marcello de Cecco, "International Financial Markets and U.S. Domestic Policy Since 1945," *International Affairs* 52 (1976): 381-399.

[36] Richard J. Barnet, *The Roots of War* (Baltimore: Penguin, 1971); Gabriel Kolko, *The Roots of American Foreign Policy* (Boston: Beacon, 1969).

[37] Henry Kissinger, "Domestic Structure and Foreign Policy," in *International Politics and Foreign Policy*, rev. ed., ed. James N. Rosenau (New York: Free Press, 1969), pp. 261-275, and works cited below.

it is obviously of less use when the subject is the changing behavior of a single state. To note that authority is fragmented under the U.S. constitution, as compared with that of Japan or France, gives few clues about which of several alternative policies regarding international liquidity or exchange rates the United States will pursue or why these policies might change.[38] If it could be demonstrated, however, that the foreign economic policy of France or Japan is generally more coherent than that of the United States, then differences between "strong states" and "weak states" might be used to explain this difference, as opposed to explaining policy substance itself and its variations.[39]

One change in domestic structures during the early twentieth century added an indirect constraint on international monetary policies that was fairly constant through the period after World War II. In the United States and other countries, labor was organized and incorporated into the political party system. Thereafter, the forces opposing deflationary domestic policies were clearly stronger than they had been during the gold-standard period. This means of avoiding exchange-rate changes over very long periods became more expensive politically.

Domestic structure is sometimes said to include the country's ideology, with ideology treated as one building block interlocked with others such as the nation's constitutional division of authority and the relative strengths of public and private sectors. But more discriminating analysis is pos-

[38] Stephen D. Krasner, "U.S. Commercial and Monetary Policy: Unravelling the Paradox of External Strength and Internal Weakness," *International Organization* 31 (1977): 635-672, features domestic structure prominently, but in fact explains little of international monetary policy with it. Krasner defines policy as the goals of the chief executives, which he finds to have been constant over the years, while the behavior of the U.S. government was changing. In his discussion, he is eventually forced to turn away from his main theories and to refer to ideology and perceptions to explain variations in behavior.

[39] Peter J. Katzenstein, "International Relations and Domestic Structures: Foreign Economic Policies of Advanced Industrial States," *International Organization* 30 (1976): 1-46.

sible when ideology is treated as a separate, cognitive variable. While the distribution of authority among governmental units is relatively constant, the reigning ideology may vary. Few ideologies are shared unanimously within a society, and in practice some tenets are often rejected or discounted by a substantial element of the national political elite. These people can come to office, sometimes without changes in other dimensions of domestic structure. U.S. politicians are not all equally hostile to state intervention in economic activity; French leaders are not all equally enthusiastic about it. Britain has its Wilsons and its Thatchers; China has its Mao Xedongs and its Deng Xiaopings. When the reigning ideology changes, striking policy changes often result. In addition, the relative salience of an individual's ideological beliefs may vary, giving way, for instance, to a security fear or a domestic political calculation on particular occasions. Once the policy beliefs of incumbent decision-makers are recognized as constituting an alternative general explanatory perspective, then treating ideology as a variable cognitive element along with other beliefs becomes more appealing than considering it a fixture of domestic structure.

Another objection to the domestic-politics perspective might be that the line between domestic policy and foreign policy has become blurred in the last generation. In the monetary area, it can be argued that U.S. domestic monetary policy—credit conditions and the rate at which the Federal Reserve allows the money supply to grow—is as important to the rest of the world as the positions the Treasury Department takes in international exchange-rate negotiations. So, for that matter, are fiscal policy and all other factors that affect macroeconomic conditions within the United States. Yet domestic macroeconomic policy may be more responsive to domestic politics than external policy appears to be.

This "blurring" thesis is certainly valid. In many countries, what is nominally domestic policy has important causes and effects abroad, and what is nominally foreign policy has important causes and effects at home. A description of either without mentioning the other is likely to be deficient, although it is also true that our knowledge about these linkages and their magnitudes is not based on sufficient systematic study. But this does not mean that the best way to analyze these complex relationships is to tackle them all in every study. That can lead only to superficial treatment of them all. My preference is to define domestic policy and foreign policy in the conventional manner, according to whether the nominal or primary or immediate target of an action is domestic or foreign/international, and to select some sections of the complex puzzle for careful study. Other causal relations may be suggested and illustrated in the presentation but otherwise left to other participants in the larger analytical enterprise. The phenomenon of domestic inflation is too central to this study to escape frequent mention, yet too large a problem to permit a serious analysis in its own right. Economists specializing in this problem are in disagreement, and efforts to bring some order to the theoretical tangle are still in process. The articulation of sociological and domestic political explanations for inflation is in its early stages.[40] This book concentrates on monetary policy as an aspect of foreign policy, without denying the significance of other elements of the problem.

ORGANIZATION AND INTERNAL BARGAINING

A fourth analytical approach dwells on a special domestic factor, the organizational structure of the government and the internal bargaining among officials. The several versions of this familiar perspective all begin by rejecting the premise implicit in most international-level approaches, namely that governments are unitary actors. Modern governments are instead seen as huge administrative conglom-

[40] See *The Political Economy of Inflation*, ed. Fred Hirsch and John H. Goldthorpe (Cambridge, Mass.: Harvard University Press, 1978).

erates. Different agencies are designed to perform different and sometimes conflicting national missions, and a given
policy issue will always touch the concerns of several agencies. This approach expects that organizations will compete
with each other for resources, and that they will typically
recommend different policies or priorities. One high priority for each will be the preservation and promotion of that
agency and its special mission. The first distinctive insight
of this perspective is captured by the aphorism, "Where
you stand depends on where you sit."[41]

Policies are then shown to be results of bargaining among
these divided officials, rather than command decisions. Even
in a country with a presidential structure, like the United
States, presidents are weaker in relation to their subordinates than the formal hierarchy would suggest. Fragmentation of authority gives other officials a base from which
to force the President to bargain.[42] Presidents compromise
their preferred strategies in order to build support at home;
other participants also accept less than they desire; policy
substance then becomes an inconsistent mixture desired
initially by no one. Or the President may permit or require
decisions to be made at lower levels, and the bargaining
occurs there. In any case, no one is really in charge. One
might suppose that this view is even more valid in parlia-
mentary structures lacking a directly elected chief executive.[43]

---

[41] Graham T. Allison, *Essence of Decision: Explaining the Cuban Missile
Crisis* (Boston: Little, Brown, 1971), p. 176. For another important review
of this approach, see Robert Art, "Bureaucratic Politics and American
Foreign Policy: A Critique," *Policy Sciences* 4 (1973): 467-490.

[42] Samuel P. Huntington, *The Common Defense: Strategic Programs in National Politics* (New York: Columbia University Press, 1961), p. 148; Richard E. Neustadt, *Presidential Power* (New York: Wiley, 1960), pp. 10, 33.

[43] Comparisons are found in Kenneth N. Waltz, *Foreign Policy and Democratic Politics: The American and British Experience* (Boston: Little, Brown,
1967); Richard E. Neustadt, *Alliance Politics* (New York: Columbia University Press, 1970); I. M. Destler, Haruhiro Fukui, and Hideo Sato, *The
Textile Wrangle: Conflict in Japanese-American Relations, 1969-1971* (Ithaca,
N.Y.: Cornell University Press, 1979).

A slightly different variant derives from cybernetic analogies. Here the emphasis falls less on top-level decisions and bargaining, and more on the standard operating procedures of autonomous bureaucracies in the absence of such decisions or during the intervals between them. In this conception, each organization focuses on only one or a few of the many objectives of government, and the agency develops a set of programmed responses for dealing with occasions when the "critical variables" it monitors move outside their acceptable ranges. Just as a thermostat monitors temperature and reacts to change by activating a heating or cooling mechanism, so a nation's finance ministry monitors inflation and government budgets, and reacts to change by recommending adjustments in expenditures and taxes. Meanwhile, the foreign ministry may be monitoring alliance cohesion and foreign requests for economic assistance, and making commitments accordingly. It is assumed that top leaders are unable to impose more than occasional, loose coordination on the conglomerate, and that otherwise each agency will push "policy" in the direction indicated by its own program.[44] This variant's core implication, then, is that policy substance as a whole will appear partially self-contradictory.

Related is the claim that the established bureaucratic machinery limits the choices of senior policy makers. They may fail to consider policies that would have been expected on other grounds, because they rely on information collected and processed by official bureaucracies, which have an interest in shaping reports so they do not reflect unfavorably on the organizations. Whether or not agencies distort information flows, a limited inventory of policy instruments available at a given time may bias choice away from responses that would have been expected on other grounds. It is further argued that when leaders are able to order a preferred new measure, the machine may later distort this

[44] John D. Steinbruner, *The Cybernetic Theory of Decision: New Dimensions of Political Analysis* (Princeton: Princeton University Press, 1974).

policy by delaying or by using delegated discretion more in keeping with old routines.

This organization perspective is narrower than the notion of "bureaucratic politics" has often been in practice. If defined broadly enough, it could "explain" every case, but at the risk of tautology. Some observers have stretched the notion to cover situations in which leaders' "stands" differ but for reasons unrelated to their organizational positions. Some have exaggerated the influence of "pulling and hauling" among bureaucrats on policy content by overlooking rival hypotheses, such as the ideas and influence of the President himself.[45] Internal struggle does produce compromised policy in some cases, but in others in which such struggle is ended by a President persuaded to adopt one player's view and reject the rest, the decisive variable is the President's thinking, not the organizational structure or process. Sometimes "bureaucratic politics" is stretched to include incumbents' attitudes and the arrival of new incumbents while organizational structures remain unchanged. But to confound structural change with personnel turnover is to risk confused analysis. The two can vary independently. Since a sharply defined perspective does help explain some important cases, it is important not to dull the edge of this analytical tool.

Many of the best-documented instances of U.S. bureaucratic politics arise in the military realm or in the intersection of military and economic affairs—such as setting military strategy and the national budget in the late 1940s, responding to Soviet missiles in Cuba in 1962, and deploying the anti-ballistic missile in the late 1960s.[46] If these

---

[45] For example, see Jessica Einhorn, *Expropriation Politics* (Lexington, Mass.: D. C. Heath, 1974).

[46] Warner R. Schilling, "The Politics of National Defense: Fiscal 1950," in *Strategy, Politics, and Defense Budgets*, ed. Warner Schilling, Paul Y. Hammond, and Glenn H. Snyder (New York: Columbia University Press, 1962), pp. 1-266; Allison, *Essence of Decision*; Morton H. Halperin, "The Decision to Deploy the ABM: Bureaucratic and Domestic Politics in the Johnson Administration," *World Politics* 25 (1972): 62-95.

instances were reinterpreted in light of the foregoing distinctions, it could be shown that even there, the influence of organization and internal bargaining was less—and the role of the President and policy ideas was greater—than has sometimes been thought.

In foreign economic policy, a bargaining process in which the President is forced to accept a compromise recurs on issues involving legislation and congressmen as well as bureaucrats—foreign economic assistance, for example. Loose coordination and diverging agencies played their part in the "Great Food Fumble" of 1972, according to I. M. Destler. In that year, huge and initially secret Soviet grain purchases from U.S. companies contributed to sharp food price inflation for Americans and increasing burdens on the developing countries that relied on U.S. foreign aid. Washington's policies in 1972 seemed almost designed to exacerbate these problems. For weeks after it was evident that these sales were driving up prices, the government continued export subsidies encouraging further sales, at great cost to the Treasury. Not until six months later were changes made in the acreage policies that were holding down grain supplies. Destler's explanation is that food policy was largely left to the Secretary of Agriculture, who was pursuing a predictably narrow strategy of increasing U.S. farmers' prices and exports. President Nixon and his National Security Adviser, Henry Kissinger, were also using grain trade to help improve relations with the Soviet Union. The Council of Economic Advisers and others charged with inflation policy did not participate heavily enough or early enough to avert the "fumble." The following year, U.S. policy lurched in the other direction, with an export embargo on U.S. soybeans for anti-inflation reasons, damaging farm and foreign policy interests.[47]

[47] I. M. Destler, "United States Food Policy 1972-1976: Reconciling Domestic and International Objectives," *International Organization* 32 (1978): 617-654. Destler's interpretation places heavy weight on intellectual changes and lags as well as on agency interests. The treatment of the President's views and participation is sketchy.

In the monetary field, Richard Gardner points to "defective liaison" between the Treasury and State Departments in explaining the creation of the Bretton Woods institutions, particularly their limited funds when compared to the magnitude of the reconstruction needs that became apparent after 1944. Treasury planning concentrated on monetary stabilization, to the relative neglect of the problem of immediate postwar reconstruction. State Department officials warned that the plans of Harry White, deputy to the Treasury Secretary, were based on the unrealistic assumption that reconstruction would somehow be taken care of, but their own plans for a separate solution to that problem were hampered by Treasury's jurisdictional supremacy.[48] Treasury has maintained that supremacy over other agencies on international monetary matters down to the present time.

A third variant of this approach emphasizes "transgovernmental relations," or direct contacts between middle- and lower-level bureaucrats in different countries and international organizations, far removed from close control by chief executives and cabinets. Specialists dealing with the same problem develop a common expertise and to some extent similar priorities vis-à-vis other functional areas. Engaging in frequent international policy coordination, it is said, these officials develop a transnational camaraderie that can lead to less conflicting policy. Students of common markets report that this sense of professional comradeship produces more flexible bargaining and more extensive coordination than would have been the case among governments operating as unitary actors.

Transgovernmental effects may also operate through coalitions formed by bureaucrats from various governments and international secretariats, through which an American official obtains the support of foreign officials (or vice versa) to influence the policy process in the U.S. or its outcome.

[48] Richard N. Gardner, *Sterling-Dollar Diplomacy: Anglo-American Collaboration in the Reconstruction of Multilateral Trade* (Oxford: Clarendon Press, 1956), chap. 5.

For example, the official U.S. position in the United Nations Conference on the Law of the Sea in Geneva was to oppose broadening the jurisdiction of coastal states over the continental shelf and to defend traditional freedom of the seas. Meanwhile, however, delegates from the Interior Department joined oil companies and others from foreign countries in a coalition lobbying for broader jurisdiction.[49] Thus, considering agencies as actors on the world stage introduces complex possibilities for policy change not suggested by the other two variants.

The most obvious sites for transgovernmental relations involving U.S. monetary policy are the meetings of financial officials at the International Monetary Fund and the central bankers' confidential gatherings at the Bank for International Settlements in Basel, Switzerland. Speaking before the 1971 annual meeting of the IMF Board of Governors, Britain's Chancellor of the Exchequer, Anthony Barber, hinted at a transnational sense of comradeship when he joked:

> Whatever differences we Finance Ministers may have, to be together with one's fellow sufferers and far away from one's spending colleagues at home is a most agreeable experience which only we can share![50]

Coordination among central bankers independently of their national governments was most consequential during the 1920s. During the 1950s and 1960s, notable communication occurred among the financial bureaucrats of 11 major financial nations, but it did not significantly modify governments' monetary policies. Robert Russell finds also that, while central banks successfully coordinated foreign-exchange market interventions and arranged short-term credit

[49] Robert O. Keohane and Joseph S. Nye, Jr., "Transgovernmental Relations and International Organizations," *World Politics* 27 (1974): 45-46; Keohane and Nye, *Power and Interdependence*, p. 149.

[50] International Monetary Fund, *Annual Meeting of the Board of Governors: Summary Proceedings 1971* (Washington: IMF, 1971), p. 27.

facilities, the formation of transgovernmental coalitions did not have much effect on national economic policies.[51] In one exceptional case, the West German Economics Ministry hinted, at a meeting of a committee of the Organization for Economic Cooperation and Development, that a favorable recommendation from the committee would aid the Ministry on a matter already rejected by the German cabinet. The committee made the recommendation, and the German cabinet later accepted it.

These variants of an organization perspective do not tell us what the content of policy is likely to be. They do identify conditions that could impose a drag on any policy change. If prevailing policy is a bargained package, then an attempt to modify one element will risk disturbing all the other elements and the advocates of each, including those not especially concerned about the specific problem at issue. Even though external conditions may change, a corresponding policy element may not change if it is embedded in an internal package. If prevailing policy is the product of standard operating routines, then a new situation is likely to evoke first an attempt to apply a standard response, not to create a new one. If existing routines prove ineffective, the next likely response would be an incremental modification. Organizational considerations as such do not prepare the observer to expect sharp shifts of policy direction, as long as the organizational structure remains basically unchanged.

Implicit in the three variants, finally, is the proposition that a change in that structure may cause a change in policy content. Following this logic, one presidential commission after another in the United States has proposed to solve policy problems by means of organizational reforms, whether dismantling or creating agencies or White House posts, transferring authority from one agency to another, or rear-

---

[51] Robert W. Russell, "Transgovernmental Interaction in the International Monetary System, 1960-1972," *International Organization* 27 (1973): 431-464.

ranging responsibilities for coordination. Interest groups have also urged structural changes to bring about policy more favorable to them. Farmers' complaints, for instance, led in 1962 to the transfer of responsibility for trade negotiations from the Department of State to a new office, the Special Representative for Trade Negotiations.[52]

IDEAS

Content of the Perspective

Each of the approaches discussed thus far identifies an element of the policy-maker's situation as an influence on policy content. But according to many commentators, behavior depends not on reality but on how reality is perceived and interpreted. A fifth and final perspective, then, focuses attention on the substantive ideas held by top policy makers and advisers as decisive or necessary elements of explanation. The core claim of this cognitive approach is that changes in reigning ideas help produce changes in policy content.

Before this approach is elaborated, some important assumptions and distinctions should be noted. One key assumption is that ideas, while affected by interests, are not simply determined by them. Ideas have more complex origins, and they can have independent effects on policy content. Thus, theories relying on interests alone will be inadequate for predicting or explaining policy changes. It is also assumed that, while generalizing about such matters is difficult, attention to policy ideas need not be an entirely

---

[52] Anne H. Rightor-Thornton, "An Analysis of the Office of the Special Representative for Trade Negotiations: The Evolving Role, 1962-1974," in U.S. Commission on the Organization of the Government for the Conduct of Foreign Policy, *Appendices*, 7 vols. (1975), vol. 3, pp. 88-92. See other volumes in this set, as well as I. M. Destler, *Presidents, Bureaucrats, and Foreign Policy* (Princeton: Princeton University Press, 1972), and Stephen D. Cohen, *The Making of United States International Economic Policy* (New York: Praeger, 1977).

ad hoc exercise. Some cognitive approaches to policy formation have made systematic use of cognitive psychology,
emphasizing the effects of recurring cognitive processes on
policy.[53] The present perspective takes account of this line
of analysis, but goes beyond it. The central emphasis here
is on the *content* of ideas rather than on cognitive *processes*.
Efforts to discover patterns in cognitive content are only
beginning, but the results are promising.

The claim that ideas matter may seem perfectly obvious
to some. A cognitive perspective could be stated so strongly,
in fact, as to be a truism. That is, one could deny that
behavior has any meaning at all except in the terms through
which the actor himself understands it; one could build an
explanation insisting on "act meaning" to the complete exclusion of "action meaning," to use Abraham Kaplan's
terms.[54] Every policy change would be explained by describing the beliefs, perceptions, and values of the policy

[53] For major reviews, see Steinbruner, *Cybernetic Theory*; Robert Jervis,
Perception and Misperception in International Politics (Princeton: Princeton
University Press, 1976); and Joseph de Rivera, *The Psychological Dimension
of Foreign Policy* (Columbus, Ohio: C. E. Merrill, 1968). The process of
dissonance reduction, including the shaping of current perceptions to fit
prior beliefs, has probably received the most attention from political scientists. Research indicating that high stress erodes most aspects of cognitive performance has been applied to foreign policy decision making;
see Ole R. Holsti, *Crisis, Escalation, War* (Montreal: McGill-Queen's University Press, 1972). Irving Janis finds that a process of small-group dynamics, labelled "groupthink," tends to differentiate between foreign policy fiascoes and successful decisions; see *Victims of Groupthink: A Psychological
Study of Foreign Policy Decisions and Fiascoes* (Boston: Houghton Mifflin,
1972). The simplicity or complexity of a policy maker's cognitive map is
significant in shaping the sort of recommendation he makes, according
to Michael Shapiro and Matthew Bonham, "Cognitive Process and Foreign
Policy Decision Making," *International Studies Quarterly* 17 (1973): 147-174.
John Steinbruner (*Cybernetic Theory*, p. 317) explains the otherwise puzzling survival of an American political-military policy by reference to the
interaction between two cognitive patterns, "theoretical thinking" on the
part of the internal advocates and "uncommitted thinking" on the part
of the President.

[54] Abraham Kaplan, *The Conduct of Inquiry: Methodology for Behavioral
Science* (Scranton, Pa.: Chandler, 1964).

makers at the time of decision. Such an epistemology seems too extreme; it implies rejection of much persuasive social science and may impose unnecessary burdens on investigators. It undoubtedly conveys an exaggerated impression of the policy maker's actual room for maneuver. The cognitive perspective used here follows instead the more conventional social-science assumption that behavior has meaning given it by the analyst's theory as well as "act meaning." Behavior is a product of some combination of environmental and internal factors.

An emphasis on ideas often elicits skeptical materialist counterarguments. Analysts of foreign policies have been reluctant to embrace this approach, for historical and other reasons.[55] In principle, explanations focusing on situational factors could be more persuasive than one using a cognitive approach, to the point that the latter would be unnecessary. It may be that a given international security threat or international market imbalance would have evoked the same response from any state in that situation, regardless of the national culture or the outlooks of particular leaders. In that case, we would expect to find evidence of very little disagreement among the state's leaders. If the beliefs and perceptions of the leaders are in this sense virtually determined by the external situation, then a cognitive perspective is superfluous. If policy content seems to vary regularly

[55] The debates among early international relations scholars were lost by the idealists and won by the realists, thanks especially to Hitler and Tojo. Realist teaching held that foreign policies reflect national interests, not sentiments, and many political scientists became realists. In addition, some of the early forays into the subject by psychologists and anthropologists were silly, and in reaction many political scientists rejected all psychological approaches somewhat hastily. More important, the difficulties of collecting direct information about the beliefs of individual decision makers and the equally serious problems of interpreting such information were daunting. Many political analysts prefer to avoid such research, arguing that more parsimonious explanations, without cognitive factors, are adequate. Or else claims about attitudes or perceived interests are swept quickly into the discussion of situational factors on the assumption that the lack of evidence about perceptions is not important.

with the political party in control of the government, a domestic political explanation would be appropriate, whether or not the covariation is recognized by decision makers. If leaders' views tend to differ regularly by organizational position, then a case fitting this pattern can more properly be explained by an organization perspective than by a cognitive approach. If we can assume that a satisfactory explanation can always be provided by one or more of the situational approaches, then investigators can avoid the task of gathering detailed evidence on the beliefs, perceptions, and priorities of top leaders. Such research is costly in time and effort, yet making inferences about motives and perceptions without collecting evidence and cross-checking and interpreting it introduces substantial risks of bias. In the absence of direct or indirect evidence, claims about motives and perceptions must be regarded as intelligent speculation at best. So the advantage of the foregoing perspectives is not a trivial one.[56]

We know from considerable research, however, that many

[56] These problems are discussed in Ole R. Holsti, "Foreign Policy Formation Viewed Cognitively," in *The Structure of Decision*, ed. Robert Axelrod (Princeton: Princeton University Press, 1976), pp. 18-54; and in *Contending Theories of International Politics*, ed. Klaus Knorr and James Rosenau (Princeton: Princeton University Press, 1969). It is partly because of the importance of collecting this different type of evidence that a cognitive perspective is presented separately here, rather than classifying President Johnson's or President Nixon's domestic political expectations, for example, as part of "domestic politics." We do not know enough to assume that given situations, whether of a domestic or international nature, regularly produce given motives or perceptions in politicians. The situation and the cognition of it may vary independently. A study including independent investigation of beliefs may combine the several analytical approaches when applying them. But failing to distinguish these different variables at the outset creates the risks of making inaccurate claims about beliefs and drawing confused analytical conclusions. In addition to works cited below, see Alexander George, "The Operational Code: A Neglected Approach to the Study of Political Leaders and Decision-Making," *International Studies Quarterly* 13 (1969): 190-222; Michael Brecher, Blema Steinberg, and Janice Stein, "A Framework for Research on Foreign Policy Behavior," *Journal of Conflict Resolution* 13 (1969): 75-101.

cases of foreign policy do not fit such patterns. All but the most extreme policy situations seem highly complex and uncertain; policy makers typically disagree among themselves as to diagnosis and prescription, or later analysts uncover evidence and reasoning that support more than one plausible interpretation of the national interest. Conflicting schools of thought cutting across interest groups, political parties, and bureaucracies are often evident. Policies sometimes seem to vary to a greater extent with the rotation of these schools of thought through the offices of government than with other variables. The cognitive analyst may argue that for a given case, a change in reigning ideas would have made a greater difference for policy content than conceivable changes in other factors. Situational factors may explain the rejection of an old policy, the timing of a policy change, or the degree of policy coherence, but contain no explanation for the choice of a new policy from among the alternatives. Actual policy changes may come in packages, having some elements that seem virtually inevitable in the light of situational changes but other elements that require a different explanation. In Hugh Heclo's words, "governments not only 'power'; they also puzzle."[57]

It is useful to distinguish between specific beliefs and general beliefs. Specific beliefs are an individual's causal map of the immediate situation—for example, a belief that the Soviet Union erected missiles in Cuba last month because the U.S. had appeared weak last year during the Bay of Pigs incident, or that if a central bank raises its discount rate this week, the effects will include an immediate run on the nation's currency, because international markets will interpret the action in present circumstances as a sign of panic. The individual may interpret a situation by specific analogy, believing that the cause of the current episode is X because the cause of a previous episode was a comparable X. According to this perspective, identifying such specific

[57] Heclo, *Modern Social Politics*, p. 305.

calculations is essential for explaining why a government rejected certain courses of action in favor of others. Specificity of a belief, incidentally, does not imply idiosyncrasy. In principle, a given specific belief can be peculiar to a single individual or shared by every observer of the situation.

General beliefs, theories or ideologies for example, may play a direct role in policy formation. A theory such as Ricardian free-trade theory or Leninist imperialism theory might be applied directly and literally by a decision maker in choosing policy at a given moment. Or a new economic theory devised by a particular writer might be explicitly cited as the source of a policy experiment. Similarly, a cognitive perspective might lead to the finding that one or another ideology—a belief system claiming a very wide range of application, having a tightly interrelated internal structure, usually having an authoritative promulgation, and pointing the way to the attainment of the highest human values[58]—has been directly applied in a given case.

More often, however, general beliefs and values have a more indirect role. They appear as predispositions that policy makers bring with them when they take office. Rather than dictating specific policy moves, these predispositions influence behavior by shaping and coloring the way new information is processed. As Robert Jervis puts this hypothesis: "Decision makers tend to fit incoming information into their existing theories and images. Indeed, their theories and images play a large part in determining what they notice."[59] A general belief or attitude may make an individual more sensitive to information supporting his predispositions than to information contradicting them. For

[58] See Edward Shils, "Ideology," *International Encyclopedia of the Social Sciences* (1968); and Clifford Geertz, "Ideology as a Cultural System," pp. 47-76, and Philip E. Converse, "The Nature of Belief Systems in Mass Publics," pp. 206-261, in *Ideology and Discontent*, ed. David E. Apter (New York: Free Press, 1964).

[59] Robert Jervis, "Hypotheses on Misperception," *World Politics* 20 (1968): 455.

example, Secretary of State John F. Dulles's general negative predisposition toward the Soviet government deeply
colored the way he processed new specific information about
Soviet foreign policy. An increase in friendly Soviet behavior was interpreted in a manner that reduced dissonance and preserved Dulles's predisposition and the stability of his hard-line policy.[60] To take another example,
this perspective might hypothesize that persons educated
primarily in economic theory and those educated primarily
in diplomatic history tend to develop different predispositions concerning foreign economic policy. In any given
international power or market situation, and regardless of
their bureaucratic location, the former will be predisposed
to notice the efficiency costs of a given policy option more
than the implications for political allies and security, and
the latter vice versa.

If predispositions reduce the range of policy options considered seriously, they provide the analyst with a way of
grouping individual policy participants into "schools of
thought" in advance, provided information is available, thus
reducing the range of policies most likely to be adopted by
a given administration or set of leaders. The limits of this
relationship between predispositions and an individual's
specific diagnosis of a situation are difficult to specify, however. Although "barefoot empiricism" seems impossible to
find in policy-making, there is also evidence of careful consideration of discrepant information under some conditions. And minds do change.

Policy debates sometimes turn less on the nature of the
facts, or beliefs about them, than on the question of which
facts are to be considered most important. Some changes
in U.S. international monetary policy may be traced to
changes in belief content from one period to the next, while
others may reflect instead changes in the *relative salience* of
different cognitions, all of which are acknowledged as valid

[60] Ole R. Holsti, "Cognitive Dynamics and Images of the Enemy: Dulles
and Russia," in David J. Finlay, Ole R. Holsti, and Richard R. Fagen,
Enemies in Politics (Chicago: Rand McNally, 1967).

by all. Salience can be defined as the prominence of a cognition in an individual's awareness.[61] Individuals A and B may favor different policies not because A doubts the validity of B's argument that a given policy would have a certain desirable effect X, but because A, though agreeing with that argument, cares little about X and cares very much about Y instead. During the 1960s, some Americans believed that Communism in North Vietnam had been oppressive, proving the wisdom of U.S. military intervention that would have the effect of defeating Hanoi. To other Americans, the sins of Saigon were more salient, leading them to oppose U.S. policy that supported the South Vietnamese government.

The individual's belief salience ordering may vary with the situation; he may ignore each wheel until it squeaks. In other cases, his analytical emphasis may be more predictable, shaped by professional experience. Relative salience may also reflect values. For example, some leaders place a higher value on reducing unemployment than on reducing inflation, if forced to choose. Some give priority to enhancing international alliance cohesion over providing additional help to national business. The higher value can be expected to concentrate thinking more on the effects of a policy for that value than on its other effects. Leaving aside relative salience, the very content of a causal belief may of course be penetrated by an obvious or hidden value premise as well. In the monetary arena, one hears such value-laden beliefs as "the international use of the dollar gives America an inordinate privilege in the monetary system," or "the currency was undermined by excessive wage increases."[62]

One further clarification is crucial. It would be a mistake

[61] See M. Brewster Smith, Jerome S. Bruner, and Robert W. White, *Opinions and Personality* (New York: John Wiley, 1956), p. 35.

[62] Fritz Machlup and Burton G. Malkiel, in *International Monetary Arrangements: The Problem of Choice* (Princeton: International Finance Section, Princeton University, 1964), attempt to sort out disagreements among economists, and they attribute some of the differences to subtly different values and different hunches about the future.

to understand this intellectual perspective as simply an argument that the idiosyncrasies of individual leaders are important in history. This perspective includes but is not limited to that form of argument. Ideas vary in the breadth of their acceptance. Some cultural assumptions are shared by an entire nation. Some ideological tenets are believed by a majority, while a given economic theory may be accepted only by a minority. Probably very few effective policy ideas are truly peculiar to a single individual. Some may be, and in some cases a cognitive perspective might find that an idiosyncrasy was decisive in producing a particular policy direction. But the emphasis is on ideas, regardless of how widely they are shared. To use individual leaders' beliefs as evidence is not necessarily to claim that policy would have been different without those particular individuals. The usual claim, rather, is that policy would have been different unless *some* member of the same school of thought had been making policy.

To summarize, a cognitive perspective claims that the content of reigning ideas has independent effects on policy content. The core claim is not construed so broadly as to be valid by definition. Distinctions are made between specific beliefs and general beliefs, and among beliefs according to their relative salience. The emphasis is on ideas, not idiosyncrasies.

But can the approach be elaborated further, and can it help the observer anticipate future policy changes? Does it explain how change takes place, or which new ideas are more likely and less likely to prevail? For that matter, where do policy ideas come from? Obviously, such questions will not be resolved in any single study. But a few hypotheses can be suggested.

Sources of Policy Ideas

CLASS

One source of beliefs and predispositions is social class. Officials and potential leaders differ in previous occupation and income level. By one classic hypothesis, the governing elite's social class indicates the range of policy ideas to be expected, particularly on some economic issues. Class-based interpretations have had very little to say about international monetary policies, however. For reasons discussed below, this connection is largely left for other investigations.

GENERATION

Members of a given age cohort share a common historical experience during the stage of life when individuals often form their fundamental substantive beliefs and values. The generational background of leaders and potential leaders may give loose clues as to which predispositions are more likely, and which policy options are least likely to be taken seriously.

PROFESSIONAL EDUCATION AND TRAINING

Impressionistic evidence suggests that individuals' policy predispositions are correlated with their university background or occupational experience. Admittedly, careful study might show that there is no simple or direct connection between studying at the University of Chicago or Cambridge University, or working for years in a central bank, on the one hand, and policy predispositions on the other. But such considerations might help narrow the range of policy ideas to be expected in a government.

Conditions and Directions of Change

A proposition of cognitive psychology holds that established beliefs, whatever their sources, shape perceptions of new information so as to help maintain those prior causal beliefs and preferences. Basic orientations toward international politics and toward economic problems tend to group themselves into recognizable schools of thought, some schools containing distinct sub-schools. Consequently, when adherents of a different ideology or school of thought come to office (or are ousted), an analyst could expect policy change toward (or away from) that school's characteristic prescription. Personnel change is one mechanism of change in governing ideas. Of course, incumbents sometimes change their minds, or form specific beliefs for the first time, while in office. One circumstance in which cognitive change is more likely is a vivid event that is clearly inconsistent with established beliefs.

CULTURE AND IDEOLOGY

New policy ideas that are more consonant with the nation's culture or with a major ideology are more likely to spread and affect policy than those that are more dissonant or alien.

SIMPLICITY

New ideas expressed in clear, simple terms are more likely to spread than those expressed only in a highly complicated form or that are more difficult to grasp.

ASSOCIATION

Ideas associated psychologically with negative symbols, such as past policy disasters, are less likely to be accepted in the present or future than proposals free of such coloration or associated with positive symbols, like prestigious thinkers or famous universities.

ORGANIZATION

Those policy options promoted by organizations through active public campaigns and mass media are more likely to be adopted and to influence policy content than schemes which are not.[63]

[63] See Peter A. Hall, "The Political Dimensions of Economic Management: A Study of the Formulation and Implementation of Macroeconomic Policy in Great Britain, 1970-1979" (Ph.D. diss., Harvard University, forthcoming).

Illustrations

The cognitive approach as defined here is not common, but isolated explanations of this type are scattered through the literature of policy history and analysis. Typically, little effort is made to evaluate rival hypotheses. To judge from the following examples, this approach may be as applicable to security policies as to economic ones.

Ideological predispositions have an independent importance for policy in the United States, according to Anthony King. He confronts the question of why the direct operating role of government in the United States is so strikingly different from what it is in three European countries and Canada. He finds that the contrast cannot be explained by differences in the countries' elites, differences in mass demands for state activity, different interest-group strength, or unique political institutions. King concludes that the most satisfactory explanation lies in Americans' distinctive beliefs and assumptions about government.[64]

During the mid-nineteenth century, free-trade policies spread across Europe. These changes had many causes, Charles Kindleberger points out, but he finds that the most satisfactory explanation is that "Europe as a whole was motivated by ideological considerations rather than economic interests."[65] During the 1830s, economic liberalism "burst forth as a crusading passion."[66] Many British landlords themselves finally agreed to repeal of the Corn Laws. "Manchester and the English political economists persuaded Britain, which persuaded Europe—by precept and example."[67]

[64] Anthony King, "Ideas, Institutions, and the Policies of Governments: A Comparative Analysis," *British Journal of Political Science* 3 (1973): 291-313 and 409-423.

[65] Charles Kindleberger, *Economic Response: Comparative Studies in Trade, Finance and Growth* (Cambridge, Mass.: Harvard University Press, 1978), p. 65.

[66] Karl Polanyi, *The Great Transformation: The Political and Economic Origins of Our Time* (Boston: Beacon, 1944), p. 137.

[67] Kindleberger, *Economic Response*, p. 65; see also Joseph A. Schum-

Other examples point to the beliefs of a particular generation in history, beliefs shared almost universally among the informed public of a given era. After World War I, Britain pushed sterling back up to its prewar parity. This policy is puzzling from a mercantilist perspective. Given its declining economic power and payments problems, a mercantilist Britain determined to expand exports would have adopted an *under*valued currency. William Adams Brown, Jr., accounts for the paradox with a cognitive factor. After the war, certain widely-held "concepts of normal" obscured the true breakdown of the prewar gold standard, he shows. Prices in different countries had diverged, and pent-up demand and capital movements were to put additional unanticipated pressure on the "normal" currency parities implied by prewar legislation. Brown traces the return to parity in 1925 basically to "moral considerations, combined with faith in the mechanisms of the pre-war gold standard system based upon long experience. The British paper pound was a promise to pay a certain weight of gold, and this promise had to be redeemed."[68] In 1925, it was expected, falsely, that the return to gold would set in motion corrective international forces that had traditionally adjusted payments imbalances. In a similar vein, Charles Kindleberger attributes policy responses in the Great Depression a few years later to widespread "economic illiteracy."[69]

But analysts have also identified ideas shared less widely

---

peter, *History of Economic Analysis* (New York: Oxford University Press, 1954), pp. 397-398.

[68] William Adams Brown, Jr., *The International Gold Standard Reinterpreted 1914-1934*, 2 vols. (New York: National Bureau of Economic Research, 1940), vol. 1, pp. 165-174, 177-178, 282-287, and 385-390. Active opinion in Britain was almost unanimous: "gold at any rate other than $4.86 was unthinkable" (D. E. Moggridge, *The Return to Gold, 1925: The Formulation of Economic Policy and Its Critics* [Cambridge: Cambridge University Press, 1969], pp. 80-88). See also Stephen Clarke, *The Reconstruction of the International Monetary System: 1922 and 1933*, Princeton Studies in International Finance, No. 33 (Princeton: International Finance Section, Princeton University, 1973).

[69] Kindleberger, *World in Depression*, pp. 23, 237, 297-298.

during a given era. Nations become divided into rival schools of thought when interpreting national interests, both military and economic. Replacing one school with another would have been expected to produce policy change. During the 1930s, for instance, American officials who agreed about German strength and hostility were divided in their beliefs about international conflict. Some believed that American refusal to join Europe in the League of Nations had prevented war. Others believed that isolation, given German strength and hostility, was encouraging war.[70] If the isolationist view had been replaced by the alternative view, U.S. policy would have been different.

During the origins of the Cold War, Washington was divided between the traditional "universalist" school and the "sphere of influence" school.[71] A later shift in U.S. military doctrine, to cite a final security example, came about when President Kennedy brought into office the strategists who had been criticizing Eisenhower's doctrine of "massive retaliation" and who then proceeded to substitute their idea of "flexible response."

Certain "lessons" of the past have affected economic as well as security policies.[72] Richard Gardner maintains that U.S. economic planning for the post-World War II period was deeply imprinted with three lessons American leaders drew from World War I peacemaking experience. The unpreparedness of the U.S. delegation to Paris, the American failure to join the League, and poor handling of economic

[70] Stefan H. Leader, "Intellectual Processes in Foreign Policy Decision-Making: The Case of German-American Relations, 1933-1941" (Ph.D. diss., State University of New York at Buffalo, 1971).

[71] Arthur Schlesinger, Jr., "Origins of the Cold War," *Foreign Affairs* 46 (1967): 22-52. For an example from another state, see the contrast between the "Ben Gurionists" and Sharett in Israel during the 1950s, in Michael Brecher, *The Foreign Policy System of Israel: Setting, Images, Process* (New Haven: Yale University Press, 1972), chap. 12.

[72] For lessons affecting American security policies, see Ernest R. May, *"Lessons" of the Past: The Use and Misuse of History in American Foreign Policy* (London: Oxford University Press, 1973).

problems had all led to subsequent breakdown of the international order. Gardner also credits a resurgence of liberal thinking in Britain for the collaboration that produced the Bretton Woods institutions.[73]

In economics, Keynesianism was doubtless the most influential school of thought created during the first half of the twentieth century. The process through which its distinctive ideas penetrated and changed American macroeconomic policy is what Herbert Stein calls "The Fiscal Revolution in America." The revolution is symbolized by the contrast between the policies of 1931 and 1962. In both years, unemployment was a problem and a federal budget deficit was in prospect. President Hoover recommended a tax increase; President Kennedy proposed a tax reduction. Stein summarizes in the following way his explanation for the eventual adoption of the principle of compensatory fiscal policy, particularly deliberate budget deficits:

> The policy changed because the view of the economic and political world changed, and the view changed partly because the facts changed [the budget became a much larger influence in the national economy]. . . . The way we thought about the facts also changed. This was partly the result of experience [namely, proof after 1929 that depressions could last a long time, and repeated experiences of budget deficits without collapse]. But changes in the factual situation and accumulating experience seldom lead unequivocally to particular changes in policy. The facts and the experience have to be interpreted in some way. In part the fiscal revolution was propelled by the development of new ideas with which to understand the facts, new or unchanged, and the experience.[74]

A Keynesian school had coalesced in the United States in the late 1930s, and by the 1950s Keynesianism dominated

---

[73] Gardner, *Sterling-Dollar Diplomacy*, chap. 1.

[74] Herbert Stein, *The Fiscal Revolution in America* (Chicago: University of Chicago Press, 1969), pp. 4-5.

professional economics. Eisenhower's 1958 deficit helped
to undermine further the "budget balancing religion" among
businessmen and other laymen. By 1962, the inflation problem was less salient to the authorities, who feared deterioration in output and employment.

By the late 1970s, economists and the public agreed in
recognizing what had come to be called stagflation as the
central macroeconomic problem. But on the question of
how much stimulus, if any, the government should inject,
there was, as Marina Whitman observed in 1977,

> a wide range of disagreement among reasonable and
> honest people. . . . How one answers it depends partly
> on one's diagnosis of what caused the problem in the first
> place. . . . Competing explanations of what has caused
> the current stagflation generate very different prescrip-
> tions for the conduct of macroeconomic policy during
> the current stage of recovery.[75]

In some cases, policy change reflects ideas shared by only
a small circle. The New Deal devaluation of the dollar, as
one illustration, is another puzzling shift, from the stand-
point of international power and market conditions. In
1933, the United States was arguably the dominant world
monetary power, and it had had a trade surplus for years.
On these grounds one would have expected an effort to
lead a multilateral response to the depression, or at least
not the unilateral competitive depreciation that broke up
the London Economic Conference. The evidence suggests
the influence of domestic political changes and the flow of
new ideas into Washington—generally, a belief in the merits of greater government management of money, and specifically, one professor's theory.

During 1933 and early 1934, the United States embar-

---

[75] Marina v.N. Whitman, "The Search for the Grail: Economic Policy
Issues of the Late 1970s," in *Economic Advice and Executive Policy: Recom-
mendations from Past Members of the Council of Economic Advisers*, ed. Werner
Sichel (New York: Praeger, 1978), pp. 80-81.

goed payments of gold to Americans and to foreign countries, first in March 1933 as an emergency measure, then in April as a definite but defensive abandonment of the gold standard. Later in the year, the dollar was actively pushed downward by means of gold purchases, and in January 1934 the dollar was fixed again at $35 an ounce—a very large devaluation.

At the time of Roosevelt's inauguration in 1933, domestic banks were in crisis, and during that year, farmers and other domestic forces desperate for a recovery of prices were active in Congress and elsewhere. "The dead weight of debts contracted at higher price levels threatened to collapse the whole economy,"[76] and furthermore, much of the initial New Deal legislation was seen as deflationary. The Committee for the Nation agitated for monetary inflation and devaluation. The external trade balance, however, was not in deficit, high tariff protection already having been enacted.

After shoring up the banks, Roosevelt moved from one monetary experiment to another with the problem of domestic prices uppermost in his mind. He told a press conference in April that he had little idea where his monetary policy would lead; he could plan only one move at a time and then watch what happened. Many of his advisers were taken by surprise by his 20 April decision abandoning the gold standard temporarily. Roosevelt professed fears of a foreign run on the gold reserves, but the stocks were sufficient for normal demands, unlike British stocks in September 1931. To explain his decision, he referred reporters to an article by Walter Lippmann. Lippmann had argued that since 1931 no nation had been able both to maintain internal prices and to keep up the value of the currency abroad; the automatic gold standard could depress internal prices.

By the time of Roosevelt's brusque July message to the

[76] Arthur Schlesinger, Jr., *The Coming of the New Deal* (Boston: Houghton Mifflin, 1958), p. 195.

London Economic Conference rejecting international currency stabilization, he was developing an interest in managed money, and particularly in the theories of Professor George Warren, an agricultural economist at Cornell. Warren's maverick idea was that the supply and demand for gold were the most important determinants of commodity prices. Therefore, by devaluing the dollar and pushing up the price of gold, the government could raise farm prices directly. Roosevelt's close friend, Henry Morgenthau, Jr., had studied under Professor Warren. Morgenthau introduced the two and presented Warren's charts to Roosevelt during a Campobello vacation, and Roosevelt decided to reject his other advisers' plan for a loose international stabilization agreement.

For some weeks after the April gold embargo, the floating dollar depreciated and domestic commodity prices rose. But prices fell back again during the summer. In October, amid threats of farmers' strikes and over the protest of his more conservative advisers, Roosevelt decided to try Warren's clear-cut gold-purchase plan. He insisted that personal compassion for human suffering, not political pressure, made inaction unconscionable.

In the event, Warren's theory was discredited. By the end of January 1934, the gold price had risen about 69 percent, but wholesale commodity prices were up only slightly more than 20 percent. Roosevelt fixed the dollar and turned away from Warren's theory, without, however, abandoning his more general and more salient idea that control over money had to be wrested away from Wall Street.[77] Referring to Roosevelt's administration, G. Griffith Johnson, Jr., concludes: "The central decisions in monetary policy must be explained in terms of the attitude of the President and the influences and opinions which have been brought to bear thereon."[78]

[77] Schlesinger, *New Deal*; Crawford, *Monetary Management under the New Deal*; Herbert Feis, *1933: Characters in Crisis* (Boston: Little, Brown, 1966).
[78] G. Griffith Johnson, Jr., *The Treasury and Monetary Policy, 1933-1938*

CONCLUSION

The major omission from this discussion of analytical approaches is the Marxist tradition. I have not presented a Marxist approach here because I doubt that it would be either necessary or convincing for explaining changes in American foreign monetary policy. There seem to have been very few efforts to apply Marx's concepts to international monetary phenomena.[79] Marxism has certainly been used to explain relations between rich and poor nations, and to analyze the effects of transnational corporations on social conditions in both.[80] Perhaps political economists bet-

---

(Cambridge, Mass.: Harvard University Press, 1939), p. 208. Related works on the role of ideas in economic policy formation include the following and works cited therein: Robert A. Packenham, *Liberal America and the Third World: Political Development Ideas in Foreign Aid and Social Science* (Princeton: Princeton University Press, 1973); Tony Killick, *Development Economics in Action: A Study of Economic Policies in Ghana* (London: Heinemann, 1978); Jeffrey A. Hart, "Cognitive Maps of Three Latin American Policy Makers," *World Politics* 30 (October 1977): 115-140; Nathaniel Leff, *Economic Policy Making and Development in Brazil, 1947-1964* (New York: Wiley, 1968); Ernst B. Haas et al., *Scientists and World Order: The Uses of Technical Knowledge in International Organizations* (Berkeley and Los Angeles: University of California Press, 1978); Joseph A. Pechman, "Making Economic Policy: The Role of the Economist," in *The Handbook of Political Science*, 8 vols., ed. Fred Greenstein and Nelson Polsby (Reading, Mass.: Addison-Wesley, 1975), vol. 6, pp. 1-78; Richard N. Goodwin, "Awaiting the Copernican Question," *The New Yorker*, 6 January 1975, pp. 38-49; Paul A. Samuelson, "Economists and the History of Ideas," *American Economic Review* 52 (1962): 1-18; Daniel Bell, *The Coming of Post-Industrial Society* (New York: Basic Books, 1973).

[79] A. Stadnichenko, *Monetary Crisis of Capitalism: Origin, Development* (Moscow: Progress Publishers, 1975); Ernest Mandel, *Decline of the Dollar: A Marxist View of the Monetary Crisis* (New York: Pathfinder, Monad, 1972). Block, *Origins of International Economic Disorder*, reports the most careful empirical research on this subject informed by a revisionist framework.

[80] Some simple tests of some imperialism theories for explaining variations in U.S. military policies indicate that the theories are valid in some respects and not in others; see John Odell, "Correlates of U.S. Military Assistance and Military Intervention," in *Testing Theories of Economic Imperialism*, ed. Steven Rosen and James Kurth (Lexington, Mass.: D. C. Heath, 1974), pp. 143-166. Cheryl Payer, *The Debt Trap: The International*

ter educated in the subtleties of Marxist analysis could produce a persuasive model that would put international monetary policies in a new light. Such an approach would probably begin by asking fundamentally different questions.[81]

The questions asked here do not seem to demand a class-based interpretation. There is little evidence for supposing that a strictly working-class government in the United States would have designed a different international monetary policy during this period. At the same time, there is considerable evidence that informed high-income Americans were significantly divided in their preferences for policy in this field. Distinctions other than class seem more fruitful and interesting for these questions.

Nor is it clear that more structural Marxist or neo-Marxist approaches would add significantly here. One may assume that the United States is a capitalist state, regardless of the class origins of incumbent officials. Then the problem would be to show that it was the changing interests of this capitalist state that produced the observed monetary policy changes. This would not be accomplished by flights of abstraction that are not connected to concrete phenomena. But more concrete efforts seem likely—judging from available work[82]— to lead back to the very factors with which we begin: payments imbalances ("contradictions"), political power, and ideologies and perceptions.

This chapter proposes five general perspectives for ana-

Monetary Fund and the Third World (New York: Monthly Review Press, 1974), argues that the IMF operates as a link between its capitalist masters and Third World repression and inequality. Also see Roberto Frenkel and Guillermo O'Donnell, "The 'Stabilization Programs' of the International Monetary Fund and their Internal Impacts," and Barbara Stallings, "Peru and the U.S. Banks: Privatization of Financial Relations," in *Capitalism and the State in U.S.-Latin American Relations*, ed. Richard R. Fagen (Stanford: Stanford University Press, 1979), pp. 171-253.

[81] Also see John H. Goldthorpe, "The Current Inflation: Towards a Sociological Account," in Hirsch and Goldthorpe, *Political Economy of Inflation*, pp. 186-216, for interesting ideas in the tradition of Karl Polanyi.

[82] See Block, *Origins of International Economic Disorder*.

lyzing changes in U.S. external monetary policies of the 1960s and 1970s. Each views the state's actions from a different angle, emphasizing, respectively, the pressures of international market conditions, the international structure of power and rivalries among states, shifts in the domestic political situation, government organization and internal bargaining, and the beliefs and priorities of the leadership. The five perspectives may also prove useful for understanding policies on other economic issues and in other democracies.

The next challenge is to explore how these alternative approaches might be applied simultaneously to specific cases of policy change. In that process, these imperfect theories must be rendered concrete and as precise as possible, and their explanatory value must be assessed and compared. The goal in each instance is to arrive at the simplest possible explanation that corresponds with the empirical evidence. Often, unfortunately, convincing explanations of international reality are not very simple. But the next three chapters will show that these analytical tools can help greatly to reduce the apparent complexity. These American monetary cases also illustrate some general relations among the explanatory variables themselves. In the concluding chapter, we will be in a position to discern some of those connections and to identify the more and the less important sources of policy change.

3

Creating a New International Money

ON 10 July 1965, Secretary of the Treasury Henry Fowler announced in a public speech in Hot Springs, Virginia, that the United States stood ready to participate in the first international monetary conference since Bretton Woods, for the purpose of reforming the world's arrangements for providing international liquidity. Six months later, the U.S. government presented to the other major financial powers its plan for creating a new synthetic international reserve asset, a rival to the dollar. Fowler's speech stunned the international financial world, since the United States had labored for several years on behalf of a balance-of-payments policy that would avoid fundamental changes, and it had specifically and repeatedly rejected rival liquidity schemes. The speech was not preceded by advance consultations with continental European governments. Not the least surprised were members of the Treasury staff, who continued for months to send up memos recounting the many reasons not to follow this course, arguments they had been refining for four years.

This reversal of American policy was, in retrospect, one of the most significant shifts of the last two decades. It ushered in a lengthy multilateral negotiating process that finally, in 1969, created the SDR (for "Special Drawing Rights" on the International Monetary Fund) along the lines of the American plan. This step, the creation of money through an international organization, carried within itself a far-reaching potential to change international relations. Little of that potential had been actualized by the end of the SDR's first decade, because events following its birth were nothing like those envisaged by its makers, but that part of the story will emerge at a later point.

This chapter deals with the 1965 shift of U.S. policy. Why did policy change in the direction it did? Why did the change deal with liquidity rather than exchange rates? From the vantage point of 15 years later, it might seem that the depreciation of the dollar was inevitable, and one might wonder why so much effort was expended to postpone the inevitable. The answers are considerably less simple than the questions. An instructive way to probe for the answers is to compare the 1965 policy with that of the early Kennedy administration. But before describing Kennedy's initial direction, we must first review the preceding events and the international political and economic setting in 1960.

THE BRETTON WOODS INTERNATIONAL MONETARY REGIME

The extraordinary military and economic strength of the United States at the close of World War II made it possible for the Americans, along with the British, to design a new monetary regime for the world and to win wide acceptance for the framework.[1] An international monetary regime may be defined as a

> set of rules or conventions governing monetary and financial relations between countries. . . . A monetary regime specifies which instruments of policy may be used and which targets of policy are regarded as legitimate,

[1] Communist countries are here considered to be outside the international monetary system for most purposes, because of the low level of their transactions with the rest of the world during this period. Exceptions include the role of the Soviet Union in world gold trade; the membership of Yugoslavia and, much later, of Romania, Vietnam, and Laos in the International Monetary Fund; and Eastern European links to Western private banks. This effort to explain U.S. policy also largely omits attention to less developed states, not because they were unaffected by these events, but because they too had little influence on the policies analyzed here.

including of course the limiting cases in which there are no restrictions on either.[2]

In the present case, the rules were embodied in the Articles of Agreement of the International Monetary Fund (IMF) and the World Bank, international organizations of sovereign states, and they took effect in 1946. Their broad purpose was to protect national and world prosperity from the perceived evils of the gold standard and government behavior of the 1930s. The Americans were particularly keen on removal of government restrictions on payments for current international transactions, which blocked the growth of world trade, including U.S. exports. One rule therefore outlawed discriminatory currency practices and current exchange restrictions, with an exception permitting the latter during a "transitional period." Controls over capital movements were not discouraged, however.

To avoid competitive exchange depreciation, a second rule required pegged exchange rates and declared that the determination of exchange rates was a matter for joint international decision. To join the IMF, a state was required to declare a par value for its currency in terms of gold or the U.S. dollar, to make the currency convertible in the above sense of ending current exchange restrictions, and to act to prevent its exchange value in actual trading from deviating from its (dollar) parity by more than one percent in either direction. In practice, the dollar was pegged to gold and all other member currencies were then pegged to the dollar. Washington indicated that it would continue the prewar policy of freely exchanging dollars and gold at $35 an ounce upon demand by foreign governments. This was the practice whereby the United States satisfied the obligation to promote exchange stability. (No obligation to do so by converting dollars or any other currency into gold was written into the Articles of Agreement.) Under these

---

[2] Richard Cooper, "Prolegomena to the Choice of an International Monetary System," *International Organization* 29 (1975): 64-65.

arrangements, the United States did not initially trade in foreign currencies in New York, since each other government was obliged to act. The only provision for U.S. action to change U.S. exchange rates involved changing the dollar-gold price. At the time and thereafter, it was assumed that the United States was providing the world with a stable international money, stable in terms of other currencies and also in terms of American goods and services.

Given a prohibition on current exchange restrictions and a presumption against exchange-rate change at least in the short run, some other provision had to be made for adjustment to imbalances in international payments. Britain was insistent on preserving national autonomy sufficient to insulate her economy from gold-standard pressures to correct deficits by suffering higher unemployment. An international fund was therefore established to provide a standing, official source of short-term credit to which governments in difficulty could turn in order to finance a deficit. They would then have some time to wait to see whether the problem would correct itself, or to apply gradual domestic adjustment measures. The United States was willing to underwrite an international fund that could be used to induce "responsible" international economic behavior from those seeking access to its sources. But as the largest prospective creditor of the day, the U.S. refused to agree to as generous a pool of resources as the British had proposed.

For cases where no other remedy was sufficient, the rules allowed exchange-rate change to eliminate imbalances. As the Articles of Agreement put it: "A member shall not propose a change in the par value of its currency except to correct a fundamental disequilibrium." A change could be made "only after consultation with the Fund [the IMF]." "Fundamental" was not defined explicitly. As suggested by the negative form of this rule, the chief concern in 1944 was with the temptation of governments to devalue solely for competitive gain, without having developed a fundamental deficit. The rule was silent about the obverse case of a state that achieves a fundamental surplus and *declines* to "propose" that its currency be revalued upward. Americans were less concerned about this second side of the problem as long as they were a surplus country.[3] In general, the Bretton Woods regime left open the crucial political issue of the allocation among governments of responsibilities for adjustment to international payments imbalances.

Apart from IMF quota increases and transactions with the Fund, the Articles had little to say about the size and composition of international liquidity. One provision allowed the membership to increase the official value of gold reserves, the technique of increasing liquidity practiced in the 1930s, by means of a "uniform change in par values." The provision of international reserves was not covered by intergovernmental management.

The "transitional period" mentioned in the Articles of Agreement lasted until 1961, much longer than anticipated, and during that time many external restrictions were maintained. But by 1961, much of the regime had come into force for the major countries, though it was hedged with unplanned additional conventions. The Fund's resources turned out to be far from adequate to deal with the imbalances of the late 1940s, and the United States therefore devised the Marshall Plan. On the other hand, major exchange-rate changes did not occur frequently. International liquidity was augmented in practice through

[3] Keynes, representing a probable deficit country, did manage to get the Americans to incorporate a provision to give deficit countries some leverage over surplus countries, fearing a repeat of the American behavior of the 1920s and 1930s. The scarce currency clause (Article VII) provided that the IMF could formally declare that a currency is "scarce" if the Fund itself were running short. This would give states authority to impose exchange controls against the surplus country, presumably the U.S. at that time. This clause became virtually a dead letter because, despite huge postwar international imbalances, the Fund in fact loaned out very few of its dollars, on the ground that these imbalances were not of the temporary sort for which the IMF was created. With dollar scarcities outside the Fund, the U.S. acquiesced in controls against dollar goods and provided dollars through the European Recovery Program.

accumulations of U.S. dollars and gold by countries earning payments surpluses, as encouraged by Washington. Backed by the military security and economic strength of the United States, the dollar became a key international currency in three senses, in addition to its role as numéraire for other currencies: (1) It served as a medium of payment for much international trade, including many transactions not involving the United States. (2) Because of its wide transactions use, the dollar was also the currency that governments traded for their own currencies when necessary to keep their exchange rates within the required one-percent margins. And (3) reserve dollars also served as a store of value for governments, along with sterling and the French franc for a few countries.

The year 1958 was notable for several reasons. It saw the strengthening of the Bretton Woods regime by the first decision to enlarge IMF resources and through reductions in European exchange restrictions. It was also the year in which the U.S. balance of payments dropped sharply into deficit (see Chart 1 and Table 1). The trade balance worsened in 1958 and again in 1959 seemingly for cyclical reasons, as the United States recovered from recession faster than Europe; in addition, increases in U.S. imports, especially of cars, suggested shifts in comparative productive strength. Furthermore, in 1958, gold began to leave the Treasury in substantial volume. The large gold stock, after growing by $305 million and $795 million worth in the previous two years, sustained a decline of $2,275 million worth in 1958.

But not all of the surplus dollars were converted. Some were accumulated by foreign firms and governments, so that foreign liquid claims on the U.S. also continued to rise as U.S. liquid foreign assets began to fall (see Chart 2). In 1960, the U.S. returned to recession while Europe was booming, but the cyclical reversal was insufficient to return the country to overall external balance. A new element now was a large outflow of short-term capital, as U.S. interest

CHART 1. U.S. Overall Balance of Payments, 1950-1965

Annual data, liquidity basis

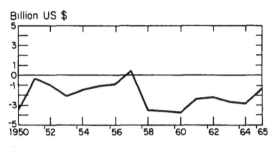

Quarterly data

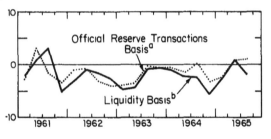

ᵃ Equals changes in liquid and nonliquid liabilities to foreign official holders and changes in official reserve assets consisting of gold, convertible currencies, and the U.S. gold tranche position in the IMF.

ᵇ Equals changes in liquid liabilities to foreign official holders and changes in official reserve assets consisting of gold, convertible currencies, and the U.S. gold tranche position in the IMF.

SOURCE: *Economic Report of the President 1966*, pp. 161, 301.

rates fell relative to those abroad. During this third year of substantial deficit and gold drain, financial markets became notably uneasy amid much discussion of the dollar's weakness and even of the chance of devaluation. In late October 1960, the price of gold on the London exchange shot out of its typical narrow range near $35 and touched $40 before receding. Gold in this case had its usual potent symbolic

TABLE 1. SELECTED U.S. BALANCE-OF-PAYMENTS ACCOUNTS, 1955-1969 (billions of dollars)

	Exports	Imports	Balance of Trade	Military Transactions, Net	Investment Income, Net	Balance on Goods and Services	U.S. Govt. Grants & Capital, Net	U.S. Private Capital, Net Long Term	Short Term	Foreign Capital, Net	Errors, Omissions	Liquidity Balance[a]	Official Reserve Transactions Balance[b]	U.S. Reserve Assets, Net (End of Period)
1955	14.4	-11.5	2.9	-2.7	2.3	2.2	-2.2	-1.1	-.2	.3	.4	-1.2	—	22.8
1956	17.6	-12.8	4.8	-2.8	2.5	4.1	-2.4	-2.6	-.5	.6	.4	-1.0	—	23.7
1957	19.6	-13.3	6.3	-2.8	2.6	5.9	-2.6	-3.3	-.3	.5	1.0	.6	—	24.8
1958	16.4	-13.0	3.4	-3.1	2.6	2.4	-2.6	-2.6	-.3	.2	.4	-3.4	—	22.5
1959	16.5	-15.3	1.1	-2.8	2.7	.3	-2.0	-2.3	-.1	.7	.3	-3.9	—	21.5
1960	19.7	-14.8	4.9	-2.8	2.8	4.1	-2.8	-2.5	-1.3	.4	-1.2	-3.9	-3.4	19.4
1961	20.1	-14.5	5.6	-2.6	3.6	5.6	-2.8	-2.6	-1.6	.7	-1.1	-2.4	-1.3	18.8
1962	20.8	-16.3	4.5	-2.4	4.1	5.1	-3.0	-2.9	-.5	1.0	-1.2	-2.2	-2.7	17.2
1963	22.3	-17.0	5.2	-2.3	4.2	5.9	-3.6	-3.7	-.8	.7	-.5	-2.7	-2.0	16.8
1964	25.5	-18.7	6.8	-2.1	4.9	8.5	-3.6	-4.4	-2.1	.7	-1.1	-2.8	-1.6	16.7
1965	26.5	-21.5	5.0	-2.1	5.3	7.1	-3.4	-4.5	.8	.3	-.6	-1.3	-1.3	15.5
1966	29.3	-25.5	3.8	-2.9	5.4	5.2	-3.4	-3.9	-.4	2.5	-.5	-1.4	.3	14.9
1967	30.7	-26.9	3.8	-3.1	5.9	5.1	-4.2	-4.4	-1.2	3.4	-1.1	-3.5	-3.4	14.8
1968	33.6	-33.0	.6	-3.1	6.2	2.5	-4.0	-4.3	-1.1	8.7	-.5	.2	1.6	15.7
1969	36.4	-35.8	.6	-3.3	6.0	1.9	-3.8	-4.7	-.6	4.1	-2.8	-7.0	2.7	17.0

a Equals changes in liquid liabilities to foreign governments, changes in liabilities to other foreign holders, and changes in official reserve assets. This balance, discarded after 1971, was regarded until 1966 as the overall measure of deficit in the balance of payments.
b Equals changes in all liabilities to foreign governments and changes in official reserve assets. This balance was published from 1966 to 1975 as a measure of official intervention to maintain par values. Figures for 1960 to 1965 were calculated later; figures for 1955 to 1959 have not been calculated.
SOURCES: Economic Report of the President 1971, Table C-87, and 1974, Table C-88.

CHART 2. U.S. Liquid Foreign Assets and Liabilities,
1950-1965

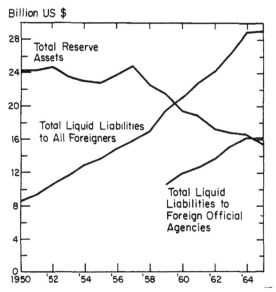

Billion US $

SOURCES: *International Economic Reoport of the President 1973*, Table
20, and *1974*, Table 33.

effect. The price break touched off a wave of currency
speculation against the dollar. Weekly news stories of
Treasury gold sales moved to the front pages. One of the
reasons cited for the gold price episode was bankers' concern over the American election and the possible economic
policies of a Kennedy administration "full of academics."
Candidate John Kennedy felt it necessary to issue on October 31 a proper policy statement on the balance of payments, including the pledge: "If elected President I shall
not devalue the dollar from the present rate. Rather I shall
defend the present value and its soundness." The Bretton
Woods monetary system had passed from an early postwar
structure based on a U.S. surplus into one with what was

beginning to seem a more than marginal or transitory American deficit.

U.S. POLICY IN 1961-1962

The response of the U.S. government to this historic change in the international financial market was essentially to re-affirm the central direction of prevailing policy, to ignore or reject radical changes, and to improvise new operational techniques for fending off challenges to the dollar's exchange rate and its world liquidity role. The Kennedy administration's initial steps were presented in a balance-of-payments message to Congress in February 1961. In addition to other mild measures to promote recovery from recession, the administration sought to allow long-term interest rates to decline while keeping short-term rates high to attract international capital flows. Intentions were declared and some measures were taken to stabilize prices and costs; to promote exports, foreign tourism in the United States, and inward foreign investment; and to continue and tighten the Eisenhower administration's efforts to limit overseas government spending by directing Defense Department procurement and foreign-aid receipts to the U.S. market. (Additional operational initiatives abroad will be described below.) The President's message expressed an interest in studies of ways to improve international institutions for furnishing increases in international reserves. Major changes of policy—such as devaluation of the dollar, floating exchange rates, stopping U.S. private foreign investment, retrenching on overseas military commitments, or creating new international monetary institutions—were avoided.

The reasons for this initial policy response need to be examined for the limited purpose of uncovering the roots of the policy of the mid-1960s and the sources of difference between the two. These decisions are best understood when first placed in their surrounding intellectual context.

Contending Diagnoses Outside Government

The evolution in international finance and politics up to the early 1960s, which in retrospect seems significant as the beginning of the recurrent political-monetary turmoil of the following two decades, had little impact on even informed elite opinion in the United States at the time. Americans were only beginning to be educated about what a balance of payments is and to learn that it could constitute a problem for their country. Few people paid attention to international monetary affairs, and even fewer expected any major changes. But the changing facts were being observed in a few government and university offices, and they gave rise to a wide range of conflicting diagnoses and prescriptions.

Several analysts perceived fundamental and persisting flaws in U.S. policy or in the international monetary system as a whole, and they therefore proposed radical changes. Professor Milton Friedman reiterated his breathtaking ideas in an articulate and confident style, but he failed to generate more than a tiny following at the time, even among academic economists, let alone bankers or merchants. The problem, Friedman told a Congresssional committee in 1963, was quite simple.

> As long as we and other countries continue to try to maintain fixed exchange rates and also to retain independence in domestic monetary policy, an international monetary crisis is always a possibility. . . . The single and only effective way to make a crisis of this kind impossible is to introduce a system of free market exchange rates. That would provide an automatic and effective adjustment mechanism for changes in international trade. . . . We should proceed on our own to set free the price of the dollar in terms of other currencies to find its own level in world markets. . . . A system of floating exchange rates would render the problem of making outflows equal inflows into the market where it belongs and not leave

it to the clumsy and heavy hand of government. It would leave government free to concentrate on its proper functions. . . . In conclusion, a word about gold. . . . Personally, I favor selling it off . . . and simultaneously removing all present limitations on the ownership of gold and the trading in gold by American citizens. There is no reason why gold, like other commodities, should not be freely traded on a free market.[4]

This diagnosis centers on the foreign exchange market and the dollar's exchange rate, a market price that has been fixed by government. The United States has an international payments deficit, and the reason is that the exchange rate is set too high.

Other economists examining empirical data in the early 1960s also came to the conclusion that the dollar was overvalued and thus should be devalued, without going as far as Friedman to urge that the practice of pegging rates be abolished altogether. As evidence of overvaluation, Professor Hendrik Houthakker of Harvard University calculated the values of the dollar and the German deutsche mark in terms of a similar bundle of consumption goods—that is, the purchasing power of each. The ratio of the two would then give the purchasing-power parity, or what was

---

[4] Statement by Milton Friedman, in U.S., Congress, Joint Economic Committee, *Contingency Planning for U.S. International Monetary Policy: Statements by Private Economists*, 89th Cong., 2nd session, 1966, pp. 30-31, 36. Friedman had earlier published his classic theoretical paper, "The Case for Flexible Exchange Rates," in his book, *Essays in Positive Economics* (Chicago: University of Chicago Press, 1953). There he had argued that wild instability of rates would not be the result of his proposal, unless fundamental economic conditions were highly unstable in the first place. Otherwise, he wrote, with no distortion of the markets caused by central bank trading, private traders would govern their behavior according to the long-run prospects for each currency. Thus, if a temporary disturbance pushed a basically strong currency below its equilibrium value, far-sighted private traders would go against the tide, seeing an opportunity to buy low and sell high later. To act otherwise would be to lose money. Their buying would bid the currency back up to its equilibrium value, keeping exchange rates fairly stable without government intervention.

assumed to approximate a true market value for the dollar vis-à-vis the mark. While at the official rate the dollar was worth DM4, figures for 1962 indicated that in terms of purchasing power the dollar was worth about DM3.12, or 22 percent less. As the cause of the overvaluation, Houthakker and others pointed to excessive devaluations of foreign currencies in 1949. The U.S. current account surplus was not large enough to cover outflows of private capital and military and foreign-aid programs. Furthermore, he argued, the payments deficit would be even larger were it not for import restrictions and, most important, the stagnation of the domestic economy. Houthakker maintained—and this was his central contention before Congress—that domestic unemployment and the international deficit were both caused by overvaluation of the dollar. Devaluation could be avoided only at a high price. "A choice will have to be made between maintaining exchange rates and reviving the economy." Houthakker offered a supporting historical analogy, one that differed from Robert Triffin's better-known reading of the same history. The pound sterling had been overvalued during the 1920s, he noted. The sequel to this period, when Britain was afflicted by both domestic stagnation and external deficit, was the collapse of sterling in 1931. Houthakker felt that allowing rates to float freely, however, would have serious ill effects, and he recommended instead devaluing the dollar against gold. He disputed the common assumption that European governments would devalue in response and frustrate parity adjustment, reasoning that in the current economic circumstances this would be competitive depreciation, which would risk punishment by the IMF.[5]

[5] H. S. Houthakker, "Exchange Rate Adjustment," in Joint Economic Committee, *Factors Affecting the United States Balance of Payments: Compilation of Studies*, 87th Cong., 2nd sess., 1962, pp. 287-304. Houthakker's Harvard colleague Jaroslav Vanek supported the diagnosis that the dollar was overvalued, judging from the existence of a sizeable deficit for several years even with domestic slack. Vanek attributed this overvaluation to technological progress and faster growth of productivity abroad, and re-

Houthakker and perhaps a few others raised the question of devaluation with U.S. economic officials during the early Kennedy administration, but the chief response apparently was a hostile glare. Many economists regarded purchasing-power-parity theory as fundamentally flawed, or inappropriate, for example in its disregard of the capital account. More important, at the time the United States still enjoyed a surplus on current account and what seemed to many to be a favorable price performance compared with competing countries. But in any case, to those who felt pride in the dollar and in America's role as world banker, suggesting devaluation had a psychological effect analogous to proposing appeasement of the Soviet Union. The proposal almost raised doubts about the speaker's patriotism.

Other economists, while uncomfortable with either fully flexible exchange rates or dollar devaluation, also ran against the grain of official discussion by calling for greater flexibility of exchange rates, and in general for emphasis on permitting markets to adjust international payments positions rather than on searching for new ways to finance deficits. A group of 21 American and European economists offered this point of view in a statement issued three weeks after the first U.S. plan for a new reserve asset was unveiled in early 1966. They advocated an international rule that would allow governments unilaterally to change their par values gradually and frequently, and they recommended that pegged exchange rates be allowed to fluctuate in a wider band around parities. The signers included four men who would later be chosen as members of or consultants to the Nixon administration: Houthakker, Friedman, Gott-

---

sulting rises in U.S. prices relative to Europe's, as well as to other causes. Vanek did favor a floating exchange rate. He argued that an improvement in U.S. employment could come about without impoverishing Europe, because the European economies were simultaneously suffering from excess demand and inflationary pressures, also due to the improper parities. ("Overvaluation of the Dollar: Causes, Effects, and Remedies," *Factors Affecting U.S. Balance*, pp. 267-285.) Both these scholars dismissed the diagnosis of a scarcity of international liquidity.

fried Haberler, and William Fellner.[6] The discussion of exchange rates and the merits of greater flexibility was, however, still very much a fringe activity until the late 1960s.

A quite different diagnosis of the international monetary situation came to dominate intellectually in the early and mid-1960s. Robert Triffin, professor of economics at Yale University and adviser to many governments and international organizations, was the first to call widespread attention to a world liquidity problem, and he authored one of the most carefully elaborated and widely discussed plans for monetary reform. The return to currency convertibility in Europe at the end of 1958 moved Triffin to gloomy reflection about the earlier return to convertibility in the 1920s, the debacle of 1931, and what he saw as the essential parallel between past and present. When he looked at the facts, Triffin saw an "unorganized, nationalistic gold exchange standard" in each period. The central weakness was reliance on national currencies, sterling before and the dollar now, as international reserves. International reserves are needed by every country, in some rough ratio to imports, Triffin thought, for financing imbalances, as collateral on which to borrow, and as a store in case of war. But production of gold long ago ceased to provide as large an increase in liquidity as governments collectively desired. Since World War II, many governments had chosen to accumulate foreign exchange alongside gold to increase their reserves. They had not agreed to international rules sufficient to regulate the world's official money supply.

It was Triffin's contribution to point out that continued reliance on this unplanned, decentralized process led inescapably to a painful dilemma. The more the reserve-currency country builds up its liabilities or pays out its reserves, in response to the decisions of the other governments, the

---

[6] *New York Times*, 21 February 1966, p. 63. Other early advocates of greater exchange-rate flexibility included Professors Fritz Machlup and James E. Meade, whose views are represented in *Factors Affecting U.S. Balance*.

less confidence foreign depositors will have in its ability to redeem these commitments, and hence the greater the danger of a panic in which the foreign-exchange component of world reserves is wiped out, as in 1931. On the other hand, the United States could balance its payments and stop the gold outflow, but with consequences almost equally unpleasant. Unless some other way of providing increases in world reserves were devised, world liquidity would fall short of rising world needs. The result could be deflation by deficit countries, competitive depreciations, and controls on trade and capital. The gold-dollar standard of necessity created either a confidence problem or a liquidity problem.

To escape this dangerous dilemma, Triffin boldly proposed abandoning the decentralized international regime and replacing it with a centralized one, as all industrialized countries had done domestically with their banking systems long before. Gradually gold and foreign exchange accretions would be replaced by deposits at the International Monetary Fund as the major source of world reserve increases. In Triffin's prescription, the function of increasing and managing world official liquidity would be lodged in an international organization, so that the world's supply would not be a casualty of decisions taken unilaterally in reserve-currency countries or of instabilities due to shifts in confidence in national currencies and gold. Triffin's plan, building on a 1942 plan of John Maynard Keynes, had all member countries agreeing henceforth to hold all of their reserves in gold and IMF deposits. Each would oblige itself to accept IMF deposits for the settlement of all international claims without limit. Members would have the right to convert some of their IMF balances to gold, subject to the limit that each member would hold at least 20 percent of its reserves in the new deposits. Some of the existing dollar and sterling reserves would be paid in to the IMF to cover this minimum obligation initially, and the new reserve asset would be made attractive so as to entice central banks to retire the rest of their national-currency reserves as well.

The new balances would be backed by the member governments' commitments to accept them in payment, and also by the gold guarantee. They would be fully liquid and they would earn interest, unlike gold. Furthermore, they would be free of the risks associated with national currency reserves—inconvertibility, devaluation, and blocking of withdrawal (assuming, that is, that the international organization did not collapse). The IMF would be authorized, like other banks, to lend some of its balances to deficit countries, and through its lending operations it could enlarge total deposits every year. The expanded IMF would be empowered to create money that could then finance transfers of real resources; it would also have authority to operate in national money markets. Thus, the world would collectively increase international liquidity in accordance with world needs for non-inflationary growth. Inflationary excesses could be prevented by a rule limiting the rate of increase to, say, 3 percent per year except by a vote of something like three-fourths of total IMF voting power (presumably allocated disproportionately to creditor states).

The Triffin plan meant that the United States would give up its role as banker for the world, along with its freedom to finance deficits by printing dollars. The U.S., like other IMF members, would have to cover deficits by drawing on its reserves or by explicit borrowing. Moreover, the United States would have some obligation to the IMF to pay off the existing dollar "overhang" due to earlier deficits. The U.S. would lose whatever bilateral political leverage it was able to exercise by virtue of its banker role. New York banks would lose the deposits and other business of foreign central banks. But clinging blindly to the prevailing haphazard practice would ultimately be worse for America, Triffin insisted. Moreover, his plan meant that the U.S. would be relieved of the burdens of maintaining a reserve currency, especially the pressure to restrict domestic monetary conditions more than was appropriate on domestic grounds. On the other hand, the plan was in essence the outline of

a world central bank, and it thus required radical infringe-
ments on individual states' sovereignty, without indicating
how a world state to back the bank was to emerge. Triffin
campaigned simultaneously for the less ambitious application of his ideas on a regional basis in Europe.[7]

Professors Friedman, Houthakker, and Triffin represented the more radical academic viewpoints in the air at
the time the Kennedy administration realized that it was
going to face a balance-of-payments problem. Other economists found lesser fault with existing rules and practices
and made recommendations for less sweeping reforms. Some
of these will be mentioned later.

President Kennedy took a more intense and sustained
personal interest in the balance of payments than any other
president had done since World War II, and his advisers
brought into the Oval Office some of the disagreements
among international monetary analysts. Nonetheless, the
outcome of these internal debates was that U.S. policy reflected the position of the Treasury Secretary, as has usually
been the case. For this reason, and also to permit comparison with later key advisers, let us then consider how the
situation was perceived by Treasury Secretary C. Douglas
Dillon and Under Secretary for Monetary Affairs Robert
V. Roosa, who was the senior operating officer in this field.

---

[7] Triffin's diagnosis and prescription were first published in the *Banca
Nazionale del Lavoro Quarterly Review*, March and June 1959, and they were
reprinted in *Gold and the Dollar Crisis: The Future of Convertibility*, rev. ed.
(New Haven, Conn.: Yale University Press, 1961). Both the diagnosis and
the prescription came under professional criticism and met a number of
competing proposals. See *World Monetary Reform: Plans and Issues*, ed.
Herbert G. Grubel (Stanford, Cal.: Stanford University Press, 1963), and
International Monetary Arrangements: The Problem of Choice, ed. Fritz Machlup and Burton G. Malkiel (Princeton, N.J.: International Finance Section,
Department of Economics, Princeton University, 1964). In 1978, Triffin
observed that the intervening events had proven him a fairly successful
prophet of the collapse of the Bretton Woods gold-dollar standard, but
an unsuccessful adviser. *Gold and the Dollar Crisis: Yesterday and Tomorrow*,
Essays in International Finance, no. 132 (Princeton, N.J.: International
Finance Section, Princeton University, 1978).

Views of Douglas Dillon and Robert Roosa, 1961-1962

Neither Dillon nor Roosa was new to this subject, though they had traveled different routes. Dillon was chairman of his family's investment banking firm, Dillon, Read and Company, and an active Republican. In the Eisenhower administration, he had served as ambassador to France and later in the State Department's second-ranking post. He had dealt with the IMF and the 1960 gold episode.[8] Roosa had earned a Ph.D. in economics in 1942 and had worked at the Federal Reserve Bank of New York from 1946 until moving to the Treasury Department in January 1961. During his last four years at the Reserve Bank, Roosa was vice president in charge of the research department.

Dillon and Roosa came to office with three strong general beliefs. One, widely shared among informed Americans, was that the existing U.S.-sponsored international economic regime had contributed enormous benefits to the free world as a whole. They shared the article of faith of their generation that after World War II, the United States, throwing off its earlier unfortunate isolationism, had courageously used its resources to pay for reconstruction and mutual defense, and had led the way in establishing international arrangements to insure against a repetition of the economic debacles of the interwar period. The dollar's link to gold and its position at the center of the monetary system were part of the American contribution. The rapid expansion of foreign economies and international trade under stable exchange rates, and the resumption of convertibility abroad, could be traced to this international regime and to U.S. efforts. Dillon and Roosa considered the role of world banker a burden and a responsibility that needed to be borne, and one which other countries were not willing to shoulder, since it did expose the reserve center alone to the risk of sudden withdrawals of gold. "The free world's monetary system, as it has evolved since World War II,

---

[8] Gilbert Burck, "A Dillon, a Dollar," *Fortune*, February 1961, pp. 93ff.

rests inescapably on the full acceptability of the dollar as a supplement to gold in financing world trade. No practicable alternative is in sight," Dillon declared at the Rome conference of the American Bankers Association in 1962.[9]

Dillon and Roosa also brought to office the related widely-shared assumption that going off gold or devaluing the dollar could well have disastrous economic consequences for the free world as a whole, amounting to destroying the international monetary system. In the past, going off gold and devaluing were associated with calamitous inflation and trade destruction, as during the interwar period. These two options were thus associated psychologically with strongly negative symbols; as in many cases, widespread causal beliefs about policy were heavily influenced by the most dramatic events. When forced to think about it, Dillon and Roosa also argued that devaluation would not in fact produce dollar depreciation. Other governments would in turn devalue against gold, restoring exchange rates among currencies to their former values. Besides, after such long and strenuous efforts to convince dollar holders that it could never happen, one had to face the likelihood that devaluation would prompt a massive wave of conversions, pushing the U.S. off gold. The process might destroy as much liquidity (in dollar form) as it created (by writing up the value of gold). Exchange rates forced to float could not be expected to remain stable. Few shared Milton Friedman's degree of faith in the invisible hand in this market. According to the conventional financial wisdom, private speculators could not be counted on to forecast long-term trends accurately and take the short-term risk of buying currencies under heavy selling pressure, or to forgo efforts to manipulate rates in the short term for speculative gain. Floating would mean chaos.

Dillon and Roosa shared a third general belief, one re-

[9] U.S., Department of the Treasury, *Annual Report of the Secretary on the State of the Finances 1962* (hereafter *Treasury Annual Report* followed by year), p. 439. See also Robert V. Roosa, *Monetary Reform for the World Economy* (New York: Harper & Row, 1965), p. 39.

lating to the national interests of the United States rather than to the free world as a whole. They believed that, although performing the role of world banker had its costs and risks, the existing regime also bestowed unique and valuable benefits on the United States. These benefits were probably more salient to Dillon, Roosa, Treasury officials, and bankers than to private economists and others, who acknowledged them but gave them less weight.[10] First, Roosa explained to a Congressional committee in 1962, the American balance of payments is strengthened by the substantial earnings the country receives from "borrowing short and investing long" abroad. U.S. foreign investment earnings far exceeded the interest paid on foreign holdings of dollars in the U.S. Roosa also felt that continuation of the functions of the dollar in private banking transactions depended on continuation of the official reserve function, at least on the scale that had been reached up to this time.[11] Furthermore, the reserve center enjoyed the unique ability to run a payments deficit if necessary without losing reserves, insofar as other governments absorbed and held the excess dollars as part of their reserve increases.

> The credit standing of a banking center is such that it can, in effect, borrow to meet its needs in almost an imperceptible fashion, without the necessity of arranging and negotiating loans as other borrowers must do. The trouble only comes, and people are only likely to begin to raise questions about undesirable aspects of the banking role, when this facility for borrowing from others is overused. That, of course, is what has happened to the United States.[12]

[10] James Tobin, *The New Economics One Decade Older* (Princeton: Princeton University Press, 1974), p. 31.

[11] Stephen D. Cohen, *International Monetary Reform, 1964-1969* (New York: Praeger, 1970), p. 49; James Tobin, *National Economic Policy* (New Haven: Yale University Press, 1966), p. 198.

[12] Statement by Roosa submitted on 13 December 1962 to the Joint Economic Committee, in *Treasury Annual Report 1963*, p. 371.

Roosa and Dillon were certainly not eager to encourage a U.S. deficit—quite the opposite. The disequilibrium must be ended, they said, but that would also be true if the U.S. had somehow given up the international roles of the dollar. In that case, indeed, the pressure to take painful medicine would have been felt earlier and more urgently. In laying down this role the United States would lose a kind of freedom.

All three of these predispositions were colored by no small amount of national pride, which frequently showed through in the discussions and even in the very language of the debate. The dollar must be "defended," like the flag. Devaluation might be defined technically as merely changing the currency's price, but it also carried the clear connotation of shameful failure. Devaluations are calamities that befall improvident countries that live beyond their means, debase their money, and fail in world commercial competition. Roosa argued that the country gained in prestige and influence from the international use of the American dollar, and Dillon wanted to solve the payments problem "without taking steps prejudicial to U.S. prestige." Servicing the payments requirements of the world, Roosa maintained, "is a role which naturally accompanies our leading economic and political position."[13] From the vantage point of a later, different era, it is important not to forget the pride and confidence of the American official outlook at this time, expressed in perhaps an exaggerated but vivid manner by McGeorge Bundy, President Kennedy's Special Assistant for National Security Affairs, in a 1965 interview. Bundy had been asked how his view of American diplomacy differed from his perspective before working in the White House. He replied that he had acquired a larger respect for the role of the United States in the world. And he had come to accept what he had learned from Dean Acheson, "that, in the final analysis, the United

[13] Burck, "A Dillon, a Dollar," p. 222; Robert Roosa, *The Dollar and World Liquidity* (New York: Random House, 1967), pp. 29, 107.

States is the engine of mankind, and the rest of the world is the train—explaining that he was not expressing chauvinism but simply passing judgment on the usefulness to the world of American energies." For Robert Roosa, the question of whether the United States ought to abandon the world banker role because of its costs suggested "the Wordsworthian nostalgia of an adult wishing he could be a child again."[14]

These general predispositions shaped the specific calculations Dillon and Roosa made about the international financial situation in 1961-1962, and both the general and the specific beliefs help explain their policy recommendations, which became U.S. policy. Their specific diagnosis of that situation had two main elements. First, they were certain that the dollar was not seriously overvalued. Notwithstanding the enlarged deficit and accelerated gold outflow since 1958, they expected that as their policy measures took effect, the U.S. would achieve balance or even surplus in a few years, and that some gold would return and rebuild U.S. liquid reserve assets.[15] No change in the exchange rate would be necessary. Expectations about the future are indispensable elements of every policy decision, and they depend on complex and necessarily unknowable influences; like many other policy makers before them and since, Dillon and Roosa resolved this uncertainty for the time being in the manner least disturbing to their predispositions.

Second, they saw no world liquidity shortage and they saw little reason to expect one in the future. More specifically, Roosa believed that other major governments might agree to international credit arrangements that would support further expansion of the dollar's role as a source of liquidity in years to come. For the present, Dillon told a Congressional subcommittee in June 1961,

[14] Henry F. Graff, "How Johnson Makes Foreign Policy," *New York Times Magazine*, 4 July 1965, p. 17; *Treasury Annual Report 1963*, p. 371.

[15] Roosa, *Dollar and World Liquidity*, p. 220.

our problem is the correction of imbalances and the handling of excessive shifts of liquid funds, rather than a shortage of overall liquidity. Indeed, in several countries the problem is to direct some of the excess liquidity into longer term finance through long-term capital exports. New reserves injected into the present payments situation would simply move to the centers which already have excess reserves. In the final analysis there is no substitute for balance-of-payments discipline in this or any economy. . . .[16]

Rather than thinking of new ways to create additional liquidity in the form of owned reserve assets, it would be better for the international community to concentrate on reducing imbalances and improving the mechanism for lending excess funds from surplus countries to deficit countries. Writing later, Roosa explained that at this time their "preoccupation, clearly, was with credit facilities" rather than creating new injections of owned reserves. If the system and individual countries stressed ways of piling up primary reserves to meet all possible contingencies, "the self restraint and discipline inherent in any system that relies on credit" would be undermined. As late as the Tokyo meetings of the IMF in September 1964, Dillon and Roosa reiterated the need "to shift the emphasis toward credit" within the existing regime.[17]

To the extent that any changes were needed, Roosa acknowledged after leaving office, "our first preference, quite understandably I would suppose, was to find ways in which the strength of other currencies could be mobilized to give peripheral support to the dollar." No other government was prepared to undertake the commitments necessary for its currency to become an additional reserve currency. "We therefore turned to ways of enlisting some of the other leading currencies in various short-term arrangements" for

[16] *Treasury Annual Report 1961*, p. 378.

[17] Roosa, *Dollar and World Liquidity*, pp. 258, 151-154; U.S. Department of State, *Bulletin* 51 (1964): 446-447.

joint resistance to speculative challenges to the key currencies while deficits were being rectified.[18]

In response to speculation in gold in late 1960, the major central banks experimented with supplying official gold to the London market to keep the price from spiraling out of control. Six foreign countries later agreed to form the London Gold Pool to share the pressure on the U.S. Movements of "hot money" between currencies were touched off by the small upward revaluation of the German mark in March 1961, again raising fears of attacks on sterling and the dollar. For the first time since World War II, the United States resumed operations in foreign-exchange markets, selling marks forward in New York to try to hold the price down until the storm passed. Partly to acquire foreign currency temporarily for such operations, the Federal Reserve negotiated a network of bilateral "swap" arrangements with major central banks. A "swap" amounted to a line of three-month credit between two central banks, which either of them could activate. The U.S. or another country under pressure could draw on official funds from abroad in a joint maneuver to recycle short-term capital flows arising from transitory disturbances. The U.S. could also use swaps more directly to protect its gold stock from conversions. If, for example, the Dutch central bank accumulated more dollars than it preferred to hold, the Federal Reserve could activate the swap line and use its borrowed guilders to buy the excess dollars, in effect giving the Dutch cover against the risk of a dollar devaluation for the duration of the credit. The United States was no longer in a position to expect all its financial partners to accumulate uncovered dollars without limit.

For flows that did not prove reversible in a short time, the technique of refinancing the credits at medium term by issuing Treasury bonds denominated in foreign currency was inaugurated—another way to reduce incentives for foreign central banks to purchase gold. In addition,

---

[18] Roosa, *Dollar and World Liquidity*, pp. 29-30.

Roosa suggested that several European governments make voluntary contributions to the IMF, to increase the capacity of this existing channel for conditional medium-term credit to the U.S. This they declined to do, but a series of negotiations did result in what was called the IMF's "General Arrangements to Borrow." Ten major countries, known later as the Group of Ten, agreed in 1962 to establish a contingency facility for lending to the IMF in an emergency. Despite heated objections by the IMF staff and by states excluded from the inner circle, the Europeans insisted on retaining a veto over whether the fund could lend the money to a particular borrower.[19] These techniques strengthened what Roosa called the dollar's "perimeter defenses."

Further in the future, according to Roosa's vision at the time, any needed increases in owned reserves could be provided by gold, "supplemented from time to time by controlled increases in dollars."

> Once the United States has its balance of payments fully under control, the rate of increase in the supply of dollars available to serve the international liquidity requirements in the world can also be managed. . . . Additional increases in the supply of dollars can rest upon an accumulation by the United States of incremental amounts of the currencies of other leading countries. These other currencies, while not equally capable of serving the multitude of functions required of a reserve currency, can, as the United States acquires holdings of them, be brought into a further mutual sharing of some of the responsibilities which the international reserve system must itself carry.[20]

[19] Susan Strange, *International Monetary Relations*, vol. 2 of *International Economic Relations of the Western World 1959-1971*, ed. Andrew Shonfield (London: Oxford University Press, 1976), pp. 105-117; Roosa, *Dollar and World Liquidity*, p. 228.

[20] Roosa, *Dollar and World Liquidity*, pp. 108, 229.

He hoped he could meet "future needs for additional reserves by issuing dollars against a 'bouquet' of currencies
acquired by the United States," expecting that with the
deficit ended, this U.S. reserve base underlying liquidity
creation would no longer be subject to the threat of gold
withdrawals and that the gold stock might even increase
again. Dillon and Roosa did not believe that Triffin's dilemma existed.

They consequently rejected the plans of Triffin and others
for creating new reserve assets. A new asset was not necessary, and it was positively harmful if it would displace
the dollar. The Treasury was particularly determined to
oppose the scheme for a Composite Reserve Unit (CRU)
put forward by the French government in 1963 and 1964.
This proposal was recognized as an attack on the dollar's
role, and it increased Roosa's reluctance to countenance
full-dress international negotiations on the liquidity question. In an earlier, more modest plan, suggested by E. M.
Bernstein, sterling and dollars would continue to serve as
reserves, but a CRU would provide the Europeans an alternative. Industrial countries would pool some of their
currencies, and against this pool they would issue multilateral Reserve Units to themselves. Discipline would be
maintained by the obligation of each country to redeem its
currency on demand in gold and RUs in a ratio of two to
one.[21] In the French version, the new assets would be distributed according to how much gold each government
already held, and central banks would be barred from any
further accumulation of dollars.

Roosa foresaw that such a regime would produce precisely what he was working diligently to avoid. The distribution would reward countries which kept a large fraction
of their reserves in gold, and the regime would create a
strong incentive to trade dollars in order to get gold for

[21] Statements of E. M. Bernstein, in Joint Economic Committee, *Guidelines for International Monetary Reform: Hearings*, 89th Cong., 1st sess., 1965,
part 2, pp. 230-256.

making settlements. "The gold-link would be tantamount to a devaluation of all the dollar holdings of the contributing countries in terms of gold," he believed, and might lead to a rush to convert dollars while they were still convertible at $35 an ounce. The French CRU proposal, advocated in Tokyo in 1964, "would, we thought, quickly consume the gold base of the dollar and destroy much of the existing liquidity hinged to the dollar," Roosa later wrote.[22]

President Kennedy's Position

From the beginning of the Kennedy administration, Dillon and Roosa had to contend with another faction within the President's circle of close advisers, which urged him to embrace more fundamental international monetary reform. A pre-inaugural task force on the balance of payments, chaired by George Ball and including Robert Triffin, urged that the administration study new schemes for increasing world reserves. This side of the internal debate was carried by Ball, as Under Secretary of State for Economic Affairs, and James Tobin, a member of the Council of Economic Advisers, supported by Walter Heller of the CEA and Carl Kaysen of the National Security Council. This group argued a New Deal domestic diagnosis of the balance-of-payments situation. Ball and Tobin were especially indignant at what they saw as a struggle over general financial policy between the national government on the one hand and, on the other, European bankers supported by domestic conservatives who had always opposed Democratic administrations. The bankers were using the gold loss as a means to throttle expansionary domestic economic policies that they opposed anyway. It was important to get the domestic economy employed and moving again, the group emphasized, but efforts were hampered by pressure for "discipline" exercised by occasional European withdrawals

[22] Roosa, *Dollar and World Liquidity*, pp. 244-245, 37, 195-198. See also Cohen, *International Monetary Reform*, pp. 32, 48-53.

of gold. As long as liquidity remained tight, this "loss of confidence" would be a source of concern. Tobin pushed for a multilateral agreement to vest the reserve creation function in an international institution, lifting from the U.S. the burden of the reserve currency and enlarging American freedom to give priority to domestic recovery.[23] Money was only a means, after all. Concern over money and the balance of payments should not become so dominant as to lead to policies that interfered with otherwise feasible improvements in real growth and living standards.

Tobin and others labored long trying to teach the President their economic lessons and to convince him that there were things worse than an international payments deficit. At a September 1963 meeting in the White House, John Kenneth Galbraith made an urgent appeal for stronger measures in the direction of exchange controls. Tobin had given Kennedy in advance a memo arguing that, contrary to the conventional wisdom, there was another way out, and that the risk of using it was less damaging than what Galbraith proposed. Tobin broached the idea not of devaluing the dollar but of simply letting the dollar float free from gold and giving the Europeans the choice of allowing the dollar to depreciate—the step President Nixon eventually took in August 1971. Kennedy, obviously having read this memo, challenged Galbraith and Dillon, using this argument. They responded heatedly, and the meeting ended without a decision.[24]

But gold and the balance of payments were a constant

[23] Arthur Schlesinger, Jr., *A Thousand Days* (Boston: Houghton Mifflin, 1965), pp. 651-655.

[24] James Tobin, notes appended to recorded interview of the Council of Economic Advisers by Joseph Pechman, 1 August 1964 (Boston, Mass.: John F. Kennedy Library, Oral History Program). The New Deal precedent of quickly suspending convertibility was evidently not suggested to President-elect Kennedy before his inauguration. (Paul Samuelson, Pechman interview of CEA, pp. 62-63.) Tobin reports that, by 1963, President Kennedy had become convinced that some measures to save the dollar were worse than suspending convertibility (*New Economics*, p. 29).

worry to Kennedy. He told his advisers that the two things
that scared him most were nuclear war and the payments
deficit. "Few subjects occupied more of Kennedy's time in
the White House or were the subject of more secret high-
level meetings."[25] In Kennedy's own beliefs, two considerations seemed most salient, one international and one
domestic-political. He felt constrained in foreign affairs
and at a disadvantage.

> I know everyone else thinks I worry about this too much.
> But if there's ever a run on the bank, and I have to
> devalue the dollar or bring home our troops, as the Brit-
> ish did, I'm the one who will take the heat. Besides it's
> a club that DeGaulle and all the others hang over my
> head. Any time there's a crisis or a quarrel, they can cash
> in all their dollars and where are we?[26]

Theodore Sorensen adds:

> Privately some advisers told the President that even de-
> valuation was not unthinkable—a drastic change in the
> system but preferable to wrecking it altogether. But the
> President emphasized that he did not want that weapon
> of last resort even mentioned outside his office—or used.
> By disrupting the international monetary system that we
> had done so much to create, devaluation would call into
> doubt the good faith and stability of this nation and the
> competence of its President.[27]

It was difficult to persuade Kennedy to deviate from
orthodox financial policies, partly because of his beliefs
about foreign policy and partly because of his beliefs about
his own domestic political situation. Like most other politicians, he assumed that to devalue the currency would be
to inflict a grievous political wound on himself. Kennedy

[25] Theodore Sorenson, *Kennedy* (Harper & Row, 1965), p. 405. See also
Schlesinger, *Thousand Days*, p. 654.

[26] Sorenson, *Kennedy*, p. 408.

[27] Sorenson, *Kennedy*, p. 408.

had been elected by an extremely small margin of the 1960 popular vote, and he was willing to have his new administration go to considerable lengths to avoid any actions that could be characterized as Democratic "tinkering with the money." There was some evidence for the suspicions on the part of those close to Kennedy that

> the gloomy rumors which triggered the gold withdrawals of 1960 had been deliberately spread by American bankers to embarrass him politically, and he did not want to be vulnerable to the same tactic in 1964.[28]

And so, while Kennedy was

> intellectually sympathetic to the reformers, it seemed to him, as he once said to Kaysen, that, when they put up their ideas, Dillon regularly and gracefully shot them down. He saw Dillon's continuation in Washington as his best insurance against a gold panic in New York. When he was satisfied that the Treasury recommendations were serious and solid, he would not go against them.[29]

MARKET PRESSURE AGAINST THE DOLLAR

In 1965, the United States reversed its previous opposition to creating a new form of international money, and indeed took the lead in a lengthy multilateral negotiating effort. Washington also turned to restrictions on American capital outflow, first announced in July 1963 and progressively intensified in 1965 and 1968. Why did policy make an about-face? Why did it take this particular new course rather than conceivable alternatives, such as dollar depreciation? Are

[28] Sorenson, *Kennedy*, p. 408.
[29] Schlesinger, *Thousand Days*, p. 655. Robert Roosa writes that, in a conversation before the inauguration, Kennedy told him that he wanted to postpone international consideration of overall monetary reform "until the position of the dollar itself had been reasonably secured" (*Dollar and World Liquidity*, pp. 13-14).

there any analytical tools that could have enabled an observer to anticipate this shift?

Most of the more familiar perspectives would have left the observer puzzled or positively misled. International market conditions seemed to be pushing Washington in a direction not taken. No significant changes in interest-group pressure, political party strength, or government organization that would account for the new policy had taken place. The international economic power structure had shifted slightly, and the recovery of Europe helps explain why the U.S. abandoned early Kennedy policies. But power changes were hardly sufficient in degree to explain a reversal. The power structure was consistent with a range of new policies different from the ones followed. The new policy resulted chiefly from intellectual sources: the continuation of some prevailing predispositions and the "encroachment" of new ideas at the top in Washington.

The dollar's international market had changed fundamentally, but the 1965 policy shift was hardly what would have been expected from a simple international market perspective. From that perspective, as developed in Chapter 2, the most obvious expectation is that when a market moves into persistent oversupply, the price will fall. A few private analysts recommended dollar depreciation at this time. But U.S. policy shifted, if anything, in the opposite direction.

The overall U.S. balance of payments had fallen substantially into deficit in 1958, and despite the initial programs of the Kennedy administration, it remained substantially in deficit, beyond what could be considered a short term. The deficit fluctuated and then turned downward again during the summer of 1962 and further downward during the first half of 1963 (see Chart 1). Throughout 1962, 1963, and 1964, the dollar traded below parity on most European foreign-exchange markets.

The downturn was traced to the private capital accounts. Commercial trade remained in surplus throughout the early

1960s, although not as strongly as it may have seemed, considering that exports financed by foreign aid accounted for half the reported trade surplus. American inflation performance continued to match or surpass that of Europe. The current account benefited also from a surplus on services. Net military expenditures and foreign aid were large negative items, but fairly constant ones over this period. On the other hand, the net export of U.S. private capital had expanded in 1956 and again in 1960. Another rise began in the latter half of 1962 and peaked in early 1963. Part of the outflow was corporate foreign direct investment, part was short-term money, and part reflected American purchases of foreign portfolio securities. The administration was attempting to hold down long-term interest rates to promote domestic investment, and foreign borrowers were taking advantage of the international difference.

In July 1963, the Federal Reserve raised the discount rate and the administration announced a policy departure, the proposal of an interest equalization tax, which was soon enacted. This tax was applied to foreign securities issued in the U.S., to encourage borrowers in developed countries to turn to other capital markets "temporarily" until the United States had achieved equilibrium. Ironically, one of the reasons the United States had sponsored a world regime of fixed exchange rates was to facilitate international trade and investment. Yet in order to maintain the dollar's rate, the U.S. was now imposing a measure that interfered with capital exports. When international market conditions were running more strongly against the dollar, U.S. policy added measures to resist these market signals rather than yielding to them.

After July 1963, portfolio capital outflows did diminish, but over the same period—late 1963 and 1964—outflows in the form of long-term bank credit ballooned. Foreign borrowers simply switched from one segment of the U.S. money market to another. In spite of a near-record commercial trade surplus in 1964, the overall deficit on the liquidity basis for that year was no smaller than for 1963, and in the last quarter of 1964 it was larger than the low point of 1963. In February 1965, the Johnson administration announced further measures to discourage capital outflows. It extended the interest equalization tax for two years, applied it to most bank loans with maturities of one year or more to borrowers in industrial countries, and urged on banks and corporations a set of voluntary guidelines for limiting the outflow. During the first half of 1965, the net outflow of U.S. private capital diminished sharply, and the overall payments position improved markedly, as shown in Chart 1. In these circumstances, the Johnson administration came out in favor of international negotiations to create a new form of international liquidity.

In sum, downward market pressure against the dollar had continued at a moderate level since the early 1960s. (This pressure would have been greater had it not been for U.S. government restraints on imports and capital outflows.) Yet the shift of U.S. policy in the mid-1960s was hardly in a direction signaled by this private market behavior. The new policy included a more active governmental effort to manage the balance of payments, and a more ambitious effort to develop intergovernmental organization, rather than a yielding to market forces.

Rising European Strength

The international market perspective would at least have raised doubts about the survival of the prevailing U.S. balance-of-payments policy, even if it could not explain the new policy. The same is true of an international power perspective. The international economic power structure shifted somewhat over the decade of the 1950s. As Europe and Japan recovered from the war, their strength rose slightly relative to that of America. By the early 1960s, Europe in particular was in a somewhat better position to resist unilateral American designs, and Europe did so.

One crude index of state capabilities is total productive and spending capacity. The six members of the European Community increased their share of world GNP between 1950 and 1960 from 11 percent to 13 percent. Japan's share rose from 1.5 to 3 percent. U.S. hegemony declined somewhat, but the structure remained centered on an economic superpower. The United States alone had produced 39 percent of world output in 1950; in 1960 it still accounted for a formidable 34 percent, and its GNP was seven times that of West Germany or Britain.[30]

Another index of a nation's relative capacity for influence on others is its share of international transactions. During the 1950s, West Germany increased its share of world imports from 4 to 8 percent, and its share of world exports from 3 to 9 percent. Japan's import share rose from 1.6 to 3 percent; her exports expanded from 1.4 to 3 percent of the world total. Here again, the United States' earlier lead eroded only slightly, leaving the U.S. still the largest trading state. The U.S. shares of world imports and exports slipped from 14 to 11 percent and from 17 to 15 percent, respectively.[31]

The United States remained the leading trader, and yet the American economy also depended on trade to a much lesser degree than any other major capitalist power. Along with its much larger GNP, the American economy was far more self-sufficient. In 1960, merchandise exports and imports together amounted to 7 percent of GNP. Proportions for other countries were: France, 23 percent; Japan, 20 percent; West Germany, 31 percent; United Kingdom, 33 percent; and Canada, 29 percent.[32] Greater reliance on the world economy reinforces the political effects of small size;

[30] U.S. President, *The United States in the Changing World Economy*, Report by Peter Peterson, 2 vols., 1972, vol. 2, Chart 1.

[31] Calculated from United Nations, *Yearbook of International Trade Statistics 1978*, 2 vols., vol. 1, Special Table A.

[32] Calculated from U.N., *Yearbook of International Trade Statistics 1978*, vol. 1, Special Table A, and U.S., *International Economic Report of the President 1977*, Table 2.

more penetrated economies are more vulnerable to disruptions in international trade and finance, and less able to resist foreign influence that is expressed through international transactions. This disparate economic influence was particularly evident in certain bilateral relations. A Canadian political leader once compared having economic relations with the United States to sleeping with an elephant.

Parenthetically, large size and relative closedness gave a country like the United States an "interest" in international payments adjustments by means of exchange-rate change at the border, rather than by means of changes in domestic macroeconomic policy and conditions. Where imports are such a low proportion of total spending, the leverage of domestic income and price changes over the balance of payments is comparatively weak. But America had this putative interest no less in the early 1960s, when its government strongly resisted exchange-rate change, than in the 1970s, when it proclaimed the wisdom of a flexible exchange rate.

Another determinant of relative state influence, at least at the margins, is the condition of the relevant international market. A government in a bargaining situation would prefer to have its trade and financial transactions in surplus rather than deficit, other things being equal. Thus the shift in the U.S. foreign-exchange market from overall surplus to overall deficit, and the counterpart surpluses in Europe, strengthened European positions relative to American, within limits. Shifting payments positions did not change the underlying capabilities just discussed. But as long as the objective of maintaining prevailing exchange rates was unquestioned, the United States was now in the position of needing to finance a deficit, while European surplus states were no longer in that position, at least for a time. The American reserve supply was still ample relative to the deficit (see Chart 2). But the U.S. could not expect as ready a compliance from her allies as during the Marshall Plan years.

Military relations among these economic powers reinforced continuing U.S. influence, generally speaking. Each of the secondary economic powers except Switzerland relied on the United States for protection in a bipolar military world. The military strength of the Soviet Union had not declined relative to the West, and in the early 1960s NATO and Japan still had no real alternative to protection by the United States.

But the economic power structure had shifted somewhat, and this permitted some changes in behavior. Enjoying their recovery and their diplomatic success in launching the European Common Market, America's allies in Europe began to question Washington's policies in both the military and the monetary spheres. NATO had become a "troubled partnership" by the time of Henry Kissinger's 1965 book of that title.[33] The national nuclear forces of Britain and France were a partial rejection of American strategic doctrine for the alliance, and in the early 1960s Europeans were expressing dissatisfaction with arrangements which gave them little control over the alliance's ultimate decisions on the use of nuclear weapons. The McNamara doctrine, that the use of nuclear weapons should be delayed in favor of "flexible responses," sounded to Europeans suspiciously like a doctrine for a war fought in Europe, from which the United States would escape. Fears about the credibility of the nuclear umbrella spread, along with suspicions of a bilateral deal behind the back of Europe, after the beginning of U.S.-Soviet detente in 1963. Washington's scheme for a multilateral nuclear naval force did not satisfy the European urge for more control over the alliance, and it

[33] Henry A. Kissinger, *The Troubled Partnership: A Re-appraisal of the Atlantic Alliance* (New York: McGraw-Hill, 1965). See also Harold van B. Cleveland, *The Atlantic Idea and Its European Rivals* (New York: McGraw-Hill, 1966); Fred L. Block, *The Origins of International Economic Disorder* (Berkeley and Los Angeles: University of California Press, 1977), chap. 7; and Cohen, *International Monetary Reform*, chap. 1.

was spurned. The fate of the multilateral force was analogous to the fate of Robert Roosa's scheme to reinforce the role of the dollar with the backing of a "bouquet" of European currencies under U.S. control.

In the monetary arena, the most prominent exercise of European constraint on U.S. policy was the use of the "gold lever," the conversion of surplus dollars into gold at the Treasury. By the late 1950s, gold losses were no longer viewed there as a healthy redistribution of reserves unneeded in the United States. But beginning at the same time, continental European governments were accumulating dollar reserves up to the point beyond which further holdings were considered too risky. Many governments maintained statutory or less formal limits on those holdings, always remembering how a large share of the foreign-exchange reserves of the Netherlands and other countries had been wiped out in 1931, when "gentleman" central bankers had trusted the British pledge to defend sterling. Until 1961, the Swiss, for example, automatically converted any dollar receipts above $100 million, though purchases were made in the London gold market as well as at the U.S. Treasury window. Even if the intention behind the conversions was often defensive, rather than a calculated effort to exert influence on U.S. policy, influence was nonetheless exerted.

European governments made further conversions after 1960, but this exercise of surplus-power should not be exaggerated. Conversions declined greatly during 1963 and 1964, and in many respects U.S. international monetary policies also met with support and with European initiatives intended to strengthen the established regime. In March 1961, Governor Guido Carli of the Bank of Italy came to New York to offer to sell $100 million worth of gold to the United States to help the recovery of market confidence in the dollar. The following month, the President of the Netherlands Bank suggested to the Federal Reserve's chief foreign exchange trader, "Why don't you get together with my Foreign Department people and see if you can't invent a way for me to avoid buying gold?"[34] Central bankers of the major Western countries cooperated in operations to defend each other's currencies.

But from their new vantage point as surplus powers, European governments did express dissatisfaction with the American deficit and exerted some pressure for policy changes. Gold purchases, whatever the motive, strengthened that pressure. In Working Party 3 of the Organization of Economic Cooperation and Development (OECD), Europeans argued that the United States was creating too much money and credit at home, allowing interest rates to remain too low, and pushing capital out and into their own countries. By 1963 and 1964, European growth had begun to carry with it price increases, and inflation was causing concern. The Americans were told that they were exporting inflation to Europe.[35] Finally, the French in particular were also becoming critical of widespread investments by American multinational firms in French industry. American leaders were shocked when President de Gaulle, after a special military deal between Washington and London in 1962, vetoed the admission of Britain into the Common Market in January 1963. These blows were in parallel with the struggle between the continent and the U.S. over who should adjust to payments imbalance.

In addition to the discussion in Working Party 3, the

[34] Charles A. Coombs, *The Arena of International Finance* (New York: Wiley, 1976), pp. 29-38.

[35] Americans responded that they could not understand, since the U.S. had lower inflation and a current account surplus. They complained, in turn, that European monetary policy was too tight. They also insisted that Europeans were being inconsistent: Europe wanted a surplus but somehow wanted the United States not to have a deficit. Americans thought Europe could solve several macroeconomic and payments problems at once by spending more of their dollars—on imports from America, contributions to mutual defense, and untied aid to developing countries—rather than accumulating reserves. See comments by Robert Solomon, *The International Monetary System, 1945-1976: An Insider's View* (New York: Harper & Row, 1977), p. 54.

Finance Ministers and central bank Governors of the Group of Ten countries agreed, in the fall of 1963, to begin quiet, middle-level talks on the long-run liquidity needs of the system. They delegated the task to their deputies, with Robert Roosa as chairman. Roosa was persuaded that this forum was the best means for retaining the initiative for the U.S. and preventing the more radical proposals from dominating official thinking.[36] During the year 1963-1964, the French proposed the anti-dollar CRU plan, while Roosa stressed the more familiar credit approach and reciprocal currency holdings. Specifically, the U.S. proposed a 50 percent increase in the IMF's resources for credit.[37] The Ten agreed on a smaller increase in Fund quotas and failed to reach agreement on any fundamental changes in the regime. The Europeans insisted on further study of the possible techniques for creating a new reserve asset, leading to the appointment of a low-level study group to report to the deputies in mid-1965. Roosa may have thought this would succeed in burying the question. He left office at the end of 1964 to become a partner in Brown Brothers, Harriman, the Wall Street banking firm, and an informal consultant to the government. The study group presented its report to the deputies on 1 June 1965.

Meanwhile, more spectacular moves had brought international monetary affairs to the front pages. In late 1964 and especially during the first quarter of 1965, the outflow of U.S. gold accelerated sharply (see Table 2). The U.S. deficit had increased markedly, with part of the outflow due to the backwash from private speculation against ster-

---

[36] Cohen, *International Monetary Reform*, pp. 31-38. At the 1962 annual meeting of the IMF, the British Chancellor of the Exchequer, Reginald Maudling, had proposed a moderate reform, the creation of a mutual currency account at the IMF that might absorb and guarantee weak currencies like the pound during crises and temporarily take some of the pressure off its reserves. At the time, this first liquidity initiative by a major government was received cooly (*New York Times*, 20 September 1967, p. 1; *The Banker*, October 1962, pp. 632-638).

[37] *New York Times*, 13 July 1964, p. 37.

TABLE 2.   U.S. NET MONETARY GOLD TRANSACTIONS WITH
FOREIGN COUNTRIES, 1960-1973 (millions of dollars at
$35 per ounce; negative figures represent net sales by the
United States; positive figures, net acquisitions)

Calendar Year (or Quarter at Annual Rate)	France	Other Foreign Countries	Total, All Foreign Countries
1960	− 173	− 1,796	− 1,969
1961	0	− 970	− 970
1962	− 456	− 377	− 833
1963	− 518	+ 126	− 392
1964	− 405	+ 369	− 36
1965	− 884	− 438	− 1,322
1964, Jul.-Sep.	− 404	+ 568	+ 164
Oct.-Dec.	− 404	− 176	− 580
1965, Jan.-Mar.	− 1,928	− 1,316	− 3,244
Apr.-Jun.	− 592	− 604	− 1,196
Jul.-Sep.	− 468	+ 52	− 416
1966	− 601	− 7	− 608
1967	0	− 1,031	− 1,031
1968	+ 600	− 1,718	− 1,118
1969	+ 325	+ 632	+ 957
1970	− 129	− 502	− 631
1971	− 473	− 372	− 845
1971, Jan.-Mar.	0	− 408	− 408
Apr.-Jun.	− 1,128	− 652	− 1,780
Jul.-Sep.	− 764	− 420	− 1,184
Oct.-Dec.	0	− 4	− 4
1972	0	− 3	− 3
1973	0	0	0

SOURCE: *Treasury Bulletin.*

ling during the 1964 crisis.[38] A greatly disproportionate
share of the conversions were made by France. After complaining for some time about the U.S. deficit and the greater
freedom from discipline permitted the Americans through
the dollar's reserve role, the French announced in January
1965 that, in addition to their practice of converting $35
million to gold monthly, the Bank of France would begin
to convert all of whatever new dollar balances accumulated

[38] U.S., Department of Commerce, *Survey of Current Business*, January
1966, p. 16.

from its surplus. President de Gaulle was asked for his views on international monetary reform at a press conference on 4 February 1965, and he astounded the financial world by seeming to endorse a return to a full gold standard. It was an opportune time, he maintained, to establish international trade

> on an unquestionable basis that does not bear the stamp of any one country in particular. On what basis? Truly it is hard to imagine that it could be any standard other than gold, yes, gold, whose nature does not alter, which may be formed equally well into ingots, bars, or coins, which has no nationality, and which has, eternally and universally, been regarded as the unalterable currency par excellence. . . . The supreme law, the golden rule— and indeed it is pertinent to say it—that must be enforced, and honored again in international economic relations, is the duty to balance, from one monetary area to another, by effective inflows and outflows of gold, the balance of payments resulting from their exchanges.[39]

The existing regime, argued the French, gave the United States an "exorbitant privilege." They found it curious that conversion of surplus dollars into U.S. gold was thought a dangerous practice. On the contrary, they claimed, the system's normal functioning requires it, to prevent deficit countries from obtaining unlimited credit.[40] De Gaulle may

[39] Quoted in Solomon, *International Monetary System*, p. 55, and in David P. Calleo and Benjamin M. Rowland, *America and the World Political Economy* (Bloomington: Indiana University Press, 1973), pp. 287-288.

[40] Cohen, *International Monetary Reform*, pp. 51-55; and *New York Times*, 2 October 1963, p. 53; 4 January 1965, p. 43; 8 January 1965, p. 39; 5 February 1965, p. 1; and 12 February 1966, p. 37. De Gaulle was listening to advice from Jacques Rueff, who had been a young adviser to Poincaré in the 1920s and had edited Moreau's diaries. Rueff's denunciation of the Anglo-Saxon gold-exchange standard had lost little of its energy in thirty years. He favored returning the system, and especially the reserve center countries, to the discipline of the gold standard, and he would have raised the price of gold to give the United States the resources with which to retire reserve dollars.

or may not have had serious concerns about the health of the monetary system.[41] But he clearly sensed an arena where the U.S. was vulnerable, and so he seized an opportunity to swing the spotlight toward France's capacity for leadership in a manner that might reduce the shadow of U.S. influence over Europe.

Other European governments had also been complaining about the American deficit and increasing their gold purchases to a lesser extent. But de Gaulle's open assault on the dollar and his proposed remedy left France largely isolated from the rest of Europe, and perhaps even found de Gaulle at odds with his own Finance Ministry. The notion of restoring the nineteenth-century gold standard did not rally any support in other capitals, and it seemed to undermine Finance Minister Giscard d'Estaing's plan for a CRU. The *Times* of London noted that the gold and foreign-exchange markets were calm, not taking de Gaulle too seriously. The deliberations of the monetary study group also demonstrated to all the governments that the French were alone in arguing for a gold-linked CRU as the only means of settlement.[42] Furthermore, at the end of June 1965 de Gaulle marched out of Brussels, beginning his boycott of the Common Market institutions.

It might be argued that a traditional power-and-interest perspective can explain the shift in U.S. policy concerning

[41] The French ambassador in Washington called on one of President Johnson's advisers in June 1965 upon returning from Paris, for the purpose of dispelling the strain in their relations. On monetary issues, the ambassador said:

When General de Gaulle talks about gold standards, he doesn't have a Council of Economic Advisers guiding him on what he says—he just has Mr. Rueff. The General does not know much about gold or international monetary matters. What he has asked for, I believe, is not a return to the Gold Standard as much as he has asked the allies to look for a better standard than what we have now. (Horace Busby, memo to President Johnson, 10 June 1965, White House Central Files, EX FI 9 [6/1/65—11/1/65], Lyndon Baines Johnson Library, Austin, Texas.)

[42] *New York Times*, 6 February 1965, p. 31, and 8 February 1965, p. 37; Solomon, *International Monetary System*, p. 77.

international liquidity in 1965.[43] In one such interpretation, the elegant academic reasoning about the needs of the world as a whole was a smoke screen. The United States had simply become a deficit country and therefore campaigned for the SDR as a means of getting more reserves for itself. Surplus countries had a different national interest; they resisted a step that would be inflationary and would thus cut the real value of their savings. Washington's policy predictably did not shift so far as to give up the existing reserve role of the dollar. According to this argument, it was the pressure of other major governments that forced the U.S. to abandon its existing policy, and the new policy was a reflection of national interest. Any administration in Washington would have been likely to do the same.

The timing might also be interpreted in terms of interstate rivalry. Secretary Fowler's call for an international conference came two weeks after France had begun its boycott of the Common Market, and some in Europe speculated that the U.S. intended to "jump the gun" on de Gaulle and draw him into negotiations while he was cut off from European support. A week later France rejected Fowler's proposal.[44]

Such a power-and-interest interpretation is only partly valid. It is true that surplus governments were able to prevent a further expansion of the dollar's role, and that the U.S. did not propose eliminating reserve dollars. The U.S. was expected to receive a share of the new assets. But the volume of assets the U.S. would receive under its own plan would not come close to plugging the payments gap. The magnitudes are not consistent with this interpretation. More important, this view requires one to assume that the interest of a deficit country will generally be in financing its deficit, rather than in embarking on alternative new policies like

[43] Parts of the following interpretation are found in Cohen, *International Monetary Reform*, and Calleo and Rowland, *America*.

[44] *New York Times*, 13 July 1965, p. 43, 20 July 1965, p. 1, and 7 September 1965, p. 55.

exchange-rate change. This is a dubious premise. Nor is it clear why one should assume that a reserve center will generally have an interest in expanding or preserving its currency's international role. That role has costs as well as benefits, about which citizens disagree.

The slippage of U.S. power and European opposition to Roosa's long-term vision would probably have led to some change. But this slippage could have explained equally well several other policies quite different from the ones chosen. One historical type of response to power decline is to form or strengthen an alliance by accommodating to the wishes of one's potential allies. But in this case the American response was not to adopt the policies urged by its surplus-nation allies, namely tighter monetary policy in the United States. Secretary Fowler's 1965 initiative was received on the European continent "with a certain reserve," in the delicate words of Herman J. Abs, head of the Deutschebank, because especially in Germany "the fear of inflationary developments was greater than the fear that business activity might ease to a slower tempo."[45] And a new U.S. policy promoting a rival to the dollar was certainly not the policy most monetary diplomats expected from Washington.

Thus, external state pressure helps explain the abandonment of old policy, but it hardly explains the content of new policy. To take another example, why did the United States respond to relative decline with a multilateral negotiating effort to enhance an international organization and create a rival to the dollar, rather than withdrawing into a unilateral course of action (as it did later, in August 1971)? *Force majeure* was equally available as an option at the earlier time. In what sense did the American national interest call for further means to finance the deficit, rather

[45] *New York Times*, 24 July 1965, quoted in Cleveland, *The Atlantic Idea*, p. 78. The U.S. did not shift its domestic monetary policy until December 1965, when the Federal Reserve's concern over spending and price increases related to the war in Vietnam led it to defy President Johnson.

than a prompt exchange-rate change by some state, or a movement to a regime of more flexible exchange rates? In what sense do power decline and national interest explain the choice of moving toward greater rather than lesser intervention in private markets? Various Americans have different conceptions of the national interest. If the Treasury had been ruled by the school of thought that governed from 1972 to 1976, the U.S. response would probably have been different. The U.S. had considerable leeway in the situation, including that permitted by the willingness of governments other than France to cooperate with U.S. positions.

Two additional difficulties weaken this argument. If the American deficit and loss of power were the reasons, why did the policy shift not come in 1959-1960? The delay is difficult to explain from this perspective. Finally, the case in question is one in which the two most active governments, the American and the French, both reversed their policies in the same year. When Secretary Fowler extolled the virtues of creating new reserve assets, Finance Minister Michel Debré responded with the arguments against. (He liked to twit his American counterparts by adding, "I got that from Bob Roosa.") Attempting to stretch the same power-and-interest perspective to explain both an earlier U.S. policy and its later opposite, both during periods of deficits, risks making the approach a tautology.

The 1965 shift in U.S. foreign monetary policy, then, is not explainable as an acquiescence to international market pressures as conceived in conventional theory. The interstate power situation contributed to some sort of policy change without forcing a particular direction. To what extent were the shift and the new policy influenced by the American domestic political situation?

DOMESTIC POLITICS

An election had taken place in the interim, but in no election campaign during these decades was international monetary policy even remotely an issue. U.S. public opinion was never polled on exchange-rate or world liquidity questions, since to all appearances few Americans had any stable attitudes on these questions. Few were aware of the possible effects of policy decisions on their personal circumstances. Neither the 1965 policy change nor the later two during the 1970s can be regarded as an echo of the voice of the people.

In the 1964 election, the voters decisively turned away the Republican challenge. It is plausible to speculate that a Republican administration would have taken a somewhat different international monetary course. It would probably have been more reluctant to impose or intensify restrictions on private capital exports, and less reluctant to tighten fiscal and monetary policy (until the next election year), than the Johnson administration, judging from historical patterns. But the party-ideology variable must be considered no more than a weak and distant influence on policy content. And beyond the effects just mentioned, a party variation probably would have made no difference at all. At the time, neither political party was hospitable to devaluation or flexible exchange rates, and neither had a position on the international liquidity issue. Each party had one spokesman in Congress on the latter, and the two of them agreed. For the analyst attempting in January 1965 to forecast U.S. policy, knowledge of which party was in power would have reduced the uncertainty only slightly.

President Johnson was reelected by a landslide. To the extent that the narrowness of the Democratic victory in 1960 had precluded fundamental monetary reform, that constraint had now been relaxed. On the other hand, economic discontent among the electorate was not pressing heavily upon Washington and creating strong incentives to look for new policies, as it was to do during the early 1970s. "As 1965 begins," boasted the President's Council of Economic Advisers, "most Americans are enjoying a degree of prosperity unmatched in their experience, or indeed in the history of their Nation."[46] Unemployment had declined to 5 percent (without devaluation) and was expected to be lower in 1965. Consumer prices were barely inching upward at the rate of 1.2 percent per year. Public expectations for the economy were relatively optimistic, and during the first half of 1965, President Johnson's popularity as measured by the traditional Gallup Poll hovered at close to 70 percent, which was quite high by historical standards.[47]

Despite the supposed interests of various economic groups with respect to international monetary questions, the 1960s and 1970s saw virtually no campaigning by organized groups on these issues. This is one of the most striking findings of this study. Unknown private contacts between officials and close associates outside government might have taken place, but not a single interviewee from the executive branch was able or willing to cite an instance of lobbying on international monetary issues. For a number of these officials the very idea appeared to be a new one. A congressional staff member recalled hearing nothing from lobbyists except a plea in 1972 in favor of an amendment to the devaluation legislation which would have legalized private ownership of gold. Research among American commercial bankers has also failed to uncover evidence of traditional interest-

---

[46] *Economic Report of the President 1965*, p. 35.

[47] At the beginning of each year, the Gallup Poll asked the following question, with the indicated results: "Which of these do you think is likely to be true of (1965)—a year of economic prosperity—or a year of economic difficulty?"

	Prosperity	Difficulty	No opinion
1965	65%	22%	13%
1971	19%	73%	8%
1973	40%	47%	13%

George Gallup, *The Gallup Poll*, 3 vols. (New York: Random House, 1972), 3: 1923, 2279; *Current Opinion* 1 (February 1973): 3. The question measuring presidential popularity is: "Do you approve or disapprove of the way (the incumbent) is handling his job as president?" The data on percent approving are given in John Mueller, *War, Presidents and Public Opinion* (New York: Wiley, 1973), p. 201.

group activity on these topics. (New York commercial bankers did mount a heavy campaign through the New York Congressional delegation in an attempt to block proposed stand-by authority for the President to restrict foreign bank loans with maturities over one year, but they failed. They did, however, persuade the government to lift its restriction on their lending from foreign branches, on the grounds that this feature gave an unfair advantage to foreign banks. Smaller banks successfully protested the original formula restricting lending from home offices, as being biased in favor of larger U.S. banks.[48])

Groups may not need to bother with lobbying if they can place their own members directly in government offices. It is certainly true that international banking and business have been successful in this respect, compared with groups favoring general protectionism, policies to halt capital and technology outflow or to redistribute more income and wealth in the United States, or substantially greater public control of industry. So in the limited sense that such other groups would have pursued strikingly different foreign economic policies, it is valid to say that their exclusion helps explain actual policy content. But of course many groups in America other than Wall Street would also have opposed a shift to widespread protectionism or socialism. And for the purpose of explaining the reversal of U.S. international monetary policy in 1965, this recruitment hypothesis has little value. The Washington financial team was drawn from the Establishment in a general sense, but its behavior was not predictable from that fact. Regarding international liquidity, international bankers and business executives were more in tune with continental European views and earlier U.S. policy than with the new direction of the American government. The *Wall Street Journal* reacted to Fowler's speech skeptically, suspecting an effort to manufacture "new inflationary stimulants under the label of augmenting liquid-

[48] Jonathan David Aronson, *Money and Power: Banks and the World Monetary System* (Beverly Hills, Cal.: Sage, 1977), chap. 3.

ity" in order to prolong the "binge" rather than "sobering up."[49] Restrictions on capital exports and international banking were almost the last thing Wall Street wanted. The AFL-CIO testified in favor of the restrictions, especially compared with domestic deflation as a balance-of-payments remedy, but the organization was not a vigorous campaigner for these programs in the mid-1960s.[50]

The role played by Congress in this case was the role of lobbyist, similar to the part it played in making military strategies before the 1960s.[51] Most members were content to ignore this arcane financial mystery, or to leave it to the specialists. The subject was hardly a lively one back in their districts. Democratic Congressman Henry Reuss of Milwaukee and Republican Senator Jacob Javits of New York chose to develop some special expertise, and their Subcom-

[49] *Wall Street Journal*, 19 July 1965, p. 8.

[50] John Conybeare, "U.S. Foreign Economic Policy and the International Capital Markets: The Case of Capital Export Controls, 1963-1974" (Ph.D. diss., Harvard University, 1976). See AFL-CIO statement, in Joint Economic Committee, *Guidelines for International Monetary Reform*, pp. 185-186. Nathaniel Samuels of the Investment Bankers Association of America and Norris O. Johnson of the U.S. Council of the International Chamber of Commerce were mildly critical of capital restrictions (*Guidelines*, pp. 187-191).

[51] Samuel P. Huntington, *The Common Defense* (New York: Columbia University Press, 1961), chap. 3. The President's general executive and policy-making authority applies on international monetary issues, but, since the Bretton Woods regime was established by treaty, changes in the IMF Articles require approval by Congress. In addition, the Bretton Woods Agreements Act of 1945, which created the machinery for U.S. participation, imposed some restrictions on the President's authority. The President was prohibited from proposing or agreeing to a change in the par value of the dollar, or approving a general change in par values, or changing the U.S. quota in the International Monetary Fund, without approval of Congress (22 USCS 286c). The President could not announce a devaluation as a *fait accompli*. The House and Senate Committees on Banking, rather than the Foreign Affairs Committees, have jurisdiction over legislation changing the U.S. quota in the IMF and changing the dollar's par value. The Joint Economic Committee has authority to investigate economic problems and administration policies and report to the full Congress.

mittee on International Exchange and Payments of the Joint Economic Committee attained a reputation for conducting serious, knowledgeable inquiries. Congressman Reuss and the subcommittee had called for each of the three changes of policy during this period before the administration effected it. As early as 1962, the Joint Economic Committee was urging the administration to take the lead in creating a new mechanism for adding regularly to international reserves. Reuss, supported by the subcommittee, consistently held that the monetary system relied too heavily on gold, and he strongly opposed any plans for increasing its role, including an increase in its price. In January 1965, Reuss introduced a bill to repeal the law requiring the government to earmark enough gold to back 25 percent of the domestic money stock.[52] He held hearings on it later in the year, and in September the Joint Economic Committee issued *Guidelines for Improving the International Monetary System*. The Committee advocated a new mechanism for creating reserves through the IMF according to universal criteria, rather than an arrangement restricted to the more wealthy countries. It also suggested study of the advantages and disadvantages of greater flexibility of exchange rates through wider bands, the earliest official move in that direction. Long before Fowler's speech, Senator Javits had been on record in favor of an international monetary conference, and his Republican colleagues Senator Bourke Hickenlooper and Representative Robert Ellsworth had recently criticized the administration for not taking up the suggestion.[53] These few Congressional voices reflected the spread of Triffinite thinking but did not constitute constituency-based political pressure.

In short, domestic political variables had less effect in producing the policy change than did international market conditions or the international power situation. The old policy was not abandoned because of domestic discontent,

[52] *New York Times*, 8 January 1965, p. 1.
[53] *New York Times*, 3 September 1965, p. 35, and 11 July 1965, p. 1.

nor was the new policy espoused by any significant domestic political movement. On the whole, parties and interest groups remained silent.

The variables contributing most to an explanation are intellectual ones. Some conceivable policies remained beyond the pale because the successors to Dillon and Roosa, along with many other Americans, shared some of their predispositions. But in other respects, older ideas defining United States interests were being displaced by newer ones, with the most decisive changes taking place in the offices of the Treasury Secretary and the President. This is a case in which a cognitive perspective is essential for explaining the hitherto inexplicable direction of the new policy.

THE SPREAD OF TRIFFINISM AND THE ALLERGY TO EXCHANGE-RATE CHANGE

Triffin's Outlook Encroaches

The idea that a reserve currency standard is inherently unstable—the idea associated with Robert Triffin—had moved into the U.S. executive branch with the Kennedy administration, but not into the Treasury Department. President Kennedy himself had not been persuaded. In 1965, however, this school of thought did penetrate the Treasury Secretary's office and the Oval Office. The spread of this idea is the single most powerful reason why U.S. policy shifted in the direction observed. If other schools of thought had dominated in 1965, different policies probably would have been followed.

The evidence for this intellectual change is unambiguous, although some of it was not publicly available immediately. President Johnson named Henry H. Fowler, an adherent of the Triffin school, to replace Douglas Dillon as Treasury Secretary, in early 1965. Johnson's relatively new White House economist, Francis M. Bator, like his predecessors, also followed Triffin. Meanwhile, Dillon and Roosa also abandoned key earlier beliefs about international liquidity after leaving office.

In considering this evidence, it is essential to keep in mind a distinction made in Chapter 2. The argument here is not that this policy change hinged on idiosyncrasies of these individuals, Fowler and Bator, or that this policy change would not have occurred unless these particular men had been in office. Fowler and Bator, along with others, were important as representatives of a school of thought. I do maintain that this policy change would not have occurred if *some* member of this school had not been in office. An analyst monitoring the circulation of ideas alone would— if he could have obtained information about the beliefs of pertinent individuals—have expected a policy change in the direction actually taken.

Several of President Kennedy's economists had advocated international reserve creation. Among them was Carl Kaysen, the economic specialist of the National Security Council staff, who was succeeded in 1964 by Francis Bator. Bator had received his Ph.D. at the Massachusetts Institute of Technology in 1956 and had taught there until 1963, when he went to Washington as an adviser to the Director of the Agency for International Development. By 1965, he held the title of Deputy Special Assistant to the President for National Security Affairs, with responsibility for both foreign economic policy and relations with Europe. Bator decided late in 1964 that a major liquidity reform could be negotiated. Because of his efforts, the President's February 1965 balance-of-payments message to Congress contained a call for early action, as noted below.[54]

In late 1964 and early 1965, Roosa and Dillon returned to private life. Roosa's successor as Treasury Under Sec-

[54] Interviews with Francis Bator. See also W. H. Bruce Brittain, "Two International Monetary Decisions," in U.S. Commission on the Organization of the Government for the Conduct of Foreign Policy, *Appendices*, 7 vols. (1975), vol. 3, p. 129. Interviewees will be identified whenever possible, as in this case. But much evidence has been gathered from interviewees who have not given permission for attribution. Such information will be used when it is important and consistent with other evidence, and in those cases notes will identify the source as an interview with some class of individuals.

retary for Monetary Affairs was Frederick L. Deming, who had been President of the Federal Reserve Bank of Minneapolis and had had little experience with international policies. Dillon was succeeded in April 1965 by Henry H. ("Joe") Fowler, a lawyer who had spent about half his previous career serving in Democratic administrations in Washington and the other half in private practice and in Democratic politics. Fowler had been named Under Secretary of the Treasury in 1961, a post he held until 1964 and in which he had had little direct part in making international monetary policy.

Fowler was convinced of the validity of Triffin's dilemma when he moved into the Treasury Secretary's office. Indeed, by that time, the idea had spread to all the President's chief economic advisers except the Chairman of the Federal Reserve Board. From the outset, Fowler knew that he wanted to promote a major international liquidity reform. He disapproved of what he regarded as previous American "foot-dragging."[55] He and Bator in particular soon swung into action.

His reasoning was based on the dilemma that Triffin discerned, as he explained later that year. On the one hand,

> if we allowed our deficits to continue, or if we lapsed back into prolonged deficit after a brief period of surplus, we would undermine world confidence in the dollar and impair its usefulness as a world reserve and leading currency. Dollars would return to our shores as claims on our gold, thus depleting instead of supplementing world financial resources. To prevent such a contraction in world liquidity and the widening circles of deflation and restriction that would surely follow, we must reach and maintain equilibrium in our payments as a matter of the highest national priority. . . .[56]

[55] Interviews with Fowler and his associates.
[56] U.S. Department of State, *Bulletin* 53 (1965): 211-212.

On the other hand, if the U.S. ended its deficits and solved the confidence problem, it would open a liquidity problem. Dollars were not a sound source of further growth. Gold supplies were erratic and depended on the quantities that two oligopolistic suppliers, South Africa and the Soviet Union, chose to put on the market at $35 an ounce. Meanwhile, as Fowler told the IMF Board of Governors,

> All our countries are fully committed to a policy of dynamic growth in a dynamic world economy. . . . If this expansion is to occur, it is reasonable to expect that the free world, including the United States, will, in the course of time, face growing needs for monetary reserves. We can hardly expect that either the industrial nations that have experienced such reserve growth or the rest of the world can be satisfied very long to limit future growth in reserves to the very modest level of new monetary gold supplies and such limited increases as come from normal IMF drawings.[57]

He spelled out the implications more bluntly a year and a half later, his frustration apparently growing.

> All countries wish to increase their reserves. This is not possible unless the total of reserves increase. . . . In a situation in which reserves are not increasing and in which it is not clear how or how much they can increase in the future, it is only possible for some countries to increase their reserves at the expense of losses by other countries. In an international competition designed to gain reserves, countries rely upon defensive beggar-thy-neighbor measures that restrain international trade and investment, and domestic growth. It is difficult to see how, in these circumstances, there can be any question as to the need for an agreed contingency plan for adding to world reserves when and as needed.[58]

[57] U.S. Department of State, *Bulletin* 53 (1965): 621-622.
[58] Henry Fowler, remarks at a meeting of the American Bankers Association at Pebble Beach, California, 17 March 1967, in *Treasury Annual Report 1967*, pp. 335-336.

He had told reporters in Washington in 1965 that even among countries that felt there was already too much liquidity,

> there is still the inevitable logic that if there is no force for additional reserves provided other than deficits in the U.S. balance of payments and those deficits don't occur, there will come a time as surely as the night follows the day in which some additional liquidity will be needed.[59]

He concluded: "These are the principal considerations that led my government to take the initiative in suggesting that it is now time to negotiate new monetary arrangements."[60]

The question did not hinge on whether liquidity was currently excessive or insufficient, nor on whether the U.S. was currently in deficit or surplus. Fowler and Bator felt, as the latter put it, that "the primary fault lies not in the dancers but in the music—in the arrangements, the set of rules and practices that have governed international finance since Bretton Woods." They felt that these rules and practices "were almost certain to land the world in hot water irrespective of the behavior of the U.S. payments deficit."[61]

Some of the data on which these ideas were based are presented in Table 3 and Chart 3. Table 3 shows that world reserves (excluding those of the planned economies) grew during the period 1951 through 1965 at an annual rate of 2.6 percent. Meanwhile, international trade had been growing at 6 percent annually. Holdings of reserve dollars grew by $10.6 billion, accounting for half the increase in total world reserves ($20.9 billion). The year 1965, however, was different. In that year, the U.S. payments deficit did not contribute to an increase in world reserves, because on

[59] Henry Fowler, press conference of 14 September 1965, in U.S. Department of Treasury, "Press Conferences 1965" (Washington, D.C.: Treasury Department), pp. 17-18.

[60] U.S. Department of State, *Bulletin* 53 (1965): 622.

[61] Francis Bator, "The Political Economics of International Money," *Foreign Affairs* 47 (1968): 51-52.

TABLE 3. GROWTH OF WORLD RESERVES, 1951-1965 (billions of dollars)

	Reserves at End of		Increase 1951-1965	Percentage Increase per Annum
	1951	1965		
Gold	33.9	41.9	8.0	1.5
Reserve positions in IMF	1.7	5.4	3.7	8.6
Currencies	13.7	22.9	9.2	3.7
Of which:				
Claims on United States[a]	4.2	14.8	10.6	9.4
Claims on United Kingdom[b]	8.2	6.7	−1.5	−1.5
Other	1.3	1.4	0.1	0.5
TOTAL[c]	49.3	70.2	20.9	2.6

[a] Covers short-term liquid liabilities to central banks and governments; foreign official holdings of U.S. government marketable securities; and foreign official holdings of U.S. government long-term nonmarketable securities for those countries that are believed to include such holdings in their reserve figures.

[b] Covers liabilities to foreign central monetary authorities, including inter-central-bank assistance.

[c] Excluding Soviet bloc and People's Republic of China.

SOURCE: International Monetary Fund, *Annual Report 1966*, p. 12.

balance it was financed not by a foreign accumulation of dollars but instead by a movement of U.S. reserves to other countries (see Chart 2). Thus, the world reserve growth rate dropped in 1965 to about half the average annual rate for the preceding decade, with the currency component actually falling by 2.4 percent.[62] Though it was universally agreed that determination of the world's need for liquidity was a particularly murky problem, depending on many variables, it was a common intuition that somehow there would be trouble if official liquidity did not keep pace with the size of world trade. The graph reproduced here as Chart 3, illustrating the divergence between reserves and trade, was published in the 1966 *Economic Report of the President*, signaling the shift in official thinking from attention

[62] International Monetary Fund, *Annual Report, 1966*, pp. 58-61, and *Annual Report, 1971*, p. 19.

CHART 3. World Imports and Reserves, 1950-1965

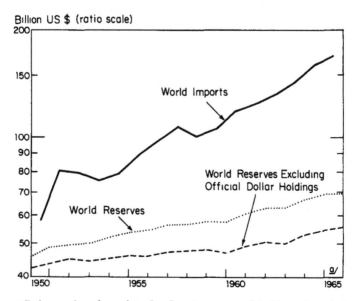

Billion US $ (ratio scale)

[a] Estimates based on data for first 3 quarters. World totals exclude centrally planned economies.

SOURCE: *Economic Report of the President 1966*, p. 157.

to the credit component of liquidity to greater salience of the reserves component.[63]

Other General Beliefs

The infiltration of the Triffinite outlook into the Treasury was a key difference from the pre-1965 period. Dillon and Roosa had been convinced that America's role as international banker was beneficial to the world and to the U.S.

---

[63] To the extent that the ratio of reserves to imports is a valid measure of reserve adequacy, these aggregate figures can be misleading. Much of the fall in this ratio reflected the fall in the ratio for the United States from 204 percent in 1951 to 67 percent at the end of 1965. The ratio of reserves to imports for all other non-Communist countries combined remained fairly stable at between 40 and 50 percent over this period (IMF *Annual Report 1966*, pp. 12-15).

itself. These general beliefs retained some hold after 1964, but the Triffin outlook reduced their salience. Fowler, Bator, and other leaders recognized benefits from continuing the dollar's reserve function, and they rejected part of Triffin's prescription—namely, eliminating the dollar's role altogether. But they differed among themselves as to the price they were willing to pay to maintain that role if it were challenged. Most of them did not see much chance of expanding it, and many, including Fowler and Bator, had decided that such a liquidity system could not be a sound one in the long run, anyway.[64]

Fowler, Bator, and other American elites also represented a political school of thought. They tended toward multilateral bargaining with allies, rather than unilateral action, as a method of alliance leadership. They were among those American leaders who are relatively sensitive to the implications of any potential action for allies' attitudes and alliance cohesion. This predisposition inclined them away from some possible courses of action which would have been more likely if a more unilateralist strain of American thinking had prevailed.

Fowler repeatedly demonstrated his preference for dealing with NATO costs and financial disturbances through multilateral and bilateral negotiation and compromise. He was quite prepared to attend the annual NATO ministerial conference and to demand that other alliance members make greater financial contributions to offset the payments effects of U.S. troops stationed in Europe. But he used the multilateral institutions to do so.

Bator was one of the U.S. officials who, during the bargaining with West Germany in 1966-1967 over military "offsets," attempted to sidetrack some stronger tactics favored by the Defense Department.[65] Any monetary moves likely to provoke conflict would have raised in his mind the

[64] Interviews with participants.

[65] Gregory Treverton, *The Dollar Drain and American Forces in Germany: Managing the Political Economics of Alliance* (Athens, Ohio: Ohio University Press, 1978), pp. 118-119.

costs to the U.S. in terms of alliance cohesion and comple-
tion of other projects like the Kennedy Round of trade
talks. In an article published in 1968, when he had again
become a private citizen, Bator explicitly raised the possibility of unilaterally demonetizing gold and "crowning the
dollar."

> It would be a bad thing for the United States to do, unless
> absolutely forced to it by others. As long as there is a
> chance for a reasonable, cooperative solution by consen-
> sus, it is wrong for a great power to settle matters by *force
> majeure*. . . . We should not accept the responsibility of
> exclusive American control of the printing press—of really
> serving as central bank to the world. Not that I worry
> much that we would misuse the power from domestic
> economic motives. . . . But it would be very unhealthy in
> terms of international politics, if for no other reason than
> that we would be constantly subject to accusations of mis-
> use.[66]

Whether to use *force majeure* or to pull back short of
strong unilateral tactics is a question that still divides Americans. During the 1960s, the United States was able to exert
even greater power than in the 1970s, and some Americans
would have been more inclined to use it unilaterally than
were these leaders. The difference will become clearer in
Chapter 4.

Allergy to Exchange-Rate Change

One major reason why the United States did not yield to
downward market pressure in 1965 goes beyond market
conditions. It is true that international market conditions
were then more favorable to maintaining pegged exchange
rates than they were 10 years later. But it is also true that
most American leaders were strongly predisposed against
dollar devaluation or floating exchange rates at that time,

[66] Bator, "Political Economics," p. 62.

such that nothing short of extreme evidence would have been sufficient to convince them to move in those directions.

Secretary Fowler was one of the strongest opponents. For Fowler and to a lesser extent for others, dollar devaluation and floating rates were bound up with a triple assumption, namely that they would be disastrous in economics, in international politics, and in U.S. domestic politics. First, many understood going off gold in light of the last such step by a reserve center—Britain in 1931. Going off gold and exchange-rate change were considered not as a policy instrument but as a form of collapse. The British collapse had been associated with exchange rate instability, destruction of official reserves and financial institutions, and a great decline of international trade. This policy course, they assumed, would amount to "destroying the international monetary system" again. The expectation of disastrous economic consequences was widespread and strong, although the events of the 1970s did not confirm these fears. Policy expectations were influenced more by simple analogy from the most dramatic precedent than by deliberate forecasting efforts. One of Fowler's associates, discussing Fowler's strong determination to support the pound sterling, commented half-seriously: "He felt that if the pound were devalued, it made it conceivable that the U.S. would have to go explicitly non-convertible. And this was almost as bad as nuclear disaster."[67]

The damage would not be confined to economic effects. Fowler and others valued gold convertibility and the par value system for foreign-policy reasons. The Bretton Woods regime enshrined the principle that exchange rates were a matter for international decision. The par values represented a visible norm of interstate cooperation, and for Fowler and many others, separately floating exchange rates were "isolationist," with the interwar connotations. A government with no obligation to maintain a particular par

[67] Interview with one of Fowler's associates.

value would be more easily tempted to act so as to injure its neighbors and provoke conflict. No one could be sure that such conflict would stop before it unravelled military alliances and provoked non-economic hostilities, as seemed to have happened earlier.

Fowler later put these fears on the record, when Richard Nixon and John Connally did the unthinkable in 1971. Testifying before a House Foreign Affairs subcommittee in September of that year, he sought "to stress some of the important foreign policy values" at issue.

> My own view is that the most important foreign policy stake involved in the present situation is the preservation and strengthening of the system of international economic and financial cooperation that has characterized, for the most part, the economic conduct of the leading nations of the free world since World War II.

The consequences of the failure to abide by "multilaterally agreed decisions that strengthen the ties that bind us" might be

> to dismantle or greatly diminish the effectiveness of the existing international monetary system, set off trade wars, refasten more tightly controls on capital in the manner of the old pre-war exchange control system of Europe, and weaken or drastically alter the alliances that have served the cause of peace and national security for much of the Free World.

He referred specifically to the events following the 1931 financial collapse and the float of sterling. When asked why the system could not operate with a regime of freely fluctuating exchange rates and automatic adjustment, Fowler replied:

> From a standpoint of foreign policy and foreign affairs, I would argue and contend that it is not the best political framework for a monetary system to operate, . . . that to go to a system of permanent floating exchange rates would be to return to a neoisolationist world in which the mar-

ket would not be the sole determinant but there would be these other nationalistic factors that cause central banks to move in from time to time. The institutionalization of an effort to work together to make a system of floating rates work would be to me a retrogressive step in terms of what I have called the practice of international financial cooperation.[68]

Devaluation was furthermore bound up with electoral fears. In the words of a senior Treasury official of the Johnson years, "Back then, we felt that any Secretary of the Treasury who devalued the dollar would be tarred and feathered."[69] The domestic consequences were discussed with President Johnson on at least one occasion. Late in 1964, McGeorge Bundy argued that if carrying on the war in Vietnam threatened the dollar's parity, then devaluation would have to be considered seriously. To William McC. Martin, then Chairman of the Federal Reserve Board, this course was inconceivable. If he had to choose, Martin said, he would rather get out of the war. No American President, he declared, could politically survive such an admission of financial defeat. Johnson did not express himself.[70] Even though no one could be certain of the electoral consequences, no political leader wanted to be the one to have to devalue. "Everyone was afraid to rock the boat."[71]

All in all, to Fowler it seemed an open-and-shut case.

I was opposed, from beginning to end, to devaluation of the dollar, by unilateral means. . . . I never heard [President Johnson] discuss it. I never discussed it with him.[72]

[68] U.S., Congress, House, Committee on Foreign Affairs, *The International Implications of the New Economic Policy: Hearings*, 92nd Cong., 1st sess., 1971, pp. 23, 35-37.

[69] Remarks to a seminar at Harvard University.

[70] Henry Brandon, *The Retreat of American Power* (New York: Dell, 1973), p. 218.

[71] Sherman J. Maisel, *Managing the Dollar* (New York: Norton, 1973), p. 197.

[72] Interview with Henry Fowler.

This strong predisposition effectively screened out serious consideration of this option, at least in the Treasury Department. According to Deming, Fowler's Under Secretary for Monetary Affairs, the administration canvassed a wide range of options on paper. But, he said, "I don't recall any serious conversation on raising the price of gold or closing the gold window—serious in the sense of something you would *do*."[73] Once in the early or mid-1960s, a State Department planner suggested devaluation of the dollar in a memorandum sent to the Treasury. State Department officials felt the matter was worth at least a discussion, but Treasury was so aghast at this breach that all copies of the memo were destroyed.[74]

A similarly strong predisposition screened out the notion of more general exchange-rate flexibility. William Dale, the American representative at the IMF, has remarked that, in those days, "Gentlemen just didn't discuss exchange rates. It wasn't done." As recalled by Frederick Deming,

> There was absolutely no acceptance of flexibility of exchange rates on the part of any responsible officials I knew. And there was not really much acceptance in the academic community. There was almost a total lack of support for them in the banking community. Now you had a few mavericks. But I can't recall any serious discussion of this; we didn't look at it all that seriously.[75]

Francis Bator had come to government from academic economics, and he had given some study to the academic debate over flexibility, as well as to the devaluation option. He regarded exchange-rate change as a policy instrument. But he agreed with the consensus that the U.S. did not

[73] Interview with Frederick Deming.

[74] Interview with a former State Department official. Just after de Gaulle's offensive in 1965, William B. Dale, the U.S. Executive Director at the IMF, sent a memo to the Assistant Secretary of the Treasury for International Affairs, indicating that the United States would eventually have to close the gold window (interview with Dale).

[75] Interviews with William Dale and Frederick Deming.

have a practical option of depreciating the dollar unilaterally by raising the gold price, since Western Europe would merely follow suit. Dollar depreciation, if needed, would have to be negotiated. He also opposed unilateral suspension of convertibility, as noted, but going off gold was thinkable. If other states forced the issue, the U.S. could simply close the window. "I do not think it would be the end of the world," he said drily in 1968.[76] He felt that, in that situation, the United States would be in a strong position relative to other states. President Johnson asked Bator about these matters in the context of sterling crises, and he did give the President these views.[77]

In Bator's opinion, the case for flexible exchange rates was not wholly inadmissible, but neither did he find it conclusive. He gave a talk on this subject at a 1962 Treasury conference, while he was a university professor.[78] He took the position that having exchange rates "locked in" was not ideal, and he warned especially against any regime that would force all pressures for international adjustment to fall on domestic macroeconomic policies. There was certainly a point, in his view, beyond which the costs of defending existing rates and the dollar's reserve role would begin to exceed the benefits. On the other hand, he shared the concern that floating rates might be upset by destabilizing speculation. Temporary payments disturbances could be handled by letting reserves rise and fall rather than by letting exchange rates move. More immediately, as long as excess dollars were hanging over the market, Bator did not see how a U.S. government could discuss exchange-rate changes without causing havoc. Finally, reform of the international adjustment process would be the most difficult one for governments to negotiate, and so regardless of

[76] Bator, "Political Economics," p. 66.
[77] Interview with Francis Bator.
[78] Francis M. Bator, "Greater Flexibility of Foreign Exchange," U.S. Treasury transcript, meeting of Treasury consultants with Secretaries Dillon, Fowler, and Roosa, February 1962 (Bator's personal files).

economic theory, the best strategy would be to launch the liquidity reform first.[79]

Laissez-faire Ideology

Related to the exchange-rate question is a very general ideological factor. Americans, despite their international reputation, are not all cut from exactly the same cloth. Two main strains can be distinguished, the "purer" laissez-faire school and the New Deal strain. An important reason why Washington moved in 1963-1965 not in the direction signaled by international markets, but toward controls and international organization, is that the purer school was not in office. If it had been in power earlier, policy would probably have changed differently. It did come to office in the late 1960s, and policy did change accordingly.

If the Chicago School exemplifies the one predisposition toward extremely strict limits on government regulation of economic activity, some regarded Henry Fowler as inclined in the other direction. Kermit Gordon once recalled Fowler's participation in domestic macroeconomic policy making during the Kennedy administration:

> Joe, largely based on his experience in the mobilization agencies in the Second World War and the Korean War, was very direct-controls oriented. You could always depend on Joe, whenever the circumstances or prospective circumstances raised the prospect of pressure on supplies and commodities or inflation, to move first with a direct-controls proposal.[80]

Clearly that is not to say that Fowler favored permanent controls or central planning. Fowler represented the New Deal ideology, which was disposed toward less strict limits

[79] See Francis Bator, "International Liquidity: An Unofficial View of the United States Case," *American Economic Review (Papers and Proceedings)* 58 (1968): 623; Bator, "Political Economics," pp. 59-60.

[80] Recorded interview of Council of Economic Advisers by Joseph Pechman, 1 August 1964, p. 403.

on government while preserving the basic institutions of the American-style free-enterprise system. President Johnson often acknowledged how much his own political-economic outlook was formed at the knee of Franklin Roosevelt.

Another clear indication of Fowler's world view appeared during his Congressional testimony in 1971, when he was reminded by a sympathizer of floating exchange rates that, after all, the marketplace was the discipline the United States accepted to a large extent. Fowler replied:

> We did up until 1933, and then we began to take a little bit of a position, I seem to recall, that marketplaces and market forces needed a degree of public or governmental intervention in order to take off the rough edges and avoid things like the depression of 1929 to 1933 and the worldwide depression that was involved. And I am still of the opinion that you don't leave economic growth, employment, unemployment and price stability and balance of payments equilibria just purely to market forces and get the best economic and social results.[81]

Specific Diagnosis

The argument so far has been that intellectual factors are essential for explaining the direction of new policy, emphasizing general predispositions concerning the Triffin dilemma, the dollar's reserve role, alliance cohesion and compromise, exchange-rate change, convertibility, and the role of government in the economy. But the new policy also depended on a specific diagnosis of the payments deficit. Professor Houthakker and a few others had concluded by 1962 that the dollar was overvalued and would have to be devalued in order to eliminate the payments deficit. By 1965, members of Congress were asking, with growing concern, how long it would be before the deficit actually came under control. However, Fowler and Bator shared the con-

[81] *International Implications of the New Economic Policy*, pp. 35-37.

sensus view that the problem was not exchange rates in this case. They expected that the deficit would disappear without the need for depreciation or permanent controls. American relative price performance and international trade performance had been strong. The U.S. competitive position in merchandise trade had not yet eroded. A 1963 forecast by the Brookings Institution supported the optimistic official prognosis. Brookings expected that Western Europe would inflate faster than America, and that if the U.S. continued price stability, the basic deficit would disappear at prevailing exchange rates by 1968.[82]

The 1965 policy also depended on a specific assessment of interstate influence on this issue and the prospects for bargaining. Officials in the Treasury and other U.S. leaders assumed that the United States was in too weak a position vis-à-vis Western Europe to carry off this novel reform, and for that reason several of them opposed initiatives such as Fowler took in his July 1965 speech. Bator and Fowler did not agree with this diagnosis of the interstate situation; they were more optimistic. One might have supposed that the improvement in the U.S. balance of payments in 1965 marginally strengthened Washington's position. Actually, both Bator and Fowler would probably have worked for the policy change in any case.

European commentators at the time hypothesized that de Gaulle's diplomatic isolation that summer had enticed the Americans to propose a conference. But France was not particularly salient in the new Treasury Secretary's thinking in this connection. Unlike his subordinates and predecessors, Fowler was not alarmed by the French gold purchases and other moves. Indeed, he later said, "I somewhat shared their point of view that we needed some alternative to the United States having a privileged position. I didn't think it was a sound basis for a monetary system."[83]

[82] Walter Salant and others, *The United States Balance of Payments in 1968* (Washington: The Brookings Institution, 1963), p. 287.

[83] Interview with Henry Fowler. During the later negotiations to create

Previous Leaders Change Their Ideas

Intellectual change in this case took place not only through personnel turnover. At the same time, Dillon and Roosa were also adopting the new view. They switched their stands after leaving office and began to advocate creation of a new reserve asset. Dillon, while still at the Treasury, told incoming Under Secretary Deming that the U.S. might have to abandon opposition to the CRU, and he asked Deming to discuss the idea with Edward Bernstein. As a private citizen, Dillon devoted an address on 14 June 1965 to "the urgent need to strengthen the international monetary system, so as to insure that the needed increases in reserves will be forthcoming."[84] In May 1965, Roosa delivered lectures to the Council on Foreign Relations, spelling out his own proposal for a new asset, which were published as a book later that year.

Later, Roosa explained why the change had taken place. His previous resistance had been based on the expectation that more liquidity could be provided by expanding the dollar's role and by credit arrangements. But the behavior of recovering states led him to abandon that alternative and to accept the validity of the Triffin dilemma. In the early Group of Ten negotiations, Roosa had floated the

the SDR, the American delegation did use tactics intended to keep French opposition in isolation (interview with an American participant). In 1965, two other aspects of the specific situation encouraged Fowler and Bator in their timing. First, Fowler perceived "a rising tide of opinion in many knowledgeable and influential quarters of the free world, private and public, that our international monetary arrangements can and should be substantially improved." He had in mind criticism from the Congressional Joint Economic Committee and from several Republicans, which he considered constructive (Fowler, memo to Moyers, 9 July 1965, White House Central Files, EX SP/FG 110 [6/16/65 to 10/15/65], Lyndon Baines Johnson Library). Second, during the previous summer, the Group of Ten had commissioned the exhaustive technical exploration of alternative approaches to the creation of new reserve assets, and this joint study was now on the table, waiting for some official response.

[84] Interview with Deming; U.S., Department of the Treasury, "Speeches and Statements by Douglas Dillon 1965."

notion of additional reserves created by the United States, which would acquire a "bouquet" of European currencies and issue more dollar reserves against it. In such a scheme, European governments would have influence over reserve creation only through discussions with Washington; the only hand directly on the tap would be an American hand. Roosa learned from their resistance to this proposal that they would accept only an arrangement in which they had direct influence on decisions to open the tap, so that they could prevent the additions from becoming inflationary.[85]

Secondly, Roosa came around to the view that a shortage of liquidity was a serious prospect. While surplus countries looked unfavorably on U.S. dollar deficits as a source of primary reserves, he wrote, they "seemed determined to have more primary reserves." Despite the enlargement of credit facilities that he had successfully urged, "it was also becoming apparent that the monetary authorities would also have to do something, sooner or later, about the primary reserves themselves." Roosa joined those who were saying that failure to create an escape would lead to a contest for the inadequate reserve stock employing "protectionist and restrictive practices that would be anathema to the postwar spirit of collaboration."[86] Roosa, in short, accepted the concept of a dilemma of confidence and liquidity in a reserve currency standard.

Moreover, he saw from the early 1965 run on gold that putting out more reserve dollars might provoke some surplus countries to convert them to U.S. gold, which could destabilize the status quo itself. His earlier hope that gold might flow back to the U.S. gave way to the prospect that U.S. gold reserves might fall lower. For both international and national reasons, he wanted to protect at least the status quo, including the American role as world banker. But now, even if U.S. payments could be kept in balance,

---

[85] *Dollar and World Liquidity*, p. 226.
[86] *Dollar and World Liquidity*, pp. 216-217, 258.

no one could be sure that its reserves would remain adequate. With its own gold more likely to shrink than rise, the United States needed, as a bank, to be able to call on other liquid assets.[87]

More than this, he now believed that U.S. gold was vulnerable to what he termed "imposed strains" and "disruptive pressures," that the system was exposed to "deliberate reductions in reserves as the result of one country's policy."[88] According to Deming, de Gaulle's gold conversions at the end of 1964 were a "trigger factor."

> Until then gold really wasn't going out in large amounts. And when it became more evident that you had something like the oil weapon, that you had a gold weapon that could be used against the United States, it seemed it might be in the American interest not to pump so many dollars out, if we wanted to preserve the gold exchange standard. . . . Roosa would have "flipped" also [if he had remained in office].[89]

Thus Roosa turned to the CRU idea, which he regarded as

> a new currency unit also backed by a bouquet of currencies but issued by an entity that would have the status of an international "currency board" in which all participants (including, of course, the United States) would be represented.[90]

William Martin and the Federal Reserve

The fact of interstate rivalry did not persuade all Americans to adopt a Triffin-like diagnosis. Some continued to prefer the dollar, while others rejected the liquidity approach altogether, preferring to emphasize problems of interna-

[87] *Dollar and World Liquidity*, pp. 222, 225-226.
[88] *Dollar and World Liquidity*, pp. 245, 219-220.
[89] Interview with Deming.
[90] *Dollar and World Liquidity*, p. 229.

tional adjustment, and recommending either external or domestic adjustment measures. In the last group was Federal Reserve Chairman William McChesney Martin, Jr. Martin was a Washington fixture, having held his post since 1951. The Federal Reserve has independent authority to conduct domestic monetary policy, but has virtually no statutory authority to make international monetary policy. Still, the Chairman and his staff are included in interagency consultations and in some White House decisions.

Martin was not sympathetic to Triffinism in 1965, and he advised Fowler against making his initiative in the Hot Springs speech. He later became convinced of the case for the SDR, when the growth of world reserves had seemed to slow. But at this time, Martin was, as he said, of the school that believed that the problem in the world was not too little liquidity, but too much. The indicated remedy was greater national discipline. Through the spring of 1965 and thereafter, Martin was becoming increasingly disturbed about the economic implications of U.S. entry into the war in Vietnam, and he was conducting an intensifying public campaign for a change in fiscal policy to finance the war without inflation. By the end of 1965, when this campaign had failed, he felt compelled to defy Johnson and tighten monetary policy sharply.[91]

The New York Federal Reserve Bank was also cool to the effort to create a rival to the dollar. In 1944, the New York bank had vigorously opposed the Bretton Woods agreements themselves, favoring a key-currency stabilization approach. During the 1960s, it followed a course of defending and enhancing the dollar's role through quiet central bank coordination. Charles Coombs, special manager for foreign operations in New York, favored credit arrangements like the swap network, and privately hoped that eventually the United States would be able to close the gold window and put the world on a pure dollar standard. He doubted that an SDR would be as attractive to foreign

[91] Interview with Martin.

central banks as the dollar.[92] But by the summer of 1965, the Federal Reserve was the only major concentration of official opinion still resisting Triffinism.

President Johnson's Predispositions

Before the liquidity policy change, President Kennedy had of course been succeeded by Lyndon Johnson. At a general level, Johnson's own policy outlook corresponded, not surprisingly, with those of his advisers Fowler and Bator, as best one can tell. The change from Kennedy to Johnson was probably, if anything, marginally favorable for the observed policy shift.

Identifying Johnson's personal ideas is not easy, whether on economics or anything else. He remains a controversial figure. To some who worked with him, Johnson gave the impression that he had few economic ideas of his own and did not grasp the issues in any detail. William Martin reflected:

> I don't think he had strong policy views of his own on anything except interest rates. As he said, he was basically á populist. He was a visceral thinker. At a meeting he would be sitting over there, and people would be sitting around here. . . . And he wouldn't even be listening to the person who was making the presentation. He would be looking at you, looking at me, asking himself, "I wonder which one of these guys knows the most about this." Then later he would be impressed by something. But if you had asked him afterward to write an account of what went on in the meeting, he probably couldn't have written a thing.[93]

To others, Johnson gave a very different impression. Francis Bator has observed:

[92] Coombs, *Arena*, pp. 20, 190-191.
[93] Interview with Martin.

There is a tendency by people who did not work closely with President Johnson to picture him as a provincial who could not understand technical issues. That is rubbish. Behind that colorful mask there was a very strong and sharp mind. Johnson had spent years in the U.S. Senate mastering the minute detail of a host of highly technical issues. In the White House, he did of course stay out of technical detail whenever there was no need for him to get into it. But he probed and tested substantive staff like me for months, before he would rely on us, to find out what one's biasses were, whether I was concerned about *his* problems, on the Hill, with the budget, with other heads of government. How accurately did I report the views of Cabinet officers I didn't agree with, or of Congressmen? At the first, he would even pick up the phone while I was standing right in front of him, to doublecheck what I had just told him. He probed whether I would be insistent enough in facing him with technical detail, or uncomfortable evidence, when the sharp detail or evidence was essential—whether I would persist even in the face of his own resistance. Of course, he didn't want to show his hand to everyone, and some people probably never saw him in a decision facing mode. Most meetings began with an Act I, with a lot of story-telling and moralizing and fun and games about the Hill, the officials present, the British or Germans or the French and de Gaulle, Texas, God knows what. You could never tell what was in his mind unless you saw him switch into an Act II mode, when he would seriously explore the issues and decisions, cross-examining officials with standing. When he was engaged on an issue—when it mattered to him—he was sharp, thorough, and did his homework.[94]

Johnson did bring to office some strong predispositions. He was disturbed especially by high interest rates and by unemployment, not unlike Kennedy. Of course, this was

[94] Francis Bator, personal communication to author, 1981.

an era in which U.S. inflation was extremely low. Second, he was in favor of using government to solve economic problems. In fact, "President Johnson *liked* to manage money."[95] Thus, reform advocates faced no ideological barrier to creation of a new money or restriction on capital outflows; these measures were more likely under Johnson than under other presidents.

Third, on international monetary matters, Johnson, more than Kennedy, "felt that gold was an anachronism, a kind of money printed by the South Africans· and the Russians."[96] Johnson was probably also more receptive to monetary innovations like creation of an alternative form of liquidity. By the same token, according to Bator, there was a point beyond which Johnson would not go to defend the dollar and convertibility. He certainly did approve a series of measures designed to resist markets and improve the payments balance. And like others, Johnson

> worried about the economic and political consequences of a unilateral U.S. devaluation of the dollar vis-à-vis gold, and did not think the other major countries would accept it. But he knew that, if a gold revaluation was forced upon the United States, it would not be the equivalent of war, or anything like it, that things could probably be worked out. On that last, he differed from the anxieties of someone like, say, Bill Martin or even Joe Fowler.[97]

During a discussion in his office in the fall of 1966, Johnson leaned across his desk and told Martin:

> Bill, if you think I am going to go protectionist, twist our foreign aid programs worse, or change the main lines of our defense and foreign policy, just so the French can buy gold from us at $35 an ounce, you've got another think coming.[98]

[95] Francis Bator, seminar at Harvard University, 1975.
[96] Bator, personal communication to author, 1981.
[97] Bator, personal communication to author, 1981.
[98] Interview with Bator.

But in 1965, Johnson was not presented with any radical recommendations like devaluation. Indeed, he heard little internal controversy over the liquidity initiative that June. This was apparently a case in which the President did not get deeply into technical detail, and thus we have little information about his views on other dimensions. The President had little difficulty accepting the Fowler-Bator recommendation. He had had no personal role in making the old policy, and the new one went in the direction of his inclinations.

But what, in fact, was the process through which the decision was reached, and did that process shape policy content? Could one perhaps have anticipated the change from the nature of government organization, as opposed to the ideas of the incumbents?

POLICY-MAKING ORGANIZATION AND PROCESS

The organization perspective elaborated in Chapter 2 maintains that foreign policies are shaped by government structures, agency stakes, and internal compromise. This approach highlights the forces that impede policy change. But it leads one to expect that a change in organization structure will produce change in policy content. Furthermore, in response to other sources of change, agency leaders are expected to differ internally, according to their respective agency interests. The President will have to bargain with them, and the new policy will therefore be a compromise not entirely congruent with any single definition of the national interest. This approach in fact adds little to an explanation of the 1965 policy change, although it does help account for the subsequent international implementation of the new ideas.

There was little reason to look for a policy change flowing from organization structure, since no major changes in the assignment of responsibilities had taken place between the early Kennedy period and July 1965.[99] There had been a change in Treasury's stand, but this hardly seems attributable to a change in agency interests. Specifying such interests is not easy in cases which do not directly involve budgets or the creation or dismantling of offices. But cer-

[99] While the detail of organization form was apparently of only peripheral importance, some of that detail should be noted. The Treasury owns most of the international reserve assets of the United States, and in 1934 Congress further appropriated resources for an Exchange Stabilization Fund and authorized the Secretary, with the approval of the President, to trade in gold and foreign currencies for purposes of influencing the dollar's exchange rate. The Treasury also played the largest American part in drafting the plans for the Bretton Woods institutions, the IMF and the World Bank. The 1945 Bretton Woods Agreements Act designated the Treasury Secretary as Chairman of the National Advisory Council on International Monetary and Financial Problems, whose other members were the Secretary of State, the Secretary of Commerce, the Chairman of the Board of Governors of the Federal Reserve System, and the President of the Export-Import Bank. The Council was established to coordinate all agencies which engage in international financial transactions and to develop the positions to be expressed by U.S. permanent representatives to the IMF and the World Bank. Informal patterns tended to reinforce Treasury's dominance. The Secretary was routinely named the U.S. Governor of the IMF and of the World Bank. The U.S. Executive Director of the IMF, appointed with the consent of the Senate, was a career Treasury official and reported to the Treasury. In 1966, the President formally delegated to the Treasury Secretary the authority to instruct these U.S. representatives, after consultation with (not necessarily the concurrence of) the Council. When the Group of Ten countries began meeting after 1961 on international monetary questions, the U.S. representatives were the Secretary of the Treasury and the Chairman of the Board of the Federal Reserve, or their deputies.

Few other organizations had sufficient expertise in this field to rival Treasury's bureaucratic muscle. The Secretary was supported by an Under Secretary and an Under Secretary for Monetary Affairs, each with broad responsibilities. Most of the Department's resources were devoted to domestic functions, but staff in the Office of the Assistant Secretary for International Affairs developed and monitored balance-of-payments programs, monitored gold and foreign-exchange markets with the Federal Reserve, and monitored economic and governmental developments in other countries through a set of country desk officers. Another office dealt with multilateral development assistance. International monetary matters were assigned chiefly to the Under Secretary for Monetary Affairs and involved relatively few personnel. In addition to controlling repre-

tainly the Treasury and the Federal Reserve were oriented toward defending the international role of the dollar more than toward promoting alternatives to the dollar. One of the least likely crusaders for the reform, on organization grounds, was the Secretary of the Treasury.

In general, senior officials' stands did not vary according to their agency locations as much as according to their

---

sentation in multilateral forums, Treasury conducts bilateral diplomacy directly. Its International Affairs bureau had financial attachés in 11 U.S. embassies in 1975, performing all the functions of diplomats: reporting, representation, negotiation, and policy advice. Some of these attachés had supervisory responsibilities over Foreign Service officers. Some stayed for long terms and developed extensive contacts in their countries, important sources for economic intelligence.

The Federal Reserve has virtually no statutory authority in external policy making, but its domestic actions, not formally subject to veto by the President, tangibly affect international flows. International operations and technical negotiations are implemented by the New York Federal Reserve Bank, and the Federal Reserve staff contains much of the remaining official expertise in this field. Naturally, the Chairman and staff are included in interagency coordinating and decision groups, though the decision authority on external matters rests with the President and the Treasury Secretary.

The Department of State chaired the internal committees that instructed U.S. representatives to the U.N., its economic bodies, and the OECD, and its delegates attended internal meetings concerning monetary affairs. But aside from a small Office of International Financial Analysis, the State Department lacked the expertise and interest needed for a more active role in monetary affairs.

President Kennedy assigned the principal coordinating responsibility for foreign economic policy as a whole to the National Security Council staff, in particular to Carl Kaysen, who was succeeded by Francis Bator. The NSC staff had little capacity for detailed research and policy development, but it could be more selective and flexible than the cabinet departments, having no operational responsibilities of its own. During the mid-1960s, the Cabinet Committee on the Balance of Payments became important. Chaired by Treasury, it affected foreign aid, government procurement, and foreign investment flows as part of the effort to defend the dollar. Finally, presidents came to rely on a "troika" of top economic advisers to coordinate economic advice and research; its members were the Treasury Secretary, the Chairman of the Council of Economic Advisers, and the Budget Director. This group was known as the "quadriad" when the Federal Reserve Chairman participated.

substantive predispositions. To be sure, the Federal Reserve's resistance to the policy change was not surprising, given its mission of managing exchange rates and defending the dollar. In addition, the National Security Council is assigned to deal with foreign states' reactions on many noneconomic issues, and these concerns were reflected in Bator's opposition to some alternative policies. The Council of Economic Advisers, lacking any stake in administering old programs, could be expected to be a source of pressure for policy departures, and in this case it was. On the other hand, the new idea also penetrated other offices. The Federal Reserve Chairman himself changed his position during the subsequent negotiations. Meanwhile, the "foreign policy" agencies, contrary to conventional expectation, did not primarily argue a brief for foreign countries. The main West European concern was more restrictive domestic economic policy in the United States. Less developed countries wanted larger foreign aid allocations and larger influence over international decisions.

The decision process was a highly centralized one. The President was not forced to accept policy elements he opposed in order to secure internal support; nor was this a case in which uncoordinated policy components were emitted by separate bureaucracies, each following its distinct standard operating procedures. Nor was it a product of transgovernmental relations. Policy was controlled from the top at this decisive turning point and thereafter.

The process of change began in early 1965. Bator, in the Executive Office, saw the February 1965 balance-of-payments message as a vehicle for promoting the languishing reform idea. The Treasury draft message mentioned only a possible need for a new reserve asset at some indefinite future time. Bator wrote a somewhat stronger draft, and Dillon agreed to accept it. (The Federal Reserve expressed reservations, but these were not effective.) As noted above, Dillon's ideas were beginning to change at that time. The President's message thus read: "We must press forward with our studies and beyond, to action . . . ," and it warned,

"Unless we make timely progress, international monetary difficulties will exercise a stubborn and increasingly frustrating drag on our policies for prosperity and progress at home and throughout the world."[100]

When Fowler was sworn in as Treasury Secretary in early April, he, too, made similar statements. Then in June and early July, a handful of men turned U.S. policy around. A secret memorandum from the President to the Secretary of the Treasury, dated 16 June 1965, constituted the first formal statement of the new liquidity policy. This memorandum, titled "Forward Planning in International Finance,"[101] was the product of discussions among Bator, Fowler, and Deming. It declared that the free world would need a new way of systematically producing additional liquidity. A secret middle-level decision group was established to develop specific American positions toward the various means of expanding world reserves, and also to consider ways of reducing U.S. vulnerability to political and economic pressure through dollar conversions into gold. The decision group was to be chaired by Under Secretary Deming.

In early July, Fowler and Bator met with President Johnson to secure his approval for Fowler's speech. By this time, the only remaining senior-level opposition was at the Federal Reserve. Dillon, the erstwhile leading opponent, was now in support. The new policy fit Johnson's own predispositions. He agreed readily, asking only that the speech be reviewed by the Secretary of State and by Under Secretary George Ball.[102] A different organization might have presented the President with a more forceful statement of the opposing arguments. But even then, it is unlikely that

---

[100] U.S. Department of State, *Bulletin* 52 (1965): 288; interview with a participant.

[101] Reprinted in Lyndon B. Johnson, *The Vantage Point* (New York: Holt, Rinehart and Winston, 1971), pp. 597–598.

[102] Interviews with participants.

a person of Johnson's views would have rejected the recommendation.

At the time of the speech, Washington had not decided on a specific American blueprint or negotiating strategy. The Deming Group subsequently developed the initial U.S. plan, and continued to formulate international monetary policies during the SDR negotiations and until the Johnson administration left office. Bator designed an atypical bureaucratic arrangement for a specific purpose. Washington interagency committees typically meet at the staff level, where participants have little flexibility to deviate from agency positions. Rarely does a member have personal access to the President to reinforce his position. The predecessor to the Deming Group, the Long-Range International Payments Committee, had been dominated by Roosa and the Treasury staff, which opposed a new asset and doubted it could be negotiated. Roosa had used this committee essentially as a seminar for discussing his ideas. Bator wanted to insure that opponents in Treasury or elsewhere would not be able to dilute the new initiative. Thus, the Deming Group was limited to five principal members: Anthony M. Solomon, Assistant Secretary of State for Economic Affairs; J. Dewey Daane, a Governor of the Federal Reserve; Arthur Okun, a member of the Council of Economic Advisers; and Deming and Bator. The principals themselves met frequently in secret with few staff present. Most important, this committee was established by Presidential directive and included a presidential assistant, Bator, as a central member. By all accounts, its deliberations were not limited to reiterations of agency positions.[103] Secretary Fowler himself appreciated this mechanism and worked closely with the group. This group was not responsible for the 1965 policy shift itself, but it may have helped prevent the policy from being undermined later. Without this arrangement, it is conceivable that Fowler and Bator would have had more difficulty negotiating a full-fledged reserve asset after 1965.

[103] Interviews with participants.

Interestingly enough, advocacy on behalf of developing countries, such as it was, came from unexpected quarters. Among major finance ministries and central banks, the common assumption at the outset was that the bulk of the demand for reserves would come from the wealthiest countries, and accordingly any new reserve arrangement should be restricted to them. Less developed countries would be in deficit and would spend any new assets they received rather than adding to reserves. They would need foreign aid, but that was not a monetary problem. If given a voice in controlling the new money, they would vote in an inflationary manner. Therefore, in order to create an asset that would appeal to European central banks, the developing countries would have to be excluded. They could be allowed an expansion of drawing rights at the IMF, providing them with more repayable credit rather than with new owned reserves. Anthony Solomon, the State Department's representative on the Deming Group, favored distributing a share of the new reserve assets to developing countries later, but opposed giving them a voice in control. The principal advocates of a universal arrangement were Robert Solomon of the Federal Reserve staff and William Dale of the Treasury and the IMF. They argued that blatant discrimination would be unwise foreign policy. The initial detailed U.S. proposal to the Group of Ten in January 1966 included elements from both the exclusive and the universal approaches.[104]

[104] Interviews with Frederick Deming, Anthony Solomon, and William Dale; Robert Solomon, *International Monetary System*, p. 129. The first American plan was a submission by the United States Deputies to the Group of Ten, "Outline of a Possible Dual Approach to the Creation of Reserve Assets," January 1966 (U.S. Treasury Department files). It was described in the new *Economic Report of the President*, in *New York Times*, 28 January 1966, p. 1, and 31 January 1966, p. 31; and in Frederick Deming, "Updating our International Monetary System," address at Washington University, St. Louis, 16 February 1966 (U.S. Treasury Department files).

CONCLUSION

The mid-1960s witnessed the major non-crisis turning point in postwar American international monetary policy. During the same period, many political and economic conditions were changing, while others remained constant. The two strongest influences on the new U.S. policy were interstate rivalry and power, and the changing ideas in Washington. Three other influences were weaker or ambiguous.

The rejection of earlier policy, and the shift toward capital export restrictions and multilateral creation of a new official monetary asset, owed little to the particular organizational structure of the U.S. government or to the sort of internal bargaining found in studies of bureaucratic politics. Under most proposed plans for reorganizing the policy-making machinery—if, for instance, the structure had included a presidential assistant with authority to coordinate foreign economic policy—the course of policy would probably have been much the same. Changing the individuals so as to bring different substantive ideas before the President, regardless of their organizational positions, would have made much more difference.

A similarly weak influence on policy change was exerted by domestic politics. Only one dimension of domestic politics had changed since 1961: The President's domestic political strength was much greater. But other things equal—including the external situation and the substantive beliefs of the President and his close advisers—a weaker domestic political position in 1965 would probably have made little difference for international monetary policy. In 1971, when Richard Nixon was in a weak position and approaching an election, policy again took a bold turn. When John Kennedy was weak just after his election, policy was cautious and conventional. When Lyndon Johnson was strong and not approaching an election, he adopted the bolder recommendations that had been avoided earlier. Other factors appear to be decisive.

In other respects, domestic political conditions did not

vary during this period. The Democratic party remained in control of the White House and Congress. Nothing comparable to the strong inflationist monetary lobby of 1933 or the strong protectionist pressure of other periods arose. Neither a grass-roots Congressional movement nor a discreet campaign by pin-striped financiers had supported the idea of the SDR. If the Republican party had taken office in 1965, however, it would have brought with it a different set of predispositions regarding economic policy, and the observed policy mix might have been somewhat different. A Republican administration would probably have been somewhat less hostile to tightening money and budgets at home and to yielding to the pressure of surplus dollars on the foreign exchange market. But a radically different policy is difficult to imagine, given the nature of the balance of payments and the common financial and political attitudes of the time. The Triffinite diagnosis of the gold-dollar standard was not peculiar to either party.

A third perspective traces changes in foreign economic policies to changes in international market conditions. Given the persisting imbalance in the dollar's foreign exchange market after 1957, a market analyst would have expected some departure from prevailing policy, and a new policy more in conformity with market signals. The most obvious possibility would have been dollar depreciation by some means, as proposed at the time by a few observers. Washington did depart from prevailing liquidity policy, and this might not have happened if U.S. payments had remained in surplus. But the new monetary policy was nearly the ·opposite of that expected from a market perspective. Capital controls and a new reserve asset were hardly predictable from market signals. The market situation was not extreme, and it left scope for varying American perceptions of the market to influence policy content. In fact, even if the payments position had righted itself, the genuine force of the Triffin idea might well have led the U.S. to propose the liquidity reform in any case.

A gradual shift in the international economic power structure is important in explaining the departure from prevailing policy, but leaves unexplained the choice of new policy. European states, especially West Germany and France, had recovered and during the early 1960s enjoyed payments surpluses. As a power analyst might have expected, their behavior began to become somewhat more independent, including a refusal to agree to the Dillon-Roosa vision of further expansion of the dollar's role in world liquidity. At the beginning of 1965, France dramatically used the "gold lever" in the interstate influence process. On these grounds, a power perspective might have anticipated U.S. policy changes in response. But the structural change had been no more than a modest erosion; the United States remained by far the dominant economic power in relations with any of its allies or even Europe as a unit. The structure left the United States with the capacity to undertake a range of new policies. The power erosion was hardly sufficient to explain not only a shift of direction but an about-face. Political and economic "interests" did not fully determine ideas.

The strongest influence explaining the new American policy was an intellectual one. The United States reversed its liquidity policy, to the surprise of many close observers, partly because a relatively new diagnosis of the international monetary system as a whole was spreading among elites. Central policy makers became convinced that this diagnosis, identified with Robert Triffin, pointed persuasively to a wiser conception of the American national interest. For this reason, the U.S. would probably have embarked on the new course in 1965 whether the balance of payments had remained in deficit or returned to surplus, and whether or not President de Gaulle had launched his assault on the dollar. If alternative political and economic predispositions had prevailed in Washington, policy might have shifted in a different direction or remained unchanged. Some American commentators in 1965 were critical of the emerging consensus on a Triffinite diagnosis, as was the case regarding the "new economics" in fiscal policy. If in the same external situation, a different school of thought had prevailed, a new strategy emphasizing exchange-rate adjustment, "crowning the dollar," or tighter monetary policy at home would probably have been adopted instead. As in other cases, like the New Deal devaluation, the response to the market and power situations depended very much on how they were interpreted.

At this stage, the American consensus supporting the Bretton Woods regime was not quite as complete as the London consensus concerning sterling in 1925. As events unfolded during the late 1960s, the conventional wisdom came under further strain, though right up until 1971 the unthinkable was still largely unthought. Political and economic developments during the interim nevertheless progressively undermined some of the critical assumptions on which the 1965 policies were founded, creating the need for another decisive choice.

4

Going off Gold and Forcing
Dollar Depreciation

ON Sunday evening, 15 August 1971, American television viewers watched one of the most stunning presidential addresses of recent years. From his desk in the Oval Office, President Richard Nixon proclaimed a "New Economic Policy," suddenly embracing vigorously two policies that he and his predecessors had always just as vigorously denounced. On the domestic side, the administration was freezing wages and prices and was going to seek tax and spending reductions to spur the private sector to reduce unemployment. On the external side, the United States was going off gold.

President Nixon began his address by declaring that national prosperity required new action on three fronts: "We must create more and better jobs; we must stop the rise in the cost of living; we must protect the dollar from the attacks of international money speculators." He went on to say, "We are going to take that action—not timidly, not halfheartedly, and not in piecemeal fashion."

He began with the "jobs" component, announcing a 10 percent tax credit for businesses investing in new machinery and equipment, elimination of the 7 percent excise tax on automobiles, and acceleration of planned cuts in personal income taxes. He also announced measures to offset the revenue losses, including cuts in the numbers of government workers and foreign economic aid. As for inflation, Nixon claimed that progress had been made, but that "the time has come for decisive action. . . . I am today ordering a freeze on all prices and wages throughout the United States for a period of 90 days."

He then turned to the intensifying international monetary crisis. "Who gains from these crises?" Nixon asked.

> Not the workingman; not the investor; not the real producers of wealth. The gainers are the international money speculators. Because they thrive on crises, they help create them. In recent weeks, the speculators have been waging an all-out war on the American dollar. . . . Accordingly, I have directed the Secretary of the Treasury to take the action necessary to defend the dollar against the speculators. I have directed Secretary Connally to suspend temporarily the convertibility of the dollar into gold or other reserve assets, except in amounts and conditions determined to be in the interest of monetary stability and in the best interests of the United States.

Nixon added that he was taking a second step to protect the dollar, to improve the payments balance, and to increase jobs for Americans. "As a temporary measure, I am today imposing an additional tax of 10 percent on goods imported into the United States." He emphasized that

> this import tax is a temporary measure. It isn't directed against any other country. It is an action to make certain that American products will not be at a disadvantage because of unfair exchange rates. When the unfair treatment is ended, the import tax will end as well.

Nixon referred to financial aid America had earlier provided to the major industrial nations when they were weaker.

> But now that other nations are economically strong, the time has come for them to bear their fair share of the burden of defending freedom around the world. The time has come for exchange rates to be set straight and for the major nations to compete as equals. There is no longer any need for the United States to compete with one hand tied behind her back.[1]

[1] U.S. Department of State, *Bulletin* 65 (1971): 253-57.

Such words had not been familiar in American foreign policy; they signaled a sharp turn.

In August 1971, the U.S. dropped its traditional practice of energetic opposition to dollar depreciation, in favor of an equally energetic effort to force other major financial powers to *accomplish* a dollar depreciation (that is, to revalue the yen, the deutsche mark, and other currencies). Likewise, Washington abandoned for some months its previous policy of managing international monetary affairs through multilateral negotiations and international organization, in favor of a new unilateral démarche involving public economic coercion directed at its allies. There was no prior bargaining with or even warning to foreign governments in this case, in contrast to monetary events earlier and later, in 1968 and 1973, for instance. The shock in foreign capitals was, as intended, considerable (coming, incidentally, a month after Nixon had revealed he had accepted an invitation to visit Peking). For not only had the United States formally suspended the dollar's convertibility into gold for the first time since 1933, an eventuality that had been on the minds of monetary diplomats for some months. It had also halted all other American measures for supporting the dollar, in plain defiance of IMF rules, which had been written largely by Washington. These rules did not actually require that the U.S. convert dollars into gold, but every IMF member state did have a central obligation to act in some way to keep its currency stable. "Closing the gold window" would have been a dramatic change in any event, but its magnitude seemed greater because of the U.S. refusal to state any conditions under which it would take up its obligations again.

President Nixon and Treasury Secretary John B. Connally embarked on a forceful campaign to coerce major foreign governments into revaluing their currencies against the dollar. This campaign was added to Connally's earlier and now more explicit demands for trade concessions from Japan and Western Europe and for their increased sharing of military alliance costs. Nixon and Connally put teeth into their demands by imposing the 10 percent tariff surcharge on dutiable imports into the U.S., to be lifted when "unfair" exchange rates had been appropriately altered. Also, foreign producers were excluded from the benefits of the reinstated investment tax credit.

The President declared that there would have to be historic changes in international relations. But he did not propose a plan for a new monetary regime. Nixon and Connally also refused to devalue the dollar themselves. In effect, the U.S. government deliberately gave the international monetary foundation a sharp jolt, knocking loose a central pillar, and then, rather than erecting a new one, they paused for other major states to respond. The world had become accustomed to relying on a fixed dollar, but now perhaps the yardstick itself could change. The brinkmanship and the sticks without carrots were interpreted by many abroad as almost a declaration of economic war on one's friends. They wondered whether the United States was decisively shifting away from its leadership of an open world economy for the first time in postwar history.

Four months later, a process of hard bargaining was brought to an end when the Group of Ten nations met at the Smithsonian Institution in Washington. They reached a compromise agreement on the first joint realignment of major currencies since 1949, giving the United States a dollar depreciation of approximately 8 to 9 percent. This was considerably less than the U.S. had demanded, but far more than other governments had been prepared to contemplate in August. In return, Washington devalued the dollar against gold after all, and revoked its import surcharge. Following this four-month period of floating, exchange rates (except for the Canadian dollar) were again pegged. The year 1971 was thus not the end of Bretton Woods; the foundation was partially rebuilt. President Nixon went before the cameras at the Smithsonian building to proclaim "the conclusion of the most significant monetary agreement in the history of the world." But the United States itself made no promises to resume defense of the dollar against challenge. The dollar remained inconvertible into U.S. reserves. Two broad questions—the future international role of the dollar, and the norms under which future payments imbalances were to be avoided or reduced—remained unanswered at the end of the Smithsonian conference. There was nevertheless some hope that further negotiations would improve the trade and monetary systems and that exchange stability and interstate harmony could be preserved without additional upheaval. This latter hope was to be buried by events in 1973, as currency traders and governments interacted to bring about the collapse of the par value regime.

This chapter dwells on the causes of the historic reversal of 1971, searching for the effects of international market conditions, interstate rivalry, domestic politics, policy ideas, and government organization and internal bargaining. The conclusions will be that in this case, the strongest influences were the change in market conditions, the circulation of unconventional policy ideas in Washington, and the superpower's eroding but continuing lead in the international power structure.

The search must begin with a discussion of certain developments that intervened between 1965 and 1971. During the late 1960s, the monetary regime and the dollar came under renewed strain, which was followed by a pronounced relaxation. It was in these circumstances that the Nixon administration made its initial policy choices. These intervening developments shaped the conditions that prevailed in 1971.

THE LATE 1960s

Military and Monetary Power

The six years that had passed since 1965 had been eventful ones. In retrospect, some of the most momentous military events had been unfolding precisely while Henry Fowler and Francis Bator were reversing U.S. international liquidity policy. Between February and July 1965, the United States began the large-scale use of American force in Vietnam. The steep rise in overseas military spending swelled the international payments deficit. This shift of military policy, together with associated domestic macroeconomic policies, touched off the American inflation that eventually brought down the dollar.

Although the long-run consequences undermined both U.S. welfare and its power to lead the world economy, decisions on guns and butter were at the time deliberately kept on separate tracks. Economic officials were not major participants in decisions regarding Vietnam. According to Arthur Okun, Chairman of the Council of Economic Advisers, President Johnson did not ask the Council to calculate the domestic economic effects of war decisions until March 1968, when Johnson was considering a turn away from further escalation and toward negotiation.[2] Treasury Secretary Fowler was a particularly firm adherent of the view that the United States should not restrain its security policies to any fundamental degree because of balance-of-payments considerations. Military planners advised that it would be a short war—that budget planners should assume it would end by July 1967.

By 1965, the domestic economy was moving gradually toward full utilization, with an inflation rate (GNP deflator) averaging 1.8 percent over the preceding two years. In 1966, the inflation rate would exactly double. The President's economic advisers had become convinced by the end of 1965 that a surge in aggregate demand had made it necessary to apply restraint, and they recommended that Johnson seek a general tax increase or face economic difficulties. But Johnson later claimed he was told that, in an election year (1966), a tax bill could get only four favorable votes out of 25 in the key Congressional committee. Chair-

[2] Interview with Arthur Okun.

man Wilbur Mills of the House Ways and Means Committee is said to have told Johnson that his price for passage of a tax increase would be major reductions in Great Society social programs. To introduce a tax would have also provided a vehicle for opposition to the war itself. Defense Secretary Robert McNamara argued strongly against the economists. Johnson's decision was not to seek a general tax increase.[3] During fiscal year 1967, military spending not only rose but in fact exceeded even the Pentagon's enlarged budget by a massive $10 billion. The President did propose a tax surcharge in January 1967, but the Congress delayed action until the spring of 1968, after a major international dollar-gold crisis. By that time, the inflationary process was becoming implanted in the economic structure, while costs were rising more slowly in competitor countries. If America's relative power in the world eroded during the 1960s and 1970s, one major reason for the decline must be traced to these choices as to how to use available power resources.

Creation of the SDR

Throughout the late 1960s, high-level talks continued to deal with the question of supplying the world's needs for international liquidity. Finally, on 1 January 1970, the International Monetary Fund created the first Special Drawing Rights (SDRs). The new monetary rules embodied many of the attributes the United States and other countries had sought, but Washington made two compromises. The Group of Ten nations had agreed in August 1967 to create a new contingency mechanism in the IMF for generating additional synthetic reserve assets if the need should arise. The

[3] Matthew J. Golden, "The 'No-Tax Decision' of 1966," in U.S. President, Commission on the Organization of the Government for the Conduct of Foreign Policy (Murphy Commission), *Appendices*, 7 vols. (1975), vol. 3, pp. 185-195. Note that separation of military and economic policy was due not to presidential inaction and bureaucratic inertia, but to a highly centralized, deliberate decision process.

European Community insisted on voting rules that would ensure to its members the ability to prevent activation of the mechanism if they voted together. Treasury Secretary Fowler in the end accepted this provision. He also agreed that the new "facility" would be given the label "drawing rights," connoting access merely to credit rather than to an owned reserve asset, mainly in recognition of the switch in the French position. (The French were now opposed to creating an owned asset, believing that it would be an alternative to gold rather than an alternative to the dollar.) Nevertheless, the U.S. and other states opposed any obligation to repay these "drawing rights." The final outcome settled on a compromise figure: IMF members would be required to pay back 30 percent of their SDR drawings. Thus, the SDR would be mostly an owned asset usable somewhat like gold or reserve currencies, and backed by the commitment of all IMF members to accept them, up to certain limits.

This experience is interesting analytically for the behavioral evidence it provides about the structure of interstate influence among the industrial capitalist states. The structure, discussed below, was still centered on a superpower, even though one whose degree of superiority vis-à-vis Western Europe and Japan was eroding. Foreign policy behavior and the bargaining outcome corresponded to what one would have expected on grounds of power and dependence. The superpower adopted a policy of initiating multilateral bargaining over new global monetary rules—bargaining with partners who each had clear incentives to negotiate cooperatively with Washington. The U.S. no longer had sufficient relative strength simply to dictate to the other major powers, if it ever did occupy such a position. Continental European governments had vetoed Robert Roosa's early ideas for harnessing the growing strength of their currencies to the dollar. Most were also cool to the 1965 American proposal. They remained skeptical about the need and the possible inflationary consequences. The U.S. payments balance continued in deficit (except for 1966), and European delegations repeated the refrain that America should first cure its deficit. They resisted schemes that might grant the U.S. an escape from balance-of-payments discipline. These powers were now strong enough to extract two concessions from Washington, the 30 percent provision and the joint European veto capability. But the main point is that they nevertheless accepted the basic American initiative. This case demonstrates that the United States continued to enjoy a superpower's capabilities for influence when Washington chose to test them in compromise bargaining.

Ironically, the birth of the SDR occurred just before a sudden explosion of the world's stock of reserve dollars, underlining the limitations of this reform. The reform had not dealt with the adjustment problem, nor had any international arrangement for controlling the currency component of world liquidity been created. The United States and the dollar remained in a unique position.

Market Pressure against Sterling and the Dollar

Signs of strain in the Bretton Woods regime had been increasing during the mid- and late-1960s. Late 1967 and early 1968 in particular brought heavy market pressure against the dollar, concentrated (as in 1960) in the London gold market and triggered by the devaluation of sterling.

Much of the markets' attention at this time was fastened on the weakness of sterling. Britain's efforts to expand the domestic economy were continually hampered by the weakness of its balance of payments. In response to a deterioration of payments in 1964, the new Labour government decided against devaluation and in favor of an import surcharge and an export rebate. Financial markets did not regard the associated domestic fiscal policy as sufficiently convincing, and heavy speculation against sterling ensued, eliciting from the government an angry denunciation of "the gnomes of Zurich." When the Bank of England ex-

hausted its short-term credit abroad, the United States and
the other major financial powers put up a large package
of $3 billion more, and the speculation and hedging sub-
sided for a time. This episode was evidence supporting the
belief that sufficient central bank cooperation could impress the markets and maintain stability long enough to
permit policy adjustments.

Britain's dilemma remained, however, through 1965 and
1966, which saw new programs to restrain domestic demand, a successful international bear squeeze in 1965, and
continued weakness in sterling. The United States strongly
opposed devaluation of sterling, for fear that yielding to
markets in the case of one weak reserve currency would
encourage them to attack the other. Nevertheless, facing a
large trade deficit and a stagnant domestic economy, the
Wilson government finally decided to throw in the towel.
The pound was devalued by 14 percent on 18 November
1967.

Long-time fears about the consequences for the dollar
were confirmed by subsequent developments. President
Johnson immediately issued another declaration that the
$35 price of gold would not be changed, but purchases of
gold in London turned into a stampede all the same. The
U.S. balance of payments had suffered another sharp drop
in 1967, especially in the capital account, while military
spending rose and the debate over a tax increase dragged
on. Domestic monetary policy had eased, encouraging larger
net capital outflows while the current account surplus was
also declining.

The Gold Pool of seven central banks had been supplying
bullion in London since 1966 to try to suppress this potential trigger of speculation and hedging. Revelations in the
French press in 1967 added to doubts about British and
American policies, and gave the impression that the French
government was using the press as a weapon. As the volume
of gold sales grew in late 1967, operators began to bet on
abandonment of the sales and upward movement of the
price, which fueled even further purchases. During the

fourth quarter, the U.S. lost $953 million worth, most of it going to the private market.

On 1 January 1968, the Johnson administration announced a major new balance-of-payments program, whose centerpiece was a mandatory prohibition on further outflows of U.S. dollars to finance corporate direct investment in developed countries. The measures also dealt with bank lending abroad, trade, and tourism. But these steps and the sales of the Gold Pool were not sufficient to forestall another furious wave of speculative gold buying in early March 1968. Gold appeared to be flowing out, never to return. Newspaper reports and editorials featured the "gold rush."

European central banks were anxious to stop this drain. Governor Guido Carli of the Bank of Italy had proposed ending the Gold Pool and beginning a two-tier gold market, with the London price freed to rise above the official $35 price, which would still be effective in gold transactions among central banks. Governments would segregate monetary gold from private gold. More generally, European financial communities were becoming more exasperated with the continued reluctance of the United States to compensate for the economic effects of the war in Vietnam by tightening domestic economic policy.

Chairman William McC. Martin of the Federal Reserve Board was in accord with this view. He continued his public cries against inflation, budget deficits, and payments deficits, warning in March 1968 that "the heart of the budgetary problem is that this country is overextended and overcommitted" militarily around the world. Warming to the subject, he went on:

> I say flatly that it's time that we stopped talking about "guns and butter," it's time that we stopped assuming that this is just a "little war" in Vietnam, and face up to the fact that we are in a wartime economy.[4]

[4] William McC. Martin, "Good Money is Coined Freedom," address before the Economic Club of Detroit, 18 March 1968.

Many Europeans and the Federal Reserve were deeply committed to preserving the Bretton Woods monetary system and feared that United States policies were threatening to undermine it.

By this time, some American officials outside the Treasury had begun to suspect, or had even become convinced, that the time had come for fundamental monetary changes. Sherman Maisel, one of the Governors of the Federal Reserve system, insisted privately in March 1968 that the United States clearly had a fundamental payments disequilibrium. The dollar was overvalued. He contended that the Europeans should be pressed to allow a depreciation of the dollar against their currencies, and that if they refused the U.S. should stop gold sales and virtually end support for exchange rates.[5] Maisel and two colleagues were outvoted. The U.S. response to the deficit and the rapid gold drain in 1968 was to reject radical change, to reaffirm support for the dollar at its prevailing exchange rate, but to abandon the effort to hold down the gold price in the private market. In return, Washington secured an important concession from major European states.

When the run on gold accelerated again, the Federal Reserve, on 14 March 1968, authorized a large increase in bilateral foreign borrowing to finance further defense of the dollar. At two White House meetings that day, President Johnson approved a plan for closing the gold markets and calling a conference of the Gold Pool central banks in Washington over the coming weekend. The messages of invitation rejected in advance the idea of raising the dollar price of gold, favored by Great Britain. One participating American official maintains, "Since then there has been a lot of talk about the dollar being overvalued, but it was not all that evident at the time."[6]

[5] Sherman J. Maisel, *Managing the Dollar* (New York: W. W. Norton, 1973), chap. 9.
[6] The discussion of the events of early 1968 is based on interviews with seven participating U.S. officials and on accounts in the *New York Times*

At this weekend conference, the United States, Italy, West Germany, Britain, the Netherlands, Belgium, and Switzerland agreed to end sales of gold to the private market, permitting the market gold price to rise above the intergovernmental price. The United States again reaffirmed the convertibility of the dollar into gold for other governments at the $35 price. All the governments sensed, nonetheless, that an era was coming to an end. Although there were evidently no explicit agreements by the Europeans to limit their demands for U.S. gold, it was becoming apparent that to press for large conversions would provoke dispute and possibly the end of convertibility. The American gold stock had fallen from over $13 billion at the beginning of 1967 almost to the $10 billion level by March 1968. That level had been mentioned informally by a few Americans as a necessary permanent "war chest." In practice, after March 1968 relatively little U.S. gold was paid out, despite huge deficits.

The European governments at the conference also agreed to the U.S. call for a pledge to end purchases from, as well as sales to, the private gold market. As part of the negotiations to create the SDR, they agreed, with some equivocation, that they would freeze the role of gold in international reserves and rely instead on the SDR for future increases. It should be noted that France was not present.

The rapid and heavy U.S. gold outflows in late 1967 and early 1968 probably affected U.S. military policy. In Vietnam, early 1968 was the period of the Tet offensive and the effort by the U.S. military leadership to raise troop levels in Vietnam from 500,000 to around 700,000. Domestic opponents of the war were able to use the vivid alarm touched off by the gold drain as a device to stop the escalation. Several Senators and the Assistant Secretary of

---

and the following books: Maisel, *Managing the Dollar*; Robert Solomon, *The International Monetary System, 1945-1976: An Insider's View* (New York: Harper and Row, 1977); Charles Coombs, *The Arena of International Finance* (New York: Wiley, 1976).

State for Economic Affairs, Anthony Solomon, argued that the crisis proved that the U.S. could not send more troops at least until taxes were increased.[7] On the day following the 14 March gold decisions, President Johnson held a meeting in the Cabinet room to consider a request from the Pentagon to call up 98,000 reservists. Johnson, citing financial concerns, delayed action on the request.[8] At the end of March, he decisively rejected escalation and turned to the Paris armistice negotiations.

After the March 1968 turning point, market pressure against the dollar subsided for two years. A tax increase was enacted in the summer of 1968. Even though the American current account fell into deficit, controls and substantial improvements in the capital account as compared with 1967 were enough to push the official settlements balance into a small surplus for 1968.[9] After private gold markets reopened, the price fluctuated between $38 and $43 an ounce. As President-elect Richard Nixon assembled a new administration at the end of the year, he was not faced with any immediate international dollar crisis.

Also during the late 1960s, international payments imbalances not directly involving the United States gave rise to market pressures against other par values as well. It was only two months after the Washington conference of the Gold Pool that the May 1968 Paris uprising shook France. The French balance of payments deteriorated, and during

[7] Interview with Anthony M. Solomon; Michael Hudson, *Super-Imperialism: The Economic Strategy of American Empire* (New York: Holt, Rinehart, and Winston, 1972), p. 227.

[8] Lyndon B. Johnson, *The Vantage Point: Perspectives of the Presidency, 1963-1969* (New York: Holt, Rinehart and Winston, 1971), pp. 406-407.

[9] Some of the capital account improvement was due to mere accounting legerdemain. The Treasury Department had persuaded some foreign official dollar-holders to switch from short-term instruments to 366-day notes. Any obligation over one year in maturity could be counted "above the line," as an autonomous foreign investment in the United States rather than as evidence of a U.S. deficit, and so Treasury was able to report an overall surplus rather than a deficit.

1968 and 1969 France was compelled to sell gold back to the United States.

In November 1968, at a tense and highly publicized meeting in Bonn, finance ministers including Secretary Fowler attempted a multilaterally negotiated shift in the Franco-German parity. While France was moving into deficit, West Germany was experiencing a large current account surplus. In early November, additional speculative flows into Germany had become heavy. The United States took the position, shared by the central banks of a number of other countries, that the French franc was not in fundamental disequilibrium, and that the German mark should be revalued. But German ministers publicly urged France to take responsibility to act, which evidently did not please General de Gaulle. He refused to devalue, and the meeting accomplished little.[10] The public haggling among governments during this currency crisis, however necessary, had added rumor and uncertainty to already disturbed currency markets. The episode raised further questions, following sterling's long struggle against devaluation, about the adequacy of international arrangements for smooth payments adjustment.

As mentioned in Chapter 2, the new French government did devalue the franc by 11 percent in August 1969, and after the German elections the mark was revalued by 9 percent in October 1969. German financial officials were apologetic about allowing the mark to float in the interim between the voting and the installation of the Brandt government, in view of their formal international obligation to maintain exchange stability. But in the event, when the DM market was freed, the exchange rate moved upward fairly smoothly and seemed to provide a convenient indicator to the new government as to an appropriate new par value. First in pounds, then in gold, and now in francs and marks, currency operators had been presented with cheap opportunities to speculate on parity changes, and they had

[10] *New York Times*, 26 November 1968.

found that such speculation was nicely rewarded. In retrospect, we can see how the ground was being prepared for the huge movements of funds in the crises of the early 1970s.

Intellectual Currents

While strains on the Bretton Woods regime were growing during the late 1960s, the policy debate among specialists produced new ideas, some of which were to affect government behavior. Even before the currency crises of 1967-1969, the persistence of payments imbalances was leading many academic economists to decide that some technique for greater flexibility of exchange rates was needed. Both reserve centers had deficits, but because of their reserve status they found it difficult to discuss, let alone carry out, par value changes. Surplus governments delayed taking the unpopular step of revaluation.

New techniques were being proposed and discussed in obscure academic journals. Some called for widening the narrow 2 percent band around parity within which exchange rates were free to vary. In this way, without abandoning the par value framework, the theoretical ability of price fluctuations to equilibrate trade accounts would be allowed to operate to a greater extent. In particular, it was argued that a wider band could discourage destabilizing speculation in capital accounts. The chance that a strong currency might drop through a wider band in the future would constitute a greater risk for a bull speculator, assuming that the currency was not in fundamental disequilibrium.

In addition, it was argued, particularly in light of the events of 1967-1969, that major countries were indeed likely to develop fundamental needs for parity changes, as contemplated at Bretton Woods but contrary to the assumptions of many central bankers in the 1960s. Academic economists pointed out that the advantages of presumably fixed exchange rates were actually being lost. Britain's long effort to save its fixed rate of $2.80 had led to prolonged economic and political turmoil, and in the end she was forced to devalue anyway, and by a large jump. Some suggested that the prevailing regime ought to be labeled not fixed parities but "jumping parities." The assumption that currencies were likely to get out of line with market conditions led some to propose a regime of "gliding" or "crawling pegs"—that is, a rule that would maintain par values but permit a government to move its peg frequently by small amounts up to a limit of perhaps 3 percent per year. Merchants and investors, the argument went, would be better able to absorb uncertainty in the form of frequent but small changes than in the form of the infrequent but large jumps actually occurring.

These new ideas looked toward greater but not unlimited flexibility. Even among academics, there was still much doubt that free floating would be workable. But by 1968 it seemed that to one degree or another, "the great majority of academic economists are in favor of flexibility of exchange rates," according to two American economists writing at the time. "This represents a radical shift of professional opinion since the time of Bretton Woods."[11]

The large-scale U.S. private sector became more concerned about balance-of-payments policy after the 1968 capital outflow restrictions were imposed, and some began to explore exchange-rate flexibility as an alternative to controls. While bank and corporate opinion remained largely orthodox, some banks and individuals participated in the growing transnational debate. There was no organized campaign to press for flexible rates. But First National City

[11] Gottfried Haberler and Thomas Willett, *U.S. Balance of Payments Policies and International Monetary Reform* (Washington, D.C.: American Enterprise Institute, 1968). For proposals and exchanges in the flexibility debate, see *Approaches to Greater Flexibility of Exchange Rates: The Bürgenstock Papers*, ed. George N. Halm (Princeton, N.J.: Princeton University Press, 1970). An exhaustive history of the crawling peg idea is found in John Williamson, "The Crawling Peg in Historical Perspective" (Rio de Janeiro: Pontifícia Universidade Católica, 1979).

Bank joined Milton Friedman in an early and lonely advocacy of a flexible regime, perhaps foreseeing the handsome profits international banks were to realize in their currency trading departments during the 1970s. Bank of America was an early advocate of widening the bands. During late 1968 and 1969, the *Wall Street Journal* and the *New York Times* editorialized in favor of greater flexibility, and the U.S. Chamber of Commerce suggested serious study.[12] A transnational gathering of commercial and academic specialists in Bürgenstock, Switzerland, in mid-1969 may have promoted a shift of attitude. According to one participating advocate of greater flexibility, at the outset only one banker or businessman was favorable to a more flexible regime, and by the end only one remained firmly opposed.[13] A majority of those present declared themselves in favor of some combination of wider bands and crawling pegs. Most of the advocates of these changes were Americans, and most assumed that the dollar would remain the fixed star of the system. Their plans called for other governments to do the changing.

Officials, however, remained highly cautious, since most of them gave high salience to the belief that the slightest sign of official interest in exchange-rate changes would itself cause disorder. Even so, during 1968 the same reasoning about the problems of the existing system began to percolate through the U.S. Treasury and Federal Reserve. Internal study groups discussed the academic plans, and the *Economic Report* of the outgoing Democratic President, issued in January 1969, included the first official U.S. discussion of these possibilities.

In the period after the 1965 SDR initiative, in short, the U.S. government demonstrated its continuing potential for monetary leadership by cajoling its capitalist partners into accepting the SDR. At the same time, Washington com-

---

[12] *New York Times*, 2 December 1968, p. 46; 28 February 1969, p. 53; 27 May 1969, p. 62; *Economist*, 14 December 1974 (world finance survey).
[13] Interview.

mitted the nation's power resources in Vietnam in a manner that accelerated inflation at home and ensured continued or growing external deficits. The war, the deficit, and sterling's devaluation led to a run on U.S. gold. In response to the most serious market pressure against the dollar since 1960, the Johnson administration in 1968 decided to abandon the Gold Pool and raise taxes. American specialists began to study techniques by which the parities of other countries could be made more flexible.

BIFURCATION OF THE EARLY NIXON POLICY

The Nixon administration took office in January 1969, during a time when the dollar was not under great market strain. Whether for this reason or in spite of it, the change of administration did not produce an immediate reversal of U.S. international monetary policy. One of Nixon's closest advisers did urge him to seize this moment for radical change, but he declined to do so. Instead, international monetary policy soon dropped to a much lower priority in the executive branch, giving way to other issues. U.S. international monetary policy became bifurcated into two partly inconsistent lines. Both lines avoided high-level diplomatic bargaining on monetary issues. For the first two and one-half years of this administration, the President allowed U.S. foreign monetary policy to emerge through the loose decision-making process predicted by organization theories of policy formation. The consequences of this early Nixon policy are a part of the explanation for 1971.

Nixon's Predispositions

President Nixon hardly came to office with a clear determination to change U.S. international monetary policy. Quite the opposite: Nixon and his National Security Adviser, Henry Kissinger, like many diplomats, regarded most international economic problems as "quartermaster corps stuff," as one observer has put it. Nixon and Kissinger were both

grand thinkers with a fairly clearly articulated world strategy, but one which at that time largely neglected economic
issues in favor of traditional military-political ones. For them,
the most perilous challenges to mankind and to American
power arose in the relationship between the United States
and the Soviet Union. The triangular relation between the
two superpowers and China was to be the basis for con-
structing a "stable structure of peace." Not only was it essential to contain superpower rivalries and develop some
forms of cooperation, but this relation could also be used
to dampen military conflicts involving third parties, as in
Vietnam and the Middle East. "The new administration,
like its predecessors, saw in the great-power relationship
the masterkey to world order."[14]

Such a strategy required that the United States execute
subtle, controlled manipulations of positive and negative
incentives directed at Moscow and Peking to move them in
desired directions. One implication was that America's allies in Europe and East Asia had to be kept in line, and
that, once the possibility of détente between adversaries
was taken more seriously, relations with allies became in-
strumental and secondary rather than ultimate ends. Nixon
and Kissinger were sensitive to alliance cohesion in this
context. Their predisposition was to attend to international
economic concerns only to the extent that such issues affected the success of their global military-political strategy.

Another implication was that potential domestic American sources of resistance or contrary signals had to be
neutralized, which led them to employ a tightly closed decision-making process in Washington. Decisions on matters
of high priority to them were restricted to the two plus a
few staff members, with much of the bureaucracy and the
Congress kept in the dark or occupied in researching long-
range questions until the announcement of dramatic break-
throughs. The two men attempted to remain personally in

[14] Stanley Hoffmann, *Primacy or World Order: American Foreign Policy
Since the Cold War* (New York: McGraw-Hill, 1978), p. 44.

control of details on military-political issues. Yet the day has only 24 hours, and because of the President's intellectual priorities, international economic issues were left largely to other leaders before 1973.[15]

President Nixon arrived in office with a weaker personal interest in the balance of payments than President Kennedy or President Johnson in his earlier years in the White House. Nixon evidently had no firm attitudes on international arrangements for exchange rates or liquidity. One economic adviser has said:

> He had a lawyer's mind. He was able to absorb complex arguments quickly. You didn't have to explain things to him very long. But after things got in his mind, they didn't necessarily stay there too long.[16]

Nixon is reported to have thought that financial experts much exaggerated the importance of foreign-exchange crises, and that their job should be to eliminate such crises.[17] The new President did not bring to office a firm set of beliefs about the Bretton Woods regime salient enough to form a serious barrier to policy change.

A segment from Nixon's secret White House tape recordings provides a glimpse of his attitude toward international monetary issues. According to the transcripts, Chief of Staff H. R. Haldeman asked Nixon on 23 June 1972 whether he had received the report that the British had just floated the pound. "That's devaluation?" Nixon asked. "Yeah," Haldeman replied, and he proceeded to try to

[15] Nixon and Kissinger established a mechanism for foreign policy planning and coordination under the National Security Council, which was aptly termed "the Kissinger operation." For a discussion, see I. M. Destler, *Presidents, Bureaucrats and Foreign Policy* (Princeton, N.J.: Princeton University Press, 1972), pp. 118-137; and John Leacacos, "Kissinger's Apparat," *Foreign Policy* no. 5 (Winter 1971-72):3-27. The effects of organization on policy content are discussed below.

[16] Interview.

[17] Elizabeth Stabler, "The Dollar Devaluations of 1971 and 1973," in *Appendices*, vol. 3, p. 141.

present the major points of a report prepared by Peter Flanigan, Executive Director of the White House Council on International Economic Policy. "I don't care about it," said Nixon. "Nothing we can do about it." Haldeman told him that Flanigan argued that the British float showed the wisdom of U.S. refusal to consider resuming convertibility until "we get a new monetary system." Nixon: "Good. I think he's right. It's too complicated for me to get into." Haldeman persisted, saying that Arthur Burns expected a 5 to 8 percent devaluation of the pound against the dollar. Nixon: "Yeah. O.K. Fine." Haldeman: "Burns is concerned about speculation about the lira." Nixon: "Well, I don't give a [expletive deleted] about the lira. [Unintelligible]." The President then asked how "the House guys" were reacting to some (unintelligible) development, possibly Nixon's decision that week to remove quotas on meat imports for the rest of the year to check rising meat prices. Haldeman responded that "all our people . . . think it's a great—a great ah . . ." Nixon: "There ain't a vote in it. Only George Shultz and people like that think it's great [unintelligible]. There's no votes in it, Bob." And thus the President ended the morning's discussion of economic topics.[18]

Judging from this bit of evidence, Nixon was inclined to remove himself from the daily events of this policy field, and even from analysis of their significance, at least unless he was shown plainly that the event could immediately affect the United States or his own electoral strength. (In actual fact, seven months later the lira was part of the foreign-exchange squall that touched off Nixon's second devaluation of the dollar.) Reforming the international monetary regime was "too complicated for me to get into."

There is no doubt that for Nixon, as for most political leaders, beliefs and expectations about domestic politics were among the most salient. Later evidence will suggest that in particular Nixon shared the common vague assumption that devaluing the currency would invite dam-

[18] *New York Times*, 7 August 1974, p. 47.

aging domestic political attack by his rivals. This expectation may do much to explain the tendency for international exchange-rate policy changes to lag behind market indicators. As we will see, such an expectation is not necessarily accurate, and it may even be a self-defeating prophecy.

The change from President Johnson to President Nixon clearly did bring a change in reigning ideology, in the direction normally associated with the party leadership groups. Nixon and therefore his administration as a whole were inclined to be more hostile to government intervention in the economy. Often during his career, Nixon had deplored the evils of bureaucracy and controls on markets. "Ideologically he hated controls," said one adviser. Referring to Kennedy's and Johnson's restrictions on international capital outflow, the adviser added, "I recall one meeting when he wanted to abolish all of them with one stroke of the pen, in effect."[19] In selecting his advisers and administrators, Nixon repeatedly turned to men with notably strict laissez-faire views, such as George Shultz, Herbert Stein, and William Simon. An analyst monitoring policy ideas during the 1968 transition would have anticipated policy changes in laissez-faire directions, away from quantity and price controls.

Kissinger's predispositions regarding international economic issues fit easily with those of his chief. Kissinger acknowledged some years later in his memoirs that, before the fall of 1971, he had paid little attention to such issues.

From the start I had not expected to play a major role in international economics, which—to put it mildly—had not been a central field of study for me. Only later did I learn that the key economic policy decisions are not technical but political. At first I thought that I had enough on my hands keeping watch on the State and Defense Departments and the Central Intelligence Agency without also taking on Treasury, Commerce, and Agricul-

---

[19] Interview.

ture. . . . On the whole I confined myself to a watching brief.[20]

In short, the 1968 presidential election brought to the White House an ideological tendency toward greater hostility to government intervention in the economy. This rightward shift in policy leanings could be expected to shape perceptions of subsequent events and the range of policy options considered seriously. But this was only a background factor. With specific regard to international monetary policy, the new President was disposed to leave such matters to subordinates. Nixon and Kissinger, unlike some American leaders, were not receptive to suggestions that they take the lead in negotiating international economic reforms.

The Orthodox Line

The result was that for the first two and one-half years of the Nixon administration, the United States sent conflicting or ambiguous signals in the international monetary field. On the one hand, it appeared to follow an orthodox line. Washington signaled opposition to major changes, especially of the dollar's external value, and it adopted tight money at home and proclaimed continued adherence to the Bretton Woods regime and prevailing exchange rates. On the other hand, other aspects of U.S. official behavior during this time indicated that Washington wanted major changes.

Critical of the persistent inflation and payments deficit, the new administration set its initial economic course in the direction of a strong budget surplus and monetary restraint. The Congress had passed an income-tax surcharge in mid-1968, and domestic monetary policy had been tight through most of that year. During 1969, the federal government had a budget surplus (on the full-employment

[20] Henry Kissinger, *White House Years* (Boston: Little, Brown, 1979), p. 950.

basis) of $12 billion, while the Federal Reserve steadily slowed the increase in the money stock, driving interest rates up to nominal levels not seen since the Civil War. The rate on three-month Treasury bills rose from a 1968 average of 5.3 percent—the highest annual average up to that point— to a peak of 7.9 percent in January 1970. This credit squeeze drew in foreign capital and buoyed the dollar in currency markets. The administration maintained that domestic inflation and the external deficit required the same treatment, the orthodox tight-money policy that Europe had been calling for. Nixon's initial balance-of-payments message in April 1969 emphasized these domestic measures, and also mentioned export expansion, encouraging foreign tourism and investment in the United States, and fair sharing of military burdens by U.S. allies. Upon assuming office, the new Secretary of the Treasury, David M. Kennedy, speaking for the President, had said, "It will be our purpose to maintain a strong dollar both at home and abroad." He repeated the canon that the dollar-gold price would not be changed.[21]

The Treasury, in the absence of close presidential guidance, continued to follow previous external policy regarding the international monetary regime and the American payments balance—at least verbally. The Treasury was cool initially to schemes to reform the international adjustment process through greater exchange-rate flexibility and was reluctant to press for changes of particular major rates. The new chief U.S. monetary diplomat, Treasury Under Secretary for Monetary Affairs Paul A. Volcker, referring to the plan for a wider band of fluctuation around parities, said that there had been "a lot of discussion [of these ideas] in academic circles, and that's where they can stay."[22]

When, after 1969, the overall U.S. payments position returned to deficit, the U.S. to some extent resorted to standard operating procedures to mitigate the effects. The

[21] *New York Times*, 28 January 1969, p. 1.
[22] *New York Times*, 13 February 1969, p. 63.

Federal Reserve drew on the swap network to absorb some of the dollars then accumulating in foreign central banks, and the Export-Import Bank also borrowed Eurodollars from foreign subsidiaries of U.S. banks in order to intercept these dollars before they reached the central banks. These measures were far from sufficient to cover the deficit. When some foreign central banks pressed demands for gold, the U.S. observed the rules until 15 August 1971. Gold sales to foreign governments amounted to $631 million in 1970 and $843 million in 1971 (see Table 2). During the first eight months of 1971, U.S. total reserves declined by $2,359 million, or 16 percent.[23] The Treasury took the public position, for example in a statement on 4 April 1971, that the dollar flow was a short-term problem and that the U.S. had no desire for parity changes by other countries.[24] Least of all did the Treasury act to promote dollar depreciation during this period.

This orthodox Treasury line reflected the continuing diagnosis that the dollar was not fundamentally out of line and that radical changes were therefore not appropriate. But if U.S. policy had been dominated consistently by orthodoxy, the line would have been carried much further. Actually, Secretary of the Treasury Kennedy was much less active on international matters than Fowler and Dillon had been. In a statement before Nixon's inauguration, Kennedy had refused to pledge in advance that the incoming administration would rule out a devaluation—an uncommon outbreak of ministerial candor that sent flurries through the European gold markets. Nixon apparently was not pleased, and thereafter Kennedy, like the President, largely avoided international monetary matters.[25] After all, the President was not putting priority there. Thus, these matters were

[23] U.S. Department of the Treasury, *Treasury Bulletin*, February 1972, Tables IFS-6 and IFS-1.

[24] *New York Times*, 5 April 1971, p. 49.

[25] *New York Times*, 18 December 1968, p. 1, and 19 August 1971, p. 35; interviews with U.S. officials who worked with Kennedy.

left to middle-level officials, not all of whom favored an orthodox line.

Another orthodox tenet common among bankers and international economists was that, for technical reasons, the only feasible way to change exchange rates was by unilateral action. If governments attempted to negotiate a realignment, they would immediately throw the financial markets into turmoil. If markets were kept open in the presence of obvious payments surpluses and deficits, traders would mercilessly exploit central banks during the bargaining. Behind this tenet was the assumption that avoiding negotiations would foster less instability than engaging in them.

This technical argument for avoiding currency negotiations is more useful politically than it is persuasive. It helps rationalize a policy of currency defense that is actually pursued out of domestic political fear. It is also useful in justifying unilateral action when negotiation might require compromise. But the claim that avoiding negotiations fosters stability is dubious. Foreign exchange markets have plainly been subject to much instability during the last two decades whether policies were unilateral or negotiated. Multilateral monetary negotiations can be and in fact have been conducted successfully in secret, and markets can be and have been temporarily closed without drastic harm to the world economy. One of the chief causes of actual instability is delay in needed exchange-rate change, and a major reason for delay is that major payments imbalances are often manifestly two-sided or multi-sided phenomena. The evidence is at least equally supportive of the view that, in the end, instability is less when international adjustment is attempted through timely multilateral negotiations than when it is done through delayed, uncoordinated unilateral jumps.

"Benign Neglect"

Other elements of U.S. action and inaction during this period seemed inconsistent with an orthodox line. Eventually it became apparent that a very different school of thought was simultaneously having influence—largely constraining—on policy. The conflicting diagnosis was formulated explicitly during the 1968 election campaign by Nixon's task force on international monetary affairs, chaired by Professor Gottfried Haberler of Harvard University. This task force, or at least some of its members, believed that the world's reserve center had developed a clear fundamental payments imbalance, and that a major exchange-rate change was desirable. The U.S. dollar was fundamentally overvalued, and it should be depreciated. According to a leading member of the task force and an original member of Nixon's Council of Economic Advisers, Hendrik S. Houthakker, the early Nixon policy was one of "benign neglect" and "was aimed at forcing a depreciation of our overvalued dollar."[26] (The more orthodox within the administration were certainly intending no such thing.) This faction deplored the alternative measures that had been imposed to stave off dollar depreciation, particularly the capital restrictions. They were disturbed by growing domestic pressure for protection from imports, which were being stimulated by the overvalued dollar and ought to be reduced by depreciation. These interferences with international markets were only short-sighted palliatives, in their view, worse on grounds of efficiency than the depreciation they were designed to prevent.

In this diagnosis, a traditional dollar devaluation in terms of gold would not accomplish depreciation, because other major financial powers, even surplus countries, would offset it. Houthakker traveled to Europe in April 1969 as a member of an official American economic delegation. In Brussels, he asked the European Community official in charge of international monetary affairs what Europe would do if the dollar were devalued under the Bretton Woods rules. "He stated flatly that all European currencies would

---

[26] Hendrik S. Houthakker, "Cooling Off the Money Crisis," *Wall Street Journal*, 16 March 1973.

be devalued by the same percentage on the same day."[27] But if devaluation was not workable, free floating was not desirable. Most of the early Nixon advisers preferred to preserve the Bretton Woods par value regime, but to do so by making it more flexible.

From this diagnosis, they derived a strategy of "benign neglect." Underlying it was the premise that an American-dominated system was still the most efficient one possible. Given the size of the American economy and its relative insulation from world trade, the greatest U.S. contribution to the international economy would be to provide a stable dollar as world money. The dollar could continue to perform its unique international function as long as the U.S. refused to devalue it outright and meanwhile prevented inflation at home. Thus, their first emphasis was on domestic economic policies to stabilize the U.S. economy. Domestic policies would not be made more restrictive than domestic conditions indicated, solely in order to reduce an external deficit. The U.S. would adopt a passive policy toward its balance of payments, justifying it as a service to the world. As long as some countries actively sought payments surpluses, others would necessarily have deficits, the reasoning went. The United States, by willingly accepting the role of the "nth" country, could absorb the net imbalance in the system and thereby reduce policy conflict.

According to this viewpoint, major exchange-rate change was needed. However, since the American dollar had to be kept aside because of its special function, other countries would have to move their currencies against the fixed dollar. No doubt this was music to the ears of an American political leader like President Nixon. It meant that there was no need to devalue the dollar or to engage in high-level monetary bargaining. Instead, the strategy would rely

[27] Hendrik Houthakker, "The Breakdown of Bretton Woods," in *Economic Advice and Executive Policy: Recommendations from Past Members of the Council of Economic Advisers*, ed. Werner Sichel (New York: Praeger, 1978), p. 54.

on international markets to force a major adjustment in the system. With the U.S. neglecting its deficit, the markets would force on each surplus government the choice of either continuing to accumulate more and more dollars, or allowing its currency to appreciate separately against the dollar. If surplus governments chose to absorb more dollars, that would be compatible with the benign-neglect policy. If they demanded gold, ultimately the U.S. could suspend convertibility and continue its passivity. Houthakker, an advocate of this line within the administration, expected that most surplus states would probably opt for exchange-rate change as the lesser evil within about a year, and without the U.S. having to engage in explicit negotiations or make diplomatic concessions to get it. Evidently this faction did not expect responses in the form of direct controls on inflows or other retaliation.[28]

The benign-neglect group also favored new IMF rules permitting greater exchange-rate flexibility. Some were uncomfortable with a reliance on market forces to produce the change. C. Fred Bergsten, then Kissinger's deputy for economic affairs, was especially eager for the United States to continue its leadership of monetary reform. Bergsten agitated internally for a change toward more flexible rates and substitution of the SDR for the dollar as reserve currency. He was convinced that maintaining the reserve role was contrary to the purely American interest as well as to the world's interest.[29] But Bergsten was never able to persuade Kissinger to act on this issue.

There was also a third strategy being espoused at the outset of the Nixon administration. Arthur F. Burns, Nix-

[28] This account is based on interviews; *Business Week*, 28 December 1968, pp. 72-74; and Gottfried Haberler and Thomas D. Willett, *A Strategy for U.S. Balance of Payments Policy* (Washington, D.C.: American Enterprise Institute, 1971), in which the essential themes of the Haberler task force report were published.

[29] Interview with Bergsten; and C. Fred Bergsten, *The Dilemmas of the Dollar: The Economics and Politics of United States International Monetary Policy* (New York: New York University Press, 1975).

on's long-standing adviser and coordinator of the pre-in-
auguration task forces, urged him to devalue immediately.
Burns had preceded Houthakker on a tour of European
banks before the election, and he had formed the opposite
conclusion—that is, that Europe would "understand" and
accept a dollar devaluation rather than offsetting its effect.
Burns told Nixon that his first month in office would be a
politically opportune moment.[30] The task force did not
endorse the idea, and Nixon did not take it up.

Thus, Kissinger and Nixon heard several ideas for major
policy changes, and they rejected them. It is not clear whether
Nixon ever read the Haberler task force report, or precisely
what posture he adopted toward exchange-rate changes at
the time.[31] In any case, he made no dramatic changes and
he also did not resolve the difference between the two main
lines. While the Treasury continued to send orthodox signals, outcroppings of the "benign neglect" strategy also
began to appear. Domestic policies of the passive sort were
adopted; a more active incomes policy was rejected. In a
series of steps, the new administration began to undo the
measures taken earlier to restrain the payments deficit. In
April 1969, it relaxed international capital controls. Statis-
tical window-dressing techniques were scrapped; foreign
aid was "untied" from U.S. export promotion. Kissinger
ordered that less pressure be put on West Germany for

[30] Interview with Burns.

[31] The President's major exposure to international monetary issues prior
to 1971 came in June 1969, at a White House meeting where the operative
question was whether and how many SDRs should be created. The time
seemed favorable for activating the new SDR mechanism. After the many
years in which American deficits injected liquidity into the system, that
stream seemed to run dry. In 1968 and 1969, the U.S. was in official-
settlements surplus, and in 1969 both Germany and France found themselves in deficit. In reality, the dollar was being strengthened by unsus-
tainable capital inflows. But the U.S. decided to propose distributing $20
billion worth of SDRs over five years. The European Community favored
$7.5 billion. The compromise was for $9.5 billion in SDRs over three
years.

military offset payments. These steps were taken piece-meal, not packaged openly as "benign neglect."

High-level American diplomacy withdrew altogether from the international monetary system rather than extending Fowler's reform campaign. The sort of vigorous pressure for exchange-rate change that Fowler had directed at West Germany in 1968 was not repeated. The President made no attempt, even secretly, to negotiate a parity adjustment with Japan or any other state before 15 August 1971. He indicated clearly that he was most concerned about other international issues. The only high-level foreign economic policy initiative before August 1971 was a strenuous (and eventually successful) effort to extract from Japan an agreement to limit exports of synthetic and wool textiles to the United States.[32]

Mid-level officials attempted to go forward without active high-level support toward new exchange-rate rules. While Paul Volcker was relegating schemes for greater flexibility to the ivory towers, Houthakker was touring Europe officially seeking support for those very schemes. (He found sympathy in the German and Italian central banks but little receptivity elsewhere. Britain and Japan were strongly opposed.)[33] After several months of debate within the Volcker Group, successor to the Deming Group, Treasury agreed in 1969 that the U.S. Executive Director at the IMF, William

---

[32] This textile trade was quite small in balance-of-payments terms. Japanese exports of all textile and apparel products (including cotton) amounted to 1.4 percent of U.S. import value in 1968 (computed from U.S. Bureau of the Census, *U.S. General Imports: Commodity by World Area*, FT 150, 1968, Tables 1, 2, and 3). Even in sectoral terms, Japan's textile and apparel sales in the United States in 1969, measured in dollar values, were only about 1 percent of American production and 4 percent of Japanese production. Yet the campaign involved two summit meetings between Prime Minister Sato and President Nixon, two cabinet-level ministerial conferences, and nine other major negotiations before Japan submitted to an agreement in October 1971. See I. M. Destler, Haruhiro Fukui, and Hideo Sato, *The Textile Wrangle: Conflict in Japanese-American Relations, 1969-1971* (Ithaca, N.Y.: Cornell University Press, 1979), p. 8 and throughout.

[33] Interview with a former American official.

Dale, could propose that the IMF Board discuss wider bands and crawling pegs. Dale carried out this mission, while simultaneously the Treasury Secretary and Under Secretary insisted publicly that nothing radical was being considered and that they were not at all convinced that any of these ideas would be technically feasible or wise.[34] Bilateral discussions of flexibility were also initiated at the technical level with several governments. The largest changes discussed officially would have created long-term adjustments in IMF rules, remaining within the par value framework. None dealt with early one-time exchange-rate realignments of the magnitudes in fact negotiated in the fall of 1971. Evidently American officials did not suggest any major U.S. policy concessions as a means of building support for multilateral reform. The outcome of these mid-level initiatives, as discussed below, was stalemate.

Perhaps the most telling sign of benign neglect from a foreign point of view appeared in 1970. An unprecedented American payments deficit led to no major new American balance-of-payments programs. That year the trade balance improved, but the previous year's huge inflow of liquid capital reversed itself. Early in 1970, the Federal Reserve began to ease monetary policy. Interest rates declined steadily, more so than rates in Europe. The differential created sufficient incentive to move large sums abroad through the Eurocurrency banks and eventually into European central banks. The U.S. official settlements balance plunged from a rare surplus, in 1969, of $2.7 billion to a deficit of $9.8 billion in 1970. A drop of only $3.7 billion in this figure in 1967 had driven the Johnson administration into a flurry of politically unpopular activity, yet the Nixon administration held back. Its orthodox financing measures were small in proportion to the deficit.

As 1971 began, the deficit deepened and the bifurcation continued. John B. Connally became Secretary of the

---

[34] Interviews; IMF, *Summary Proceedings 1969*, pp. 53-55; *New York Times*, 26 September 1969, p. 51.

Treasury and the United States became more assertive, but not on behalf of monetary adjustment. Far from demanding that foreign governments give serious thought to exchange-rate changes, Connally at first consistently denied that "our international financial problems can be taken care of by some sort of monetary magic. Money itself cannot produce, increase efficiency, or open markets abroad."[35] Speaking before the U.S. Chamber of Commerce in late April 1971, Connally explicitly rejected a policy of benign neglect.[36] Shortly thereafter, exchange-market pressure led the West German government to abandon its peg and let the mark float upward, lifting the hearts of the supporters of benign neglect. Connally, however, criticized the German float. In Munich in May 1971, he warned:

> The danger is plain. To revert to the use of exchange rates as a supplementary tool of domestic policy is fraught with danger to the essential stability and sustainability of the system as a whole.[37]

Connally used this Munich platform to deliver his first comprehensive external policy statement. With a bluntness unusual in international monetary gatherings, he declared that his country's economic policies had consistently had an outward orientation responsive to the needs of others, but that other countries were not reciprocating in an equitable manner. His complaints were aimed at trading arrangements and the share of military costs borne by U.S. allies. He said:

> The persistent underlying balance of payments deficit . . . is more than covered, year in and year out, by our net military expenditures abroad, over and above amounts received from foreign military purchases in the United States. . . . No longer does the U.S. economy dominate

---

[35] U.S., Congress, Senate, Committee on Finance, *Foreign Trade: Hearings*, 92nd Cong., 1st sess., 17 May 1971, p. 21.

[36] *New York Times*, 28 April 1971, p. 63.

[37] Department of State, *Bulletin* 65 (12 July 1971):42-46.

the free world. No longer can considerations of friend-
ship or need or capacity justify the United States carrying
so heavy a share of the common burdens.[38]

Here, as in Treasury statements at home, exchange-rate
policy remained orthodox.

The original choices made by the Nixon administration
as a whole are an essential if indirect part of the explanation
for the dramatic policy reversal that took place in 1971.
These choices were partly responsible, as elaborated below,
for the stalemate among the major financial powers in 1971.
At the end of the 1960s, market pressure against the U.S.
dollar had seemed to ease and even reverse. This might
have been an opportunity for negotiations, but it was des-
tined to evaporate soon. In 1971, the favorable financial
tide ebbed, revealing starkly the steady erosion that had
been taking place in underlying trends.

SWELLING DEFICITS AND DOLLAR DEPRECIATION

The international market perspective on foreign economic
policy hypothesizes that if supply and demand in the relevant market become fundamentally imbalanced, policy will
change by yielding to market pressure in the appropriate
direction. This perspective does identify the leading source
of change in the 1971 case. Beneath the cyclical ebbs and
flows of the late 1960s, underlying conditions in the foreign
exchange markets had actually been moving fairly steadily
toward a dollar depreciation. For years, the overall balance
of payments had shown deficits; in 1971 the imbalance
became extreme, and there was renewed selling pressure
on the dollar. Such market signals would have led an analyst
using the international market perspective to anticipate a
halt to dollar defense (including market intervention and
foreign borrowing) and a shift to a policy of depreciation
by some means. From this perspective the most likely re-

[38] Department of State, *Bulletin* 65 (12 July 1971):42-46.

CHART 4. Trends in Unit Labor Costs in Manufacturing,
1960-1972 (index based on costs in U.S. dollars)

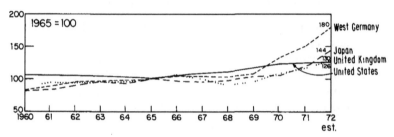

SOURCE: *International Economic Report of the President 1973*, p. 39.

sponse would have been either of two ways of yielding to the market. Either the deficit country would devalue its dollar, or it would suspend formal convertibility and exchange controls and allow private markets to operate. More active exchange-rate diplomacy, the surcharge, and U.S. nonmonetary demands, however, are difficult to explain from market conditions alone.

One partial index of trends in the dollar's underlying market value was comparative unit labor costs in manufacturing. Chart 4 shows the trends for four major countries. During the early 1960s, the relative U.S. position improved. But from 1965 until the exchange-rate adjustments of 1969-1971, U.S. costs rose faster. Partly as a result, U.S. exports ran into sales difficulties, while American demand drew in a surge of imports. Contrary to Henry Fowler's hope, 1964 turned out to be a peak year for the U.S. trade balance (see Chart 5). Thereafter, this indicator, too, showed a steady decline, interrupted by a brief recovery in 1970. The broader and economically more meaningful balance on current account and long-term capital, or basic balance, showed the same general pattern.

The acceleration of U.S. inflation relative to that of other countries was due to a combination of private-market processes and government-policy choices. Among the latter, the

CHART 5. U.S. Trade Balance, 1960-1972 (annual data,
1960-1970; semi-annual data at annual rates,
1971-1972)

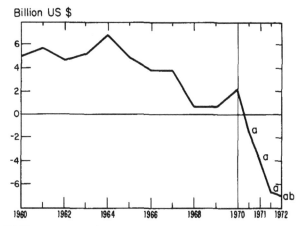

^a Half-year at annual rate.
^b Preliminary.

SOURCE: *Annual Report of the Secretary of the Treasury on the State
of the Finances 1973*, p. 427.

U.S. intervention in Vietnam and the failure of macroeconomic policy to compensate for the additional expenditures by noninflationary means, have already been mentioned. To these should be added the early Nixon
administration's unsuccessful efforts to decelerate the price
rises.

Before 1971, these so-called underlying trends were mixed
with sufficient "noise" to make an unambiguous prognosis
impossible. In the late 1960s, aggregate unemployment declined. Short-term capital inflows helped produce overall
payments surpluses in 1968 and 1969. Then, in 1970, interest-rate differentials opened in favor of Europe, and
some widened in 1971, prompting U.S. capital outflows that
for once reinforced trade movements rather than offsetting
them. The trade balance also slumped in late 1970, and in
the second quarter of 1971 it dropped sharply into deficit.

When these figures became available during the summer, they indicated that the United States would have a yearly trade deficit in 1971 for the first time since 1893. During the first half of 1971, the total payments balance plunged from an already unprecedented 1970 deficit of $9.8 billion to a spectacular $22 billion deficit on an annual basis (see Chart 6 and Table 4).

The dollar was on the floor in most European markets by early 1971, and "overt speculation began to appear . . . in March, further swelling the torrent of dollars flowing to

CHART 6. U.S. Overall Balance of Payments, 1960-1972 (annual data, 1960-1969; quarterly data at seasonally adjusted annual rates, 1970-1972)

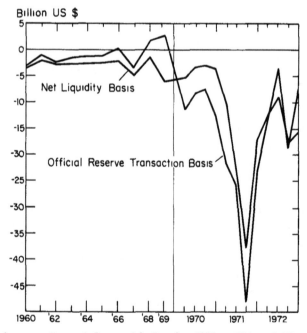

SOURCES: *Economic Report of the President 1973*, p. 294, and *1974*, p. 351.

TABLE 4. U.S. BALANCE OF PAYMENTS, 1946-1973 (millions of dollars)

Year or Quarter	Merchandise[ab]			Net Military Trans- actions	Net Investment Income		Balance on Current Account
	Exports	Imports	Net Balance		Private[c]	U.S. Govern- ment	
1946	11,764	−5,067	6,697	−493	750	6	4,885
1947	16,097	−5,973	10,124	−455	997	50	8,992
1948	13,265	−7,557	5,708	−799	1,177	85	1,993
1949	12,213	−6,874	5,339	−621	1,200	73	580
1950	10,203	−9,081	1,122	−576	1,382	78	−2,125
1951	14,243	−11,176	3,067	−1,270	1,569	151	302
1952	13,449	−10,838	2,611	−2,054	1,535	140	−175
1953	12,412	−10,975	1,437	−2,423	1,566	166	−1,949
1954	12,929	−10,353	2,576	−2,460	1,899	213	−321
1955	14,424	−11,527	2,897	−2,701	2,117	180	−345
1956	17,556	−12,803	4,753	−2,788	2,454	40	1,722
1957	19,562	−13,291	6,271	−2,841	2,584	4	3,556
1958	16,414	−12,952	3,462	−3,135	2,416	168	−5
1959	16,458	−15,310	1,148	−2,805	2,658	68	−2,138
1960	19,650	−14,758	4,892	−2,753	2,825	16	1,801
1961	20,108	−14,537	5,571	−2,596	3,451	103	3,069
1962	20,781	−16,260	4,521	−2,448	3,920	132	2,456
1963	22,272	−17,048	5,224	−2,304	4,056	97	3,199
1964	25,501	−18,700	6,801	−2,133	4,872	3	5,783
1965	26,461	−21,510	4,951	−2,122	5,274	20	4,306
1966	29,310	−25,493	3,817	−2,935	5,331	44	2,320
1967	30,666	−26,866	3,800	−3,138	5,848	40	2,051
1968	33,626	−32,991	635	−3,143	6,157	63	−443
1969	36,400	−35,807	593	−3,344	5,820	155	−1,050
1970	41,964	−39,788	2,176	−3,374	6,374	−115	416
1971	42,768	−45,466	−2,698	−2,918	8,929	−957	−2,790
1972	48,769	−55,681	−6,912	−3,558	9,751	−1,889	−8,353
1973[ı]	67,001	−67,655	−653	−2,841	11,927	−2,952	344
Seasonally Adjusted							
1971: I	10,872	−10,743	129	−677	1,942	−113	151
II	10,791	−11,708	−917	−707	2,358	−178	−728
III	11,522	−11,907	−385	−715	2,051	−306	−678
IV	9,583	−11,108	−1,525	−818	2,577	−360	−1,538
1972: I	11,655	−13,475	−1,820	−894	2,290	−399	−2,343
II	11,539	−13,313	−1,774	−954	2,252	−461	−2,364
III	12,362	−13,935	−1,573	−846	2,447	−497	−1,893
IV	13,213	−14,958	−1,745	−864	2,763	−531	−1,751
1973: I	15,320	−16,280	−960	−825	2,954	−645	−592
II	16,778	−17,022	−244	−730	2,888	−777	−367
IIIᴾ	18,153	−17,439	714	−576	3,103	−792	1,217
IVᴾ	20,048	18,748	1,300	—	—	—	—

TABLE 4 (*cont.*)

Year or Quarter	Long-Term Capital Flows, Net U.S. Government[d]	Private[e]	Balance on Current Account and Long-Term Capital	Non-Liquid Short-Term Private Capital Flows, Net[e]	Allocations of Special Drawing Rights	Errors and Omissions, Net
1946	—	—	—	−253	—	155
1947	—	—	—	−236	—	861
1948	—	—	—	−131	—	1,115
1949	—	—	—	158	—	717
1950	—	—	—	75	—	−124
1951	—	—	—	−227	—	354
1952	—	—	—	−41	—	497
1953	—	—	—	183	—	220
1954	—	—	—	−556	—	60
1955	—	—	—	−328	—	371
1956	—	—	—	−479	—	390
1957	—	—	—	−174	—	1,012
1958	—	—	—	−145	—	361
1959	—	—	—	−89	—	260
1960	−889	−2,100	−1,188	[h] −1,405	—	−1,084
1961	−901	−2,182	−15	[h] −1,200	—	−1,037
1962	−892	−2,606	−1,042	[h] −657	—	−1,166
1963	−1,150	−3,376	−1,328	[h] −968	—	−418
1964	−1,348	−4,511	−76	−1,643	—	−978
1965	−1,532	−4,577	−1,804	−154	—	−520
1966	−1,469	−2,575	−1,724	−104	—	−322
1967	−2,423	−2,932	−3,304	−522	—	−857
1968	−2,158	1,191	−1,411	231	—	−431
1969	−1,926	−70	−3,046	−640	—	−2,395
1970	−2,018	−1,429	−3,031	−482	867	−1,205
1971	−2,359	−4,401	−9,550	−2,347	717	−10,784
1972	−1,339	−152	−9,843	−1,637	710	−3,112
1973[i]	−832	1,803	1,315	−3,989	—	−6,428
			Seasonally Adjusted			
1971: I	−642	−895	−1,386	−517	180	−949
II	−575	−1,691	−2,994	−492	179	−2,391
III	−598	−2,018	−3,294	−822	179	−5,511
IV	−544	201	−1,881	−516	179	−1,933
1972: I	−289	−1,143	−3,775	−535	178	944
II	−95	604	−1,855	310	178	−940
III	−366	−393	−2,652	−430	177	−1,626
IV	−586	781	−1,556	−982	177	−1,490
1973: I	−336	−16	−944	−1,822	—	−3,891
II	75	−317	−609	−1,404	—	425
III[p]	−363	1,685	2,539	234	—	−1,355
IV[p]	—	—	—	—	—	—

TABLE 4 (cont.)

Year or Quarter	Net Liquidity Balance	Liquid Private Capital Flows, Net^c	Official Reserve Trans- actions Balance	Changes in Liabilities to Foreign Official Agencies, Net^f	Changes in U.S. Official Reserve Assets, Net^g	U.S. Official Reserve Assets, Net (End of Period)
1946	—	—	—	—	−623	20,706
1947	—	—	—	—	−3,315	24,021
1948	—	—	—	—	−1,736	25,758
1949	—	—	—	—	−266	26,024
1950	—	—	—	—	1,758	24,265
1951	—	—	—	—	−33	24,299
1952	—	—	—	—	−415	24,714
1953	—	—	—	—	1,256	23,458
1954	—	—	—	—	480	22,978
1955	—	—	—	—	182	22,797
1956	—	—	—	—	−869	23,666
1957	—	—	—	—	−1,165	24,832
1958	—	—	—	—	2,292	22,540
1959	—	—	—	—	1,035	21,504
1960	^h −3,677	^h273	−3,403	1,258	2,145	19,359
1961	^h −2,252	^h904	−1,348	742	606	18,753
1962	^h −2,864	^h214	−2,650	1,117	1,533	17,220
1963	^h −2,713	^h779	−1,934	1,557	377	16,843
1964	−2,696	1,162	−1,534	1,363	171	16,672
1965	−2,478	1,188	−1,290	67	1,222	15,450
1966	−2,151	2,370	219	−787	568	14,882
1967	−4,683	1,265	−3,418	3,366	52	14,830
1968	−1,611	3,252	1,641	−761	−880	15,710
1969	−6,081	8,820	2,739	−1,552	−1,187	16,964
1970	−3,851	−5,988	−9,839	7,362	2,477	14,487
1971	−21,965	−7,788	−29,753	27,405	2,348	12,167
1972	−13,882	3,542	10,340	10,308	32	13,151
1973	−9,103	−1,639	−10,741	10,443	299	ʲ14,378

			Seasonally Adjusted			Unad- justed
1971: I	−2,672	−2,958	−5,630	4,948	682	14,342
II	−5,698	−647	−6,345	5,686	659	13,504
III	−9,448	−2,434	−11,882	10,688	1,194	12,131
IV	−4,151	−1,749	−5,900	6,087	−187	12,167
1972: I	−3,188	−288	−3,476	3,047	429	12,270
II	−2,307	1,456	−851	1,082	−231	ᵏ13,339
III	−4,531	7	−4,524	4,579	−55	13,217
IV	−3,851	2,367	−1,484	1,595	−111	13,151
1973: I	−6,657	−3,842	−10,499	10,279	220	12,931
II	−1,588	1,923	335	−352	17	12,914
IIIᵖ	1,418	690	2,108	−2,095	−13	12,927
IVᵖ	—	—	—	—	—	ʲ14,378

TABLE 4 (*cont.*)

ᵃ Excludes military grants.

ᵇ Adjusted from Census data for differences in timing and coverage.

ᶜ Includes fees and royalties from U.S. direct investments abroad or from foreign direct investments in the United States.

ᵈ Excludes liabilities to foreign official reserve agencies.

ᵉ Private foreigners exclude the International Monetary Fund (IMF), but include other international and regional organizations.

ᶠ Includes liabilities to foreign official agencies reported by U.S. Government and U.S. banks and U.S. liabilities to the IMF arising from reversible gold sales to, and gold deposits with, the United States.

ᵍ Official reserve assets include gold, special drawing rights, convertible currencies, and the U.S. gold tranche position in the IMF.

ʰ Coverage of liquid banking claims for 1960-63 and of nonliquid nonbanking claims for 1960-62 is limited to foreign currency deposits only; other liquid items are not available separately and are included with nonliquid claims.

ⁱ First 3 quarters on a seasonally adjusted annual rates basis (except reserve assets are for end of December).

ʲ Includes increase of $1,436 million resulting from change in par value of the U.S. dollar on October 18, 1973.

ᵏ Includes increase of $1,016 million resulting from change in par value of the U.S. dollar on May 8, 1972.

ᵖ Preliminary.

SOURCE: U.S. *Economic Report of the President 1974*, Table C-88.

foreign markets."[39] Transnational money managers sometimes moved quickly in response to an official hint of a possible parity change. In early May, some German officials commented sympathetically about a report recommending a German appreciation. Foreign liquid funds surged into Frankfurt. On the morning of 5 May, the Bundesbank, in order to hold the mark at its ceiling, had to purchase $1,000 million in the first 40 minutes of trading. Then, horrified at the inflationary consequences, the Bank withdrew from the market and allowed the mark to float, taking with it the Dutch guilder. The Swiss franc and Austrian schilling were also revalued. The Canadian dollar had been freed to float upward on 31 May 1970. Even so, by July 1971 the U.S. dollar's effective exchange rate had declined only 2.5

[39] Charles A. Coombs, "Treasury and Federal Reserve Foreign Exchange Operations," Federal Reserve Bank of New York *Monthly Review* 53 (October 1971).

percent from its May 1970 value.[40] Nixon's mixed strategy had accomplished little adjustment. Markets remained nervous and alert.

The extreme clarity of the renewed payments hemorrhage sealed the fate of the traditional dollar defense. Now, in contrast to 1933, there could be little question that the United States was in fundamental disequilibrium. By August 1971, hardly any commentator still maintained that the external imbalance could be rectified at tolerable economic cost without substantial exchange-rate change.[41] This was particularly so in view of the fact that the American economy was already underemployed. The United States in 1971 presented a manifest case of the textbook "dilemma" pointing toward the need for exchange-rate change. More hopeful diagnoses of the deficit were overwhelmed by contrary data.

[40] According to the Treasury index reported in *Economic Report of the President 1974*, p. 222. This index gives a weighted average exchange value of the dollar against 22 OECD currencies, with weights derived from each country's share of U.S. trade. The Morgan Guaranty Trust Company index, computed by a similar method from a sample of 14 major currencies, showed a depreciation of 3.2 percent by July 1971 (*World Financial Markets*, 17 December 1974).

[41] Evidence of the spreading acceptance of this diagnosis is abundant. At mid-summer, Treasury technicians projected the U.S. balance of payments for 1972, assuming no policy changes, and concluded that the U.S. would have a $4 billion deficit in the current account. Treasury decided that a current account surplus of at least $9 billion would be needed for overall balance (U.S., Congress, House, Committee on Foreign Affairs, *The International Implications of the New Economic Policy: Hearings*, 92nd Cong., 1st sess., 21 September 1971, p. 82). The research staff of the IMF had also begun in early 1971 to calculate the size of exchange-rate changes that would be necessary to rectify fundamental disequilibria. When the executive directors met on 16 August to respond to the United States, the staff was ready with a forecast that an average dollar depreciation of about 10 percent would be required (Margaret Garritsen de Vries, *The International Monetary Fund 1966-1971: The System Under Stress* [Washington, D.C.: IMF, 1976], vol. 1, pp. 537-538). During the summer an OECD working paper also implied that some form of parity change would be necessary (*New York Times*, 2 July 1971, p. 45). For further evidence, see *New York Times*, 25 July 1971, p. III-5, and the *Financial Times* editorial of 14 August 1971.

Thus, the extreme market conditions made it probable that any American administration would by this point have made a shift away from the old policy and toward some means of dollar depreciation—whether within or without Bretton Woods, and whether or not accompanied by non-monetary measures. The economic costs of not adjusting, both for exporting and import-competing industries in the United States and for international monetary stability, had become insupportable. The weight of economic irrationality was close to sinking the dollar, regardless of whether foreign governments demanded more U.S. gold or domestic political groups demanded economic policy changes. If the underlying indicators and the payments deficit had somehow improved in 1971, then the international power structure, domestic political pressures, and new ideas in Washington would not have been likely to produce the observed policy change. In this sense, the market deterioration must be regarded as the leading source of change in this case.

But market analysis is not sufficient. Some market analysts would have expected a dollar depreciation much earlier. There was still debate in the U.S. as to whether specific steps such as going off gold, dollar devaluation, or floating exchange rates could be avoided, and as to whether Washington should proceed unilaterally or through negotiations. The surcharge especially is puzzling. By discouraging imports, a surcharge would be expected to retard, rather than encourage, a dollar decline in the market.

POWER SHIFT AND SOVEREIGN STALEMATE

Public figures and academic theorists have explained the policy change of 1971 as a function of the international power structure. Some of these power interpretations have been confused or exaggerated. An international power perspective does provide important elements of an explanation, but the evidence indicates that it is inadequate and in some respects misleading.

American leaders began in 1971 to proclaim the thesis that the structure of international economic power among the industrial capitalist countries had shifted, to the advantage of Western Europe and Japan and to the disadvantage of the United States. We have seen examples of this official line in John Connally's Munich address and President Nixon's 15 August speech. According to this thesis, Europe and Japan had become much stronger since the 1940s, yet they continued to follow selfish policies, requiring the United States to bear disproportionate burdens for the international system. They ought to give more. The power shift was cited to justify American unilateralism and withdrawal from leading joint efforts. Americans, preoccupied and frustrated in Vietnam, found this view appealing.

It was after 1971 that American academic theorists devised the hypothesis of hegemonic decline mentioned in Chapter 2. This may be an instance of princes whispering in the ears of professors rather than the reverse. These theories were given greater validity by subsequent changes, especially in U.S. relations with OPEC countries. But with reference to the political-monetary events of 1971, they are less persuasive.

International Military Power Structure

Before dealing with the economic power structure, we should note briefly that an analysis of the world military structure would not have led one to expect this sharp change in U.S. international monetary policy. On several occasions, shifts in the distribution of military power have led to shifts of foreign economic policy; the realignments by France at the end of the nineteenth century and by Britain in the mid-1930s were mentioned in Chapter 2. But no major structural change took place during the period leading up to 1971. It is true that there had been changes since World

War II: Germany had rearmed, and minor nuclear arsenals were built in Britain, France, and China. In many developing countries, decolonization and modernization altered the utility of force, and regional military balances shifted. The gap between the superpowers narrowed as the Soviet Union improved its nuclear weapons, delivery vehicles, and conventional forces. Despite these adjustments, however, it was still the case in 1971 that no power in the world came close to rivaling the military strength of either superpower. America's allies remained clearly dependent on the United States for security. This dependence remained especially marked, in fact, for precisely that country from which Washington wanted the largest monetary adjustment—Japan. At the global military level, the power structure remained essentially the same as it had been since World War II.[42]

Thus, on such grounds one would have had little basis for expecting a major U.S. foreign economic policy shift in 1971. Moreover, within a bipolar structure, power shifts are less likely to lead to realignments among the actors than in a multipolar structure, since addition or subtraction of an "ordinary" power has relatively little strategic consequence for a superpower. If anything, the rise of the Soviet Union relative to the United States during the 1960s would have led a military power analyst to expect U.S. foreign economic policies that were at least equally if not *more* solicitous of her allies during the 1970s, rather than the observed shift toward unilateralism.

Power structures do not determine security attitudes completely, however. Changes in behavior—the movement away from overt confrontation in Europe after the early 1960s, as well as specific arms control and other negotiations—reduced fears of war between the superpowers. East-West détente, by reducing NATO's sense of external threat, permitted NATO allies to feel relaxed enough to press their

[42] For an elaboration, see Kenneth N. Waltz, *Theory of International Politics* (Reading, Mass.: Addison-Wesley, 1979).

economic conflicts against each other, conflicts that before had been suppressed by the high tension of the Cold War.[43] It is plausible to suppose that if the same tension had prevailed in 1971, Washington and her allies would have avoided the actual degree of monetary conflict.

This hypothesis is qualified by two considerations, however. West European and Japanese weakness vis-à-vis the Soviet Union probably helped the U.S. gain their compliance with American economic designs during the Cold War. Yet it seems equally likely that their weakness vis-à-vis the U.S. also contributed to that result, along with allied economic gains attracting them toward cooperation with those designs. Second, East-West détente was only a change of degree. It will be seen below that Soviet-American structural rivalry continued to exert a constraint on U.S. international economic policy. In the fall of 1971, the prospect of bargaining with its adversaries led the United States to settle the dispute it had just opened with its allies.

For an explanation of the policy change that occurred in August 1971, a security and military power perspective adds only two background elements. The U.S. intervention in Vietnam disturbed the U.S. economy and balance of payments. East-West détente somewhat relaxed one incentive for allied cooperation.

Superpower in a Crowd

Economic capabilities did become somewhat more evenly distributed among capitalist industrial states over the postwar period. But the erosion of American dominance over the other major states by 1971 has been much exaggerated in the U.S. Not only did those states remain dependent on the U.S. for military protection, but the system's economic structure also remained centered on an economic superpower.

[43] Richard N. Cooper, "Introduction," in *A Reordered World: Emerging International Economic Problems*, ed. Richard N. Cooper (Washington, D.C.: Potomac Associates, 1973), pp. xxi-xxii.

The United States alone controlled an extraordinary 39 percent of the world's total productive capacity and spending power in 1950. The subsequent recovery of Western Europe and Japan increased their shares, but in 1970 the American share of world GNP was still 30 percent. The European Community as a whole controlled 15 percent, Japan 6 percent.[44]

A country's relative economic capabilities for influencing the behavior of others are indicated more directly by its share of international transactions and its dependence on those transactions. One of those capabilities is international purchasing power. In 1950, the United States purchased 14 percent of world imports. Even then, Britain was a close second, with a 12 percent share. During the 1950s, the U.S. share slipped to 11 percent, and it rose slightly during the 1960s. Over the same two decades, the American share of world exports declined from 17 percent to 14 percent (see Table 5). In terms of aggregate buying and selling capacity,

TABLE 5. SHARES OF WORLD TRADE (percent)

	A. Shares of World Imports			
	1950	1960	1970	1976
United States	14.4	11.2	12.1	12.7
West Germany	4.4	7.5	9.1	8.7
United Kingdom	11.8	9.6	6.6	5.5
France	4.9	4.6	5.8	6.3
Japan	1.6	3.3	5.7	6.4
	B. Shares of World Exports			
	1950	1960	1970	1976
United States	16.9	15.9	13.6	11.4
West Germany	3.3	8.9	10.9	10.3
United Kingdom	10.5	8.3	6.2	4.7
Japan	1.4	3.2	6.2	6.8
France	5.1	5.4	5.7	5.6

SOURCE: United Nations, *Yearbook of International Trade Statistics, 1978*, Special Table A.

[44] U.S., President, *The United States in the Changing World Economy*, Report by Peter G. Peterson, 2 vols. (1972), vol. II, chart 1.

the United States continued to swing heavy weight in the world economy.

The critical dimension distinguishing the superpower from other leading economic powers was its relative self-sufficiency. In 1970, U.S. exports plus imports were still only 8 percent of GNP, which contrasted with the proportions of other major states in roughly the same pattern as in 1960.[45] The U.S. remained in a much better position not only to exert influence but also to resist foreign influence based on trade dependence.

The actual use of power takes place perhaps most often in bilateral relations. Each of America's major trading partners was much more dependent on the American market than was the U.S. on that country's market. As a rough indicator of bilateral economic vulnerability, Table 6 shows the proportion of U.S. GNP exported to each country and the share of the country's GNP exported to the U.S. By this crude measure, Japan, for example, was six times more

TABLE 6. BILATERAL EXPORT DEPENDENCE BETWEEN THE U.S. AND OTHER MAJOR ECONOMIC POWERS, 1970

		Canada	United Kingdom	Japan	West Germany	France
A.	Country's export dependence on U.S.[a]	.134	.018	.030	.017	.006
B.	U.S. export dependence on the country[b]	.009	.003	.005	.003	.002
C.	Foreign country dependence/U.S. dependence (A/B)[c]	14	7	6	6	4

[a] Country's exports to U.S./country's GNP.
[b] U.S. exports to the country/U.S. GNP.
[c] Discrepancies are due to rounding.
SOURCES: IMF, *Direction of Trade*; World Bank, *World Bank Atlas 1972*.

[45] The 1970 proportions for other countries were: Japan, .19; France, .24; U.K., .32; West Germany, .36; and Canada, .37. Computed from U.N., *1978 Yearbook of International Trade Statistics*, 2 vols., vol. 1, Special Table A, and World Bank, *World Bank Atlas 1972*.

dependent on the U.S. market than America was on Japan's market. A serious interruption of these transactions would have caused far more harm to the partner than to the United States in every case.

Another basis of influence is the relative capacity to export capital, to control the international allocation of credit, and—when there is a preference for pegged exchange rates—to finance a payments deficit.[46] Here again the United States stood out among the industrial states. Shortages of savings relative to domestic need in most other industrialized countries limited their capacities to export capital, while the extraordinary size, depth, and efficiency of the U.S. private capital markets facilitated foreign borrowing in them. American firms also dominated by far among direct foreign investors in 1970.

One partial index of relative capability to control international credit allocation, focusing on official short-term capital, is a country's IMF quota and voting power. During the first years of the IMF's operation, the U.S. weighted share of votes, based on quotas, was 31.5 percent, followed by Britain with 15 percent, China with 6.5 percent, and France with 6.2 percent. By early 1971, the U.S. share had declined, but was still dominant at 22 percent. The other leading financial member states were Britain (9.2 percent), West Germany (5.3), France (5.0), and Japan (4.0).[47]

In short, the extraordinary American position in the international economic power structure had eroded somewhat over the first postwar generation, but the amount of the decline hardly seems sufficient to explain the dramatic reversal of 1971. If a hegemonic state stands to reap a large share of the collective good of international monetary stability, and if the U.S. was in such a position in 1950, then the United States in 1971 still had a substantial "interest" in sustaining that good.

[46] See Bergsten, *Dilemmas of the Dollar*, chap. 2, for one of the best discussions of monetary power.

[47] IMF, *Annual Reports* for 1947 and 1971.

An international economic power analysis conducted at the end of the 1960s would have expected that the United States, no longer a surplus country, would bargain with its more dependent partners on behalf of regime modification, seeking dollar depreciation and new rules shifting more of the burden of initiating international adjustment to surplus countries. Because of the basic continuity in the global military and economic structures, it would be expected that the other major states would bargain with Washington. But the slippage in the U.S. position implied that Japan and Western Europe would be able to resist one-way dictation and to insist on American compromises. The relationship would be one of bargaining, not dictation.

It would not have been far-fetched to expect a high-level American initiative toward a compromise agreement on exchange-rate adjustment within the Bretton Woods regime. Some American officials advocated such initiatives at the time. The campaign by Fred Bergsten of the National Security Council, the middle-level talks within the IMF Executive Board, and Arthur Burns' recommendation of devaluation have been mentioned. Furthermore, in late July 1971, the Federal Reserve Board's director of international finance, Robert Solomon, sent a memorandum to Arthur Burns, then Chairman of the Reserve Board, and to Treasury Under Secretary Paul Volcker, proposing that a bargaining initiative be taken at the 1971 IMF annual meeting. This plan, with the purpose of bringing about a concerted revaluation by other industrial countries, would have had the U.S. offering to negotiate a reform in which it would agree to give up the reserve role of the dollar.[48] Another, probably more strongly felt, foreign demand for an American concession was the call for more active domestic measures against inflation. Here too, various American elites had been urging the Nixon administration in the same direction well before August 1971, for purely domestic reasons. None of these recommendations was accepted by top

---

[48] Solomon, *International Monetary System*, pp. 183-184.

leaders before 15 August. Yet the United States did take some of these measures later, anyway. After a lag of some three to four years Washington's top leaders would signal that they had decided that serious monetary reform bargaining was not contrary to American interests after all.

Nor would it be unreasonable to suppose that the United States had had the power to extract an agreement from its allies earlier with a mix of incentives and threats. Japan, Germany, Britain, and other countries were much more dependent on the U.S. militarily and economically, and on the Bretton Woods regime, than was the U.S. on them. Their monetary behavior seemed to confirm such a power analysis. In the SDR negotiations, they insisted on U.S. concessions, but by and large they accepted the American initiative. They further cooperated with the U.S. Treasury after 1968 by restraining their gold purchases. When the U.S. deficit and foreign surpluses grew, surplus governments allowed by far the largest part of their surplus dollars to accumulate in their central banks, rather than converting them. During 1970 and the first seven months of 1971, U.S. liabilities to foreign governments ballooned by no less than $21 billion, while U.S. reserves, including gold, declined by only $3.7 billion. Some did resume gold purchases at low levels. Total gold outflow from January 1971 through 15 August came to $845 million, but half of that was part of transactions with the IMF. The surplus countries did not try to push the United States off gold, because of their greater general dependence on the monetary system, and because they had no alternative to American leadership. It would have been more difficult for Washington to achieve their agreement to exchange-rate changes than to the SDR and gold restraint. But the evidence does not indicate that they resisted because the U.S. was too weak to bring about agreement. The evidence indicates that the President did not try.

Several years later, a key Japanese policy maker was asked to speculate about the consequences if in early 1971 the

American President had sent a secret message to Tokyo, demanding a large yen revaluation, offering to discuss the possibility of a dollar devaluation against gold, and threatening an import surcharge if no agreement were reached. After a pause for reflection, he replied slowly:

> I believe Japan would have had to accept the yen revaluation if, as you said, a surcharge would have been the alternative, if it was inevitable that the United States was going to have one or the other. The Europeans would have demanded an increase in the gold price, but this was not crucial for Japan. . . . I believe I would have been inclined to accept, because from a yen appreciation we would gain in lower prices on imported raw materials and so forth, while with the surcharge we would just be giving money to the United States. The problem, of course, was to convince Tanaka, the Minister of Trade and Industry. I am not so sure that one could have convinced Tanaka.[49]

If the overall structure of economic power is not adequate to explain the actual course of U.S. policy, then how is it to be explained? Why did the United States pursue passivity, mixed with orthodoxy, followed by unilateral coercion?

Issue-Specific Analysis

It has been argued that, although an overall structural interpretation is inadequate, an issue-specific power analysis can explain at least the suspension of convertibility. While the U.S. continued to enjoy a strong position in terms of general capabilities, it was experiencing a sharp decline in the specifically monetary capabilities that were relevant under a convertibility regime. Robert Keohane and Joseph Nye point to shares of world reserves as indicating relative

---

[49] Interview.

monetary power under Bretton Woods rules.[50] The American share of world reserves fell from 50 percent in 1950 to 15 percent at the end of 1970, and then to 11 percent in August 1971.[51] In this view, American ability to defend convertibility was rapidly weakening. But U.S. ability to change the rules, based on nonmonetary capabilities, remained high. The growing disjunction between overall power and monetary power would have led one to expect the U.S. to attempt to change the rules. Keohane and Nye argue that the new policy to be expected from an issue-structural perspective would have been the one the U.S. followed, in particular the unilateral suspension of convertibility.

The utility of this distinction between general and special capabilities is subject to doubt on both theoretical and empirical grounds so far as international monetary policies are concerned. It does have greater promise elsewhere. One would expect that countries having the largest shipping fleets, or the largest capacities to export coffee, would have the greatest influence over policies on shipping or coffee, with less regard for the general military and economic power structure among states. But international monetary policies are inherently macropolicies. Exchange rates cut across all sectors of international transactions in goods, services, and capital. A change in international monetary policy necessarily has much wider effects—both at home and on world financial stability—than a change in shipping policy or coffee-export policy. Therefore, theoretically one would expect that a country's monetary policies will reflect its general strengths and vulnerabilities to a greater extent; monetary power should coincide with general power more than is the case in other "issues." The capabilities needed to deter or induce another state to change

[50] Robert O. Keohane and Joseph S. Nye, Jr., *Power and Interdependence: World Politics in Transition* (Boston: Little, Brown, 1977), pp. 132-143. See also the discussion in Chapter 2 of the present book.

[51] These data are taken from the Peterson Report, vol. II, chart 11.

its external monetary policies are likely to include more than narrowly monetary ones.

Empirical evidence mentioned above seems to confirm this hypothesis. During the 1960s, the putative "reserve power" of several states rose. By 1972, both Germany and Japan had greater monetary power than the U.S., according to Table 7. On a monetary-structural analysis, rising states would have been expected to change their monetary policies. Yet Japan and Germany did not make more active use of their apparently increased monetary power. Their policies continued to conform fairly closely to the Washington line as it was made known to them officially. This is not surprising, because their monetary power had increased less than their share of world reserves had. Their net influence over monetary policies was diluted by their continuing general dependence on a relatively closed U.S. economy. Conversely, real U.S. monetary power fell by less than its reserve share. The evidence indicates that Washington was still able to deter other governments from forcing it to abandon convertibility as of 13 August 1971.

Issue-specific analysis defined in this manner can in fact be misleading, and not only because the monetary arena is so heavily affected by the general power structure. There are also strictly monetary dimensions other than reserve share. The ability to defend a parity and convertibility is a function not only of reserves but also of capacity to borrow abroad, and this varies in part with the overall, nonmonetary strength of the country. A country with more prom-

TABLE 7. SHARES OF WORLD OFFICIAL RESERVES (percent)

	1957	1967	1972
Germany	9	11	15
Japan	1	3	12
United States	40	20	8
France	1	9	6
United Kingdom	4	4	4

SOURCE: International Monetary Fund, *International Financial Statistics*, as reported in Robert Keohane and Joseph Nye, *Power and Interdependence*, Table 6.3.

ising export industries is likely to have better access to foreign credit than one with less, even though the former may have a payments deficit or already significant foreign debt levels. Large countries may receive balance-of-payments loans (for example, Britain in the 1960s) because abrupt adjustment actions by a large country would be unwelcome to foreign lenders. Furthermore, a country that operates a key international currency derives short-term credit, in effect, from the willingness of foreigners to accumulate its money. Britain in 1913 held a meager 3 percent of world reserves,[52] but this seeming limit on monetary influence was significantly offset by Britain's external financing capabilities. The United States enjoyed the same compensation during the apparent decline shown in Table 7. Thus, a broader conception of the issue-specific power structure also reveals a stronger America.

For that matter, it may be questioned whether a nation's comparative monetary power varies with its *share* of world reserves. The ability of country A to defend its parity bears no obvious relation to the ratio of A's reserves to country B's reserves. A's ability is a function of the ratio between A's reserves and the demands on those reserves (leaving aside borrowing). Demand for reserves is likely to be a function of the size of A's deficits and, particularly if A is a reserve center, the size of foreign liquid claims on its reserves.

Formulated in this way, a monetary-power analysis does tell us something additional. It is plausible to expect that, other things being equal, the lower a reserve center's official liquidity ratio (official reserves/liabilities to official foreigners), the greater the likelihood of a suspension of convertibility, either temporary or lasting. There is presumably some ratio above zero at which the center will close the

[52] Robert Triffin, *The Evolution of the International Monetary System: Historical Reappraisal and Future Perspectives*, Princeton Studies in International Finance No. 12 (Princeton, N.J.: International Finance Section, Princeton University, 1964), Table 10. On this point, see Bergsten, *Dilemmas of the Dollar*, pp. 35-36.

window. So even if the monetary arena is strongly affected by the overall structure, specifically monetary capabilities may make *some* independent difference in a reserve center's relations with short-term creditor states.

What would this sort of analysis have led one to expect of the United States? The U.S. official liquidity ratio fell steadily from its high level of 212 percent in 1959 to 95 percent at the end of 1967. Over the next two years, it rose again to 142 percent. After a year of benign neglect and foreign dollar accumulations, it stood at 72 percent in 1970, and fell further to 40 percent by the end of July 1971.[53] In 1970 and thereafter, the United States could not have satisfied all foreign governments if they had demanded to convert all their swelling dollar reserves at once. But how low is too low? In 1913 the comparable ratio for the Bank of England was 38 percent.[54] A simple comparison of ratios

[53] U.S. total reserve assets divided by U.S. liquid liabilities to official institutions of foreign countries, computed from *Treasury Bulletin*, February 1972, Tables IFS-1 and IFS-2. These figures do not include U.S. liquid liabilities to private foreigners, including Eurodollar banks. Total dollar liabilities to all foreigners first surpassed U.S. official reserves in 1959, and thereafter the gap steadily widened. In principle, these private foreign dollars could always have been transferred to foreign central banks, as long as the official institutions chose to continue absorbing them rather than allowing their currencies to float. The private "overhang" was of course always in the immediate background of intergovernmental relations. Equally important, however, private financial confidence was subject to influence by official policy; this was always the basis on which any international reserve currency with fractional backing could operate in the first place. At present the focus is on state-to-state influences, and so the official liquidity ratio as defined here is the most appropriate indicator. Only foreign governments could present dollars for U.S. reserves.

[54] The Bank of England's gold reserves were valued at $165 million, while foreign official holdings of sterling were $432 million, both in 1913 dollars (Peter H. Lindert, *Key Currencies and Gold 1900-1913*, Princeton Studies in International Finance No. 24 [Princeton, N.J.: International Finance Section, Princeton University, 1969], Tables 1 and 2). Some differences between the two situations imply greater power for England than for the later U.S. government: Other British banks also held gold, and the Bank of England could keep the balance of payments from departing too far from equilibrium by manipulating the bank rate. The same is true for the United States more recently, but since the 1930s central banks

cannot be taken as meaningful alone, given the differences between the two environments. But it seems reasonable to argue that the American situation in 1970-1971 was much less clearcut than it may seem through hindsight. The U.S. liquidity ratio vis-à-vis foreign governments was still not obviously unmanageable, other things equal. The U.S. had not lost all its capacity to deter foreign governments from withdrawing gold during an adjustment. There remained a significant probability that the United States would choose a new policy that included a formally open gold window. American leaders, as we will see, were divided on this point. They were not on the ropes. Thus, even a redefined monetary-power analysis is still insufficient to predict or explain a U.S. decision to throw in the towel.

Indeed, it is arguable that in closing the gold window, Washington reduced rather than increased its influence over foreign monetary policies, contrary to the contention of Keohane and Nye. Their analysis overlooks the influence Washington derived from the *threat* to close the window. Before 15 August, this lever was present; afterwards, it was gone.

To summarize, "interests" and power, even with the issue-specific refinement, are not sufficient for explaining the shift of U.S. policy from dollar defense mixed with passivity to unilateral coercion rather than to alternative policies.

Allies' Policies and Interstate Stalemate

Contrary to what a power analysis would have implied, Washington maintained its orthodox line after 1968 and

---

have been more constrained by domestic policy consequences than before 1914. Other differences, however, imply a stronger position for the United States than for England. In 1913, private citizens as well as governments could demand gold for sterling. The British economy was more dependent by far on foreign countries than the American. Both reserve centers exercised some political hegemony over foreign holders, but Britain did not have the alliance relation supporting the major power claimants that the U.S. had more recently with Japan and West Germany.

avoided giving any sign, even secretly, that the President was prepared to negotiate a major exchange-rate adjustment. Some of his advisers quietly hoped that market forces would bring about an historic adjustment without high-level government bargaining. But in the absence of a lead from the superpower with the deficit, a power analyst would have been surprised to see any of the other states sponsor a move toward negotiations or take the politically unpopular adjustment measures alone. The benign neglect idea was premised on a miscalculation of foreign state reaction, judging at least from actual experience up until Nixon scrapped the passive policy in August 1971. The result was an interstate stalemate, which was partially responsible for the magnitude of the imbalance and foreign dollar accumulations in 1970 and 1971.

A U.S. initiative would have been necessary for avoiding a stalemate, but it would probably not have been sufficient. Supporting decisions in allied governments would also have been required. They had less influence than the U.S., but initiatives on their part, or greater willingness to discuss exchange rate-flexibility, would have made American advocates of negotiation more persuasive in Washington.

Among these allies, the exception was Canada, the state most dependent on the United States and also America's leading trade partner. In early 1970, Canada's current account moved into large surplus, while at the same time strong inflows of long-term and short-term capital, mainly from the U.S., were enlarging the money supply and threatening to accelerate inflation. The Canadian government decided to release its dollar to float upward in May 1970, to the great distress of the IMF staff.

Japan was second only to Canada as a trade partner for the United States. And the payments imbalance between Japan and the United States accounted for by far the largest single share of the 1971 global American deficit. Of a total U.S. deficit of $9.3 billion in the basic balance; this bilateral relation accounted for $4.3 billion.[55] The stalemate here was the most consequential of all in payments terms. Here the strategy of silence (or of vigorous action on the small textile sector rather than on exchange rates) had its most conspicuous failure.

Japan's response to surplus was quite different from that of Canada. The Japanese had accomplished remarkably rapid economic recovery and growth after the early 1950s, thanks in part to international trade. During 1968, Japan also achieved a striking reversal from extreme deficit to surplus. This performance earned admiring praise from the IMF Executive Directors during routine consultations. Exports expanded rapidly thereafter. During 1970, Japan's overall surplus grew suddenly to a record $1.2 billion (see Table 8), increasing her small stock of international reserves by 32 percent in a single year. It was becoming more apparent to all, including Japanese officials, that the surplus was not transitory. Japan, insisting that it did not seek to maintain such a large surplus, announced steps in 1970 to ease its formidable barriers to imports and to liberalize capital outflows. Yen appreciation was hardly mentioned.

In IMF debates, Japan's delegates were consistently among the most negative regarding new rules to make exchange rates more flexible. As seen by Finance Minister Takeo Fukuda at the 1970 meeting of the IMF Board of Governors in Copenhagen, the chief problems of the international monetary system were global inflation and disruptive movements of short-term capital. He endorsed domestic disinflationary policies and expressed a firm preference for direct controls on capital movements rather than exchange-rate flexibility.[56] Meanwhile, the Japanese government maneuvered tenaciously to avoid yielding to the Nixon administration's demand for new textile export restrictions.

Despite the measures taken in 1970, Japan's current ac-

---

[55] U.S., President, *International Economic Report of the President 1973*, Table 17.

[56] IMF, *Summary Proceedings 1970*, pp. 72-74.

TABLE 8. OVERALL PAYMENTS POSITIONS AND CURRENT
ACCOUNTS OF SELECTED COUNTRIES, 1961-1973[a]
(billions of U.S. dollars; negative figures represent
deficits; positive figures, surpluses)

	Average 1961-65	1968	1969	1970	1971	1972	1973
U.S.							
overall	−1.8	1.4	2.7	−9.8	−29.8	−10.4	−5.3
current	6.0	1.4	0.7	2.1	−1.2	−7.0	3.0
Germany							
overall	0.1	1.7	−3.0	6.3	4.4	5.0	9.2
current	0.5	3.9	2.7	1.7	2.0	2.8	6.6
Japan							
overall	0.0	0.9	0.8	1.2	10.4	3.1	−6.1
current	−0.2	1.2	2.3	2.2	6.0	7.0	0.1
Canada							
overall	0.2	0.3	0.1	1.6	0.9	0.3	−0.5
current	−0.7	0.1	−0.7	0.9	0.3	−0.5	0.0
U.K.							
overall	−0.6	−3.0	1.2	3.2	6.5	−2.9	0.7
current	0.4	−0.3	1.5	2.0	3.0	0.8	−2.1
France							
overall	0.9	−3.7	−1.1	2.1	3.4	1.8	−1.7
current	0.7	−0.8	−1.7	0.1	1.0	1.0	−0.1
Primary-producing countries							
overall	0.8[b]	2.6	1.5	4.3	8.7	18.2	15.0
current	−8.3[b]	−8.7	−8.3	−11.3	−11.4	−4.8	−2.1

[a] Overall positions are measured by net changes in official gross reserve assets (gold, SDRs, reserve positions in the IMF, and foreign exchange assets) and in certain reserve-related liabilities (such as Fund credit and various liabilities to foreign official institutions).

[b] 1967.

SOURCES: International Monetary Fund, *Annual Reports* 1969 through 1975, using latest revisions.

count surplus continued to increase the following year. But until late August 1971, the government adamantly rejected yen revaluation. Some dissenting voices in Japan did begin to raise the question. The respected Japan Economic Research Center published a study at the end of 1969 predicting massive payments surpluses during the 1970s unless Japan made major policy changes, possibly including yen revaluation to increase real consumption and avoid inflation.[57] But among most bankers and officials, yen revaluation was a distant hypothetical notion until the May 1971 currency crisis. When Germany ended support of the dollar, many in Tokyo were incredulous. The yen was now exposed as the obvious remaining candidate for upward pressure, and earlier assumptions that there was plenty of time for response were undermined.[58] Some major exporting companies began to change their export contracts to protect themselves against losses in the event of revaluation.[59] But Prime Minister Eisaku Sato and Finance Minister Fukuda continued to rule out the possibility.

One reason, apart from U.S. behavior, was the widespread Japanese belief that Japan was still a less-than-fully-developed country, an isolated island critically dependent on imports of food and fuel for its economic survival. Memories of the struggle to overcome payments deficits remained fresh, and the need to promote exports was still taken for granted. Yen revaluation was understood as a blow to exports. (Little attention was paid to the fact that currency appreciation would also aid exports to the extent that they were fabricated from imported inputs.) The rate of Y360 to the dollar was a fixture, having been established by General MacArthur in 1949. Related to this was the widespread image of the United States as a strong, rich, benevolent protector. A country able to send men to the moon ought to be able to aid its weaker partner without demanding equal concessions. The U.S. had long made clear its willingness to do so.

In the spring and summer of 1971, the Japanese government made incremental policy changes to deal with the payments question. The domestic economy was in the midst of a slowdown, and the government argued that recovery

[57] Lawrence Krause and Sueo Sekiguchi, "Japan and the World Economy," in Asia's New Giant, ed. Hugh Patrick and Henry Rosovsky (Washington, D.C.: The Brookings Institution, 1976), pp. 429-430.

[58] Far Eastern Economic Review, 22 May 1971, pp. 77-81; Financial Times, 12 May 1971, p. 20.

[59] Japan Times, 20 May and 21 May 1971.

by itself would reduce the external surplus. In June, the government announced additional plans in an "Eight Point Program for Avoiding Yen Revaluation." Underlying this program was the argument that a major reason for the seeming undervaluation of the yen was that the economy was still surrounded by formidable controls on imports and capital outflows. The eight points were: (1) reduction in the number of import quotas to twenty by October 1971; (2) preferential tariffs for imports from less developed countries; (3) additional general tariff reductions; (4) liberalization of capital movements; (5) reduction of certain non-tariff trade barriers; (6) increased aid to less developed countries; (7) abolition of preferential financing of exports and of special tax benefits for exporters; and (8) monetary and fiscal policies designed to stimulate the domestic economy. Thus, the surplus was to be whittled down more by allowing increased imports than by holding back exports. Washington's complaints were aimed at these controls, not at the exchange rate.

Another reason for avoiding a yen appreciation was that it would cause huge capital losses for the Bank of Japan, which had cooperated by holding most of its reserves in dollar form, and for many of the big companies close to the governing Liberal Democratic party. Japan's export industries held large export contracts denominated in dollars, and unlike German firms, they were unable to hedge against exchange risk, because of Japan's exchange controls. Incidentally, these tight controls over inflows of foreign hot money also gave Japanese financial officials confidence that such surges could not force them off their parity, as had occurred in Germany.

Finally, many Japanese felt that correcting the imbalance was not solely or even primarily a Japanese responsibility.

The Japanese surplus had its counterpart in the American balance of payments deficit. If the Japanese contribution to this imbalance had been organization, hard work or abstinence, many Japanese felt, the American side had complemented these exemplary virtues with inflation and overextended international involvement. Surely some kind of moral responsibility for taking difficult action rested with the American government.[60]

Through the summer of 1971, the Bank of Japan continued to take in more and more international reserves at the 360 rate. The current account surplus was not showing signs of shrinking; on the contrary, it nearly tripled between 1970 and 1971.

The other major surplus countries in 1970 and 1971 were West Germany, France, and Great Britain. The West German government had dealt with its surplus in 1969 by allowing the mark to float and then repegging it at a higher value. Speaking at the 1969 IMF annual meeting during the float, Bundesbank President Karl Blessing emphasized that this technique was only a temporary measure. He greatly preferred stronger and more flexible domestic policies, rather than more flexible exchange rates, to correct international imbalances. Afterward, German representatives became somewhat more favorable to limited exchange-rate flexibility. But at both the 1969 and 1970 annual meetings, Germany lectured on the peril of worldwide inflation and

[60] Gary Saxonhouse, "A Review of U.S.-Japan Economic Relations," *Asian Survey* 12 (September 1972):743. The prominent Japanese economist Ryutaro Komiya wrote in 1973 that the international rules provided for a workable and superior means of international adjustment, and that the United States was responsible for the collapse of the IMF regime. "If the U.S. had proposed a depreciation of the dollar in view of a fundamental disequilibrium in its balance of payments, either in August 1971 or preferably much earlier, the IMF would have agreed and a multilateral exchange rate adjustment would have been properly effected." Komiya agrees that a yen revaluation would have been better than a dollar devaluation for Japan and the system; but, pointing out that the international rules did not obligate Japan to act, he maintains that the U.S., facing a stalemate, should have chosen devaluation to preserve the international regime, rather than smashing it. (Ryutaro Komiya, "Recent U.S. Foreign Economic Policy from a Japanese Point of View," in *Toward a New World Trade Policy: The Maidenhead Papers*, ed. C. Fred Bergsten [Lexington, Mass.: Lexington Books, 1975], pp. 359-363.)

the need especially for the United States to strengthen the dollar by domestic action.[61]

Despite the revaluation, West Germany found itself in 1970 with an enormous overall payments surplus and rapid inflation at home. The basic balance was approximately even, but German authorities faced large, unwelcome inflows of foreign short-term money occasioned by international interest-rate differentials. In May 1971, speculation concentrating on Germany added to the inflationary inflow, and the mark was allowed to float again. Economy Minister Karl Schiller blamed this crisis and policy defeat on the extraordinary U.S. deficit and the policy of benign neglect.[62] By July, the mark had appreciated effectively by 4 percent.

France's domestic restraint and her 1969 devaluation brought about prompt and steady improvement in her current account and overall payments position, at the cost of some increase in unemployment. Finance Minister Valéry Giscard d'Estaing was among the most determined opponents of changing the Bretton Woods charter to allow greater exchange-rate flexibility. It would be a mistake, he intoned, to seek "an easy way out—as it were, a sort of monetary LSD." The blame was placed on the United States for not following more effective anti-inflationary policies. Giscard d'Estaing was more direct than most in expressing the common European view that the benign neglect approach was unfair in that it attempted to shift the burden of adjustment from "countries in disequilibrium" to the "countries that have made the greatest efforts to restore or maintain their equilibrium."[63] The United States, he said in July 1971, should finance further deficits by borrowing from the IMF

[61] IMF, *Summary Proceedings 1969*, pp. 198-202; *Summary Proceedings 1970*, pp. 35-39; de Vries, *International Monetary Fund*, vol. I, pp. 503-504; interview with William Dale.

[62] *New York Times*, 9 May 1971, p. 28.

[63] IMF, *Summary Proceedings 1969*, pp. 59-60; *Summary Proceedings 1970*, pp. 81-87.

under the usual conditions, as other countries did.[64] The British balance of payments also showed strong gains and surpluses in 1970 and 1971 on both current and capital accounts.

The chief European complaint about the American deficit was directed at domestic economic policy. The 1970 annual report of the Bank for International Settlements joined other international bodies in calling for "a more direct wage/price policy, formal or informal."[65] Another complaint arose from U.S. prosecution of the war in Vietnam. By this time, many Japanese and Europeans, including financial officials, regarded this war as an American blunder carried out without their consent, and they resented being told that they had to finance the U.S. deficit arising from it.[66]

Not only were European Community (EC) countries suspicious that schemes for greater exchange-rate flexibility were American devices for escaping proper responsibility for the U.S. balance of payments. They were also cool to such schemes because the EC was at the same time moving in the opposite direction internally. In an effort to narrow or eliminate exchange-rate fluctuations among the members, the EC states embarked in 1969 on an ill-fated plan to establish an Economic and Monetary Union. The plan's other long-term aims included pooling reserves and creating mutual credit facilities, harmonizing domestic policies, and forging common external monetary policies towards the United States and the rest of the world. For the smaller and more open economies, exchange-rate fluctuation was much more disruptive than for the United States. Moreover, the 1969 European parity changes had upset the EC program to establish common agricultural prices— the principal political glue holding the Community to-

---

[64] *New York Times*, 20 July 1971, p. 41.

[65] Bank for International Settlements, *Annual Report 1970*, p. 189.

[66] *New York Times*, 30 September 1970, p. 59; Michel Garibal, "A Warning to the Dollar," *New York Times*, 3 December 1970, p. 47; interview.

gether. Movement in the direction of a European currency and central bank was also partly stimulated by desires to free Europe from dependence on the dollar and on American policies, and to enhance EC external bargaining strength. EC representatives at the IMF cited this project as a reason for delaying IMF discussions of greater flexibility.[67]

In March 1971, the EC Council of Ministers authorized the first step toward Economic and Monetary Union. Immediately, before the agreement could be implemented, however, it broke apart during the May 1971 dollar-mark crisis. Germany, after withdrawing from the exchange market, attempted to bring her partners along in a joint upward float against the dollar. Besides holding the Community together, a joint float would avoid the damage to German exporters' competitive position in Europe that would result from a unilateral float. Italy and France were strongly opposed to allowing their currencies to appreciate. Most EC governments preferred to erect capital controls to ward off speculative inflows. France insisted that the U.S. should deal with its own deficit via devaluation or controls or both. But controls were anathema to Economy Minister Schiller of Germany, and Germany's geopolitical objectives led her to minimize clashes with Washington. Thus the EC split. The German and Dutch currencies were floated, while the other governments defended prevailing rates with new capital controls. The quarrel on the continent continued through the summer.[68]

America's allies, then, took no initiatives of their own

[67] Testimony of Under Secretary of State for Economic Affairs Nathaniel Samuels, in House Committee on Foreign Affairs, *International Implications*, p. 99. The multiple forces behind this EMU project are dissected by Loukas Tsoukalis, *The Politics and Economics of European Monetary Integration* (London: George Allen and Unwin, 1977), and Robert W. Russell, *"L'Engrenage*, Collegial Style, and the Crisis Syndrome: Lessons from Monetary Policy in the European Community," *Journal of Common Market Studies* 13 (1975): 61-86.

[68] Tsoukalis, *Politics and Economics*, pp. 112-115; *Washington Post*, 28 April 1971, p. A19.

toward exchange-rate adjustment, and they were cool to middle-level American suggestions toward that end. This was because of the nature of high-level U.S. policy as well as for European and Japanese reasons. Parenthetically, if these states had major interests in preservation of the Bretton Woods system, as they felt they did, then their behavior reflected miscalculations only somewhat less consequential than the American. Few anticipated American behavior of the sort that occurred in the summer and fall of 1971. If Japan or West Germany had shown less resistance to exchange-rate flexibility by negotiation, American advocates of joint decision making would probably have been in a somewhat stronger position in 1971 or before. Furthermore, during the fall of 1971 these allied governments bargained hard for every percentage point of exchange-rate adjustment, as a power analysis would have predicted. This, too, may have reflected a miscalculation on their part. As will be seen in Chapter 5, they found themselves a year later agreeing to a further dollar depreciation. That is, it was because of their decisions that the dollar was adjusted in a jerky two-step manner rather than in a single decisive step in 1971. If instead they had agreed to the U.S. Treasury's wish for a one-time 15 percent depreciation in 1971, it is conceivable that the U.S. might then have been persuaded to support the new rates. In any case, currency market expectations might then have been favorable and stable long enough to permit the negotiation of a regime providing greater flexibility within an agreed framework. As it was, market operators saw parities declared, challenged, and abandoned repeatedly, and this changed the operators' behavior. In the end, the allies got not only revaluation but also collapse.

In August 1971, in sum, the United States still had the power to select from a range of domestic and external policies as methods for ending the existing stalemate. Objective international market conditions and international power relations shaped but did not determine the elements of a new policy package. They did not determine whether the response would be confined to domestic policy, or confined to external measures, or would include both. Objective international conditions did not impose an answer to the question of whether the United States would continue to adhere to the Bretton Woods framework or repudiate it by suspending convertibility and all other support for the dollar. The market and power perspectives are unable to explain why the new external strategy took the form of an import surcharge and unilateral demands rather than compromise bargaining, either bilateral or multilateral, such as the U.S. had used on other occasions. Can a domestic politics perspective help explain these outcomes?

DOMESTIC DISCONTENT AND DOMESTIC POLICY RESPONSE

The present case is similar to the 1965 policy shift in that domestic political conditions were among the weaker influences. They help explain some of the policy details and the domestic policy changes, but an analyst monitoring only public opinion, electoral struggles, and group pressures would have had virtually no clue that a change in international monetary policy was imminent. Instead, this analyst would have anticipated a shift in trade policy that did not occur. Domestic political challenge was not the source of pressure on the Nixon administration to depreciate the dollar or go off gold.

The 1968 elections had produced a change in party control of the White House. That certainly was not because of voters' attitudes on international monetary issues. But Chapter 2 hypothesized that alternations among party elites having different ideological leanings tend to cause corresponding policy shifts. Republicans were expected to be somewhat more likely to yield to international market pressure on exchange rates, and to be somewhat less concerned about domestic political backlash from devaluation, than Democrats.

It is true that Democrats had resisted and Republicans yielded. (The contrast is clouded by the fact that the Treasury Secretary in 1971, John Connally, was a Democrat, though he did switch parties a few years later.) A 1969 Democratic administration might have followed an interventionist domestic economic policy earlier, and might have been more disposed to continue capital controls and dollar defense. Although there is some chance such efforts would have saved the dollar, this party change was probably no more than a marginal influence. Many Republicans had also favored strong dollar defense. Democrats, regardless of predispositions, would have also had to face the medium-term erosion of the dollar's base and, by 1971, stark evidence of fundamental disequilibrium. Either party would then have had to make choices, concerning the Bretton Woods regime and diplomatic strategy, for which party differences provide little guidance. And even if Democratic presidents fear domestic attack for departing from financial orthodoxy even more than Republicans, the following pages will show that Nixon was nevertheless highly sensitive to that possibility.

After taking office, the new administration experienced a decline in political strength, by some measures. The economy deteriorated, Nixon's popularity dropped, and rivals were demanding changes in macroeconomic policy. From this situation, a domestic political analyst might well have expected some of the 1971 changes in *domestic* policy, but not changes in international monetary policy.

In the 1968 election, Nixon had won with only a minority of the popular vote, and the Republican party had been unable to take control of either house of Congress. In 1970, the domestic economy went into a recession. The unemployment rate rose (to 6.2 percent in December 1970) without a slackening in the rate of consumer price inflation (5.9 percent for 1970). The results of the 1970 midterm elections were disappointing for the Republicans. They failed to increase substantially their strength in Congress, while the nation's governorships suddenly turned from a Republican to a Democratic majority.

The economy's performance through the middle of 1971 remained worrisome. During the first four months, the rate of consumer inflation stopped rising and even dropped off, but from April through July it accelerated again. The GNP grew, but more slowly than expected, so that the unemployment rate at midyear remained stuck at its elevated level rather than beginning to fall as predicted. The balance-of-payments deficit was increasing.

This economic environment weakened the administration's domestic political position. The public's expectations for the economy were much more pessimistic than in early 1965; nearly three-fourths of those questioned in a Gallup poll said they expected a year of "economic difficulty" rather than "prosperity." President Nixon's handling of his job was disapproved by an increasing fraction of the public; his popularity rating dropped to 50 percent.[69] Congress and organized labor increasingly criticized the administration's gradualism in fiscal and monetary policy. The chief demands were for a more active domestic incomes policy and for comprehensive import controls. In December 1969, Congress, over strong opposition from Nixon and other Republican leaders, passed a bill authorizing the President to control credit. In August 1970, Congress passed the Economic Stabilization Act, giving the President authority to impose controls on wages, prices, and rents. In March 1971, the Joint Economic Committee scorned the administration's economic projections as unrealistic and urged faster tax reduction together with a clear wage and price control program. Organized labor complained loudly about the unemployment problem, advocating increased government spending for public-service jobs and welfare programs.

[69] George Gallup, *The Gallup Poll,* 3 vols. (New York: Random House, 1972), 3:1923, 2279; John Mueller, *War, Presidents and Public Opinion* (New York: Wiley, 1973), p. 201.

Even business organizations added their voices to the calls for an incomes policy. The U.S. Chamber of Commerce remained opposed to any form of wage-price controls, but in late 1970, the Committee for Economic Development issued a statement proposing a government board to give wage and price guidance to labor and business. The Business Council, a group of executives of large corporations, in its semi-annual commentary in October 1970, suggested that the administration explore new tools for stopping inflation.[70] By 1971, some Republicans, including Federal Reserve Chairman Arthur Burns, began to speak critically about the administration's refusal to consider more active anti-inflationary programs.

In early 1971, the administration endorsed deficit spending through the concept of the "full employment budget," and the Federal Reserve eased credit and began to lower interest rates. But at midyear, Nixon still faced an unsatisfactory economic performance, the increasing isolation of his initial domestic policy, and an approaching election. Nixon and Connally seized the political high ground abruptly and dramatically with their wage-price freeze and fiscal stimulus. This domestic politics analysis explains nicely the shift in *domestic* policy.

The domestic political situation included, in addition to dissatisfaction with macroeconomic conditions, a host of pressures by specific interest groups. Much of this group activity was on behalf of changes in trade policy rather than in monetary policy. Monitoring changes in interest-group activity, one would have anticipated moves toward higher trade barriers. Some years earlier, a few industries, notably petroleum, textiles, and some agricultural sectors, had succeeded in obtaining protective arrangements. Then, in 1967, immediately after the conclusion of the Kennedy Round of tariff-reduction negotiations, a rash of bills was introduced in Congress to legislate new restrictions for steel,

[70] Linda S. Graebner, "The New Economic Policy, 1971," in Murphy Commission *Appendices*, vol. 3, pp. 160-169.

textiles, shoes, lead and zinc, electronics, chemicals, meat, dairy products, and other commodities. Perhaps the most significant shift in the domestic political situation, as far as influences on foreign economic policy are concerned, was the gradual reversal of the traditional anti-tariff stance of the American Federation of Labor-Congress of Industrial Organizations.[71] As competition from imports became stronger in traditional manufacturing at prevailing exchange rates during the 1960s, organized labor became a leading force for general protection, creating a domestic situation much different from that when the Trade Expansion Act had been passed in 1962.

This shift in domestic pressure was not sufficient, however, to produce a general change in trade policy toward increased protection. The textile industry, led by Senator Strom Thurmond of South Carolina, achieved the most politically notable success. During the 1968 presidential campaign, Thurmond led his delegation and other Southern Republicans into the Nixon camp at the Republican nominating convention, three weeks after Nixon had promised further protection for the textile industry.[72] The result was the long international struggle with Japan and other Asian exporting states, ending in the 1971 agreement to limit shipments.

But legislative campaigns for more general protection were defeated. In 1970, the House Ways and Means Committee approved a bill that would have imposed mandatory quotas on imports of textiles and shoes, and would have established a formula requiring quotas on other products when imports were shown to damage domestic industry. After a long battle, the bill died in the Senate.[73] In the fall of 1971, the AFL-CIO expressed dissatisfaction with exchange-rate realignment and began promoting the Burke-

[71] The shift is chronicled in *National Journal* 4 (1972):108-119.

[72] Destler and others, *Textile Wrangle*, pp. 68-70.

[73] *New York Times*, 15 July 1970, p. 1; 21 July, p. 1; 14 October, p. 1; 20 November, p. 1; 29 December, p. 1.

Hartke bill as its foreign economic policy. This bill would have placed ceilings on nearly all imports, limiting them to the average level of 1965-1969. It would also have created a strong new agency to regulate imports and would have eliminated a wide range of tax advantages for companies operating in foreign countries. But the bill did not pass.

It is also true that corporations and banks hindered by capital export restrictions complained about them in Washington, especially following the January 1968 program. The Republican victory and this pressure probably helped bring about the steps relaxing those restrictions in April 1969.[74]

In 1971, the Administration did impose the import surcharge, and one might be tempted to attribute this to interest-group pressure and public opinion. But Nixon reversed this measure after only four months, and before the 1972 election was held. Giving constituents a political plum and then taking it away before the election is hardly what domestic political analysis would anticipate. There is another interpretation that can account for the temporary import surcharge—namely, that policy makers believed that it was a necessary bargaining tool to influence other states to revise *their* trade barriers and exchange rates. Evidence for such a belief will be considered below.

What was most striking in domestic politics was what did not occur. Various interest groups had stakes in international monetary policy, as suggested in Chapter 2. Yet none of them spoke out, on either side. For example, farmers, producers of high-technology exports, and textile and apparel makers all stood to gain in international trade from a dollar depreciation, and to lose from continuation of prevailing policy. On the other hand, workers in service industries, government employee unions, and consumer organizations would benefit from prevailing policy and lose from depreciation. One could suggest offsetting costs and benefits to qualify these supposed interests, but these basic suppositions seem reasonable. Yet in this case interest groups

[74] Interview with a Nixon White House economic adviser.

did not act upon their presumed special interests. All remained silent about international monetary policy, apart from capital controls. Some general conditions that might explain this paradox are discussed in Chapter 6.

In summary, changes in the American domestic political and economic situation were important sources of change in domestic economic policy in 1971. Changes in both domestic and external policy were bound together in this instance, but this is not because the two change together of necessity. They may vary independently, and they may respond to somewhat different influences, even though they clearly also influence each other.

Regarding external policy, a domestic politics perspective would have been misleading. Political party turnover may have added marginally to the policy shift. But the main expectations would have been a change in the direction of higher direct trade protection, which did not materialize, and continuation of prevailing international monetary policy. Above all, no public opinion polls, major political challengers, or interest groups were pressing for a sharp alteration in exchange-rate policy or for unilateral economic diplomacy. The major sources of this American departure did not lie in objective domestic political conditions.

It may nevertheless be true that the President's *expectations and calculations about* domestic politics were salient influences. Consideration of this possibility requires a different type of evidence, which is best introduced together with evidence on other intellectual influences.

THINKING THE UNTHINKABLE AND USING COERCION

In the international situation of mid-1971, at least two external American strategies were conceivable. Neither was inevitable and the difference was substantial. A more active policy to achieve dollar depreciation could have taken the form of either a bargaining initiative or a unilateral move. In the former case, the U.S. would maintain its traditional commitment to collective decision-making under the aegis of Bretton Woods. Washington would propose, perhaps secretly, a bilateral or multilateral compromise. The initiative would hint at the possibility of American concessions, perhaps including domestic measures or devaluation. At the same time, the United States would threaten sanctions if negotiations failed. The domain could be limited to immediate exchange-rate realignment or it could include changes in monetary rules and trade practices as well. Dollar-gold convertibility could be continued nominally, or the U.S. might suspend it temporarily during the bargaining. Such a suspension would be communicated to other governments privately as a transitional necessity, along with public assurances that the United States remained committed to Bretton Woods norms and was prepared to fulfill her obligations under satisfactory conditions. The U.S. had used bargaining strategies of this sort before, and it used one again in the policy shift of 1972-1973. Some American officials advocated essentially this approach in 1971.

The second option was a unilateral move announcing the end of dollar defense, demanding concessions by surplus countries, and actually imposing penalty sanctions rather than threatening to do so. This strategy would attempt to coerce foreign governments into accomplishing the exchange-rate realignment without having the American President make any serious concessions. It would be a strategy of all sticks and no carrots.

The choice made between the alternatives permitted by the international and domestic situations can be explained by adding a cognitive perspective on foreign economic policy. An analyst of policy ideas with access to the appropriate information would have been in a good position to explain the earlier Nixon policies that appeared puzzling from a power perspective. This analyst would have noticed a striking change that has not been discussed so far—the disappearance of old attitudes toward the Bretton Woods system, not only from the White House but, in 1971, from the office of the Secretary of the Treasury, whence came crucial monetary advice. Changes in the general predispositions of the governing leadership and in their specific perceptions and calculations explain the 1971 choice of diplomatic strategy: the suspension of convertibility, the imposition of the surcharge, and later the retreat from unilateralism.

A cognitive analyst would have known in 1968 that the incoming President would be predisposed to be sensitive to alliance relations but would have expected him to have little interest in international monetary matters. In the latter respect, Nixon was quite different from President Kennedy and several European heads of government, though not very different from other American political leaders. We have seen that Nixon and Kissinger behaved according to their predispositions, disregarding monetary matters on the whole. This high-level attitude helps explain the early conduct of the Nixon administration—the bifurcation of U.S. policy for two years.

This general predisposition was reinforced by the specific diagnosis that has been called "benign neglect," which held out the prospect that reliance on market forces alone would bring about a major exchange-rate adjustment within the Bretton Woods framework. This diagnosis, insofar as it pertained to interstate relations, proved to be one of the more critical miscalculations of the decade. But along with Nixon's priorities, it explains why the superpower did not attempt to use its still considerable strength to bargain over new rules more favorable to adjustment.

A cognitive analyst would also have expected the switch from Democrats to Republicans to bring a shift in executive-branch predispositions toward a purer free-market ideology, and it did. The effects appeared initially as opposition to domestic and international economic controls. Nor was it surprising that Nixon brought into office a group of advisers more sympathetic to Milton Friedman's theoretical argument for freely floating exchange rates in particular. They included Herbert Stein, a member of the

Council of Economic Advisers, and George P. Shultz, then Director of the Office of Management and Budget. (They entered an official milieu where intellectual opposition to floating did, however, remain quite strong.) A cognitive perspective would thus have expected that the U.S. would be somewhat more likely to adopt a policy of flexible exchange rates. Policy did indeed change in that direction, though not all the way to endorsing a system of completely flexible rates. This the United States never did before the par value regime collapsed entirely in 1973.)

Yet the connection between the arrival of "ideological floaters" and the August 1971 policy change is more coincidental than causal. The floating idea was not decisive with the President. Nixon was acquainted with the debate between fixed and flexible rates, but it left him ambivalent. During the one recorded policy deliberation on the topic before the 15 August measures, Nixon at one point interjected:

> In reading over the years on this subject, I have never seen so many intelligent experts who disagree 180 degrees. George [Shultz] and others like the floating idea. Arthur [Burns] says to get in a good negotiating position and then deal. . . .[75]

Far more influential were the different ideas brought by two new leaders who joined the administration at the beginning of 1971. President Nixon appointed Peter G. Peterson, president of the Bell and Howell company, to the new post of Assistant to the President for International Economic Policy. Peterson was not central to international monetary policy, but his outlook did affect the thinking of the President and others in the administration. At the same time, Nixon also replaced his chief international monetary

---

[75] From notes taken at the meeting and published by William Safire, *Before the Fall: An Inside View of the Pre-Watergate White House* (Garden City, N.Y.: Doubleday, 1975), p. 514.

policy-maker, appointing John Connally as Secretary of the Treasury.

Connally was a prominent politician, and that is the main reason Nixon chose him. Connally's first exposure to politics came when he worked for Congressman Lyndon Johnson from the late 1930s until 1941, while Connally was finishing law school. Through the late 1940s and 1950s, he made his fortune managing business enterprises for a pair of wealthy independent oil and gas operators in Fort Worth, Texas. He lobbied for them in Washington, while remaining close to Johnson, and was vice chairman of the Texas delegations to the Democratic national conventions in 1956 and 1960. After one year as Secretary of the Navy in 1961, he resigned to undertake the first of three successful campaigns for the Texas Governorship. He led the state government from 1963 through 1968, when he joined a Houston law firm and several corporate boards. As a director of Texas Instruments, Inc., Connally may have become more sensitive than before about foreign competition and foreign investment restrictions.

In late 1970, after Republican disappointments in the midterm elections, and with the economy still performing unsatisfactorily, Nixon's electoral advisers were gloomy. "It's all even for '72, and maybe even trending uphill if we don't deliver on the economy and inflation," one White House staff member told a visitor. "We're in trouble in the ten largest states, and in some of them the situation won't get any better. The ones that really matter are Texas and California. Without them, you can forget it in '72." The aide's telephone buzzed three times, announcing a call from the Oval Office.

> During the brief, one-sided conversation, the aide said almost nothing: his reaction showed in his expression, which changed from surprise to astonishment to utter disbelief. As he put down the receiver, he slowly settled back in his chair. "The Old Man's decided to do something about the Texas situation," he said, shaking his

head. "And you won't believe who he's got to help him do it."[76]

Not long after Connally's arrival, Nixon was spending more time with the colorful, self-assured Texan than with almost any other adviser, which made possible even greater influence over policy than Connally's formal post carried. By June 1971, Connally succeeded in having Nixon publicly designate him chief economic spokesman for the administration.

In choosing Peterson and Connally, whatever the reasons, the President was tapping a minority school of thought about foreign economic policy. If he had depended upon or appointed representatives of the majority school, the United States would probably have acted differently in 1971. Many financial and business leaders, and many prominent politicians from the sunbelt, would have urged that higher priority be given to preserving the Bretton Woods system. Most would not have campaigned for economic sanctions against allies. Most politicians would have been much less likely to override determined arguments from experienced

[76] Richard J. Whalen, "The Nixon-Connally Arrangement: The Continuing Adventures of a Trader in Horses and Presidents," *Harper's Magazine*, August 1971, p. 29. It might be suggested that domestic political conditions were an indirect cause of the external policy shift, after all. It is true that the President's political strength declined in 1970; Nixon evidently selected Connally in the expectation that this would help Nixon in Texas politics; and Connally played a prominent role in the policy shift. But that is a rather loose linkage to international monetary policy, and not only because it overlooks the influences of international markets and power. Domestic political weakness could have led an observer to expect any number of responses besides appointments. Even supposing that politics caused the incumbent to appoint an ally from the sunbelt, he was not thereby compelled to pick a Treasury Secretary, or one with distinctive attitudes toward international economic diplomacy. The ideas Connally brought did affect policy, but as far as electoral politics was concerned, Nixon could as easily have chosen a politician devoted to Bretton Woods. Domestic politics as such, without changes in leaders' beliefs and priorities, would not have produced this policy change. Nor was politics necessary for a change in reigning ideas; Peterson's arrival was not due to politics.

Treasury officials, as Connally did with respect to the import surcharge and the U.S. negotiating strategy.

Change of Predispositions

With the selection of the new Treasury Secretary, it was evident that intellectual barriers to a major change in international monetary policy had fallen. In Connally's mind, some of the general beliefs that had been crucial for Douglas Dillon, Robert Roosa, and Henry Fowler were much less salient. The new Secretary found it easier to think the unthinkable. In the first place, he did not bring to office a devotion to the world banker roles of the dollar. Another official, arguing later against suspending convertibility, mentioned that such a blow to private confidence would undermine the international transactions function of the dollar. "Think about all those contracts denominated in dollars," the official said. Connally shot back: "Forget about those Arabs."[77] Connally, then, did not begin with a predisposition to preserve the Bretton Woods monetary regime. Neither did he strongly believe in an alternative international monetary arrangement, as Henry Fowler did when he arrived in 1965. Such matters as the foreign policy consequences of floating exchange rates were simply of low salience to him. Connally's associates have reported a dazzling capacity for mastering and manipulating complex new arguments quickly and confidently under fire. But his ability in this field, as one of them remarked delicately, "did not come from profound knowledge, great study, or strong convictions."[78]

Nor did Connally represent a fixed position concerning the degree of government involvement in economic activity. While his instincts were often manifestly conservative, it would be a mistake to picture Connally as governed by a strong commitment to laissez faire, let alone floating exchange rates. Long-time Connally-watchers made com-

[77] Interview with this official.
[78] Interview.

ments like the following, offered during his 1979 campaign for the Presidency:

> John likes to do things. He likes to get his hands on everything. That's why you had wage and price controls at the Treasury. That's why you had his university building program [while he was Governor of Texas]. If all those business people supporting him think he'll let them and the economy alone, they're going to be real surprised.[79]

In 1971, Connally simultaneously urged wage-price controls at home and withdrawing the central bank from management of the dollar abroad.

Connally once commented directly on international trade theory, in response to a Congressional worry about the liquidation of American industries unable to compete with wage levels in Hong Kong.

> Senator, that is an economic theory of comparative advantage. In the first place, the reason I do not understand it is that I am not an economist. But if I were an economist I would not want to understand it, because I do not believe it is going to work. . . . I know of no nation that practices it. . . . Monetary decisions are not made in a political vacuum.[80]

Connally's selection meant a noticeable shift, compared with some of his predecessors, with respect to predispositions on the trade-off between alliance cohesion and U.S. national gain. Chapter 3 showed that Henry Fowler and Francis Bator exhibited greater reluctance than some of their contemporaries about taking unilateral steps that would ruffle their European allies. Examples below illustrate that, in 1971, Connally was clearly prepared to pay a higher cost in alliance cohesion than Fowler, Bator, and other Americans in the same situation.

[79] *New York Times Magazine*, 18 November 1979, p. 182.
[80] Senate Finance Committee, *Foreign Trade: Hearings*, 1971, p. 58.

Changes in Specific Ideas and Choices

The arrival of Connally and Peterson meant a shift not only in general predispositions but also in specific beliefs. During the first half of 1971, Connally, Peterson, Treasury Under Secretary Paul Volcker, and eventually Nixon himself acquired or strengthened several beliefs that pointed toward a policy reversal and choice of a coercive strategy.

FOREIGN COUNTRIES ARE HARMING AMERICA

One of Connally's most salient perceptions was that the allies of the U.S. were hurting U.S. business. Out of the mass of evidence on the nature of the situation, Connally fixed on domestic and international trade matters more than monetary ones, on signs of declining U.S. competitiveness, and on the foreign as opposed to American causes for this trend. He told a Senate subcommittee in May 1971 that what disturbed him more than the overall payments deficit was "the underlying trend in our trade and current account position."[81] Connally was convinced, at a time when few other Americans were saying such things, that the structure of the world had fundamentally changed with the recovery of Western Europe and Japan.

> Much of the condition that we find ourselves in today is the result not of our actions but the actions of other nations who have strengthened their own position, and during the last decade both Germany and Japan have immeasurably strengthened their position.[82]

They had done so by efficient and diligent private effort but also, he maintained, by government action. Connally complained repeatedly in private and in public about foreign trade policies and investment restrictions. For example:

[81] Senate Finance Committee, *Foreign Trade: Hearings*, p. 20.
[82] Senate Finance Committee, *Foreign Trade: Hearings*, p. 80.

Many of these nations impose competitive disadvantages upon us. Japan, for instance, sets very strict quotas on United States high technology products such as computers. What Japan does allow imported, they tax heavily. And Japan's restrictions on foreign investment make it all but impossible to circumvent these barriers. . . .[83]

As Connally saw it, foreigners had taken advantage of the high cost of American production and their own lower standard of living, yet they were becoming more rather than less protectionist. The European Community's common agricultural policy as a barrier to American farm exports was a particularly sharp thorn in his side. He welcomed the failure of Great Britain to enter and enlarge the Community, in contrast to the historic American position favoring European integration for the sake of long-term political gain.[84] In internal meetings during 1971, Connally was "vociferous about how the United States was getting the short end of the stick in trade matters." At one Cabinet-level meeting with the President, he delivered, according to an official who was present, "an unbelievable diatribe" against the European Community and Japan, implying that they were America's real enemies.[85] He raised the question of renegotiating the General Agreement on Tariffs and Trade (GATT), which was written when Japan and Europe were much weaker.[86] Connally was resolved to impress this general view on the foreigners themselves at the May 1971

[83] Speech given in April 1973, quoted by Sidney E. Rolfe and James L. Burtle, *The Great Wheel—The World Monetary System: A Reinterpretation* (New York: Quadrangle/New York Times Book Company, 1973), p. 119. This speech also shows Connally's belief that Americans as well as foreigners had a fundamentally outdated perception of the world political economy, which made rough tactics necessary in 1971.

[84] Henry Brandon, *The Retreat of American Power* (New York: Dell, 1972), p. 229.

[85] Interview with a participant in the meeting.

[86] Senate Finance Committee, *Hearings: Nomination of John B. Connally of Texas to be Secretary of the Treasury*, 92nd Cong., 1st sess., 28 January 1971, p. 27.

international bankers conference in Munich. Determined to make time for this foreign trip, Connally refused requests from Congressional leaders Wilbur Mills and William Fulbright and even the President to testify on the Hill.[87] In the speech, Connally told U.S. allies to do more to fulfill their responsibilities. He emphasized trade and military costs, not exchange-rate realignment, following the orthodox Treasury line.

At about the same time, Peter Peterson was bringing a related new perception into the highest level of government. While at Bell and Howell, Peterson had developed concerns about American competition in the world economy. When he became Assistant to the President and Executive Director of the new Council on International Economic Policy, Peterson presented a series of briefings to the President and other administration leaders during early 1971, portraying with graphs and data his theme of the decline of the American position relative to foreign countries. President Nixon was impressed with these arguments; he recited them to visitors in the Oval Office during this period. In the later published version of his arguments, Peterson concluded:

> To meet the new realities, not only our policies but our methods of diplomacy will have to be changed. Our international negotiating stance will have to meet its trading partners with a clearer, more assertive version of new national interest. . . . I believe we must dispel any "Marshall Plan psychology" or relatively unconstrained generosity that may remain. . . . This is not just a matter of choice but of necessity.[88]

This change of outlook in Washington is a necessary part of the explanation for the shift in 1971 toward more assertive U.S. foreign economic policies, and particularly the choice of coercion rather than the more usual bargaining.

[87] Whalen, "Nixon-Connally Arrangement," p. 36.
[88] Peterson Report, vol. I, pp. i-ii, 49.

If the ideas of those Americans who placed more of the blame on the United States had prevailed instead, the new U.S. policy would almost certainly have been less shocking. This difference in diagnosis also shaped interpretations of the events of the following autumn. Those who had seen Japan and Europe as obstinate and their nationalism as the source of international imbalance attributed the autumn standoff to the allies' continued short-sightedness. Other Americans were more inclined to the views that allied resistance owed much to earlier U.S. policy failures and one-sided positions, and that the Nixon shocks themselves deepened this resistance.

Along with beliefs about general economic weakness went a perception of a growing payments imbalance. During one of Connally's first Treasury staff briefings in late 1970, an adviser told him that over the next six months the country was going to face its gravest financial crisis since the depression. Interest rates were starting to fall; the payments deficit would grow. The suspension of convertibility was inevitable, he declared. The only choice was between picking the time and waiting for a crisis to force America's hand. This adviser pressed for closing the gold window and adopting a supporting domestic policy of restraint.[89] Connally directed a handful of Treasury officials to draw up extremely confidential contingency plans for suspension of convertibility, beginning in early 1971.

Another adviser, the long-time U.S. Executive Director at the International Monetary Fund, William B. Dale, also questioned the orthodox diagnosis of the deficit and tried to heighten Connally's perception of monetary as opposed to trade risks. On 28 January 1971, Dale sent Connally a long secret memorandum concluding that "interruption of convertibility and a major change in exchange rates would be necessary in the not-too-distant future."[90] Dale proposed a bold U.S. initiative for a bargained exchange-rate realignment, an example of the first external option. In Dale's

[89] Interview with this policy maker.
[90] Interview with William Dale.

scenario, a week before the September 1971 IMF annual meeting, the President would suspend gold sales and currency trading, and seek Congressional approval to change the dollar's par value. When the foreign finance ministers gathered for the IMF meeting in Washington, the U.S. would put pressure on them to appreciate uniformly against gold and to stand still for a U.S. depreciation back to $35. The United States should also consider proposing an international means of "deliberately working our way out of the reserve currency business," Dale suggested.[91] Thus, foreign states would be asked to accept a substantial dollar depreciation, but the U.S. would accept responsibility for taking the initiative and proposing general reforms of the monetary system. Dale hoped the negotiations could be completed and currency markets reopened in two weeks.

Meanwhile, as the American unemployment rate remained high, and inflation seemed to worsen through the second quarter, and while domestic criticism of Nixon's gradualist domestic economic policy continued to rain down, Connally decided to try to convince Nixon to abandon that policy. Nixon refused at first. In fact, after an economic conference on 26 June at Camp David, he sent Connally out as his spokesman to announce the President's "four no's": no tax reduction, no increased federal spending, no wage-price controls, and no wage and price review board. But Connally continued to hammer at Nixon's tenacity. He urged a bold package of domestic measures, together with a duty surcharge on imports to improve the balance of trade, appeal to the public, and shock foreign governments into concessions.[92]

DOLLAR DEFENSE IS DOOMED

In early July, Connally's Treasury advisers received the data on the second quarter trade balance. It was these fig-

[91] William B. Dale, "Scenario III: Exchange Rate Realignment and Related Matters" and "Time Sequence of Events for Scenario III," 28 January 1971, U.S. Treasury Department files, Washington, D.C.

[92] Graebner, "New Economic Policy," pp. 167-170.

ures that convinced Under Secretary for Monetary Affairs
Paul Volcker that time had finally run out. The refutation
of the more hopeful diagnosis led the technical advisers to
urge that policy change include radical international monetary measures, not just domestic or trade policy changes.

Volcker had succeeded Frederick Deming in his post in
1969. He had arrived by a much more conventional route
than his superior, and he had brought with him a strong
attachment to the prevailing international monetary regime. He had begun his career with the Federal Reserve
Bank of New York, had served as deputy to Robert Roosa
at the Treasury, and had worked for Chase Manhattan
Bank between tours in Washington. He had not been active
in electoral politics. Volcker was most reluctant to encourage a suspension of convertibility or dollar depreciation.
He did his best to discourage other American officials from
even discussing particular exchange-rate changes.

In late May 1971, Treasury economists completed a lengthy
study of the U.S. competitive position, which concluded
that the dollar was overvalued by 10 to 15 percent.[93] When
the June trade balance was calculated, the deficit seemed
conclusive. Volcker met in early July with William Dale and
John R. Petty, Treasury's Assistant Secretary for International Affairs, both of whom agreed that the markets might
well interpret the figures as signs that the dollar was
doomed.[94] For Volcker, the trade data were much more
important than the reserve losses for the fundamental change
in his thinking.[95] Treasury forecasters were now projecting
that the U.S. would show a trade deficit for 1971—the first
year in the twentieth century that that would happen. If
the economy returned to high employment, they estimated

[93] "The U.S. International Competitive Position and the Potential Role
of Exchange Rates in the Adjustment Process," confidential report from
U.S. Treasury Office of Financial Analysis to Under Secretary Paul Volcker,
28 May 1971, U.S. Treasury Department files, Washington, D.C.

[94] Thomas A. Forbord, "The Abandonment of Bretton Woods: The
Political Economy of U.S. International Monetary Policy" (Ph.D. diss.,
Harvard University, 1980), pp. 243-244.

[95] Interview with a key Treasury official.

the current account for 1971 would show a deficit of $4 billion. Assuming that the U.S. would continue to run its customary deficits on capital account and government account, the country would need a large surplus on current account instead. A domestic policy sufficiently contractionary to bring overall external balance was considered to be domestically intolerable. It now seemed an unavoidable conclusion that the U.S. was in fundamental disequilibrium and that the only solution was a major exchange-rate realignment, a dollar depreciation on the order of 12 to 15 percent.[96]

Allied governments, however, were resisting appreciation. The United States would have to act. Volcker felt that if the U.S. simply raised the dollar-gold price by a substantial amount, other governments would follow, and that after devaluation the U.S. would not be able to maintain convertibility, anyway. Many American officials had long opposed such a move because they did not wish to enhance the role of gold in the monetary system. Furthermore, raising the gold price would of course cause losses for foreign central banks that had held dollar reserves. How seriously U.S. leaders explored other strategies, such as that advocated by Arthur Burns in August, is not clear. Volcker, Dale, and Petty were in agreement that because of the international situation the U.S. should suspend convertibility as a means of producing realignment.

When Volcker and Petty reported the trade data to Connally and made their recommendation to close the gold window, Connally was still unwilling to "bite that bullet." Connally told them instead to prepare the technical papers for an import surcharge. Volcker and Petty argued firmly against a surcharge, regarding it as protectionist.[97]

[96] Testimony by Paul Volcker, House Foreign Affairs Committee, *International Implications*, p. 82; Stabler, "Dollar Devaluations," p. 149.

[97] Interviews with participants; Forbord, "Abandonment," p. 246. Efforts to date the sequence of decisions by Nixon and Connally have produced somewhat conflicting results. Various participants, each of whom

DOMESTIC POLICY REVERSAL

President Nixon, meanwhile, was feeling greater pressure against his domestic policies:

> In the briefing I held for congressional leaders after my July 15 China announcement, I found that for every one who expressed support of that dramatic foreign initiative, at least twice as many used the opportunity to express concern about our domestic economic policies and to urge new actions to deal with the problems of unemployment and inflation. After this meeting Connally and I concluded that the time had come to act.
>
> "If we don't propose a responsible new program, Congress will have an irresponsible one on your desk within a month," he said. I knew he was right, and I authorized him to obtain privately the views of our senior economic advisers and then to prepare a report for me that included options for me to consider.[98]

Over the following three weeks President Nixon abandoned his resistance to a wage and price freeze, and he and Connally were also persuaded, or nearly persuaded, to attempt some "monetary magic" as well. Nixon met with Paul W. McCracken, Chairman of the Council of Economic Advisers, on other matters in mid-July, at which time McCracken told Nixon that the economic front needed something of "Peking proportions." Knowing Nixon's penchant for what he called "the big play," McCracken mentioned closing the gold window and floating the dollar.

---

saw only part of the process, gave slightly different accounts in interviews. For this and other reasons, I submitted a request to the Treasury under the Freedom of Information Act for documents recording the decision process. The Treasury responded that virtually no such documents related to the international monetary decisions of August 1971 could be found in its files. At the time of writing, the Nixon White House files had not been opened to scholars. The most elaborate effort to date the sequence is reported by Forbord, "Abandonment."

[98] Richard M. Nixon, *RN: The Memoirs of Richard Nixon* (New York: Grosset and Dunlap, 1978), p. 518.

McCracken reports that Nixon reacted excitedly and called Connally and asked him to meet with McCracken soon.[99] According to Petty, Nixon told Connally in the last week of July that he would approve a bold package including the wage-price freeze and budget reductions and possibly a suspension of convertibility.[100] Nixon's decision on the freeze may have been crystallized by the wage settlement in the steel industry announced on 2 August, at which time the companies announced an 8 percent price increase. At a meeting with Connally that day, Nixon brought George Shultz, Director of the Office of Management and Budget, into the planning process. It was decided to let the issue "sit and simmer" for a while, to delay making any dramatic moves until September—after the Congress would have returned from its August recess and after Connally would have assumed chairmanship of the Group of Ten.[101]

EXPECTATION OF FURTHER GOLD LOSS

But almost immediately they changed their timetable because of a new international currency disturbance. On Friday, 6 August, the day Connally departed for a vacation in Texas, two events set off another stampede out of the dollar. The Treasury released the news that the U.S. had sustained a new decline in international reserves of more than $1 billion. And the Congressional Subcommittee on International Exchange and Payments, led by Representative Henry Reuss, published its "inescapable conclusion" that the dollar was overvalued and had to be depreciated. The report urged that the U.S. press other countries to revalue, and failing that, the nation might have no choice

---

[99] Graebner, "New Economic Policy," p. 170.

[100] Interview with Petty, conducted by Forbord and reported in "Abandonment," p. 261. Other observers doubt that Nixon was reconciled to closing the gold window until after the events of early August and the debates at Camp David, as indicated below. Precisely when he approved the surcharge is also not clear.

[101] Brandon, *Retreat*, pp. 221-22; Nixon, *RN*, p. 518; Graebner, "New Economic Policy," p. 170.

but to go off gold. The subcommittee suggested that the U.S. might resort to a transitional float followed by a return to other means of dollar stabilization. At the beginning of the summer, Representative Reuss had introduced a "sense of the Congress" resolution calling for these measures in order to end the payments disequilibrium. Senator Jacob Javits, also a member of this subcommittee, had earlier proposed an international monetary conference to deal with the payments problem. The May currency crisis had been sufficient to convince some informed members of Congress that time had run out.[102]

During the week beginning on 9 August, "$3.7 billion moved across the exchanges and into central bank hands."[103] American private bankers who had been optimistic about the U.S. balance of payments turned pessimistic, saying to reporters, "We have lost the battle for the balance of payments." "Highly placed European central bankers" told the financial press that a forced devaluation of the dollar and general realignment were serious possibilities.[104] The Federal Reserve made heavy drawings on the swap network during the week to provide devaluation cover for part of the dollar gains of four central banks.

Evidently these new events also intensified a fear in Washington that foreign central banks might soon move to protect themselves further by demanding gold itself, even though they had shown great restraint until then. Volcker and Shultz met on 10 August and agreed that they should advance the timetable in order to pre-empt any such drain, now that they were convinced that dollar defense was doomed. They called Connally back to Washington. By Thursday, the President had decided to hold a secret meeting with 15 selected officials at Camp David on Friday,

[102] Interview; *New York Times*, 4 June 1971, p. 45, and 8 August 1971, p. 1.

[103] Coombs, "Foreign Exchange Operations," October 1971, p. 215.

[104] *American Banker*, 10 August 1971, p. 1.

13 August. That day, Nixon and Connally conferred privately at length before the group gathered.[105]

Expectations of new gold losses may have been heightened by a controversial episode involving Britain. During that week, the Bank of England requested devaluation cover for its dollar reserves. During previous currency crises, various governments had asked the Federal Reserve to borrow the excess dollars back through short-term swap lines. In effect, the U.S. had undertaken a commitment to make good any devaluation loss on the dollars in question. During this August 1971 crisis, the Federal Reserve drew $2.2 billion on the swap lines, including $750 million for the Bank of England. Connally complained angrily that the British had asked for $3 billion dollars worth. British and Federal Reserve officials deny this.[106] President Nixon maintains in his memoirs that the British ambassador asked the Treasury to convert $3 billion into gold itself, and that this forced earlier action. But other sources suggest that the President had already scheduled the Camp David meeting when he learned of the British action.[107] This and the other events in August may have only accelerated the timing of decisions that had been considered in detail for weeks.

CHOOSING UNILATERALISM AND GOING OFF GOLD

At the Camp David meeting, if not before, the President decided in favor of the second diplomatic strategy and closing the gold window. But this meeting made clear that the distinctive Connally-Peterson ideas had had to do battle with more familiar beliefs—voiced, as it happened, by the Federal Reserve Chairman, and probably by Nixon himself—before winning out. After opening the meeting, Nixon gave the floor to Connally to review the package of meas-

[105] Graebner, "New Economic Policy," p. 170.

[106] Brandon, *Retreat*, pp. 224-226; Coombs, *Arena*, p. 218.

[107] Nixon, *RN*, p. 518; Graebner, "New Economic Policy," p. 170. See also Juan Cameron, "How the U.S. Got on the Road to a Controlled Economy," *Fortune* (January 1972): 74; Forbord, "Abandonment," pp. 226-229; and remarks by Connally at Camp David, quoted below.

ures that had been developed. In Nixon's words, Connally called for:

> closing the "gold window" and allowing the dollar to float; imposing a 10 percent import tax that would be mainly a bargaining chip to discourage foreign countries from depressing their currencies in order to promote their exports; reinstating the investment tax credit to stimulate the business community; providing new income tax relief; and repealing the excise tax on automobiles to encourage higher sales. He left for last the action that would be perceived by the American people as the most dramatic and significant: a ninety-day freeze on wages and prices.

Nixon further reports that,

> while there was relatively strong, though skeptical, support among those present for the freeze and the other domestic actions, there was substantial disagreement on closing the gold window.[108]

Federal Reserve Chairman Burns agreed with the diagnosis that the dollar was overvalued; he had favored devaluation as far back as 1968. But Burns objected to the Connally strategy for accomplishing the adjustment. Burns, a professional economist, had served as President Eisenhower's first chief economic adviser, and he had known Nixon for many years. He arrived at the Federal Reserve in 1970 with an attachment to the gold-dollar standard and a resolute antipathy for floating exchange rates.[109] Burns, like Henry Fowler, interpreted the interwar years as a period when exchange-rate instability played havoc with international trade. Apart from the likely erosion of trade, Burns had three other objections to floating rates: they would not last, because governments would always be pressed

[108] Nixon, *RN*, p. 519.
[109] Interviews with participating Federal Reserve officials.

into intervening to protect domestic groups against large movements; they might lead to competitive national policies and political friction; and they would add to inflation and reduce the discipline on domestic economic policies exercised by the loss of reserves under pegged rates.[110]

At this meeting, Burns opposed suspending convertibility. He insisted that it was not necessary and that it would give rise to uncertain consequences, possibly including foreign retaliation. Burns's preferred strategy was one of multilateral compromise, with the U.S. contributing a strong anti-inflationary domestic program that would stabilize the currency markets, and foreign states then contributing revaluations. Burns went along with the import surcharge, although reluctantly.

The following dialogue at Camp David shows vividly the difference between the compromise view and the unilateralist view.

> NIXON: "Arthur, your view, as I understand it, is why is it not possible to do all the things that get at the heart of the problem and then go to close the gold window if needed. The Treasury objection to that is that reserve assets will be depleted quickly."
>
> BURNS: "I think they are wrong. If they are right, you can close it a week later. You will be doing something dramatic—a wage and price policy, a border tax. You will order a cutback in government spending. These major actions will electrify the world. The gold outflow will cease. If I'm wrong, you can close the window later. . . ."
>
> NIXON: "Wouldn't they retaliate on the tax, too?"
>
> PETERSON: "If you announce you have a balance of payments problem, other countries cannot retaliate under GATT."

[110] U.S., Congress, Joint Economic Committee, *How Well Are Fluctuating Exchange Rates Working? Hearings*, 93rd Cong., 1st sess., 1973, pp. 172-173, 188; *New York Times*, 5 March 1973, p. 45; interviews.

BURNS: "If we close that window, other countries could double the price of gold. We are releasing forces that we need not release. I think Paul Volcker should go ahead and start negotiating with other countries on a realignment of currencies. . . ."

CONNALLY: "What's our immediate problem? We are meeting here today because we are in trouble overseas. The British came in today to ask us to cover $3 billion, all their dollar reserves. Anybody can topple us—anytime they want—we have left ourselves completely exposed. . . ."

BURNS: "Yes, this is widely expected. But all the other countries know we have never acted against them. The good will—"

CONNALLY: "We'll go broke getting their good will."

VOLCKER: "I hate to do this, to close the window. All my life I have defended exchange rates, but I think it is needed."

CONNALLY: "So the other countries don't like it. So what?"

VOLCKER: "But don't let's close the window and sit—let's get other governments to negotiate new rates."

CONNALLY: "Why do we have to be 'reasonable'? Canada wasn't."

BURNS: "They can retaliate."

CONNALLY: "Let 'em. What can they do?"

BURNS: "They're powerful. They're proud, just as we are. . . ."

CONNALLY: "We don't have a chance unless we do it. Our assets are going out by the bushel basket. You're in the hands of the money changers. You can see the result of this action will put us in a more competitive position."

BURNS: "May I speak up for the 'money changers'? The central bankers are important to you. They would be pleased at this action, short of closing the window."[111]

---

[111] Safire, *Before the Fall*, pp. 513-515.

Different American leaders brought to this situation different predispositions regarding international politics, which channeled them toward different courses of action. Burns, along with others inside and outside the government, was inclined to preserve the Bretton Woods institutions as long and as fully as possible, and to put some trust in the willingness of Western Europe and Japan to respond cooperatively to U.S. leadership without overt coercion. As to the immediate situation, he would gamble that they would still not demand gold in large amounts and that they would agree to adequate revaluations.

Connally, however, was much less predisposed to preserve Bretton Woods, and he further believed that attitudes about the world political economy were glaringly anachronistic, not only in foreign capitals but also in Washington. Without unilateral shock treatment, the other governments were more likely to dig in their heels and frustrate a major adjustment. Moreover, he and Volcker feared that some of them would come in for gold. He insisted, in effect, that the U.S. should "break some crockery" to show that it was serious, now demanding not only trade concessions but also exchange-rate concessions. In the end, the President was more persuaded by the Connally view.

There was also strong internal criticism of the idea of slapping a surcharge on imports; indeed, no policy maker besides Connally recommended both closing the gold window and imposing the surcharge. Economists pointed out that it would actually slow the descent of the dollar, and Treasury officials objected to it as well. Connally, however, insisted that it was necessary. He referred to the farmer in the old joke who hit his donkey on the head with a two-by-four to get his attention. President Nixon also reflected this coercion rationale for the surcharge at Camp David, when he said:

> My long-range goal is not to erect a 10 percent barrier around the U.S.—that would be retrogressive—but to set a procedure that lets us go up and down with room for

negotiation. If we could move on the authority, and at the same time close the gold window, we then provide the basis of negotiation. It gives you more stroke. . . . [On the GATT basis] the border tax is not too damned aggressive, just aggressive enough.[112]

Again the President was persuaded more by Connally.

The President was thus choosing a drastically new and risky diplomatic strategy, one whose consequences would hinge on beliefs, reactions, and domestic politics in Japan, West Germany, France, and other countries. Yet neither Nixon nor any of his assembled advisers had expert knowledge about these countries. Neither the President nor the Treasury Secretary called for political research or political forecasting comparable to the careful financial projections they received. There is no evidence that their diplomatic judgments were based on more than hunches.

The U.S. government embarked on this historic departure toward a new international monetary regime without a road map. One key official pressed Connally, outside the Camp David setting, to propose simultaneously an American plan for long-range reform of the international monetary system. Connally snapped: "Forget about it. It'll be a year before they know what the problem is."[113] Such matters were not discussed at Camp David.

On 18 August, Connally invited several American economists outside the government to give him their views at a meeting with top Treasury staff. According to one participant, Connally opened the meeting by saying, "Well, you know what we have done. What do we do next?" Most of the visitors emphasized to Connally that America now had an opportunity to reform the international monetary and trade system, particularly in the direction of more flexible rates. Connally seemed to have learned a great deal about

[112] Safire, *Before the Fall*, pp. 512, 515. Cf. George P. Shultz and Kenneth W. Dam, *Economic Policy Beyond the Headlines* (New York: W. W. Norton, 1977), p. 115.
[113] Interview with this official.

the detailed technical issues involved in monetary reform, compared with his early days at the Treasury. He asked penetrating questions and spent a full six hours with the group. Then at the end of the day, he said: "I appreciate your coming in today. And since you have shared with me, I think I should give you an idea of where I am going. My basic approach is that the foreigners are out to screw us. Our job is to screw them first. Thank you, gentlemen." And he left.[114]

EXPECTATIONS FOR DOMESTIC POLITICS

It has been argued that the electoral calculations leading to the domestic policy change were also the major reason for the international monetary policy reversal of August 1971. "As usual," writes C. Fred Bergsten, for example, "it was domestic politics rather than foreign policy which forced dramatic changes in long-standing international arrangements." From the premise that this action was not forced by a foreign run on gold, Bergsten comes to the conclusion that "concerns over domestic unemployment dominated this U.S. policy shift."[115] In this view, closing the gold window was not necessary, but was done because Connally and Nixon believed that it would win votes. Unemployment was too high, and currency depreciations are always expected to stimulate the economy's foreign trading sector and other sectors linked to it. Treasury consultant E. M. Bernstein is reported to have provided an estimate that the dollar was overvalued by an amount sufficient to account for 0.5 percent of the unemployment rate; hence, a devaluation could provide 500,000 new jobs.[116]

This hypothesis gives electoral goals more weight than they deserve. The payments imbalance was becoming enor-

[114] Interview with a participant.
[115] Bergsten, *Dilemmas of the Dollar*, pp. 91-93. This interpretation also appears in Forbord, "Abandonment," and in Susan Strange, "The Dollar Crisis 1971," *International Affairs* 48 (1972):191-216.
[116] Graebner, "New Economic Policy," p. 163.

mous. A number of academic economists as well as the Treasury's three senior staff members had advised that the dollar would have to be depreciated for international economic reasons, and they had recommended suspension of convertibility as the means. Presumably the technicians' perceptions and judgments were not based on electoral goals.

Furthermore, this hypothesis neglects the possibility of expectations of loss as well as gain. Devaluing or going off gold would be seen as admitting major defeat and violating international obligations, which could produce domestic political backlash. Many American leaders shared the hunch that a President who devalued the dollar would be "tarred and feathered" by his rivals at home.

If this case had hinged mainly on domestic political expectations, the politicians would almost certainly have continued sidestepping "monetary magic" and would have dealt with unemployment by other means. The evidence indicates that President Nixon was far more sensitive to the domestic political costs than to the gains. His concerns came out at the Camp David meeting. At one point, he mentioned to his advisers that he wanted to present the new policy in "a speech of ten minutes—concise, strong, confident: not a lot of stuff whining around that we are in a hell of a shape." He then turned to Peter Peterson. "Pete, what do you think the reaction of 'folks' to closing the window will be?"

PETERSON: "They will worry."

NIXON: " 'The President has assured the devaluation of the dollar. The dollar will be worth less.' The media will be vicious. I can see it now: 'He's devalued the dollar.' "

ARTHUR BURNS to PAUL VOLCKER: "What will happen to the price of gold?"

VOLCKER: "Everybody who speculates in gold will seize on this to make a mint. We have to come up with a proposal to demonstrate gold is not that important. Maybe we should sell some."

PAUL MCCRACKEN: "People's reaction to closing the gold window would be negative. On the other hand, they will see it as part of a program of strong action on wage-price matters."

VOLCKER: "There is a certain public sentiment about 'a cross of gold.'"

NIXON (*making a face*): "Bryan ran four times and lost."[117]

This transcript gives no evidence that anyone present was attracted to closing the gold window as a means of increasing jobs or votes. When asked about this, a Connally associate who was present at the meeting replied:

Unemployment was raised as an argument, but it really didn't enter into it. We would have been willing to tolerate more reserve losses if we had thought we could turn it around. . . . Connally clearly thought the program as a whole was a great opportunity for political gain. And it *was*. This economic program and the trip to China won the 1972 election for Nixon. Before, people were worried about the economy, and after, they were less worried about it. Connally was interested in more activist steps, but he did not think the value of the dollar was something you could casually change for employment purposes.[118]

Herbert Stein, who also participated in the meeting, commented:

At Camp David we were concerned about the unemployment problem, hence the freeze and certain tax reductions. And there was some worry that our net export position was deterring the recovery. But the exchange-rate changes were not primarily motivated by a desire to improve the domestic economy. Unemployment was a very minor consideration in closing the gold window.

[117] Safire, *Before the Fall*, pp. 514-515.
[118] Interview.

Stein added, referring to Nixon and the gold window:

> His only concern was whether people would see it as the U.S. going down the drain—not maintaining our obligations. But when he decided on how he would describe it in his speech—as an achievement, as the U.S. asserting its independence—then he decided he could do it.[119]

The evidence seems most consistent with the interpretation that Connally and Nixon decided to close the gold window because of the international situation and their beliefs about it, and that simultaneously they set about to find ways to minimize the domestic political cost. Given his acceptance of the fear that international gold losses were now likely, Nixon was unwilling to agree to Burns's alternative strategy, for domestic as well as international reasons. In response to Burns's argument that closing the gold window was not necessary, he countered:

> NIXON: "If we do all these things, speculators may say 'Next they'll close the gold window,' and there would be a run."
> BURNS: "*Then* you would close the window. What's to lose by waiting?"
> NIXON: "The argument on the other side is that domestic opinion would not give it a chance. . . . you risk appearing that your actions didn't work. . . ."[120]

If one was going to take bold actions, it would be best domestically to take them all at once.

Domestic rivals might also be outmaneuvered by a speech using Connallyesque rhetoric explaining the suspension of convertibility not as weakness but as a measure to "protect the dollar from the attacks of international money speculators." Nixon simply turned inside-out the conventional meaning of "defending the dollar." His television address directly took up "the bugaboo of what is called devalua-

---

[119] Interview with Herbert Stein.
[120] Safire, *Before the Fall*, pp. 513-514.

tion," saying that for most Americans the effect of the action would be "to stabilize the dollar," not to make it worth less. He reiterated: "Now, this action will not win us any friends among the international money traders. But our primary concern is with the American workers, and with fair competition around the world." He introduced the import surcharge as a second measure for dealing with "unfair exchange rates," declaring that "there is no longer any need for the United States to compete with one hand tied behind her back." He called upon the citizenry to end their self-doubt and to insure that the nation "stays number one in the world's economy."[121]

Domestic political calculations may help explain the Connally negotiation strategy that was subsequently pursued. A unilateral strategy of making highly publicized demands on foreign governments without suggesting compromise outcomes or American concessions could be useful in gaining approval at home.[122]

Incidentally, these techniques were successful. After 15 August, Nixon's rivals made almost no attempt to criticize him for "devaluation."

In summary, changes in leaders' predispositions and specific calculations of the U.S. interest are necessary and, along with market and power conditions, sufficient to explain the 1971 policy shift.

ORGANIZATION AND INTERNAL BARGAINING

It has also been argued that the unilateral form of the new American policy was due in part to an organizational failing. Graham Allison and Peter Szanton describe the "New Economic Policy" as "risky" and "short-sighted" foreign policy. It jeopardized the international cooperation on which economic welfare depends over the long run, for the sake of immediate domestic concerns. They use this case to il-

[121] Department of State, *Bulletin* 65 (1971):253-257.
[122] This interpretation was suggested by a Connally adviser.

lustrate their theme that "organization matters." As they explain it:

> The short-sighted character of that decision clearly reflected the unbalanced process that produced it. The group President Nixon relied upon to make the decision was dominated by a newly appointed Secretary of the Treasury, John Connally. . . . Domestic perspectives were . . . weighted heavily. But the group contained neither the Secretary of State nor the Assistant for National Security Affairs, nor any senior subordinate of either. Thus, no one was engaged whose job required him to think hard about the consequences of the decisions for larger foreign policy objectives.[123]

Allison and Szanton argue that if certain organizational reforms had been in place, and specifically if the Secretary of State and the President's Assistant for National Security Affairs had participated in the decision, then U.S. policy would have had a more farsighted character.

In fact, organizational reforms having precisely the purpose of integrating and balancing competing national objectives were already in place at this time. Few cases cast more doubt on the efficacy of organizational reform. Few illustrate more clearly the strength rather than the weakness of the President and the limitations of organizational explanations of policy content.

Upon taking office, Nixon and Kissinger were determined to impose rational control upon foreign policy making. They established under Kissinger's direction a mechanism for anticipating policy problems and formulating long-range solutions. An interagency group for international monetary affairs, led by Treasury Under Secretary

---

[123] Graham Allison and Peter Szanton, *Remaking Foreign Policy: The Organizational Connection* (New York: Basic Books, 1976), p. 145. In the odd final sentence the authors have overlooked the most important official engaged: the President. The lapse nicely illustrates a tendency of organization analysts to underemphasize the power of the chief executive.

Paul Volcker, prepared a policy study which advanced through this "Kissinger operation" to the President during 1969. Nixon also created a Cabinet Committee on Economic Policy. In early 1971, he added a cabinet-level Council on International Economic Policy, with its own staff led by Peter Peterson. The members of this new Council were the President, the Secretaries of State, Treasury, Defense, Agriculture, Commerce, and Labor, the Director of the Budget, the Chairman of the Council of Economic Advisers, the Special Trade Representative, the Assistant to the President for National Security Affairs, the Assistant for Domestic Affairs, and Ambassador-at-Large David M. Kennedy, who dealt with textile imports. Judging from the range of coordinating institutions in place, an organization analyst would have expected that policy would be carefully integrated.

But the President simply chose to ignore them all. Instead, he deputized Secretary Connally to take charge of developing policy on these issues, as mentioned earlier. Given Nixon's predispositions, and if "[Connally] was telling the President what he wanted to hear," as Allison and Szanton say, then it is difficult to imagine how different organizational arrangements could have made much difference to policy content.

Interestingly enough, Arthur Burns enunciated most of the arguments an organization analyst would have expected to come from the State Department or the National Security Council. He cautioned Nixon that Connally's program might provoke foreign retaliation and other unknown ill effects internationally, and he pleaded for preserving foreign "good will." The President nonetheless reached the personal judgment that the decision was "not too damned aggressive, just aggressive enough." As a matter of fact, the top economic official at the State Department, while opposed to suspension of convertibility, favored an even stiffer import surcharge, as a psychological and bargaining device.[124] The strongest opposition to a surcharge was in the Treasury, not the State Department.

Senior officials were divided, but their policy positions did not correlate closely to assumed agency missions and stakes. It is true that the Federal Reserve, charged with operating the instruments of dollar defense, put up the most prominent opposition to suspending convertibility. On the other hand, the Federal Reserve Chairman's first preference had been dollar devaluation, not defense of existing rates. The National Security Adviser remained silent, instead of weighing in with expected arguments on behalf of foreign governments and alliance cohesion. An organization analyst would hardly have expected radical international monetary recommendations to come from the Office of Management and Budget, nor—most important—that the strong leadership in shaking Bretton Woods would come from the Treasury Department. This is a case in which the variation in recommendations was related more closely to advisers' substantive predispositions and perceptions than to their agency roles.

Despite the division among the players, this policy was not the result of an internal bargain. The President was not compelled to compromise his own preference in order to build internal support. Nixon heard objections to Connally's package, but he was persuaded to approve the entire package and reject all the criticisms. Unlike other instances of foreign policy change, there is no evidence here that the President would have preferred some other policy on 15 August. Nor is this a case in which autonomous bureaucracies later ignored or subverted presidential decisions during an implementation phase. On the contrary, the moves on 15 August marked the end of a period of bifurcated U.S. policy and a shift to a period of high centralization. Likewise, the period from the late 1960s well into the 1970s was one in which transgovernmental relations among central bankers were superseded by direct diplomacy among

[124] Interview with an American official.

senior statesmen. Burns's August recommendation to Nixon expressed the sort of feelings associated with transgovernmental camaraderie, but they had little effect on U.S. policy at this point.

In other cases of foreign policy change, organizational factors as defined here seem to weigh more heavily as influences on policy content than they did in this case. Perhaps in this case as well, in order to make "bureaucratic" factors relevant, one could stretch their meaning to include much more—for example, which individual held a given post, officials' substantive attitudes, the fact that the President listened only to certain advisers, the fact that Kissinger did not participate before 15 August.[125] But organizational structures and procedures can change without a change of incumbents, and a change of incumbents or ideas may occur independently of organizational structure. To confound several partially independent variables makes analysis unnecessarily fuzzy and may place responsibility for policy outcomes at the wrong level. The analyst searching after an explanation and finding himself in the Oval Office has turned his back on bureaucratic analysis. In the present case, it is clear that the strongest influences were the international situation and the policy ideas of the President and others; the contribution of organizational factors was slight.

THE SMITHSONIAN COMPROMISE

In August 1971, then, the United States jolted the international monetary foundation, and then paused for other major states to respond. For four months, the result was continued stalemate. The other financial great powers, especially France and Japan, refused to yield to the sweeping American demands backed by the sudden use of economic

[125] For example, see Wilfred L. Kohl, "The Nixon-Kissinger Foreign Policy System and U.S.-European Relations: Patterns of Policy-Making," *World Politics* 28 (1975):1-43.

force, as long as the U.S. refused to offer equally visible concessions to them. They did feel compelled by the pressure of unbalanced markets and the American jolt to permit their currencies to rise grudgingly during the deadlock. By October, the dollar had depreciated by approximately seven percent from its 1970 effective level. Meanwhile, prolonged uncertainty was threatening business conditions, and America's alliances were fraying as much as at any time since the war. The President decided that the political costs of continuing the monetary stalemate would exceed the economic gains for the United States. He therefore ordered another change in negotiating strategy and accepted a compromise agreement in December.

On 15 August, the Nixon administration acted unilaterally, almost completely ignoring the IMF headquarters down the street from the White House. (Secretary Connally, glancing over his shoulder at the legal obligation to "collaborate with the Fund to promote exchange stability," invited Managing Director Pierre-Paul Schweitzer to watch the President's address on a television set in Connally's office!) On 20 August, the IMF Board announced that the United States was in violation of its obligation to insure the dollar's exchange stability. The Managing Director warned that unless prompt action was taken, disorder and discrimination could seriously disrupt currency and trade relationships, and not only for the industrial countries. Many developing countries were unsure what exchange-rate policies to follow and were calling the Fund for advice. Schweitzer asked the Group of Ten countries to meet quickly, but he was rebuffed. During the second week after 15 August, he appeared twice on television to call for a negotiated approach to adjustment. It would be normal, he said, for the U.S. to make a contribution, and a dollar devaluation against gold would be one appropriate contribution. Privately, the IMF formulated a proposed exchange rate realignment, which was leaked to the press at about this time. It envisioned a 3 to 5 percent dollar devaluation together with revaluations of several currencies, including 15 percent for the yen, 13 to 14 percent for the mark, and 7 percent for the French franc and the pound sterling. This initiative, or at least its publication, touched off irritations all around—in the U.S., where Connally wanted to suppress talk of dollar devaluation, and in other countries, where the revaluations were regarded as much too large.[126]

In Europe, the first reaction to the Nixon speech was optimistic. Some saw the suspension of convertibility as a step toward negotiation of a needed currency realignment. Perhaps the import surcharge might not be in effect long enough to affect trade flows. But the mood changed to gloom when Paul Volcker flew to London and Paris on 16 August with word that Connally was not anxious to convene a bargaining conference, and that the U.S. had no intention of devaluing the dollar.[127] Connally's initial strategy was not simply to float passively. It was to create a crisis among states, to make large vague demands, but to make no specific suggestions of the percentages of revaluation that would satisfy the United States. According to Henry Kissinger, Connally

> reasoned that the longer the import surcharge remained, the stronger our bargaining position would be. He feared that *any* American proposal would enable all other nations to combine against it even though they would never be able to agree on a positive program of their own.[128]

The EC governments immediately closed their foreign exchange markets for a week, and at a meeting in Brussels they once again attempted to agree on a joint response to the dollar problem. Again they failed. All of them expected

[126] de Vries, *International Monetary Fund*, vol. I, pp. 531-541; *American Banker*, 23 August and 24 August 1971; *Washington Post*, 25 August 1971; *New York Times*, 21 August and 24 September 1971. In September, the Council of the GATT judged the American tariff surcharge "not compatible" with the GATT (*New York Times*, 17 September 1971, p. 26).

[127] *American Banker*, 17 August, 19 August, and 23 August 1971.

[128] Kissinger, *White House Years*, pp. 956-957.

to be targets of strong speculation when they reopened their markets, and the West Germans renewed their appeal for a joint upward float. France, however, wanted the EC to segregate its foreign exchange markets into two tiers. Exchange rates for capital transactions would float in unison, while fixed rates would be maintained for trade. To tie the franc to a floating mark might pull the franc too far up and damage French trade excessively—a fear shared in Britain. Besides, if the Germans and Dutch were going to continue their float in any case, then French goods behind a fixed commercial franc would reap an increasing advantage within Europe at the expense of her partners. The joint float proposed by Germany would give the U.S. a trade advantage without an American concession. Bonn, on the other hand, was unwilling to agree to French-style exchange controls. Thus, the Brussels meeting ended in shambles. France reopened its market on the two-tier basis, and all the others, including Britain, floated without coordination. Central banks intervened separately to control these floats during the autumn, and European currencies rose by varying degrees.[129]

Imbalances of payments between France and Germany, and between Europe and Japan, made the 1971 negotiations even more complex than would have been necessary to adjust the world's key currency. The mark was undervalued not only with respect to the dollar but also relative to the French franc, meaning that payments balance would require the mark to rise somewhat more than the franc vis-à-vis the dollar. But the German government was keen to avoid appreciating any more than necessary against the franc. Each of the surplus countries, when bargaining with the United States, held back to make sure it did not get too far in front of its competitors.

---

[129] *Economist*, 21 August 1971, pp. 55-57; *Wall Street Journal*, 23 August 1971, p. 1; Coombs, "Treasury and Federal Reserve," October 1971; *New York Times*, 17 August 1971, p. 1; 19 August, p. 1; 20 August, p. 1; 24 August, pp. 1, 24.

Rivalry between Germany and France expressed itself in the issue of the gold price. One technique for bringing about realignment of exchange rates was revaluation of both the mark and the franc in terms of gold—the mark by more than the franc—assuming that the dollar/gold price remained constant. But France adamantly refused to revalue the franc against gold, for several reasons. To do so would permit the American government to escape having to devalue its currency against gold. Finance Minister Giscard d'Estaing consistently maintained that no other government had been allowed to elude political responsibility when depreciation was necessary, and that no exception should be made for the Nixon administration. More importantly, Giscard d'Estaing and others were concerned about the deflationary consequences of currency appreciation in their own countries, and they were not eager to assume the visible responsibility themselves. Another unstated reason was that the French public had a notorious taste for gold as a savings vehicle, and revaluation would reduce the franc value of their hoards. As long as France refused to revalue against gold, and the United States refused to devalue, then Germany could not revalue the mark enough to satisfy the United States without giving an excessive competitive advantage to France. Not until the U.S. agreed in December to devalue was this impasse finally broken.

Japan's response was similar. At first, the Sato government reasserted prevailing policy. The suspension of convertibility and the import surcharge came to be known in Tokyo as a "Nixon shock." It sent the Tokyo Stock Exchange into record single-day losses, shook government leaders, and drove them into emergency consultations. Amid some confusion, the government sent an emissary to Washington and Europe while insisting that the Eight Point Payments Program was still in effect. The yen would not be revalued. Unlike the EC countries, Japan did not suspend foreign exchange trading. The Bank of Japan continued to buy dollars at the 360 rate for two weeks. The government believed that it could control speculative inflows until consultations had taken place, and undoubtedly it was reluctant to yield its position any sooner than necessary. In addition, maintenance of an open window permitted Japanese companies and banks with large dollar holdings to unload them at the Bank of Japan before the dollar was allowed to depreciate. Japanese firms leaped at this lucrative opportunity. During the single month of August, the Bank of Japan soaked up $4.5 billion, an amount equal to Japan's entire reserve stock before 1971. The resulting huge capital loss for the central bank caused considerable press criticism in Tokyo. After the first week, the major trading companies and other business groups decided that revaluation was inevitable, and they urged the government to yield—but as little as possible.[130]

Japan was in a weaker power position vis-à-vis the United States than were the EC states, making her more vulnerable to U.S. efforts at coercion, particularly if the U.S. and the EC joined forces. Yet Japan was considerably stronger than in earlier years, and in this case it was the Americans who wanted something from Japan. Secretary Connally, perhaps hoping to divide and conquer, told Japan's ambassador on 18 August that the U.S. wanted to deal bilaterally with Japan prior to negotiations with other countries. A high-level meeting was scheduled for Washington in early September. But in late August, it became apparent that the EC would not come to an early settlement with Washington, and Japan's envoy reported that he found no strong pressure in Europe for an immediate yen revaluation. Japanese officials showed considerable relief when the EC failed to reach agreement in Brussels.[131]

On 28 August, the Japanese government allowed the yen

[130] *Japan Times*, 17 August through 29 August 1971; *Far Eastern Economic Review*, 11 September 1971, pp. 47-50; Krause and Sekiguchi, "Japan and the World Economy," p. 436; interviews with two Japanese officials.

[131] *Japan Times*, 20 August 1971, p. 1; 21 August, p. 5; 24 August, p. 1; *American Banker*, 23 August 1971, p. 3.

to float through its ceiling, while refusing publicly to accept the August demands as long as Washington offered no concessions. The Washington bilateral meeting in September produced heated argument but little agreement. Foreign Minister Takeo Fukuda and Finance Minister Mikio Mizuta maintained that exchange rates were not the source of the imbalance, and that the U.S. could deal with the dollar deficit by domestic measures. They complained sharply about the import surcharge and called for its removal, especially in view of the floating of the yen. Otherwise, they warned, the surcharge might provoke retaliation. After many "loud words," they finally agreed in private to the principle that the yen could be revalued as part of a multilateral agreement. At home, the Japanese government announced financial aids for industries to offset the surcharge's effects.[132]

During the days and weeks after 15 August, the United States gradually amplified on what it would require for an agreement and for removal of the surcharge. The U.S. position came to have four general planks: (1) the United States would not devalue the dollar "one iota," and it demanded (2) substantial appreciations of leading surplus currencies, (3) modification of major "unfair" trading practices, and (4) greater sharing of the financial costs of military alliance. None of the three demands was spelled out in detail, but the trade practices that had been most frequently criticized were Japan's non-tariff barriers and the EC common agricultural policy. The U.S. insisted on some

[132] Joint communiqué, in Department of State, *Bulletin* 65 (4 October 1971):350-351; *New York Times*, 10 September 1971, p. 21, and 18 September, p. 37; *Financial Times*, 11 September 1971, p. 1. Meanwhile, the U.S. stepped up its campaign for Japanese concessions on the specific issue of textile exports. On 20 September, President Nixon issued an ultimatum. If Japan did not accept new export restraints, the President would impose quotas on 15 October under the authority of the Trading with the Enemy Act of 1917. Japan accepted new textile restraints on 15 October (*New York Times*, 21 September 1971, p. 27; 26 September, p. IV-15; 16 October, p. 1).

combination of the three measures that would produce a large improvement in the American balance of payments. At a September Group of Ten meeting, the U.S. representatives put a figure on "large," and the reaction was astonishment and alarm. Volcker said that the U.S. sought a swing in its current account of no less than $13 billion from what it would otherwise be in 1972. Almost all of this $13 billion turnaround would have to come out of the trade balances of other countries. Their monetary diplomats regarded this as a tall order indeed, far more than they had been contemplating.[133]

Meeting in Brussels on 13 September, the EC Finance Ministers managed to forge a common diplomatic position, at least in general terms. They declared that the international monetary system should be reformed on the basis of fixed but adjustable parities and proper domestic policies. New measures were needed to deal with international capital movements, and these could include a limited widening of margins for currency fluctuation. International liquidity, said the Community, should be based on gold and increasingly on SDRs, without domination by any single national currency. They took up the American line in arguing that the power shift since World War II required replacing the dollar gradually with an internationally managed standard. Most concretely, the six countries put the U.S. on notice that the needed currency realignment would have to embrace the currencies of all the industrial countries concerned, "including the dollar." They demanded elimination

[133] *New York Times*, 20 August 1971, p. 1; 16 September, p. 1; 18 September, p. 1; *Financial Times*, 14 September 1971, p. 1, and 16 September, p. 1; Solomon, *International Monetary System*, p. 192. Volcker's reasoning was that, with full employment, the U.S. current account was going to show a $4 billion deficit, whereas a current account surplus of $9 billion would be needed. That is, the U.S. intended to supply approximately $6 billion in foreign aid and private capital to developing countries; unrecorded outflows would be at least $1 billion; and an official settlements surplus of $1 or $2 billion would be needed over the next several years to restore confidence in the dollar. The calculations assumed no net recorded outflows of long-term capital to developed countries.

of the import surcharge and the discriminatory investment tax credit, before serious currency negotiations could proceed. European governments were feeling mounting pressure from their industrialists to retaliate against this tax discrimination in particular.[134]

The European Commission argued that the proposed American solution, falling heavily and suddenly on trade, was indefensible. The U.S. disequilibrium, it maintained, was primarily caused not by trade developments but by the determination of American business to continue capital exports while the trade surplus declined. Rather than regulating these capital movements, the U.S. was talking of abolishing its existing restrictions. Another source of the drain was excessive military spending in Vietnam.[135] Two days after their Brussels meeting, the Six met with Secretary Connally and the rest of the Group of Ten ministers and governors in London for the first time since 15 August. These monetary conferences during the early autumn sparked much acrimony but no accommodation.

The U.S. import surcharge also came under attack by Latin American governments during the autumn. They bitterly protested application of the measure to their trade, which had traditionally provided the United States with a surplus rather than a deficit. But the U.S. refused to apply the surcharge selectively, attempting instead to convince Latin Americans that its effects on their countries would be less than they feared.[136]

Federal Reserve Chairman Burns remained worried about

[134] *Bulletin of the European Communities*, No. 9/10-1971, pp. 41-43; *New York Times*, 12 September 1971, p. 1; 13 September, p. 1; 14 September, p. 1; 18 September, p. 37; *Financial Times*, 14 September 1971, p. 32, and 16 September, p. 1.

[135] *Bulletin of the European Communities*, No. 11-1971, pp. 26-27; *European Community*, September 1971, pp. 12-14.

[136] *New York Times*, 18 September 1971, p. 37; Department of State *Bulletin* 65 (11 October 1971):382-384, and 65 (15 November 1971):561. Secretary of State Rogers wanted to lift the surcharge from Latin America. But Kissinger strongly opposed any selectivity on the grounds that it would damage relations with Japan even more severely (interview with a participating U.S. official).

the costs of Connally's strategy and maneuvered quietly to promote a settlement of the crisis. With the major governments having publicly dug in their heels, each demanding that the other concede first, Burns reasoned that a secret mediation might help bring them together. Dr. Jelle Zijlstra, the widely respected president of the Bank for International Settlements and president of the Dutch central bank, agreed to undertake the mission. Zijlstra was to fashion his personal numerical plan for a realignment compromise, based on separate, secret consultations with each of the major finance ministries and central banks. He held these meetings and produced a plan, but Connally refused to meet or cooperate with Zijlstra.[137] Connally was determined to extract larger concessions and believed that time was on his side.

Burns also began receiving reports from other countries about reactions to the surcharge and retaliations contemplated or actually taken. A number of countries were introducing exchange restrictions, and Denmark announced its intention to imitate the 10 percent surcharge. These reports became numerous enough for Burns to start a daily log. He took these signs of international conflict to Kissinger, who agreed that the two of them should meet with Nixon to express concern. Nixon appeared disturbed and told Burns to continue his log and to meet again with him in a week or two.[138]

Kissinger was preoccupied with the secret armistice negotiations with North Vietnam and the intimately related talks with Moscow and Peking. Earlier, he had also been engaged in a brief but intense struggle in Washington over North Atlantic policy, which had implications for the monetary problem. A week after the dollar-mark crisis, Senate Majority Leader Mike Mansfield revived his proposal to bring home half of U.S. forces stationed in Europe. The dollar drain had always been one of the arguments for what

[137] Brandon, *Retreat*, pp. 231-232; interview with a Key American official.

[138] Interview with Burns.

Kissinger regarded as a body blow to his entire global strategy. Kissinger, with the help of Dean Acheson and John McCloy, rushed to assemble a bipartisan array of past luminaries of U.S. foreign policy. With their endorsement, the administration was able to defeat Mansfield's amendment.

In the first days after 15 August, Kissinger did not trust his own judgment on the merits of the economic measures. In time he became convinced that Connally was correct in his political assessment that some shock would have been necessary to bring the allies to serious negotiations involving hard choices. But he also concluded—in contrast to Connally—that the passage of time would raise political costs far higher than could be justified by the economic gains to the U.S.

In early September, Kissinger asked economists Richard Cooper of Yale University and Francis Bator, then at Harvard, to brief him. These two explained that a currency realignment was necessary, but they were horrified by the prospects of an economic war within the alliance. Bator later argued their case publicly,[139] branding Connally's tactics "recklessly dangerous" as well as unnecessary. In particular, Bator said,

> As long as the surcharge is on, the strain on foreign politicians' self-restraint is bound to grow, and the President's freedom of maneuver will shrink. Time . . . is on no one's side. . . . [If] Connally does not change course soon, the other side will start shooting back. Control over events will shift to the war parties in all the capitals, and Aug. 15 will be a turning point in postwar Atlantic and U.S.-Japan history.

If a Cooper-Bator intellectual outlook had been guiding policy during this period, U.S. actions would have been significantly less shocking.

---

[139] Francis M. Bator, "Mr. Connally's War" and "Mr. Connally's Opportunity," *New York Times*, 29 November and 30 November 1971.

Bator and Cooper also warned Kissinger that the administration might be laying a trap for itself in domestic politics. The surcharge could become addictive; the longer it provided protection for domestic industry, the more painful it would be for the President to withdraw it "cold turkey." Furthermore, if the allies started retaliating with economic measures, Kissinger would have a much harder time holding the Senate together against the Mansfield proposal. They recommended an end to the surcharge and the "Buy American" discrimination as soon as possible, to clear the atmosphere for a currency agreement.[140]

Tensions continued to mount in October, as Connally still refused to initiate a specific proposal for a compromise, and as the other governments were unable to agree among themselves. Connally hinted that the U.S. might lift the surcharge selectively for West Germany. France pressed her European partners to make a serious examination of possible retaliations against the surcharge. German industry urged Bonn to reconsider the policy of relatively free floating in favor of a quick European stabilization on terms acceptable to France. In November, Connally demanded that Japan revalue against the dollar by 25 percent. Finance Minister Mizuta repeated Japan's arguments, saying that he could not go above five percent. Connally told a press conference on 13 November that world monetary uncertainty could continue for "almost an indefinite period," and that the United States would not suffer if it did.[141]

Kissinger and Burns finally decided that the U.S. should make concessions to end the monetary crisis. Sometime in November, President Nixon also decided that a proper balance between American political and economic objectives required accepting smaller currency and trade adjustments than the Treasury claimed were needed. Disarray in the

---

[140] Interviews.

[141] *Journal of Commerce*, 18 October 1971, p. 11, and 19 October, p. 1; interviews conducted by Professor Kent E. Calder, Harvard University, and provided to the author; *New York Times*, 14 November 1971, p. 1.

Western camp on the eve of his 1972 summit meetings in Peking and Moscow might weaken America's hand in dealing with its adversaries. It was Nixon's judgment that the United States should now settle for less than had been expected in August.

In a conversation with Burns, Nixon expressed his concerns about the conflict, but he indicated he was not sure how he would deal with Connally's possible resistance to a compromise.[142] At a meeting late in November with Connally, Kissinger, Burns, and Shultz, Nixon raised questions about the political costs of continuing the surcharge and the stalemate. When it became apparent that Nixon had made up his mind, Connally fell into line. The surcharge would have to be removed and Connally would negotiate the best possible bargain in return for it.[143]

In order to bring matters to a head, Kissinger recommended to Nixon that he intervene personally with European heads of state. According to Kissinger's memoirs, the U.S. first suggested a collective summit meeting. But French President Georges Pompidou

> made it clear that he was not interested; he knew he would not be able to create a common European front; in case of a stalemate [West German Chancellor Willy] Brandt would be under great pressure to side with the United States. Therefore we decided to initiate a series of bilateral talks. The key was Pompidou. [Britain's Prime Minister Edward] Heath would avoid choosing sides between France and the United States. If we lined up with Brandt, we would evoke French resentment; we could always do that if the approach to Pompidou failed. Our preferred strategy was to permit Pompidou to establish a position of leadership in Europe by negotiating the terms of a settlement with us. We always had in reserve

[142] Interview with Burns.
[143] Interviews with participants; *New York Times*, 27 December 1971, p. 27; Brandon, *Retreat*, pp. 235-236; Stabler, "Dollar Devaluations," p. 150; Solomon, *International Monetary System*, p. 201.

the threat to isolate him if he were totally intransigent. I did not think this likely. I judged that everyone would be eager to settle if an American proposal gave the opportunity. And I was confident that Nixon would not want a public impression of deadlock to emerge from meetings in which he was involved.[144]

Pompidou agreed to a meeting scheduled for 13 December, but he insisted that the U.S. not settle or discuss economic disputes with any other European leader before that.

According to one report, Prime Minister Heath demonstrated the importance of these economic issues for broader U.S. foreign policy objectives by refusing to meet President Nixon at all until the United States called a meeting of the Group of Ten for serious monetary bargaining.[145] One Kissinger associate speculates that Kissinger himself may have suggested this tactic to his counterpart in London, as a means of influencing President Nixon to rein in Connally.[146] If so, this would be a rare instance of a transgovernmental coalition of actors in different governments helping one of them to outmaneuver a domestic rival on a monetary issue. Even so, the President already had other evidence of political conflict. In any case, such evidence had its effects on policy by influencing Nixon's own calculations. During the autumn, the bureaucratic players argued and maneuvered. The stands taken by the Federal Reserve and the NSC, if not the Treasury, were understandable in light of their organizational missions. But again, there is little evidence that the President was forced to, accept a policy contrary to his own substantive judgment. As to basic trade-offs, Nixon was still in charge.

Connally called a Group of Ten meeting for 30 Novem-

[144] Kissinger, *White House Years*, p. 958.

[145] C. Fred Bergsten, *Toward a New International Economic Order: Selected Papers of C. Fred Bergsten, 1972-1974* (Lexington, Mass.: Lexington Books, 1975), p. 346.

[146] Interview. No confirming evidence for this speculation has been found.

ber and 1 December in Rome, where the U.S. first put forth specific proposals, scaling down earlier demands. The U.S. would eliminate the surcharge, Volcker said, in return for early decisions on trade concessions, progress in sharing defense costs, and an average dollar depreciation against OECD currencies of 11 percent. Such a realignment was expected to produce a balance-of-payments swing of $9 billion, rather than the $13 billion proposed earlier. During the executive session, Giscard d'Estaing complained about the American refusal to devalue the dollar. Connally interrupted, speaking slowly and savoring every word: "What would the gentleman's reply be if I suggested ten percent?" Flabbergasted silence prevailed in the room for over 30 minutes. The Europeans caucused. Connally's tactic had caught them without instructions from their governments as to specific figures for a settlement. But ten percent was a *larger* devaluation than many of them had in mind. After some further bargaining, Connally adjourned the Rome conference without a settlement, as had been agreed with Pompidou. But the impasse had been broken.[147]

The American willingness to discuss the gold price and other concessions opened the way for France and Germany to patch up their bilateral dispute. By December, the German float had carried the mark to a 10 percent appreciation against the French franc, and German industry was complaining vehemently. The German government was prepared to appreciate 4 percent against the franc. France had refused to move the franc up part way against gold to reduce the gap. But the same exchange-rate result could be accomplished if the dollar was devalued against gold, while the franc held its gold parity and the mark was upvalued slightly. President Pompidou and Chancellor Brandt met in Paris on 3 and 4 December. They worked out a

---

[147] *New York Times*, 30 November 1971, p. 1; 2 December, p. 1; 3 December, p. 69; *Washington Post*, 3 December 1971, p. 1; *Financial Times*, 1 December 1971, p. 1; Brandon, *Retreat*, pp. 239-240. Cf. Martin Mayer, *The Fate of the Dollar* (New York: Times Books, 1980), pp. 199-200.

coordinated stand to be taken in the forthcoming meetings with President Nixon, and they pledged to return to their efforts to create a European Economic and Monetary Union after the current crisis was surmounted.[148]

France and the United States struck a major deal at their summit meeting held in the Azores on 13 and 14 December. The financially knowledgeable Pompidou sat down with a nervous Henry Kissinger, carrying Connally's figures, and the two negotiated over the exchange rates of all the major countries. The United States played one of its two trump cards: The dollar would be devalued. France would accept an 8.6 percent revaluation of the franc against the dollar if the U.S. would raise the dollar-gold price from $35 to $38 an ounce. Pompidou implicitly agreed not to insist on an early return to dollar convertibility, so $38 actually became only the new "price at which the United States would not sell gold." The U.S. Treasury was unwilling to defend the new exchange rates with reserves as long as the realignment was smaller than it felt was necessary. Pompidou insisted on an end to floating rates, but he accepted a slight widening of margins. As to trade concessions, President Nixon settled for some vague language pointing to the "imminent opening of negotiations." Removal of the U.S. surcharge, the second trump, was held in reserve.[149]

The final scene of 1971 was played out in the red castle of the Smithsonian Institution in Washington on Friday and Saturday, 17 and 18 December. It was not clear that agreement would be reached even then until late on the second day. One central order of business was an agreement between Japan and the United States. Japan had agreed in principle that the yen could be revalued in the context

[148] *Financial Times*, 3 December 1971, p. 27; 6 December, p. 48; *New York Times*, 5 December 1971, pp. 6 and IV-2; 16 December, p. 1.

[149] Joint communiqué, Department of State, *Bulletin* 66 (10 January 1972):30-31; Kissinger, *White House Years*, pp. 959-962; Brandon, *Retreat*, pp. 240-241; Solomon, *International Monetary System*, pp. 204-205; *New York Times*, 15 December 1971, p. 1; *American Banker*, 15 December 1971, p. 1.

of a multilateral settlement. In private, Secretary Connally and the team led by Finance Minister Mizuta ended their tug of war at the figure of 16.9 percent revaluation of the yen against the dollar. (The weighted average appreciation of the yen against all major currencies was less, around 11 to 13 percent.)

More intractable were currency relations among the European states. Connally alternately threatened the Europeans and mediated among them. European cabinets were kept in continuous session in order to approve changes in negotiating positions. In the end, West Germany agreed to revalue by 13.6 percent against the dollar, 5 points further than France and Britain.[150]

For its part, the United States played its second trump, removing immediately the surcharge and the discriminatory feature of the investment tax credit. The U.S. did not resume convertibility or any other specific obligation to defend the dollar. Rather than its initial aim, the equivalent of a 12 to 15 percent dollar depreciation, Washington achieved an average depreciation of approximately 8 percent against all OECD currencies.[151]

The other major U.S. demands, for trade concessions and greater military burden-sharing, had been effectively separated from these negotiations. But Japan and the EC were also negotiating bilaterally with the United States on trade. Japan had accepted U.S. demands for textile export restraints in October. Connally declared in December that the administration would delay submitting to Congress the legislation to devalue the dollar on paper until further unspecified trade concessions were granted. Japanese and Eu-

[150] G-10 communiqué, Department of State, *Bulletin* 66 (1972):32-34; Brandon, *Retreat*, pp. 241-243; Solomon, *International Monetary System*, pp. 205-211; Mayer, *Fate of the Dollar*, pp. 200-203; de Vries, *International Monetary Fund*, vol. I, pp. 553-559; *American Banker*, 20 December 1971, p. 1.

[151] Testimony by Paul Volcker in House Committee on Banking and Currency, *To Amend the Par Value Modification Act of 1972: Hearings*, 93rd Cong., 1st sess., March 1973, p. 74.

ropean steel producers then agreed to tighten their "voluntary" restraints on exports to the U.S.[152] These concessions might have been made without use of the surcharge weapon.

The major states, except Canada, thus returned to pegged exchange rates. The Bretton Woods foundation was partly rebuilt, though no agreement had been reached on a set of rules to allocate future responsibilities for taking adjustment action. Pending further reform negotiations, the major states agreed that the band for legal currency fluctuation would be widened from 2 percent to 4.5 percent. The Smithsonian compromise was ratified immediately by the IMF Executive Board. President Nixon proclaimed the result "the most significant monetary agreement in the history of the world."[153]

CONCLUSION

The year 1971 witnessed a second and more dramatic turning point in U.S. international monetary behavior. In this instance, the strongest influences on U.S. policy were foreign exchange market and balance-of-payments conditions, the interstate power structure, and the predispositions and salient perceptions of the Washington leadership. These three perspectives—markets, power, and ideas—are necessary and largely sufficient for explaining the 1971 change.

As in 1965, changes in U.S. domestic politics were not a major influence on international policy content. There were changes in domestic politics after 1965, including the Republican presidential victory of 1968, an increase in protectionist interest-group pressure, and increasing demands for a more active incomes policy to deal with stagflation. A domestic politics perspective can help explain the domestic elements of Nixon's New Economic Policy. But it would have also led us to expect a general shift to higher direct

[152] *New York Times*, 16 October 1971, p. 1; Department of State *Bulletin* 66 (1972):784-785.

[153] *New York Times*, 19 December 1971, p. 1.

trade barriers, which did not occur. Moreover, neither public opinion nor major political challengers, nor even interest groups, oddly enough, were calling for the new international policies that were actually chosen. Other factors would probably have caused the observed policy changes regardless of objective domestic politics.

Still less does this case demonstrate that "organization matters." Modifications in the government's organizational structure after 1965 had little discernible effect on international monetary policy, and it is difficult to imagine that different arrangements could have made much difference. Most of the expectations of the organization perspective would have been mistaken. The various agencies produced conflicting recommendations, but the variation was not closely related to assumed agency missions and stakes. While advisers were divided, the policy was not the result of an internal bargain. The President personally made a clearcut choice in August, and it was implemented as intended until he modified instructions in November. It is true that, during the period from 1969 until mid-1971, U.S. international monetary policy was not produced by a highly centralized process. Through piecemeal actions and inaction, a bifurcated policy emerged, as would be expected by cybernetic theories of decision. But Nixon terminated that interlude with a lasting return to centralization in August 1971.

Clearly the shift in the dollar's position in international markets during the 1960s and early 1970s was the largest cause of the Nixon shock. The foreign exchange market, for several military and economic reasons, developed a persisting imbalance. By mid-1971, the American deficit had become extreme and signs of market disorder were becoming more frequent. Some major shift away from defending the dollar and toward depreciation was highly likely, whether or not surplus governments demanded gold, whether or not domestic groups demanded policy changes, and regardless of the intellectual predispositions of policy makers.

Market analysis is not sufficient, however, to explain aspects of the new policy other than depreciation. Market conditions did not determine whether convertibility would be formally abandoned, nor did they determine whether the United States would negotiate or would act unilaterally and coercively.

The postwar shift in the interstate power distribution adds to the explanation, though perhaps not to the degree often supposed. At the level of military resources, the global structure remained essentially bipolar. American power had slipped somewhat in general economic terms, but the U.S. remained a superpower. Still, Washington did not in fact behave after 1968 as would have been expected on grounds of its relative power. Instead, its high-level monetary diplomacy fell silent. During a period when financial market conditions were more favorable for negotiations, Washington waited for markets to bring about fundamental modifications within Bretton Woods. This "benign neglect" strategy, avoiding U.S. concessions, ran aground on the power structure, producing a stalemate. In the end, Washington had to change policy as well.

The issue-specific capacity of the United States to maintain convertibility also declined. Here too, however, the magnitude of the change has been exaggerated by looking exclusively at reserves as indicators of monetary power. In the summer of 1971, the official liquidity ratio was still not obviously unmanageable. The U.S. retained the power to consider at least two alternative strategies for ending the stalemate. Objective power and interest analysis is inadequate, as it often has been, for explaining policy content.

The choice of coercive unilateralism and going off gold in August can be explained only by taking into account changes in leaders' substantive predispositions, the earlier policies these produced, and the inflow of different specific ideas in 1971. In the early Nixon period, U.S. behavior was puzzling to a power analysis because of the top leadership's priorities and the "benign neglect" diagnosis. The sudden shift in 1971 from dollar defense to yielding to the market can be explained without analysis of changing intellectual outlooks. But the active, shocking character of the change was predictable, if at all, only on this basis. The departure of traditional attachments to Bretton Woods at the top level, and the salient beliefs that American problems were caused by foreign countries and that they would not change their behavior without actual coercion, convinced Nixon and Connally to reject the route of compromise bargaining in the summer. Ironically, it was these ideas, rather than the academic case for freely floating exchange rates, that were decisive in 1971. In sum, if earlier or later American leaders from different schools of thought had been in office instead, new U.S. policy in 1971 would probably have been substantially different.

Beliefs about the domestic political consequences of radical monetary change were highly salient but mutually offsetting. Given his impressions of the external and domestic situations, Nixon reluctantly embraced "the bugaboo of devaluation" while hurrying to cover it under a blanket of nationalist rhetoric and diplomatic intransigence. Fears of domestic cost may have outweighed hopes of domestic gain.

During 1972, the President's electoral strength relative to his rivals rose steadily, culminating in his landslide victory over Democratic Senator George McGovern. By this time, there were already signs of a third shift in U.S. international monetary policy.

5

Farewell to Bretton Woods

A YEAR after the Smithsonian conference ended, the United States shifted course a third time, by taking the lead in multilateral bargaining over new monetary rules once again. In an address to the annual meeting of the International Monetary Fund in the fall of 1972, the Secretary of the Treasury announced the first high-level American proposal for negotiated changes in the international monetary regime since 1965. This American plan would have created a more flexible par value system within the Bretton Woods framework. United States representatives gave signs of serious intentions to compromise in order to achieve agreement within that framework, and a process of negotiation in the IMF got under way.

Soon after it had begun, however, new currency crises erupted, and late on the night of 12 February 1973—14 months after the dollar devaluation and the much-heralded Smithsonian agreement—the Treasury Secretary called in the press to announce that the United States had devalued the dollar again by 10 percent. "Once more, Nixon does the unthinkable," remarked the *Economist*. Only a month earlier, bankers had been saying that the dollar's prospects were favorable. But in response to renewed heavy dollar selling, Washington secretly told Japan and the western European states that they should either free their currencies to float upward against the dollar, or assent to a second dollar devaluation. The Canadian dollar, the British pound, and the Swiss franc were already floating at the time. Japan decided to float the yen, the U.S. devalued the dollar, and France and Germany repegged their currencies again to reflect the dollar devaluation. The United States continued to reject any obligation to support its currency by market intervention or interest-rate changes.

The second devaluation, as carried out, proved to be a particularly significant policy shift in light of its systemic consequences. Contrary to expectations, currency traders soon began yet another and even more prodigious flight from the dollar into gold and European currencies. As a result, the continental European states also decided to float. By mid-March 1973, all major governments had abandoned the regime of agreed par values. Fourteen states met in Paris and certified what West German Finance Minister Helmut Schmidt called "the end of Bretton Woods." The international monetary system was now on a managed-floating basis.

This sequence of U.S. international monetary actions taken during late 1972 and early 1973 is treated here as a third major policy change. Little of this scenario had been predicted at the time. Why did the United States propose a negotiated monetary reform in 1972 rather than continuing the unilateralism of 1971? Why did it seek another dollar depreciation so soon after the 1971 adjustment rather than maintaining the new rates longer? The second devaluation appeared arbitrary to many observers at the time. Then, after surplus countries had again accepted new pegged rates, leading some to complain in fact that the dollar was now *under*valued, why did the Treasury Secretary make a point of announcing that the United States still refused to accept any obligation to defend these rates? (During this period, the Nixon administration also relaxed domestic price controls, and announced that restrictions on capital outflows would also be phased out.) Why did Washington invest considerable diplomatic effort in reforming and preserving the par value regime, and yet at the same time act in ways that raised questions about pegged rates and contributed to the regime's disintegration?

CHANGES IN DOMESTIC POLITICS

Changes had occurred in American domestic politics, but they were not responsible for these further policy changes. Indeed, rather than pressing the government toward further devaluation, domestic political developments were if anything moving in the opposite direction. In 1972, economic growth accelerated to a real rate of 6 percent, and the boom brought unemployment down to 5 percent. Consumer price inflation for 1972 was moderately low (3.4 percent). The public's 1971 discontent over economic prospects eased considerably.[1] In these circumstances, President Nixon was re-elected by a landslide. In early 1973 Nixon, fresh from his second inauguration ceremony, was in the process of proclaiming the long-sought armistice agreement in Vietnam. Like President Johnson in early 1965, Nixon was unusually free of domestic political constraints. An analyst monitoring mass opinion and electoral strength would not have anticipated changes in foreign economic policy.

Interest-group activity related to foreign economic policy had changed little since 1971. No major group or political challenger was calling for further monetary change, even though some groups would clearly gain from it. The AFL-CIO repeated its position in favor of general import controls, with no greater success. Some Wall Street leaders moved in parallel with Washington policy makers toward toleration of flexible exchange rates at least during a tumultuous transitional period. But policy probably would have taken the same course with or without Wall Street lobbying in Washington.

INTERNATIONAL POWER STRUCTURE

The economic power structure among the capitalist industrial states had lost its extreme concentration some years

---

[1] U.S., President, *Economic Report of the President 1974*, Tables C-2, C-26, and C-48. For public opinion data, see Chapter 3, note 47, above.

earlier, but the structure remained one centered on a relatively invulnerable economic superpower. As explained in Chapter 4, a power analysis would have expected the leading state, now a deficit country, to use its capacities to maneuver the other major financial and trading powers into a modified set of monetary rules assuring the United States greater exchange-rate flexibility. Instead, actual U.S. behavior first turned away from high-level activity in monetary affairs, then shifted to a coercive approach.

By late 1972, the United States had turned in a policy direction consistent with such a power analysis. The content of the 1972 plan seemed to acknowledge both the continuity and long-term shifts in the structure. The large size and relative closedness of the United States economy were reflected in Washington's emphasis on exchange-rate flexibility as a means of adjustment. The U.S. also sought greater symmetry of adjustment pressures. Under the proposed rules, reserve changes would trigger obligations of surplus as well as deficit countries to take adjustment measures. A state would be permitted to float, but it would then have to meet "more stringent standards of behavior in other respects."[2]

The Secretary's speech to the IMF meeting hinted that the U.S. might be persuaded to give up at least part of the reserve role of the dollar if necessary to obtain agreement. As to reserves, the United States said:

> We contemplate that the SDR would increase in importance and become the formal numéraire of the system. . . . Official foreign currency holdings need be neither generally banned nor encouraged. . . . Careful study should be given to proposals for exchanging part of existing reserve currency holdings into a special issue of SDR, at the option of the holder.[3]

The Americans were prepared to negotiate a system involving a return to dollar convertibility, albeit limited con-

---

[2] U.S., Department of State, *Bulletin* 67 (23 October 1972): 460-466.

[3] Department of State, *Bulletin* 67 (23 October 1972): 463.

vertibility, provided the other elements of the new regime fit American requirements.[4]

The 1972 proposals were not surprising from a power perspective. Neither was the American external strategy in the currency crisis in January 1973. Washington turned away from its previous attempt at dictation and returned to the strategy of high-level bargaining used in 1968 and before. But the power structure had not altered appreciably in one year. The substantial oscillations in U.S. policy in the early 1970s are anomalies for power analysis.

The significance of this lag in the American initiative should be underlined. The lag was a major reason that in 1973 the international monetary system lacked an agreed-upon set of rules that would have given traders greater confidence that payments imbalances would be adjusted in a predictable manner. Instead, uncertainty prevailed. Governments did begin negotiating toward a new regime late in 1972. If it had been closer to realization, private confidence would probably have been less fragile and more easily managed by governments than proved to be the case in early 1973. One ought not jump to the conclusion that this era demonstrated that no adjustable-peg regime is workable with open capital markets. The actual interstate stalemate was not inevitable.

If East-West détente eased the sense of external threat facing NATO and Japan, and thereby released economic conflicts among allies, nevertheless we can see from this period that these military-security relations were only a distant influence. Late 1972 and early 1973 were the very zenith of détente. Yet rather than bringing deeper allied conflict, this case revealed much smoother crisis management among governments than in 1971 or 1978.

[4] Cf. Robert Solomon, *The International Monetary System, 1945-1976: An Insider's View* (New York: Harper & Row, 1977), p. 240, and John Williamson, *The Failure of World Monetary Reform 1971-74* (New York: New York University Press, 1977), p. 79. See also *Economic Report of the President 1973* for a statement of the U.S. position.

A power perspective contributes to explaining this third case of policy change. But why, after proposing a modified par-value regime, did the United States then also send other signals tending to undermine such a regime? And why did the U.S. seek another currency adjustment, by means of negotiation or otherwise, so soon after the Smithsonian settlement?

AMBIGUOUS MARKET CONDITIONS

One might suppose that international market conditions forced the second devaluation, that 1973 was essentially an extension of 1971. Actually, during the year following the first devaluation, an international market perspective would have produced conflicting evidence, leaving no clear expectation for future U.S. policy. Balance-of-payments trends and currency market conditions were especially complex and easily subject to conflicting prognoses in 1972.

Some indicators seemed to show that the dollar remained overvalued, so that some market analysts might have looked for a further dollar depreciation. By the end of 1972, the United States was no closer to the turnaround sought in its trade account. In fact, the trade balance deteriorated from a deficit of $2.7 billion in 1971 to a deficit of $6.9 billion the following year, in spite of more favorable exchange rates. (The 1972 bilateral deficit with Japan constituted by far the largest share of the deficit, accounting for two-thirds.) Overall, the U.S. balance of payments showed a deficit of $10 billion on the official settlements basis, the largest yearly deficit on record except for 1971 (see Table 4). During most of 1972, currencies of most industrial countries traded at premiums above their new dollar parities.

On the other hand, by the end of 1972 a number of indicators led most European currency specialists to conclude that the dollar was probably on the road to recovery. Some initial worsening of the U.S. trade deficit had been expected, according to the J-curve hypothesis that the unfavorable effects of depreciation on the balance would come quickly while the favorable effects would be delayed several quarters. During the latter half of the year, monthly U.S. trade data began to show signs of belated improvement. Most important, the underlying American competitive position had improved substantially because of the exchange-rate changes and comparative inflation performances. Unit labor costs in the United States remained virtually constant during 1971 and 1972, while unit costs (converted to U.S. dollars) were rising in other major countries. These trends were reflected in export prices. Overall, the American 12-month inflation rate in early 1973 was 3.4 percent, compared with 6.4 percent in West Germany, 6.9 percent in France, 6.3 percent in Britain, and 8.1 percent in the Netherlands. As the *Wall Street Journal* noted, "on the economic fundamentals, despite the U.S. balance of payments deficits, the U.S. dollar should be relatively strong compared with other currencies, with the exception of the yen." Early in January 1973, the dollar was in fact trading at its highest level in a year. The currency crisis two weeks later took many London dealers by surprise. "It's a tempest in a gin and tonic," one said drily. Later a New York bank economist mused, "It really snuck up on us. There's no reason for it, except that most foreign-exchange dealers are manic-depressive by nature."[5]

In short, it would be difficult to explain the second dollar devaluation, let alone the 1972 diplomatic shift, from an international market perspective focusing on fundamentals, the sort of perspective used heretofore. Underlying economic conditions had not yet made prevailing exchange-rate policy obviously irrational. Instead, currency

---

[5] IMF, *Annual Report 1973*, pp. 2-5; U.S., President, *International Economic Report of the President 1973*, pp. 34-42; *American Banker*, 30 January 1973, p. 3; *Wall Street Journal*, 5 February 1973, p. 1, and 12 February, p. 1. The improvement in the American competitive position, judging from relative wholesale prices of manufactured goods adjusted for exchange-rate changes, is displayed graphically in IMF, *Annual Report 1977*, Chart 8.

traders' behavior became increasingly detached from indicators of long-term equilibrium exchange rates during 1972 and 1973.

TRANSNATIONAL ACTORS' CAPABILITIES AND CONFIDENCE

The impetus for the second dollar devaluation came not from changes in underlying economic conditions nor from a change in foreign government behavior toward the U.S., but from a more complex interaction involving a new set of actors. Over the long term, private transnational monetary actors had emerged and had increased the resources under their control. Increasingly, governments were required to take into account the expectations of these actors as much as those of other governments. Private actors' expectations had long been guided primarily by underlying market conditions. But circumstances during 1971-1973 undermined their willingness to bet on the long term. Long-lasting payments imbalances became extreme, and central banks yielded to market pressure and changed parities, yet other actions during this period also weakened private confidence that new parities would last. Above all, governments had not resolved the stalemate among themselves regarding rules to assure payments adjustment. Transnational actors' behavior therefore came to be more sensitive to day-to-day rumors and official hints of parity changes. Under these conditions, governments could not be certain how a given move would affect the fragile private expectations. But the long-term increase in private capabilities meant that the consequences could be significant.

The potential for this kind of fragmentation was rooted in earlier policy decisions and market processes, though this was not fully appreciated in 1972. At the time of the Bretton Woods conference, the international mobility of short-term capital was much more restricted. Since the 1920s, quick movements of "hot money" had been able to affect exchange rates sharply in the short run. But from the early

1930s until the late 1950s, various industrial countries had imposed controls on these international capital movements. Bretton Woods rules permitted continuation of these controls.

After 1958 major governments relaxed capital controls, facilitating greater integration of an international financial market. Simultaneously, governments unwittingly served as midwives at the birth of new types of international financial institutions—multinational corporations and banks.[6] Thus, in addition to improvements in communications technology that increased the mutual sensitivity of national economies generally, there arose commercial organizations whose very structures straddled national frontiers. The horizons of transnational money managers are necessarily global. When a corporate treasurer in New York senses that the German mark will appreciate, he can protect or enrich his firm simply by accelerating intrafirm payments due in Germany and delaying receipts due his headquarters from its German subsidiaries. These "leads and lags" accomplished through regular business links have the same manifest effects on currency markets as old-fashioned speculation, and they can swell those effects enormously. Similarly, the creation of extraterritorial Eurodollar banks provided an especially efficient pipeline for transmitting the effects of changing monetary conditions in one country to other countries. Eurobanks made available a more conven-

[6] The origins and development of the Eurocurrency market are discussed in Richard N. Cooper, *The Economics of Interdependence* (New York: McGraw-Hill, 1968), pp. 116-122, and in Susan Strange, "The Market as an Actor and Environment" (London: Royal Institute of International Affairs, 1973). The origins, size, and consequences of the Eurocurrency markets have given rise to much debate. Also see Jonathan David Aronson, *Money and Power: Banks and the World Monetary System* (Beverly Hills, Calif.: Sage, 1977), pp. 50-51; Susan Strange, *International Monetary Relations*, vol. 2 of *International Economic Relations of the Western World 1959-1971*, ed. Andrew Shonfield (London: Oxford University Press, 1976), pp. 59f; and *Eurocurrencies and the International Monetary System*, ed. Carl H. Stem, John H. Makin, and Dennis E. Logue (Washington: American Enterprise Institute for Public Policy Research, 1976).

ient source of funds for quick speculation against declared parities.

The resources controlled by these transnational actors steadily grew in relation to central banks' reserves. At the end of 1971, official reserves totalled $122 billion. The Eurocurrency market alone was estimated to have grown to $71 billion by this time. A study by the U.S. Tariff Commission estimated total short-term assets held at the end of 1971 by "private institutions on the international financial scene" at $268 billion.[7]

During the first two decades of the adjustable-peg regime, private currency traders generally took officially declared parities as measures of long-term equilibrium. They expected stability except in particular cases where fundamental economic comparisons began clearly to suggest that a parity change was overdue. Most of the time, banks and corporations accepted official assurances and held uncovered foreign currency assets. Some large banks "made a market" in foreign exchange during calm periods, acting as surrogate central bankers balancing demand and supply at the official parity.

When traders' expectations about a given currency did change, they collectively began to move funds. Because of these long-term structural changes, these flows became progressively more massive and quicker to respond. For example, on the day before the pound was devalued in 1967, the Bank of England lost $250 million. But then in a two-day period in 1969, in order to hold the deutsche mark at its ceiling, the German Bundesbank was required to purchase $2.5 billion. On the morning of 5 May 1971, the Bundesbank slammed the window shut after taking in $1 billion in the first 40 minutes of trading. The flight out of

[7] IMF, *Annual Report 1973*, Table 9; Bank for International Settlements, *Forty-Second Annual Report* (Basle, 1972), pp. 154-155; *Wall Street Journal*, 12 February 1973, p. 2. The Eurocurrency estimate excludes double-counting.

the dollar in late January and early February 1973 was estimated at $10 billion.[8]

Particular policy decisions by governments during these last years of the par-value regime helped undermine private confidence in par values. In brief, major governments begin to signal a greater willingness to change parities while simultaneously indicating an unwillingness to defend new parities strongly. Thus, even when a new parity was regarded by all actors as consistent with underlying economic conditions, uncertainty could cause the government to hold back, which in turn caused private actors to remain apprehensive and ready to move quickly on only fragments of evidence, in order to protect themselves in case of a further parity change. Banks that in earlier squalls had acted as "market makers" now lost confidence that central banks would back them if they held against the tide. Private actors were less likely to engage in equilibrating speculation.[9]

More generally, the interstate stalemate undermined private confidence. Governments had failed to negotiate modifications in the Bretton Woods rules that would provide a legitimate long-term framework in which parity adjustments could be carried out more promptly and smoothly. Lacking such a framework, governments began yielding to speculators separately in an ad hoc manner. Where it was all leading was unclear in the absence of interstate agreements. If such a framework had been in place and governments had carried out its rules, the massive currency movements of early 1973 would have been less likely.

Evidence of private actors' capabilities and the greater fragility of their confidence appeared soon after the Smithsonian settlement. In mid-1972, they attacked the pound sterling while Britain's balance of payments was still in sur-

[8] Robert W. Russell, "Crisis Management in the International Monetary System, 1960-1973," paper delivered at the annual meeting of the International Studies Association, New York City, 16 March 1973; *American Banker*, 13 February 1973, p. 3.

[9] Aronson, *Money and Power*, p. 106.

plus. The surplus was declining and there were threats of a dock strike and faster inflation, but the pound previously had weathered much worse conditions. One difference now, however, was that in his March budget message, Chancellor of the Exchequer Anthony Barber had made a statement to the effect that the home economy should not be distorted in order to defend unrealistic exchange rates. Then, on 19 June the shadow Chancellor, Denis Healy, predicted that sterling would be devalued within a month or two. Though the parity was not yet obviously unrealistic, these statements were enough to set off some selling, which itself further undermined confidence. Suddenly over the next three days, huge amounts of sterling were dumped on the market. The Bank of England, after providing intervention support totalling $2.6 billion, allowed the pound to float on 23 June 1972.[10]

This victory for speculators seemed to invite other challenges. Recognizing the profits to be made, some banks reportedly organized "rings" that would secretly enter the market with large transactions intended to move an exchange rate temporarily, drawing "greater fools" in after them, and they would then reverse the transactions and take the speculative profit. The sudden decline of the pound in the fall of 1972 has been attributed to such manipulations.[11]

The January 1973 dollar crisis similarly surprised many bankers. In this case the stimulus was not manipulations by "rings." Events in Europe having little to do with the American balance of payments nevertheless dragged in the dollar because of its international role. Traders were stirred first by the lira, about which, ironically, President Nixon had wished not to hear. On 20 January, the Italian government instituted a two-tier market, hoping to contain

[10] Charles A. Coombs, "Treasury and Federal Reserve Foreign Exchange Operations," Federal Reserve Bank of New York *Monthly Review* 54 (September 1972): 212-216.

[11] Aronson, *Money and Power*, pp. 110-111.

speculative capital flight by allowing the capital-account lira to float downward. Much of this flight was directed toward Switzerland, where banks were relying on it to help them escape a credit squeeze. A number of Swiss banks reacted to Italy's policy change by dumping some of their U.S. dollar reserves in exchange for Swiss francs. This pushed the dollar down and the franc up to its ceiling. Expectations of another central bank surrender fueled some additional speculative purchases of Swiss francs. Citing the need to maintain its domestic anti-inflation policy intact, the Swiss government quickly withdrew from the exchange market on 23 January, allowing the franc to float. "Here we go again," said the *Economist*.[12]

That even the orthodox Swiss could be pushed off their peg so readily seemed especially tempting (or worrisome). The Swiss franc promptly shot upward, and soon transnational actors had begun another flight out of the dollar. The speculation jumped to the German mark, the only strong currency still relatively free from capital controls and still pegged. There had been no sudden change in U.S. or German economic prospects, though the two governments did confirm the size of the 1972 trade imbalances during this period. Currency intervention by the Bundesbank and to a limited extent by the Federal Reserve was not sufficient to satisfy all traders about the German resolve to hold the parity. Then, over the weekend, the press reported that Finance Minister Helmut Schmidt had said that Treasury Secretary Shultz had recommended floating the mark rather than imposing controls. The two governments denied the reports, but hot money inflows swelled again, despite new German restrictions.[13] More and more oper-

[12] *Economist*, 27 January 1973, p. 71; see also *American Banker*, 31 January 1973, p. 1.

[13] *New York Times*, 4 February 1973; *Journal of Commerce*, 6 February 1973, p. 1; *American Banker*, 6 February 1973, p. 1; *Wall Street Journal*, 5 February 1973, p. 1.

ators who did not consider parities fundamentally out of line nevertheless felt unable to resist the tide.

"Ideological Floaters" Rise to the Top

At this point, Washington decided to move. The content of its new policy as well as concurrent U.S. actions were strongly shaped by the ideas circulating in Washington at the time. Intellectual changes help explain the oscillation in American monetary diplomacy. They clarify why Washington responded to ambiguous market conditions with another devaluation so soon after the Smithsonian settlement. The cognitive analyst would have been able to anticipate some of the elements of U.S. action that seemed to raise questions about the par-value regime that the U.S. was simultaneously trying to reform. After considering these factors, we will be in a position to return to the account of the complex process of bargaining among states and transnational actors, a process that ended with the collapse of the par-value regime.

The Return to Compromise Diplomacy

After the Smithsonian conference President Nixon turned back to other matters. During 1972, he had been occupied with his re-election campaign, the war and armistice negotiations with Hanoi and Saigon, and nuclear arms-control negotiations with the Soviet Union. The Vietnam armistice talks were moving toward conclusion when currency turmoil began again in January 1973. Nixon was fresh from a landslide election victory and his second inauguration. The first devaluation had certainly not cost him electoral support. President Nixon approved the major monetary moves of this period, but little is known about his personal views about them. He received some conflicting recommendations, as will be shown below, and on each occasion he approved the course of action recommended by the Treasury Secretary.

In May 1972, Treasury Secretary John Connally had resigned. To replace him, President Nixon chose George P.
Shultz. Nixon continued his practice of delegating responsibility for economic policies to an "economic czar" above
the cabinet level. Nixon formalized Shultz's supra-cabinet
status in December 1972 by naming him an Assistant to
the President as well.

Turnover in this pivotal position again signified changes
in reigning predispositions. Shultz represented a stance different from Connally's on each of two major dimensions.
First, Shultz brought back an inclination toward multilateral compromise rather than unilateral coercive diplomacy
on monetary matters. Secondly, with Shultz and his colleagues, a "purer" laissez-faire strain in American thinking
came into its own, along with salient belief in the theory of
freely floating exchange rates.

George Shultz was a professionally trained economist,
the first member of his profession to become Secretary of
the Treasury. He had specialized in domestic industrial
relations and had had no experience either as a banker or
as a diplomat. While teaching at the University of Chicago,
he and Milton Friedman had become close associates with
similar views. After serving on various labor-management
arbitration panels, Shultz was appointed Secretary of Labor
in 1969. In mid-1970, Nixon, impressed with Shultz's personal strength and firm free-market beliefs, moved him
into the President's Executive Office as Director of the
Budget, one of the President's three top-ranking economic
advisers. Before he moved to the Treasury, Shultz's duties
were almost entirely in nominally domestic matters. As one
might have expected from differences in education and
experience, he did not share some of the predispositions
that had been held by Douglas Dillon, Robert Roosa, and
others from the New York banking community. There is
little evidence that the benefits and prestige of the dollar's
world-banker role were salient or a source of pride for
Shultz.

With the elevation of Shultz, the tendency toward unilateralism and the tolerance for conflict with allies that had
characterized Connally were replaced by more familiar
American ideas about alliance leadership. Shultz was more
inclined to avoid overt conflict if possible, preferring to
ensnare allies in joint decision making. In this respect, his
predispositions paralleled those of Henry Fowler, Francis
Bator, and William Martin, as well as Arthur Burns and
Paul Volcker.

If the more coercive school of thought had remained in
control, a return to American monetary-reform initiatives
would surely have been less likely.[14] Connally had continued to stall. By contrast, soon after taking office, Shultz
met with President Nixon, in June 1972. He argued successfully that the United States should now develop a position on the future shape of the monetary system, that the
American initiative should emphasize rules for greater exchange-rate flexibility, and that it should be unveiled at the
fall 1972 IMF meetings.[15] To discuss and approve the content of the plan, Shultz formed a special senior group. He
opened the policy process to the Secretary of State, whose
outlook had been squelched under Connally. Henry Kissinger was able to attend or send a deputy, even though
he rarely did either. The group's other members were Arthur Burns, Herbert Stein (who had become Chairman of
the Council of Economic Advisers), Peter Flanigan (who
had succeeded Peter Peterson as Executive Director of the
Council on International Economic Policy), and Under Secretary Paul Volcker. The group met periodically and secretly in Shultz's office.[16]

[14] Interviews with two Shultz associates. Cf. George P. Shultz and Kenneth W. Dam, *Economic Policy Beyond the Headlines* (New York: Norton,
1977), p. 116.

[15] W. H. Bruce Brittain, "Two International Monetary Decisions," in
U.S., President, Commission on the Organization of the Government for
the Conduct of Foreign Policy (Murphy Commission), *Appendices*, 7 vols.
(1975), vol. 3, p. 134.

[16] Interviews with members of the group.

This difference between the more unilateral and the more traditional predispositions was again manifested early in 1973. Rather than announcing a fait accompli or issuing public demands or threats to foreign leaders, Shultz and his group decided to send Volcker on a secret mission to foreign capitals to bargain privately over a joint response to the currency crisis. In 1972 and 1973, U.S. "interests" could easily have been interpreted otherwise. The circulation of ideas through Washington helps explain the oscillations of American monetary diplomacy.

Some critics of the Shultz group regarded its policies as "isolationist," but this characterization was not accurate. These critics favored a particular type of international monetary coordination—the established IMF and Group of Ten arrangements requiring currency intervention and domestic policies to defend par values. Under Nixon and Shultz, the United States did refuse to intervene heavily in support of the dollar or to bend domestic monetary policy away from domestic objectives. But under them, the United States also offered a long-run plan for interstate monetary cooperation on a different basis. They began negotiations toward this end, even if at the same time they also refused some demands from foreign governments. U.S. policy was again mixed. The genuine attitudes of this leadership group were not so much isolationist as they were laissez-faire.

Laissez-faire and the Theory of Floating Rates

This brings us to the second consequential change in predispositions. Relatively pure free-market thinking penetrated further in high Washington circles. Shultz explained his own philosophy in clear, classical liberal terms soon after leaving the Treasury:

> I think no one should aspire to manage the economy— the Secretary of the Treasury or whatever. I certainly never had that idea. That is, I think the basic idea about our economy is that it manages itself. For example, the

policy of competition is one that helps the economy manage itself.[17]

In a book published soon thereafter, Shultz declared:

Leadership is all too often equated with doing something and patience equated with indecision. Indeed, one of the most difficult problems for economic policy is finding ways to "do nothing" while waiting for the lagged effects of actions already initiated to work their way through the market process.[18]

Regarding international monetary policy, Herbert Stein has said, "Shultz, Flanigan, and I were ideological floaters."[19] They believed that freely flexible exchange rates would be the ideal cooperative monetary system. The ascendancy of the Triffin school in Washington during the 1960s was giving way to the Friedman school in the 1970s. At that time, adherents to Friedman's theory were still in a distinct minority even in America. Even more, they recognized that, although their first preference was for all states to cooperate by turning exchange rates over to the market, a diplomatic initiative to that effect would be futile. Shultz regarded the reserve-indicator scheme for enforcing greater flexibility as the closest thing to floating that could be negotiated within the IMF. This technical idea was in fact suggested to him first by Friedman.[20]

Observers monitoring these cognitive changes in the Washington leadership were not surprised by several of the features of U.S. policy that interacted with other events to undermine the par-value regime, despite the simultaneous American effort to reform that regime. Mandatory domestic wage and price controls were relaxed unexpectedly soon after the 1972 elections. The most powerful champion of controls—Connally—had been succeeded by Shultz. Like

[17] Interview by Hobart Rowen, *Washington Post*, 14 April 1974, p. A21.
[18] Shultz and Dam, *Economic Policy*, p. 2.
[19] Interview with Herbert Stein.
[20] Interview with George Shultz.

Nixon, Shultz had been one of the most determined opponents of controls and predictably, he and his colleagues favored dismantling them. The administration claimed that on the empirical evidence the costs of domestic controls had been "surprisingly small during 1972." They argued that nevertheless "there was every reason to believe" that the burdens would become serious.[21] They were anxious to act, on the basis not of new evidence but of their predispositions. A different American school of thought processing the same 1972 data would have been less likely to reach the same policy inference.

Another feature of U.S. policy influenced by ideology was the use of international capital controls. Herbert Stein reports that "removing international capital controls was regarded very highly by Shultz and me as a symbol of our determination to re-establish freedom in *some* market."[22] Still another manifestation was the appearance of the first official American suggestions of floating. In early 1973, measurements of equilibrium exchange rates were ambiguous. When traders began again to flee the dollar, the Shultz group interpreted this as a market signal that governments should cease defending existing rates. During the ensuing interstate bargaining, the Treasury Secretary advanced the idea of floating more than once, even though the established American policy position centered on reform of the par-value system. In general, a major reason that the American shift in 1973 took the direction of yielding to the currency market (rather than alternative courses of action) was that the incumbent leadership was predisposed in that direction. After the second devaluation, the refusal to countenance even a general pledge to support the dollar—even when they and virtually all observers agreed that it was

---

[21] *Economic Report of the President 1973*, pp. 66-68, 80. For a participant's account emphasizing non-ideological reasons for the relaxation, see Herbert Stein, "Price Fixing as Seen by a Price-Fixer: Part II," in *Contemporary Economic Problems 1978*, ed. William Fellner (Washington: American Enterprise Institute for Public Policy Research, 1978), pp. 129-133.

[22] Interview with Stein.

then at or below its equilibrium—is also much easier to explain when one takes these ideological predispositions into account.

The idea of floating had moved into Washington at the top, but it had not taken over completely. As noted earlier, floating was anathema to Arthur Burns as well as to many others, and they were also less hostile to incomes policies and capital controls. These substantive differences help explain why the U.S. government failed to advocate a floating regime before 1973.[23] Intellectual differences manifested themselves in mixed policy.

Specific Diagnosis of the Deficit

While turnover in top offices gave greater influence to these two general beliefs, the Treasury's more specific internal diagnosis of the U.S. deficit had remained essentially the same since 1971. At that time Paul Volcker and his staff had calculated that economic fundamentals would (given certain policy constraints) require a dollar depreciation of 12 to 15 percent. Though the U.S. had agreed to a lesser amount at the Smithsonian conference, not all U.S. officials expected this adjustment to be adequate. By the earlier Treasury diagnosis, the dollar remained overvalued. In early 1973, the administration apparently expected improvement in the trade balance in the absence of further depreciation, but not sufficiently rapid improvement to avoid currency market disturbances.[24] Arthur Burns had believed in 1971 that the realignment would be sufficient for

[23] Even as late as the summer of 1973, the Nixon administration expected that in the end the United States would be part of the "center of gravity," implying a par value. See a statement by Paul Volcker, in U.S., Congress, Joint Economic Committee, *How Well are Fluctuating Exchange Rates Working? Hearings*, 93rd Cong., 1st sess., 1973, p. 153.

[24] Volcker's Congressional testimony on 27 February 1973, reprinted in U.S. Treasury, *Annual Report of the Secretary of the Treasury on the State of the Finances 1973*, p. 467; Volcker, "Press Briefing, 13 February 1973" (Washington: U.S. Treasury), pp. 13-14; Volcker, "Press Conference," New York, 16 February 1973 (Washington: U.S. Treasury), p. 22.

international equilibrium. But when markets resumed dollar selling in late January 1973, Burns and others at the Federal Reserve concurred with the judgment that the dollar was still overvalued.[25]

The earlier diagnosis provided a ready basis for interpreting new events in the context of highly mixed market signals. Not all currency traders or governments were sure that the dollar remained overvalued. But most of the U.S. administration, convinced that it was, took the new speculation to be confirmation of that diagnosis. They perceived in the maze of indicators a case for further depreciation. They calculated that a second devaluation would finally quiet the speculative pressure disturbing the exchange markets. Transnational actors could then have greater confidence that it was safe to hold dollars. After the decision, according to a key participant:

> People felt that this time we had really done it! Now there will be no question about the dollar being out of line. This problem will now be out of the way during the reform talks.[26]

In Shultz's view, they had little choice. The move was an accommodation to reality, to long-term changes in the world economy.[27] These beliefs led the Washington leadership to seek a second devaluation only a year after the first.

The Treasury's diagnosis was sharply disputed by some financial analysts at the time. The second dollar devaluation was criticized as being hasty and unnecessary for payments adjustment, damaging to confidence in the dollar, and counterproductive in that it would aggravate American inflation.[28] On this last count, the decision was evidently fa-

[25] Interviews with Federal Reserve officials.

[26] Remarks to a colloquium at the Center for International Affairs, Harvard University, 16 January 1976. Interviews with other participants confirm this point.

[27] Interview with Shultz.

[28] Leland B. Yeager, *International Monetary Relations: Theory, History and Policy*, 2d ed. (New York: Harper & Row, 1976), p. 597; William McC.

cilitated by a miscalculation: The administration underestimated the degree to which the depreciation would raise American prices.[29]

BARGAINING AMONG STATES AND TRANSNATIONAL ACTORS

The Volcker Agreement

Secretary Shultz and his senior policy group concluded in February that "the markets were telling everybody" that further exchange-rate change was needed. Shultz, Stein, and Flanigan preferred a free float, but Burns was opposed. It was decided to send Volcker by plane on a secret mission to explore the possibilities with top leaders of major governments. Shultz met with President Nixon on 6 February and secured his approval. Evidently no case against a second dollar devaluation was presented to the President.

George Shultz described the message sent to allied governments in these words:

> We put out two propositions. Either change the exchange rates in the form of a second devaluation, or have an open float—take your choice.[30]

Volcker flew first to Tokyo, knowing that the Europeans would insist that Japan appreciate the most. In 1972, Japan's current account surplus had grown further quarter after quarter, despite the 12.5 percent effective yen revaluation in 1971 and even while the Japanese economy's real growth was accelerating. Prime Minister Kakuei Tanaka

Martin, "Statement before the Subcommittee on International Finance of the Committee on Finance, United States Senate" (1 June 1973); Arthur B. Laffer, "The Bitter Fruits of Devaluation," *Wall Street Journal*, 12 January 1974; Charles A. Coombs, *The Arena of International Finance* (New York: Wiley, 1976), pp. 225-239.

[29] According to an interview with a senior participating economist. See also *Washington Post*, 14 April 1974, p. H1.

[30] Interview with Shultz.

had nevertheless pledged publicly that the government would not revalue again.

Volcker was taken to the official residence of Finance Minister Kiichi Aichi, where he presented a letter from President Nixon. Volcker requested that Japan revalue the yen immediately by another 10 percent at least, and that Japan accept a dollar devaluation of 10 percent. Washington in this case, in contrast to 1971, used a diplomatic strategy of bargaining initiated by American promises (devaluation by the United States) as well as threats. Volcker indicated that Japan would have to go further than the Europeans. He revealed, to Aichi's surprise, that European governments had already given their support to the U.S. position.

Aichi asked for more time, arguing that the Smithsonian rates had not had enough time to show their results. He said his government was preparing further trade liberalization measures. Japanese officials maintained that that moment was an awkward one for technical and political reasons having to do with the Japanese budgetary process, and they insisted that another revaluation would seriously damage Tanaka's already strained political position. Tokyo would not agree to a 10 percent yen revaluation. They said that a float was the only possible currency measure the government would take. Volcker declared that some action was necessary immediately. Otherwise, he threatened, the U.S. could be forced to turn to import barriers.[31]

Volcker then flew on to Europe, while speculative funds were flowing heavily into central banks. Meanwhile, Federal Reserve officials departed for the monthly central bank meeting in Basel not knowing about the policy switch. Volcker had a round of secret meetings with British Prime Minister Edward Heath and the Finance Ministers of Britain, West

[31] *New York Times*, 14 February 1973, p. 55; *Wall Street Journal*, 14 February 1973, p. 4; interviews with American and Japanese policy makers; interview conducted by Professor Kent Calder, Harvard University, and provided to the author.

Germany, France, and Italy. Tokyo sent Takashi Hosomi, Vice Minister of Finance, to join the others in Bonn. After three days, agreement was reached.

Finance Minister Helmut Schmidt first renewed West Germany's unsuccessful effort to assemble a joint float of the EC currencies against the dollar. To the Germans' surprise, France's Finance Minister Valéry Giscard d'Estaing was prepared to join for the first time. But Britain would not agree to repeg the pound to the DM, and so the joint float was not adopted. The European leaders then indicated their willingness to effect a dollar devaluation and continuation of pegged rates.[32]

They joined ranks with Volcker in pressing Japan to commit herself to a larger adjustment. Volcker again asked Hosomi to accept a definite revaluation or a target rate for a floating yen, but Tokyo continued to resist. Eventually Volcker accepted what were considered satisfactory assurances of a yen float with relatively little official intervention. The Europeans were satisfied and Volcker was able to telephone the result to Shultz, who went before the press in Washington to announce it.[33] The United States would devalue the dollar again, the Western European states would put the devaluation into effect, and Japan would allow the yen to float.

These interactions are best understood as traditional bargaining among states, overlaid with a sort of bargaining between states on the one hand and transnational actors on the other. The states reached agreement more easily than in 1971. One set of reasons is found in interstate relations. These countries, considered as producers, still faced conflicts of interest. But in 1973, the secret American bargaining initiative probably provoked less resistance than public unilateralism would have. At the same time, the other

---

[32] *New York Times*, 14 February 1973, p. 55; *IMF Survey*, 26 February 1973, pp. 49-53.

[33] *New York Times*, 14 February 1973, pp. 55; interviews with American and Japanese policy makers.

governments knew that American willingness to bargain
was backed by a willingness to impose trade sanctions. Some
European commentators blasted what they saw as American mercantilism. But in this case, the change did not affect
currency relations within Europe, and so French industry,
for example, received the second devaluation rather calmly.
European governments spoke approvingly of the result.[34]
In Japan as well, reporters found "quiet confidence" among
bankers and businessmen, contrasting with the gloom of
1971. Many observers believed that Japan's economy would
not be seriously hurt by further revaluation up to about 18
percent, given price inelasticities of Japanese imports and
continued non-price protective barriers.[35] After the first
revaluation, Japan's export surplus had actually increased.
Japanese leaders no doubt resented being forced into a
reversal after pledging no further revaluation. But once a
multilateral front had formed, leaving Japan isolated, they
perhaps calculated that a float was their least unattractive
alternative.

Allied governments, especially in Europe, were much less
opposed to dollar depreciation than in 1971. Indeed, according to one American leader, they "were willing to tolerate more of a devaluation than I thought was necessary."[36] They, too, were affected by financial market disorder.
Western officials were under pressure not only from the
Americans but also from the money traders. While governments bargained with each other, they were also engaged in a joint effort to influence the expectations and
behavior of transnational actors. The role of transnational
actors probably eased the interstate outcome.

Secretary Shultz's announcement on 12 February described three basic steps within the context of a need to
reform and strengthen the framework for international

---

[34] *New York Times*, 14 February 1973, pp. 1, 53; 16 February, p. 57; and
18 February, p. 1; *Economist*, 17 February 1973, p. 78; *IMF Survey*, 26
February 1973, pp. 49-53.

[35] *New York Times*, 14 February 1973, p. 1.

[36] Interview.

trade and investment. The United States, he said, was dissatisfied with the pace of improvement in payments positions and in monetary reform negotiations, and was disturbed by new restrictions moving contrary to the direction he sought. Thus, first, the further 10 percent devaluation was undertaken, expressed in terms of the SDR for the first time in an attempt to undermine the symbolic role of gold. The new rates were considered sustainable, he said. "We have, however, undertaken no obligations for the U.S. Government to intervene in foreign exchange markets." Second, the administration revealed that its proposals for trade legislation would soon be sent to the Congress, and that they would include requests for authority not only to reduce barriers but also to raise tariffs and provide "safeguards" when these would advance American interests. Third, Washington would phase out its three programs restraining capital outflow, namely the interest equalization tax, Commerce Department controls on direct investment, and the Federal Reserve voluntary foreign credit restraint program.[37]

In later statements, Treasury leaders expressed satisfaction that the new currency realignment had in general followed the outlines of the type of monetary system envisioned in the 1972 U.S. plan. Imbalances had led to market-based adjustments, with symmetrical participation by surplus countries as well as deficit countries, arranged through multilateral negotiation. They expressed the hope that by correcting the long-standing imbalances, the "Volcker agreement" would speed the reform negotiations toward a new set of rules that would make whirlwind trips unnecessary.[38]

The Paris Agreement, March 1973

Before the next meeting of the Committee of Twenty, however, this second interstate pact had also collapsed. The

[37] Department of State, *Bulletin* 68 (12 March 1973): 298-305.

[38] Paul Volcker, "Press Briefing, 13 February 1973"; *New York Times*, 14 February 1973, p. 53; *Wall Street Journal*, 20 February 1973, p. 1.

Volcker agreement lasted only 18 days. Contrary to official hopes, the second devaluation, as implemented, proved destabilizing rather than stabilizing in the financial markets. Washington made clear that it would prefer not to back private stabilizing speculators with official intervention. Indeed, rather than imposing a traditional "devaluation package" of contractionary domestic measures, the U.S. had *relaxed* domestic price controls and had announced a plan to scrap capital outflow controls. This combination of official actions damaged willingness to hold funds in dollar form, setting off portfolio adjustments.[39] Speculators' repeated lucrative successes encouraged renewed assaults on the remaining central banks still prepared to sell strong currencies for dollars. Many individual traders believed that the dollar was now undervalued. Yet, once the bandwagon got rolling again, collectively they soon found themselves again selling rather than buying. The collective behavior was different from the sum of the individual views, and it amounted to a veto of the Volcker agreement.

Immediately after the second devaluation, the commercial lira was freed to float alone, like the currencies of Canada, Britain, Switzerland, and Japan. The U.S. Federal Re-

[39] Walter S. Salant, in "The Post-Devaluation Weakness of the Dollar," *Brookings Papers on Economic Activity* (2:1973), writes (p. 485): "Because [the second devaluation] was quite unexpected, it must inevitably have raised the fear that it could happen again, especially since it was medicine that the U.S. Treasury appeared to enjoy taking. One investment adviser who believed that the dollar was undervalued explained that he did not recommend purchase of dollars because, having thought the dollar already cheap before the second devaluation and having persuaded clients to buy dollar-denominated assets, he had made a mistake that proved very costly to them. Although his conviction that the dollar was undervalued was even stronger after the second devaluation than before it, his confidence in his own judgment was naturally shaken. Many others must have felt the same way. The second devaluation appeared to be quite arbitrary; if the dollar could be devalued arbitrarily once, it could be again. This response to it, moreover, was reinforced by the U.S. government's declaration at the same time that it intended to end the controls over the outflow of capital and to refrain from market support of the dollar."

serve also remained on the sidelines, leaving Germany, France, and smaller countries pegging to the dollar. The dollar settled at about 16 percent below its mid-1970 value against a weighted average of OECD currencies.[40] On 15 February, German Finance Minister Schmidt unaccountably told the press that the Common Market had agreed in principle that in the event of another currency crisis, they could float together against the dollar. "The move is being held in reserve."[41] For a week, currency trading nevertheless remained calm, and the Bundesbank was able to unload $1 billion of its swollen reserves.

Signs of a lack of confidence continued flashing in the gold market, however. At the beginning of 1973, the London gold price had risen to about $65, and it continued on to new highs after the February negotiations. Volcker proposed to other governments that they sell gold to try to hold down the price. At least two governments were eager to do so, but France refused, and no gold was sold.[42] On 22 February, gold leaped by almost $10 an ounce to $90 in very heavy trading. That set off another deluge of dollar selling and "leads and lags." A week later, on 1 March, the Bundesbank absorbed $2.6 billion—a new record for a single day—and European governments closed their foreign exchange markets for two weeks.[43]

During these events, private bank and corporate leaders were moving toward the view that, although they were not attracted to a regime of floating exchange rates, an effort to maintain adjustable pegs at this point might produce even more disorder. More market operators were becom-

[40] Testimony by Paul Volcker, House Committee on Banking and Currency, *To Amend the Par Value Modification Act of 1972: Hearings*, 93rd Cong., 1st sess., 27 February 1973, p. 74.

[41] *Wall Street Journal*, 26 February 1973, p. 1.

[42] Interview; Solomon, *International Monetary System*, p. 321; *New York Times*, 25 February 1973, p. 1.

[43] *American Banker*, 26 February 1973, p. 1; *Wall Street Journal*, 26 February 1973, p. 1; 2 March, p. 1; *New York Times*, 23 February 1973, p. 1; 24 February, p. 1; and 2 March, p. 1.

ing convinced that floating rates might bring relief, at least temporarily.[44] The whole was different from the sum of its parts.

The next initiative for joint state action came from Europe. Over the weekend of 3-4 March, the EC Council of Finance Ministers met in Brussels, together with the central bank Governors, to discuss their response. The German government cabled Washington that the EC was moving toward agreement.

On 3 March, the monetary crisis was discussed at a White House meeting that included the President, his "quadriad" of economic advisers—Shultz, Stein, Burns, and Roy Ash, director of the budget—and Volcker. The President raised a question about foreign-policy implications and told the group to confer with Kissinger. Up to this point, Kissinger had hardly been involved at all. After reading the German cable, Kissinger told the economists that it would be unwise for the United States to abdicate leadership entirely by remaining absent from an international conference at which world monetary arrangements would be fundamentally changed and where U.S. interests might be affected. Shultz and Kissinger later conferred further with President Nixon. The United States then sought a joint meeting with the Europeans. The EC Council invited the other members of the Group of Ten plus Switzerland to attend a meeting in Paris the following Friday, 9 March.[45]

Anticipating that the EC would cease pegging against the dollar, Washington was now presented with the question that had not arisen until this time: Should the dollar be a truly floating currency? Arthur Burns reportedly accepted floating under these conditions but favored limited market intervention. He took the position that the new disturbance

[44] *American Banker*, 2 March 1973.
[45] Elizabeth Stabler, "The Dollar Devaluations of 1971 and 1973," in Murphy Commission *Appendices*, vol. 3, pp. 154-155; interview with a participating American official; *New York Times*, 4 March 1973, pp. 1 and 2; 5 March, p. 1.

reflected a confidence problem; markets were not really signaling that the dollar should depreciate even further. Burns argued that a joint announcement that governments were prepared to intervene to support the new rates would be sufficient, with perhaps a small amount of actual intervention, to calm the markets and bring back stabilizing speculators.[46] While he recommended limited intervention, Burns nonetheless shared the judgment that, for the time being, pegged exchange rates could not be maintained under the old rules. After such an undeniable series of calamities, he felt forced to accept a shift to managed floating during a transitional period. He may have been influenced by conversations with financial leaders in the U.S. during this crisis. He found that they were far less disturbed by the prospect of floating than he would have thought, and he was surprised to learn that in the circumstances some even thought it was a good development.[47]

Shultz's position remained consistent with his different predispositions. Shultz argued that a small degree of intervention would not calm the markets. Reluctant to see the chance for a clean float slip away, Shultz told the President that "we had a choice of massive intervention or floating. You had to go whole-hog one way or the other. The President decided," as Shultz put it, "to go the floating route this time, not the half-way par value route."[48]

The Paris meeting on 9 March produced little. During the intervening week, the EC had decided to defer any separate European decisions until after one last attempt to extract American concessions. In Paris they presented Shultz, Burns, and Volcker with a "shopping list" of steps the United

[46] Interview with an American participant.

[47] Burns testimony, House Committee on Banking and Currency, *To Amend the Par Value Modification Act of 1972: Hearings*, p. 116.

[48] Interview with George Shultz. Little else is known about President Nixon's personal role in these decisions. He continued to remain distant from international monetary issues, relying on Shultz. Among the reasons might be the fact that during these weeks, the Watergate scandal was absorbing more and more of Nixon's attention.

States ought to take in order to deal with the disorder. French Minister Giscard d'Estaing in particular insisted that the crisis was the responsibility of the Americans. Washington had been granted its further depreciation in February, and to let the dollar fall any further now would impose an unfair and intolerable penalty on European producers, he said. The EC called on the U.S. to intervene in support of the dollar, using its own reserves or foreign borrowings; to tighten domestic credit and restrict capital outflows toward the same end; and to take several other measures. The French reportedly urged that the Common Market retaliate against the protectionist effect of any further dollar decline by imposing a surcharge on U.S. goods.[49]

Shultz declined politely to make any commitments. He did indicate privately that American interest rates would be rising, anyway, for domestic reasons. But there would be no pledge to intervene. An additional reason, or rationalization, was provided by the ongoing reform negotiations. The Shultz group preferred to withhold that trump at least until receiving in return a satisfactory new set of exchange-rate rules. The 14 states agreed to meet again on the following Friday, 16 March.[50]

The way was now finally clear for France to accept a "European solution," even without Britain. West Germany had first proposed in 1971 that the EC countries peg their own exchange rates together while floating free of the dollar. In February 1973 France had been prepared to tie itself thus to the deutsche mark if Britain would not take advantage by staying out, but Britain had indeed refused to join. During the Brussels meeting on 4 March, Schmidt had threatened that if the joint float were still not accepted, Germany would be forced to float alone again, in order to insulate itself from imported inflation. (Chancellor Brandt

[49] *New York Times*, 4 March 1973, p. 1; 5 March, p. 1; 13 March, p. 59; *Washington Post*, 13 March 1973, p. 1.
[50] *New York Times*, 9 March 1973, p. 49; 10 March, p. 1; 12 March, p. 1; *Wall Street Journal*, 12 March 1973, p. 1.

had immediately issued a firm retraction of this threat, insisting that "we cannot afford to be anything but good Europeans.") Britain's price for joining the "snake" was very high, in the view of her partners: Chancellor of the Exchequer Barber demanded, among other things, unlimited financial support for weak currencies.[51] So six other states decided to go ahead without Britain. At a Brussels ministerial conference on 11 March, Germany, France, Belgium, the Netherlands, Luxembourg, and Denmark adopted a joint float. They were joined a few days later by Norway and Sweden. France extracted from Germany a "sweetener" in the form of a further 3 percent revaluation of the DM, but Germany vetoed the French proposal for an EC surcharge. The currencies of Switzerland, Italy, and Britain would continue to float separately, with Ireland's pound pegged to the pound sterling. Schmidt announced to the press "the end of Bretton Woods."[52]

The Paris conference on 16 March 1973 in effect inaugurated a new international monetary regime of managed floating exchange rates. The United States now had—at least temporarily—a much more flexible system, without having made explicit concessions constraining its domestic economic policies or the reserve role of the dollar. In Paris, the Americans did accept an extremely loose ground rule under which floating exchange rates could be managed. The joint communiqué of 16 March declared the determination of the 14 governments

> to ensure jointly an orderly exchange rate system. To this end, they agreed on the basis for an operational approach toward the exchange markets in the near future and on certain further studies to be completed as a matter of urgency. They agreed in principle that official intervention in exchange markets may be useful at appropriate times to facilitate the maintenance of orderly

[51] *New York Times*, 5 March 1973, p. 1; 12 March, p. 47.
[52] *New York Times*, 12 March 1973, pp. 1, 47; 13 March, p. 59; *Wall Street Journal*, 13 March 1973, p. 13.

conditions, keeping in mind also the desirability of encouraging reflows of speculative movements of funds.
Each nation stated that it will be prepared to intervene
in its own market, when necessary and desirable, acting
in a flexible manner in the light of market conditions
and in close consultation with the authorities of the nation whose currency may be bought or sold. . . . It is
envisaged that some of the existing "swap" facilities will
be enlarged.[53]

The American delegation had thus continued to refuse any
but the most highly qualified commitment to intervene.
Shultz made much of the distinction between maintaining
a given set of rates and maintaining "orderly" business conditions, saying for example that the currency markets had
"not been all that disorderly in the last couple of weeks."[54]
The U.S. agreed also to review possible actions to encourage capital inflows and reflows of Eurocurrency funds into
the United States.

The refusal to enumerate new policies more specifically
also reflected continued bargaining between governments
and speculators. Governments were anxious not to signal
where new speculative assaults could be directed.[55] Several
European governments did announce further tightening
of direct measures to discourage inflows.

At the time, these new international arrangements were
not expected to be permanent. The crises had erupted in
the midst of slow reform negotiations, which continued.
Most foreign governments were opposed to floating as a
permanent regime, and the evidence indicates that at this
stage even the American government expected a return to
a modified par value regime. At a press conference in Paris,

[53] Department of State, *Bulletin* 68 (16 April 1973): 454-455. If any
further secret commitments were made, they remain secret at this writing.

[54] "Secretary George P. Shultz Press Conference, Paris, France, March
16, 1973" (Washington: U.S. Treasury).

[55] *New York Times*, 17 March 1973, p. 1.

Shultz was asked: "Mr. Secretary, do you intend the dollar to come back to a fixed parity one day?" He replied:

Well, we have outlined in the IMF speech a system that is basically a par value system designed to be more flexible than the system has been in the past, and you can read that speech. We haven't really changed our view about that.[56]

Shultz personally believed that under the pressure of "reality," government practices would have to become more flexible, and that then interstate agreement on new rules would be easier. He looked toward a meeting of the IMF in Nairobi in September 1973 as an occasion that might catalyze a settlement. He later expressed the belief that the five major governments had been in fact moving toward agreement through a series of private conferences of finance ministers, and that they would have completed the negotiations if it had not been for the oil crisis of late 1973.[57]

In sum, the outcome of March 1973 issued from a process of bargaining between states and transnational actors. Currency market conditions were ambiguous, so that governments and private participants found it difficult to diagnose the situation and to forecast what each other would do. Each side acted according to its strongest expectation, and the interaction of expectations produced the outcome. Private confidence in pegged parities had become fragile. Meanwhile, American leaders were predisposed toward floating. They interpreted the January run on the dollar as a signal for another depreciation. But given the weak confidence, transnational actors did not react in the way expected by theoretical market analysis. Government efforts to stabilize the markets produced the opposite effect. This in turn weakened government expectations that states

[56] "Shultz Press Conference, March 16, 1973." Cf. testimony of Paul Volcker, Joint Economic Committee, *How Well are Fluctuating Exchange Rates Working? Hearings*, p. 153.

[57] Interview with an American participant.

could manage these markets, and they withdrew from intervention altogether for a time.

CENTRALIZED DECISION MAKING

One analytical question remains. Did the internal organization of the U.S. government substantially affect policy content? Was policy a product of bureaucratic bargaining? As in the earlier cases, an organization perspective makes little independent explanatory contribution here.

No notable changes in the organizational structure intervened between 1971 and 1973. Decision making remained highly centralized. In this case the President in effect deputized his economic "czar" to be the center.

One organization, the Federal Reserve, had a clear institutional stake in these decisions. Its foreign exchange branch had been largely immobilized in August 1971. In February 1973, as expected, this office strongly favored resuming intervention in currency markets and objected to a second devaluation. But in contrast to August 1971, Federal Reserve Chairman Burns did not act entirely in accordance with this organizational stake. He and other Federal Reserve officials joined in the consensus favoring a second devaluation. Subsequently, however, Burns did lean more toward intervention than other senior officials.

On the whole, senior officials did not offer recommendations that differed according to their organizational positions. During the formulation of the 1972 reform proposals, there were differences over the wisdom of a floating regime and over whether the United States had an interest in maintaining the reserve role of the dollar. These differences help explain why U.S. actions in 1972 and 1973 were partially inconsistent. But the origin of the differences was not organizational missions. Each contending view had its adherents outside government and outside the United States. Once the process is conceptualized in terms of contending intellectual schools, the weakness of an organization perspective appears in relief. In the currency crisis of January 1973, the views of senior officials hardly differed at all. All shared the hunch that a further depreciation would steady the currency markets. It is difficult to imagine how a different organizational structure could have avoided this joint miscalculation.[58]

THE UNCERTAIN SEVENTIES

What might have been a transition to a new regime of "stable but adjustable" par values turned out to be a permanent arrangement. Even though many officials remained unconvinced of the theory of freely flexible exchange rates, major currencies continued to float throughout the decade of the 1970s. One reason was that macroeconomic conditions in industrial countries became and remained more unstable, making it difficult to identify currency parities that could be expected to last. The decade was a period of accelerated inflation and also of greater divergence among national inflation rates. Between 1960 and 1970, the average annual change in GNP deflators for the seven major industrial countries had been 3.4 percent, the individual country averages ranging from 2.7 to 4.8 percent. In 1974, the same countries registered an average inflation of 12 percent, and the national rates ranged from 7 to 21 percent.[59] Economies expected to diverge to this degree would be difficult to keep within the harness of fixed rates.

More spectacular of course, and related, was the revolution in world oil trade that erupted seven months after the Paris monetary conference. The sudden oil price increases, and more generally the shift in control to the pro-

[58] Cf. Brittain, "Two International Monetary Decisions," and Stabler, "Dollar Devaluations."

[59] IMF, *Annual Report 1975*, Table 2. The pattern of dispersion continued through 1978, while the overall average declined some. Both the average and the dispersion increased in 1979 and 1980. See IMF, *Annual Report 1978*, Table 10, and *Annual Report 1981*, Table 1.

ducer governments, threw payments balances into disarray. The changes in oil trade and their reverberations affected countries in different ways. One of the effects was a steep rise in the U.S. dollar at the end of 1973. At that point the dollar was almost back up to its Smithsonian effective rate. During the second half of 1973, the U.S. official settlements deficit disappeared, giving way to a surplus of approximately $9 billion at an annual rate. Other major countries, including some that had been criticizing the United States from atop payments surpluses, found themselves suddenly sliding into deficits. Even the most vocal opponent of floating, the French government, was forced to allow its franc to float out of the European "snake" in January 1974. Concern over the inconvertibility of the dollar abruptly evaporated, as governments scrambled for reserves and loans. There were serious fears that the global financial mechanism might even collapse under the strain of petrodollar recycling. Reflecting, and adding to, these woes was the deep recession of 1975.

The turbulence in economic and political conditions in the 1970s was accompanied by considerable confusion on the part of professional analysts of these phenomema. Established theories and techniques of macroeconomic management seemed discredited, but specialists were far from agreed on a new diagnosis of the immediate problems, let alone a prognosis or a prescription. Policy was enveloped in a thicker fog of intellectual confusion than earlier.

For the remainder of the 1970s, U.S. international monetary policy essentially stayed on the new heading established in early 1973. The reluctance to intervene in currency markets continued, excepting particular occasions when the government sent a signal that fluctuations were going "too far." In July 1973 and again in January 1975, for example, the Federal Reserve entered the market briefly to counter dollar weakness that was becoming extreme enough to impede normal financial business. In other words, the policy was to float with temporary "last-ditch" intervention but without a return to pegging. In the reform negotiations that had begun in 1972, the American voice became more unified and even doctrinaire in advocating a floating regime and a long-run policy of floating the dollar. This became particularly apparent after Shultz and Volcker were succeeded at the Treasury by William Simon and Jack Bennett, respectively, in June 1974. The latter refused to agree to a new set of rules requiring a par value for the American dollar. On the other hand, France in particular would not agree to a new regime that legalized floating.

These two governments decided to suspend their dispute at a meeting in Rambouillet in November 1975. The IMF Interim Committee, meeting in Jamaica in January 1976, then put the final touches on the new regime that replaced the original Bretton Woods arrangements. France accepted a new Article IV of the IMF Articles of Agreement that permitted a member state to follow any exchange-rate practice it chose, consistent with rather general obligations of good monetary "citizenship." The only constraints on states under the new regime were requirements to collaborate with the Fund, to "aim for orderly economic growth with reasonable price stability," to "intervene in the exchange market if necessary to counter disorderly conditions," and to "avoid manipulating exchange rates or the international monetary system in order to prevent effective balance of payments adjustment or to gain an unfair competitive advantage over other members."[60] The new regime did not include any precise rules for assigning symmetrical adjustment obligations, such as the U.S. had proposed in 1972. That source of interstate conflict remained subject to ad hoc bargaining. The United States accepted at Rambouillet a new procedure which allowed the IMF to vote to return to par values but which retained a veto for the U.S.[61]

As to international liquidity policy, the settlements at

[60] *IMF Survey*, 19 January 1976, pp. 20-21.

[61] Cf. Solomon, *International Monetary System*, chap. 17; Benjamin J. Cohen, *Organizing the World's Money: The Political Economy of International Monetary Relations* (New York: Basic Books, 1977). See also Williamson, *Failure of World Monetary Reform*.

Rambouillet and Jamaica also involved compromises. The IMF Committee of Twenty agreed that the role of gold should be reduced and the SDR should become the principal reserve asset. Thus, the new agreements abolished the official price of gold. The French, however, sought to preserve a role for gold. They also proposed that some of the gold that states had originally deposited with the IMF be returned to them, at the official price, permitting national governments to reap the capital gain represented by the now-higher market price of gold. This proposal was accepted by the other governments. Another one-sixth of the IMF's gold was auctioned on behalf of a trust fund for developing countries, as proposed by the U.S. The new arrangements did little to increase the actual role of the SDR, beyond establishing a new method of valuation and a higher interest rate. At Jamaica, very little indeed was agreed about the status of the U.S. dollar as a reserve currency. Several techniques had been suggested, including creation of a substitution account in the IMF where states could retire dollar reserves in exchange for SDRs. But this issue had lost much of its steam in the conditions of 1975-1976. The capacities of international organization to manage the monetary system were weakening rather than strengthening.

At the end of the 1970s there were signs of possible new departures in U.S. external policy, but regarding liquidity they proved fruitless. Renewed discussions of an SDR-dollar substitution account in 1979 and 1980 again failed to lead to agreement.[62] Heavier intervention in currency markets in the late 1970s proved to be a change in degree but not in kind.

Specifically, President Jimmy Carter announced a package of new measures to defend the dollar on 1 November

[62] See Treasury Under Secretary Anthony Solomon, address before the Alpbach European Forum, 27 August 1979 (Washington: U.S. Treasury); *New York Times*, 8 August 1979, p. D1; *Economist*, 1 September 1979, p. 72; Federal Reserve Bank of Chicago *International Letter*, 8 May 1980.

1978. These actions evidently resulted from pressures from traders and foreign states, as viewed through the Carter administration's basic policy outlook. The floating dollar, after strengthening during the mid-1970s, had begun a renewed decline. From 1975 to 1977, the American current account had swung from a huge surplus of $18 billion to a huge deficit of $14 billion, as the United States had accelerated out of the mid-seventies recession faster than other major countries. Accordingly, the dollar began to sink rapidly during the last quarter of 1977 (see Tables 9 and 10). The decline immediately generated an international political backlash, as American allies like West German Chan-

TABLE 9. U.S. TRADE AND CURRENT ACCOUNT
BALANCES, 1973-1981 (millions of dollars;
quarterly data seasonally adjusted)

	Trade Balance	Current Account Balance
1973	911	7,140
1974	−5,343	2,124
1975	9,047	18,280
1976	−9,306	4,384
1977	−30,873	−14,068
1978	−33,759	−14,259
1979	−29,469	−788
1980	−25,342	3,723
1978 I	−11,141	−6,173
II	−8,295	−4,102
III	−7,508	−3,166
IV	−6,815	−820
1979 I	−5,114	1,408
II	−8,070	−1,493
III	−7,060	1,099
IV	−9,225	−1,802
1980 I	−10,126	−2,095
II	−6,744	−545
III	−2,902	4,975
IV	−5,570	1,390
1981 I	−4,677	3,263
II	−6,910	1,142

SOURCES: U.S., *Economic Report of the President 1981*, Table B-99, and U.S. Department of Commerce, *Survey of Current Business*, December 1981.

cellor Schmidt and friends like King Khalid of Saudi Arabia complained loudly of the effects on them. Early in 1978, the U.S. stepped up its currency intervention. But Washington's private outlook held that Japan and West Germany should stimulate their home economies to promote international equilibrium, and that failing this, exchange rates would have to change.

Nevertheless, the Carter administration eventually agreed that currency trading was going too far, relative to underlying market conditions, and was generating unacceptable costs. During 1978, the current account deficit showed substantial improvement, and at the 1978 summit meeting in Bonn, Japan and West Germany agreed to expansionary measures. Yet the dollar continued to fall, exacerbating U.S. inflation. Inflation had quickened in 1977 and again in 1978, for several reasons, and Carter announced a new anti-inflation program on 24 October 1978. Included were new forms of incomes policy but no new measures of monetary restraint, which is what the financial communities preferred. Currency traders promptly began selling dollars heavily. In light of the improvement in the current account, a new energy program, and new action against inflation, Treasury Under Secretary Anthony M. Solomon judged that the markets were becoming "very psychologically disturbed." There were a few signs that suggested the possibility of "a nineteenth century kind of financial panic," as one banker put it. The selling spilled over to the New York stock market. While the Dow Jones average plunged, reports reached Washington that "second tier" central banks were joining the private traders' attack on the dollar. Finally, the dollar's exchange rate had probably sunk further than the administration believed necessary for payments equilibrium. One participant added, "We were worried that a bank might fail somewhere."[63] Transnational actors might

[63] *Washington Post*, 2 November 1978, pp. 1, 6; *Wall Street Journal*, 6 November 1978, p. 1; *New York Times*, 13 November 1978, p. D3; *Fortune*, 4 December 1978, pp. 40-43.

TABLE 10. U.S. DOLLAR EXCHANGE-RATE CHANGES, 1973-1981 (index numbers, March 1973 = 100)

	Effective Exchange Rate[a]	Real Effective Exchange Rate[b]
Pre-June 1970 parities	118.5	
Smithsonian central rates	107.0	
1972	106.5	111.0
1973	100.0	98.0
1974	101.3	95.2
1975	101.9	98.7
1976	104.8	100.7
1977	105.6	100.9
1978	99.1	96.5
1979	98.3	96.5
1980	98.2	98.3
September 1977	106.4	101.2
December 1977	102.9	99.3
March 1978	101.5	97.6
June 1978	100.3	97.6
September 1978	97.2	94.9
December 1978	97.5	96.1
March 1979	97.9	95.8
June 1979	99.1	97.2
September 1979	97.6	95.4
December 1979	98.7	97.5
March 1980	101.3	100.6
June 1980	96.2	96.1
September 1980	96.4	96.0
December 1980	99.9	100.8
March 1981	102.5	104.8
June 1981	109.3	111.9
September 1981	110.3	111.0
November 1981	107.6	109.0

[a] The index of the effective exchange rate is a measure of the dollar's trade-weighted average appreciation or depreciation vis-à-vis the currencies of 15 other major countries. The exchange rates used in the construction of this index are the average of daily noon spot exchange rates in New York for months shown. The trade weights used are based on 1976 bilateral trade in manufactures.

[b] The index of the real effective exchange rate is the index of the effective exchange rate adjusted for inflation differentials which are measured by wholesale prices of nonfood manufactures. Exchange rates and trade weights used in the construction of this index are the same as those used for the effective exchange rate index. Annual figures are averages of months.

SOURCES: "Effective Exchange Rates—Nominal and Real, January 1970-June 1981" (New York: Morgan Guaranty Trust Company, International Economics Department, 31 July 1981), and World Financial Markets (Morgan Guaranty), December 1981.

eventually respond to signs of underlying improvement, but in the interim the costs could be excessive.

In order to stop the "bandwagon," on 1 November the U.S. government pledged massive currency intervention if necessary to encourage counter-speculation. To support this pledge, it assembled an additional pool of $28 billion worth of foreign currencies and credit lines from diverse sources. U.S. sales of gold, resumed in May 1978, were accelerated sharply, and the Federal Reserve boosted the discount rate another full percentage point. Treasury Secretary Michael Blumenthal made clear that the U.S. was not pegging the dollar but was signaling that recent trends were clearly excessive.[64]

The November 1978 package was essentially another, though larger, instance of "last-ditch" intervention, supported in this case by an increase in domestic interest rates. The actions promptly stopped the slide, and by mid-1979 the dollar had climbed back nearly to its nominal external value of March 1973 (see Table 10). The Federal Reserve had repaid its entire foreign currency swap debt by April 1979.

If international monetary policy essentially held its course, domestic monetary policy did shift substantially in 1979. Though unemployment was below 6 percent, it was widely believed that a recession was beginning, and yet inflation was accelerating further as well. For the year as a whole (fourth quarter to fourth quarter), both consumer prices and finished-goods producer prices rose more than 12 percent. The comparable respective rates in 1976 had been 5 percent and 2.7 percent.[65] On the basis of these deteriorating domestic conditions alone—leaving aside complaints of foreign governments and the behavior of foreign ex-

[64] Federal Reserve Bank of Chicago *International Letter*, 10 November 1978; *Washington Post*, 2 November 1978, p. 4.

[65] *Economic Report of the President 1981*, p. 149. Two important elements in the inflation were increases in prices of imported and domestic oil.

change markets—there was reason to anticipate some change in American domestic economic policies.

But in what direction? On the plane of ideas, the cumulative effect of the experience of the 1960s and 1970s was leading many American economic analysts to doubt the adequacy of the Keynesian consensus. As noted in Chapter 2, there was no agreement on which approach would yield better results. But it was clear that the monetarist account of inflation was spreading, and the monetarist technique— keeping money-stock growth steady and relatively slow— was gaining adherents. Whatever the evidence might indicate, the monetarist idea had the advantages of being unambiguously associated with cultural norms of faith in private markets and distrust of government, and of offering a simple and easily grasped theory and prescription. It was not obvious that the monetarist idea would triumph in the United States, but given a high-inflation environment and years of strenuous advocacy by its adherents, it was the most obvious alternative candidate-theory.

On 6 October 1979, the Federal Reserve announced a major change in domestic monetary policy, in the direction of tighter money and credit conditions and freer interest rates. The rule of controlling monetary aggregates would be implemented with a new technique, replacing the emphasis on regulation of interest rates. The sources of this action have not been explored fully, but it does appear that transnational actors and foreign states at least precipitated it. At this writing, it does not seem, however, that the United States has shifted fundamentally toward setting domestic policy in response to external conditions.[66]

The U.S. current account continued to improve substantially in 1979, reaching near-equilibrium in the second and third quarters, despite a concurrent upsurge in world oil prices and U.S. oil imports. At the same time the payments

[66] An exaggerated statement appears in Gelvin Stevenson, "The International Forces Dictating U.S. Economic Policy," *Business Week*, 5 November 1979, pp. 134-136.

positions of Japan and West Germany were dramatically weakening. Relative American price performance was not deteriorating, since inflation abroad was accelerating to a greater extent than in the U.S.[67]

Even so, trader sentiment turned strongly against the dollar in the third quarter, pushing its average value down by 2 or 3 percentage points. Attention may have focused more on the oil prices, particular bilateral exchange rates, the U.S. political scene, and the future of American inflation. Other countries increased interest rates, while in the U.S. nominal interest rates remained below the inflation rate. The international differential occasioned moderate private capital outflows. Also market participants began to suspect that some countries might fight oil price increases by pushing their currencies up vis-à-vis the dollar.[68]

Finally, the American political scene may have encouraged the expectation that government actions would permit inflation to worsen and the dollar to fall again. Presidential elections were approaching. In the summer of 1979, President Carter had scheduled a major address on energy and then had abruptly canceled it. Soon afterward, he asked for his Cabinet's resignations, and he replaced Treasury Secretary Blumenthal with G. William Miller, who had been Chairman of the Federal Reserve. Some interpreted recent events as signs that America was rudderless and that the fight against inflation would not be rigorous. The appointment of Paul Volcker as the new Federal Reserve Chairman in August calmed some anxieties, but it was not enough.

These conditions merged into a new run on the dollar, especially in September, accompanied by speculation in gold that sometimes reached frenzy. At first, the U.S. intervened on a large scale to support the dollar; then, seeing that the

[67] Morgan Guaranty Trust Company, *World Financial Markets*, November 1979.

[68] *World Financial Markets*, November 1979; "Treasury and Federal Reserve Foreign Exchange Operations," *Federal Reserve Bulletin*, March 1980, pp. 190-193.

pressure was not easing, it withdrew to conserve resources. On 29 September, Secretary Miller and Chairman Volcker stopped in Hamburg to meet with West German Chancellor Schmidt and financial officials on their way to the IMF annual meeting in Belgrade. The American leaders sounded out their allies on possible support measures for the dollar, whose value against the mark had fallen 4 percent in the preceding two weeks. West German leaders were said to have rejected any further expansion of the swap lines, through which they had been lending deutsche marks to the U.S. for intervention. They did reportedly agree to allow the U.S. to issue more bonds in German money markets for this purpose. Most foreign bankers, like most U.S. bankers, wanted a tighter U.S. domestic monetary policy. The Americans went on to Belgrade, but soon after the meetings had begun, Volcker departed unexpectedly for Washington. In Belgrade, Sheik Mohamed Abalkhail, the Finance Minister of Saudi Arabia, warned that "a continuous erosion of our financial resources, through inflation and exchange depreciation," could lead Saudi Arabia to cut oil production.[69]

On 6 October, the Federal Reserve announced three measures designed to "assure better control over the expansion of money and bank credit, help curb speculative excesses in financial, foreign exchange and commodity markets and thereby serve to dampen inflationary forces."[70] The Board signaled its concerns by hiking the discount rate another full percentage point; it also imposed a new 8 percent marginal reserve requirement on banks' increases in "managed liabilities." And the System announced that it would henceforth put greater emphasis on targeting the supply of bank reserves in its open-market operations as

[69] *Federal Reserve Bulletin*, March 1980, pp. 190-193; *New York Times*, 17 August 1979, p. D1; 19 September, p. A1; 30 September, p. 13; 3 October, p. D1; 4 October, p. D1; 5 October, p. D9.

[70] *Federal Reserve Bulletin*, March 1980, pp. 193ff; see also *New York Times*, 8 October 1979, pp. A1, D1; 24 November 1979, p. 29.

the technique for regulating monetary growth. This meant that the Federal Reserve would allow the federal-funds interest rate and other interest rates to fluctuate more widely, which would be upward in the short run. Interest rates shot upward and oscillated widely in 1980 and 1981. The October 1979 shift did not involve new external policy measures.

Members of the Board explained that credit demand was proving to be stronger than they had expected. Some had become alarmed when spectacular price jumps in gold began to spill over into commodities in plentiful supply. Even though they were also concerned about pushing the economy into recession, speculation in commodity and financial markets at home and abroad had been interpreted as an urgent warning of instability, supporting a case for new operating techniques and greater restraint.[71]

Subsequent events confirmed that American domestic monetary policy remained, as before, substantially independent of external pressures. In late 1980, short-term money market rates in the United States surged from 10 percent up to 17 percent, and through much of 1981 they remained much above rates abroad.[72] American tight-money policy pulled up rates in other countries, and it pulled up the dollar as well. The shift of the current account into surplus also helped raise the dollar. From June 1980 to its peak in August 1981, the dollar's effective exchange rate rose 17 percentage points in nominal terms and 19 points in real terms. At that stage, the dollar was 6 points above the value set at the Smithsonian conference of 1971.[73]

Once again, U.S. domestic and international monetary policies triggered a fusillade of complaints from Western Europe and developing countries. The decline of European currencies forced their governments to tighten their own policies more than they thought was desirable for their

[71] *New York Times*, 8 October 1979, p. A1.
[72] *IMF Survey*, 4 May 1981 and 22 November 1981.
[73] *World Financial Markets*, November 1981, p. 10.

already weakened economies. Developing countries with large foreign debts and floating interest rates saw their interest bills soaring. The Bank for International Settlements in June 1981 criticized the policy mix of "severe monetary restraint not supported by appropriate government policies in other areas," leading to severe misalignment of exchange rates. Late in June, the heads of government of the European Community deplored the "devastating impact" of U.S. monetary policy on the EC economy and expressed determination to press the U.S. to change it.[74] But at a meeting of seven major nations in Ottawa in July, President Ronald Reagan and Treasury Secretary Donald Regan rejected all requests for changes in domestic policy for international reasons.

Despite these sharp exchange-rate movements and foreign-state pressures, the new Reagan administration decided on a floating exchange-rate policy of strict non-intervention. In response to the currency movements of 1978-1980, the Carter Treasury and the Federal Reserve had considerably increased U.S. intervention to try to moderate exchange-rate movements in either direction. On 4 May 1981 Treasury Under Secretary for Monetary Affairs Beryl W. Sprinkel, successor to Roosa, Deming, Volcker, and Solomon, announced to the Congress a policy of "minimalist" intervention, limited to countering exceptionally disorderly conditions in emergencies, such as the shooting of President Reagan that had occurred on 30 March. Asked to define the "minimalist" policy more precisely, Sprinkel replied that "it means that when I work in the office, the markets will take care of the exchange rate and not the Treasury and the Federal Reserve."[75] From 30 March through October 1981, the U.S. government did not enter the exchange markets at all.[76] Robert Roosa and other ob-

---

[74] Federal Reserve Bank of Chicago *International Letter*, 13 March 1981 and 17 July 1981.

[75] *New York Times*, 5 May 1981, p. D13.

[76] "Treasury and Federal Reserve Foreign Exchange Operations," *Fed-*

servers criticized the Reagan policy, and how long it would continue was not clear. But for the most part, U.S. international monetary policy departed from the decade of the 1970s still traveling the floating route chosen in 1973.

CONCLUSION

The Nixon shocks of 1971 were followed a year later by a third consequential change in U.S. international monetary policy. The result of the ensuing process was "the end of Bretton Woods." These American policy shifts—the return to initiating high-level reform negotiation and the proposal to negotiate another currency realignment—were not widely anticipated at the time. In this third case, the strongest influences on U.S. policy were long-term modifications in the interstate power structure, changes and continuities in high-level policy ideas, and the behavior of transnational financial actors.

As in the cases of 1965 and 1971, domestic political change was not a major influence. Domestic changes had occurred, but if anything they relaxed constraints on the elected political leadership, rather than pressing toward further devaluation or initiatives for negotiations. Similarly, an organization perspective makes little independent contribution to explaining this case. Little change had taken place in the organizational structure. The decision making process remained highly centralized. Senior officials differed on some aspects of policy and were agreed on others, but the differences seemed not closely related to agency missions. To the extent that American policy was mixed or compromised, the reasons were other than bureaucratically based bargaining. If senior officials with the same predispositions

---

eral *Reserve Bulletin*, September 1981, pp. 687-689; *New York Times*, 4 December 1981, p. D11. For a favorable American judgment on the record of the floating policy, see the October 1979 address by Under Secretary of State Richard N. Cooper, "Flexible Exchange Rates after 6 Years' Experience," Current Policy No. 114 (Washington: U.S. Department of State).

had faced the same foreign opposition to floating, but had been in charge of different U.S. agencies, policy would probably not have been much different.

One might have supposed that an international market perspective could explain the second devaluation, as it explained the first. However, the investigation raises much doubt as to whether a second devaluation would have taken place if it had only been for reasons identified by such a perspective. The balance-of-payments situation was highly ambiguous in late 1972. Conflicting evidence provided ample basis for contradictory prognoses. In such a situation, as is often true of international politics, behavior depended much on the conceptual framework policy makers and other actors imposed on the data.

Some elements of American behavior could have been anticipated by an international power analysis, but they would have been expected several years earlier. The United States, as a relatively invulnerable superpower now in deficit, would have been expected to continue high-level reform bargaining with its more dependent partners on behalf of rules ensuring greater adjustment burdens for surplus countries. The American initiative of 1972 was consistent, though belatedly, with such an analysis. So also was Washington's return to the strategy of compromise bargaining during the 1973 currency crises. But the actual oscillations of U.S. policy during these years, so influential in these monetary developments, are puzzling from this perspective. It does not explain why, in an ambiguous market situation, the United States chose a second devaluation so soon after the first. Nor does it make clear why other aspects of American action seemed to undermine confidence in the par-value regime that the 1972 plan was designed to improve.

The second devaluation as well as other related U.S. actions would not have been so surprising to an analyst of policy ideas. The oscillations of American monetary diplomacy from bargaining to unilateral coercion and back again were caused in part by the movement of different foreign-policy predispositions in and out of top Washington circles. In addition, a predilection for purer laissez-faire policies and freely floating exchange rates had spread further. An alternative leadership group less willing to rely on market forces to reshape the monetary system would have been more likely to press for early reform negotiations among states than was the Nixon administration. A school of thought more inclined toward active monetary management, like that in authority under President Johnson or President Roosevelt, would have been likely to infer from the same mixed 1973 facts that currency markets were calling for firmer management rather than have yielded to downward pressure. A different group would have been more likely to make public pledges to support new rates, or to act to do so, or at least to avoid signaling that such support would be withheld. It would have been less eager to dismantle price controls and capital controls. Policy responses were shaped not only by these general predispositions but also by the specific diagnosis that the dollar in 1973 remained overvalued, a diagnosis shared within the U.S. government and elsewhere but disputed by many others.

Finally, the impetus for the second realignment came from nervous transnational currency traders, who both responded to government actions and influenced them. Until this time, these traders had behaved mainly in response to fundamental economic indicators, as would be expected from a market perspective. In the circumstances of early 1973, however, the fundamental indicators were mixed. Equally significant, governments were stalemated regarding international rules that would assure adjustment of payments imbalances. Meanwhile, governments gave ad hoc signals that they might yield under pressure. In these circumstances traders' expectations sometimes diverged from long-run fundamentals. The effect of state policies depended on how they affected these transnational actors' expectations and behavior. The converse was also true. In the event, the reciprocal process of interaction led to heavy assaults on the dollar. When some traders began to move, others who did not consider the dollar overvalued were nevertheless drawn into the wave in order to protect themselves. If traders had acted more on the basis of long-run expectations, there might have been no pressure for a second devaluation. Governments perceived that a further devaluation would quiet this disorder. That proved to be the second miscalculation of the period, this time in relations with transnational actors rather than in relations with states. The effect was further to disturb confidence, and the response was still heavier assaults on central banks. Thus, at the end of this sequence of moves, officials and traders had backed into the floating exchange rates that few of them had sought.

6

Conclusions: Markets, Power, and Ideas

ON three occasions during the 1960s and 1970s, the United States changed its international monetary policies in ways that decisively altered the global monetary system. Judging from this period, the most powerful sources of change in American foreign monetary policy are international market conditions, the interstate military and economic power structure, and the circulation of policy ideas through Washington. An adequate explanation or forecast of U.S. policy content will require a combination of the three corresponding analytical perspectives. None of the more familiar approaches is adequate alone. Additionally, some influence, though clearly weaker, is felt on certain occasions from changing U.S. domestic political conditions and—still less—from government organization and internal bargaining. The working assumptions of several schools of analysis are called into question by this study.

A brief review of concrete conclusions will set the stage for more general conclusions. One of my general goals here has been to improve the conceptual tools needed for explaining foreign economic policy content. Available theories are notoriously weak and imprecise. Little progress has been made heretofore towards integrating international-level hypotheses with national-level ones. These American cases in the monetary sphere reveal some important remaining theoretical ambiguities, but they also illustrate useful distinctions and hypotheses that could be applied elsewhere. The cases also hint at links among the explanatory variables themselves. These links will be developed here as part of the conclusions.

DOMESTIC POLITICS

In order to make familiar concepts more useful in a disciplined analysis, it is necessary first to sharpen them in several respects. For instance, the notion of domestic politics is likely to be more useful for developing valid generalizations if we distinguish between domestic politics and domestic political motives or expectations. Changes in domestic politics may lead to changed perceptions on the part of political leaders and in turn to policy changes, in a regular pattern. If so, focusing only on political motives or perceptions may lead to spurious conclusions. Confounding the two will simply lead to confusion. Another helpful distinction is that between relatively unchanging domestic structures and more changeable elements of domestic politics. On this basis, Chapter 2 suggested two as yet imprecise hypotheses that may be applicable in electoral democracies. One holds that changes in mass opinion and political party strength, whether at elections or between them, will lead to party alternations and corresponding shifts in policy content. The other proposes a connection between changes in the mix of interest-group pressure and changes in policy content.

Changes and continuities in political party strength and in interest-group pressures were part of the background of U.S. external monetary policies during this era but affected policy probabilities only marginally. In two of the three cases, public pressure on the President was easing rather than increasing at the time of the policy change. These cases indicate that domestic politics is one of the weaker influences. As argued in Chapter 3, the shift to Democratic Control of the White House in 1961, and its continuation in 1965, made the policy change of 1965 somewhat more likely. A Republican administration would probably have been somewhat more inclined toward contraction at home or exchange-rate adjustment, and less predisposed toward creating international reserves or imposing international capital controls, than the Democrats were.

But beyond this, support for the familiar gold-dollar standard and fixed exchange rates was widespread among both
parties' elites. Leading Republicans joined Democrats in
advocating the creation of new reserves. At the level of
mass opinion, there was relatively little sign of an increasing
demand in 1964 and 1965 for change in foreign economic
policies generally, let alone for the creation of synthetic
reserves in particular. President Johnson, fresh from a
landslide election victory, was in fact more insulated from
public-opinion pressure at the time when the shift was ordered than before.

Similarly, the Republican return in 1969 may have contributed distantly to the likelihood of a suspension of dollar
defense. (This party-based interpretation is clouded by the
central part played by Democrat John Connally, and by the
surprising adoption of wage-price controls.) What was more
important, however, was that by 1970 public opinion had
turned against the administration out of dissatisfaction with
unemployment and inflation. This domestic shift would
have led a domestic-politics analyst to expect some new
policy perhaps like the 15 August *domestic* measures, even
if it would not have predicted the international monetary
shift.

In early 1973, mass opinion was again much less disturbed about the economy, and now President Nixon, too,
was enjoying greater flexibility after his own huge re-election victory. Thus, while the election may have made it
easier for the administration to release prices from control,
there is otherwise little reason to see the international monetary changes as responses to public clamor or election
results.

A second variant of domestic politics analysis emphasizes
the shifting mix of pressures from organized interest groups.
In none of these three cases did interest groups organize
public or even private campaigns to change or influence
U.S. international liquidity or exchange-rate policy. Labor
unions were not particularly active on behalf of reserve

creation, nor did bankers particularly oppose the SDR scheme. Ironically, neither groups that stood to gain from dollar depreciation nor those that would suffer from it spoke out, for or against. Banks and corporations did lobby against capital controls after they went into effect, particularly after 1968, and this opposition contributed to the relaxation of those controls. Perhaps the longest-lasting shift in U.S. domestic politics regarding foreign economic policy during this period was the increase in interest-group activity on behalf of general import protection, beginning in 1967. On this count, however, a domestic politics perspective would have indicated a lasting change in trade, rather than monetary, policy—which failed to occur. In short, the strong influences originate elsewhere.

Here we have counterintuitive cases in which interested groups did not act on behalf of their supposed interests. What accounts for these cases? One ready explanation would be the esoteric nature of the subject of international monetary policy and ignorance on the part of group leaders. Put another way, the causal chains from "dollar devaluation" to "group welfare" are multiple and difficult for even specialists to weigh, contrary to simple assumptions about group interests. In contrast, group leaders more readily grasp the net consequences of raising and lowering trade barriers for their sectors, and they are therefore far more active on trade policy. A second, more subtle reason was that government leaders had for years conducted a campaign to identify support for the dollar with patriotism, creating a taboo against pressure to end dollar defense. In this light, thirdly, groups evidently regarded other tactics as more promising or cost-effective. But perhaps the reason for silence was not the subject matter. The relatively closed nature of the U.S. economy attenuated the actual connection between international monetary policy and group welfare. In structurally more open economies like West Germany, we might look for more widespread and intense

interest-group participation on international monetary issues.

These American cases also suggest causal links or at least
correlations among explanatory variables. For example, interest-group activity is itself affected by international market conditions. As U.S. trade balances declined in particular
industrial sectors, interest groups in those sectors mobilized
to demand protection. Political party differences are associated with policy predispositions on economic issues.
Further research and theorizing might better establish these
links, the conditions under which they appear, and the ways
in which they affect policy content.

The focus here has been on external policy. When the
focus is instead on domestic macroeconomic policy, naturally one can expect a much larger role for domestic political conditions. But that is a subject requiring much study
in itself. Some work of this type is underway,[1] but surprisingly little has been established thus far.

ORGANIZATION AND INTERNAL BARGAINING

Changes in organization and internal bargaining had the
least effect of any of the five variables. Admittedly, the
period considered does not offer us an instance of the
strongest possible experiment, a radical change in government organization for international monetary affairs.
Nevertheless, changes were made, including creation of a
new coordinating mechanism, creation of a new White House
post, and the elevation of the Treasury Secretary to supra-

[1] See *The Political Economy of Inflation*, ed. Fred Hirsch and John H.
Goldthorpe (Cambridge, Mass.: Harvard University Press, 1978), esp.
chapters by Maier and Hirsch; Edward Tufte, *Political Control of the Econ-
omy* (Princeton: Princeton University Press, 1978); Douglas A. Hibbs, Jr.,
"Political Parties and Macroeconomic Policy," *American Political Science
Review* 71 (December 1977): 1467-1487; Peter A. Hall, "The Political
Dimensions of Economic Management: A Study of the Formulation and
Implementation of Macroeconomic Policy in Great Britain, 1970-1979"
(Ph.D. dissertation, Harvard, forthcoming).

Cabinet authority. The first two of these changes, in 1969 and 1971, respectively, had little effect on policy content. The increase in the authority of the Treasury Secretary gave greater force to the ideas of the incumbent, which varied during the period, and may also have increased the coherence of policy. But after other influences are considered, these organization changes seem to have had little independent effect.

An organization perspective also points to policy formation processes within a given structure, processes which tend to constrain policy change. These cases indicate that such chains can be broken by stresses in the international market situation or by a change of ideas at the top level of government. Policy makers' divergent stands varied less by organizational position than by substantive schools of thought. And while there were such differences, the major turning points during the 1960s and early 1970s were not compromise results of an internal bargain. Presidents got what they wanted.

The period from 1969 to 1971 was an exception to this conclusion. Proceeding from the premise of benign neglect, the American President evidently concluded that international monetary affairs needed little of his personal attention. With little active leadership from the top, U.S. middle-level officials responded to the deficit in various ways, producing a period of conflicting U.S. actions. This sequence corresponds to the expectations of a cybernetic model of the decision process. President Nixon dramatically ended this interlude in August 1971.

In focusing on the major turning points, we have not found much evidence that transgovernmental coordination or coalition-building was strong enough to influence U.S. policy. Coordination certainly took place among central bankers and within the Group of Ten, the IMF, and the OECD. This interaction gave rise to attitudes of professional camaraderie. Even occasional coalition-building in this field may have taken place, as in the fall of 1971. But when major new directions were determined, the decisions were made by the President and by senior officials whose attitudes were little affected by these networks. In all three cases, the U.S. officials who most clearly represented the viewpoints of foreign central banks were pushed aside. Transgovernmental relations may have greater effects in other issue areas, but here the main directions of U.S. policy can be understood quite well without this concept.

In pointing to the limits of organization analysis, these cases suggest some conditions that may determine the utility of such a perspective. These were instances in which policy choice would affect organizations' missions but not their very size or existence. In other cases, where the allocation of resources among agencies is in question, as for example in weapons procurement decisions, one may expect policy stands to vary more closely with agency location. Second, most bureaucratic actors were in a weak position to force the President to compromise because they lacked active support from outside the executive branch, from Congressional leaders or organized interest groups. But of course, if organizational behavior is largely a reflection of conditions outside, then the utility of an organizational perspective gives way to a broader domestic-politics approach.

Above all, we see that the utility of this type of analysis in the United States depends heavily on the ideas of the President.[2] If the President assigns low priority to an issue and relegates it or details of it to other leaders, as with the allocation of the military budget for fiscal year 1950, then those features may be determined by internal bargaining or uncoordinated agency behavior. President Nixon permitted this to happen to some extent with international monetary policy from 1969 to 1971, as with food policy and trade policy toward Latin America. But when a President chooses to exercise his authority, he can cut through bureaucratic politics in some crucial cases. A fuller recog-

[2] This confirms Robert J. Art, "Bureaucratic Politics and American Foreign Policy: A Critique," *Policy Sciences* 4 (1973): 467-490.

nition of the effects of Presidential beliefs and priorities would lead to a reinterpretation of supposed cases of "bureaucratic politics." Earlier interpretations have confused analysis by treating cognitive factors as part of organization. In general, the organization approach can be sharpened and strengthened by keeping it in perspective alongside alternative approaches.

INTERNATIONAL MARKET CONDITIONS

One of the three most powerful sources of change in U.S. international monetary policy is identified by the international market perspective described in Chapter 2. Its core claim is that when market conditions change so as to make prevailing policy economically irrational, government tends to change policy by yielding and adopting a new policy more in conformity with market signals. This basic notion is in widespread popular use, and in its simplified form it can offer a powerful explanation. In the present cases, the perspective is important but not sufficient.

Conditions in foreign exchange markets and the U.S. balance of payments did exert a major influence on policy content, but American government behavior did not always respond as an international market perspective would expect. This study suggests that when market imbalance becomes extreme, the United States responds by yielding in the general direction indicated by market signals, to some extent. When market conditions are imbalanced but not extremely so, even the United States may resist market signals. The particular response depends on the predispositions of the leadership group. Market conditions may often be ambiguous enough to leave the observer with a disconcertingly wide range of likely policy responses.

During 1970 and 1971, the overall U.S. payments deficit became extreme, with the capital and current accounts reinforcing each other in the same direction. In 1971, the U.S. government swerved dramatically from defending the dollar to depreciating it, partly by means of going off gold. The international market perspective identifies the largest influence explaining this policy change. Apart from the most dramatic instance, however, the perspective is clearly inadequate. In 1963, the payments deficit, which had persisted for five years, took a further turn downward. The American response at that time was in a sense the opposite of what a market perspective would have predicted. Rather than yielding to market signals, the Kennedy and Johnson administrations turned to policies directly and indirectly discouraging capital outflows—that is, policies managing and overruling the market to a greater extent than before. The proposal to create a new international reserve asset was also hardly predictable from market signals. Policy makers sharing different policy predispositions, like those of the Nixon and Ford administrations, would probably have responded to the same situation in ways more in keeping with the expectations of the market perspective.

This approach alone is also inadequate for explaining the third case of policy change. In 1972 and 1973, the United States turned back from unilateralism to a multilateral reform initiative, and it devalued the dollar for a second time in a year. That the American balance of payments had dropped from surplus to deficit does explain why the United States had become dissatisfied with a monetary system placing few pressures on surplus countries to inititate adjustment. But market conditions do not explain the oscillations of U.S. monetary diplomacy from multilateral reform initiatives to coercive unilateralism and back again.

More generally, these cases highlight an ambiguity in the market perspective. Does liberalism in international economic arenas imply that a government under pressure will withdraw alone to a more passive laissez-faire stance toward markets, or that it will participate in active efforts to tighten interstate policy coordination and create or strengthen multilateral institutions? Further work may help dissolve this ambiguity, either within a market approach or by turning to others.

It is not clear that the second dollar devaluation would have occurred, either, if it had been only for international market conditions as traditionally conceived. Market signals during that period were mixed. On the basis of the economic "fundamentals," an analyst would probably have expected no further devaluation from the Smithsonian level. Nevertheless, on particular occasions foreign exchange traders put further heavy downward pressure on the dollar. After the Smithsonian meeting, the market situation entered a period of ambiguity. More than the market perspective, then, is needed to explain the second devaluation.

For this purpose, it was useful to supplement the market perspective with the concept of the independent transnational actor. The expectations and behavior of these actors were determined neither by underlying market conditions nor by governments. But they interacted critically with governments to produce the collapse of the adjustable-peg regime. If their confidence in the par-value regime had been greater, Bretton Woods might have been continued longer. The earlier cases, however, also reveal that this supplementary concept may sometimes be superfluous. In 1971 and before, transnational currency traders behaved quite predictably as "markets," never assaulting a currency whose payments had not been out of balance for some time. The notion of the transnational actor may be most useful in periods when governments' behavior or inaction has undermined confidence in long-term indicators of equilibrium.

The basic market hypothesis may also be contingent on several qualifying conditions other than the intellectual outlook of the official leadership. The present cases deal with an established policy that was the centerpiece of an international regime, involving international commitments by the system's superpower and commitments to states with which it also had military alliance relations. Policies less central to strong international regimes and less linked to security relations might prove more responsive to the pressure of market imbalance. These cases, secondly, deal with macropolicy. The exchange rate is the most important price of all for most economies, so that changes in exchange-rate policy will have deep structural implications for many sectors of an economy as well as for foreign military spending and sales. Moreover, the dollar was the world's single most important currency. Policies affecting a narrower domain might also yield more readily to market forces. Thirdly, technical features of financial policy inhibit advocates of change within the policy process. Premature disclosure or even discussion can be costly, for governments and private parties alike. Of course the need for secrecy is not unique to the financial field, but policy areas less sensitive to premature disclosure may be more flexible than these cases would suggest. (Other policy areas, on the other hand, may be more constrained by domestic politics than is the international monetary field, adding to the tendency to continue established policies until imbalances become extreme.) Finally, the United States had one of the most self-sufficient economies in the world. States whose economies are more heavily penetrated by international transactions simply have less capacity to resist the forces of world markets. Washington at least had a choice. The relative closedness of the American economy has effectively offset to some extent the presumption in favor of market forces built into the world views of many Americans. Policies in more open economies may be more responsive to international market changes.

These two decades of American experience suggest other links between market conditions and other explanatory variables. A country's balance of payments depends ultimately on the international security situation, so that a currency can be undermined by participation in a major war or other military policy change. Vietnam was an albatross for the U.S. dollar. Wars, for that matter, may simultaneously strengthen the payments positions of nonbelligerents, as illustrated by the cases of the United States during the Napoleonic wars and of Japan during World War I and the Vietnam war.

International financial markets are also shaped by earlier foreign economic policies and power. If international capital markets were more open and integrated by the 1970s, this was because of earlier policy decisions to open them. If private currency traders lacked confidence in the established regime in 1973, so that markets became chaotic, a major reason was the lag in official efforts to modify the rules to give assurance of prompt adjustment. Another reason was the series of statements and policy decisions made by various governments in response to currency turmoil during the late 1960s and early 1970s. In short, we see further evidence substantiating the well-known converse causal relation: power and policy shape market conditions. Disentangling these complex reciprocal relationships is an important challenge that is difficult if not impossible to meet by means of one or a small number of case studies. But given the state of our knowledge of policy formation, we advance when we at least pose the problem explicitly.

INTERNATIONAL SECURITY AND POWER STRUCTURE

Like the international market perspective, the security and power approach, taken alone, is necessary but insufficient, judging from this evidence. The core contention of this perspective is that shifts in the international distribution of power and the behavior of foreign states in the struggle for relative influence tend to produce major changes in foreign economic policies. This perspective, when refined, helps explain why the United States departed from previous policy on several occasions; but like the market approach, it is insufficient for explaining the choice of new policy.

Several variants of this perspective should be distinguished. One dwells on the global military structure and maintains, for instance, that in some circumstances a decline in a state's security or relative military power leads to realignments of foreign economic policy to strengthen alliances or weaken opposing alliances. During the era of the 1960s and early 1970s, we lack a decisive experiment or structural change to test this version of the perspective. As is pointed out in Chapter 4, the global military distribution remained essentially constant and bipolar throughout this period. Within that structure, however, the Soviet Union was closing the strategic gap between it and the United States, a move that would have implied an American foreign economic policy at least as solicitous of her allies in the 1970s as before. Thus, this variant would have led the analyst to expect either no change in U.S. foreign economic policy or a shift in the direction opposite from that observed. Broadly speaking, this was a period during which U.S. international monetary policy and security conditions seemed mostly disengaged from each other, with the exception of the Smithsonian settlement. This is not to deny that a major structural change—particularly a decline sufficient to leave the United States in a position comparable to that of France relative to Germany in the 1890s or Britain vis-à-vis Germany during the 1930s—might have re-engaged the two.

That the distribution of military capabilities remained basically unchanged was also significant for relations among the allied capitalist states. Western Europe and Japan remained dependent on the United States for security, giving Washington an additional basis for unequal influence over their policies.

A second variant of a power perspective emphasizes shifts in the overall *economic* power structure. This "hegemony" hypothesis maintains that as a system shifts away from dominance by a single state, the erstwhile leading country at some point abandons leadership policies. After the Bretton Woods conference, the diffusion in the structure of the global capitalist system and interstate rivalries did have effects on U.S. international monetary policy, even if smaller effects than is sometimes supposed. The gradual erosion of the superpower's margin of superiority was already apparent by the early 1960s. Economic recoveries and payments surpluses gave America's partners in Western Europe a stronger position from which to resist early Kennedy policies, and thus the economic power structure helps explain why the U.S. abandoned its earlier policy in 1963-65. The structural position of the U.S. also helps explain why the new policy employed a bargaining initiative rather than a unilateral démarche.

Likewise, the gradual rise in the net capabilities of Japan and Europe, though hardly approaching those of the United States, helps explain why the United States abandoned prevailing policies in 1971—namely "benign neglect" and official convertibility—and again in 1972-1973—in that case, the unilateralist coercive strategy. The secondary financial powers were strong enough to resist simple dictation and did so, producing an interstate stalemate lasting until Washington indicated that it was prepared to lead and bargain over international monetary rights and obligations.

The decline of the narrowly monetary power of the U.S., as distinguished from its general economic capabilities, also makes some contribution in the case of 1971. The ratio of U.S. official reserves to foreign official claims was falling during 1970 and 1971, at least increasing the likelihood that convertibility would have been interrupted. But the ability to defend convertibility had been rising as recently as 1969, and even by 1971 it was still as strong as, say, that of England in 1913, other things taken as equal. That is, analytically distinguishing between monetary power in this sense and the payments deficit, the official liquidity ratio per se was still not obviously unmanageable. Moreover, this narrow measure neglects U.S. borrowing capacity and its general ability to influence dollar holders.

In each of the three cases, power analysis is inadequate for explaining the content of new policy. In 1965, the United

States still had the power to adopt any of several alternative courses of action. It could have shifted in the direction of exchange-rate flexibility rather than liquidity creation. It could have employed a passive or unilateral strategy rather than proposing a blueprint for multilateral bargaining and policy coordination. The new policy was not the one preferred by the rising financial powers—namely, tighter U.S. domestic monetary policy—and the proposal to create a rival to the dollar was certainly not what foreign monetary diplomats expected to be Washington's interpretation of American national interest.

In the late 1960s, the strongest expectation from an economic power perspective would have been that the U.S. would extend its high-level diplomatic campaign to reform the international monetary regime, now maneuvering its more dependent allies into accepting new rules that placed on surplus countries more of the responsibility for initiating adjustment. The evidence indicates that the superpower's decline was much less by 1971 than is sometimes supposed, particularly considering net influence in bilateral relations with Japan, West Germany, and other allies, and that these states had incentives to bargain cooperatively. Yet bargaining was not the policy course chosen in Washington. By mid-1971, the U.S. had available at least two strategies for ending the adjustment stalemate, one leaning toward unilateral coercion and the other toward negotiation and compromise. American officials were divided on whether to suspend convertibility in addition to the other measures contemplated. The American power decline (as distinguished from the market situation) was too gradual to account for the sharp reversals of 1971.

The return in 1972 to an initiative in multilateral bargaining was consistent with the power hypothesis, though belatedly so, as was the abandonment of the unilateralist coercive strategy during the currency crises in 1973. But to a power perspective, these startling oscillations in what for so long had been the staid American devotion to or-

thodoxy are puzzling. Nor did any notable power shift intervene during the 14 months after the Smithsonian meeting that would have led one to expect a further devaluation
so soon.

Another variant of the power perspective is the hypothesis that a lower level or a decline in competitiveness leads
to a more interventionist international economic policy. The
shift toward regulation of foreign exchange during the
1960s might appear to confirm the thesis, but it took place
before the United States had begun to register much of a
decline in its trade balance. Furthermore, the actual intervention was applied not to merchandise imports but to
capital outflows—not a policy designed to reduce the competitiveness of foreign industry. During the 1960s, the United
States further *liberalized* most of its industrial trade. Then,
during the 1970s, when a decline in competitiveness was
clearly evident, Washington first went through a phase of
greater intervention (wage and price controls and a short-
lived import surcharge), followed by sharp *liberalization* of
exchange rates and capital flows. (This was accompanied
by a trade policy of small tariff reductions combined with
selective protection for a few industries.) On the whole, this
experience casts doubt on the "competitiveness" variant of
the power perspective.

The events of this period point to some links between
the international power structure and other explanatory
variables. One of these is that a state's influence can be
affected by international market conditions, at least at the
margins. On the sectoral level, a state seeking to export
coffee, for example, is in a stronger bargaining position
vis-à-vis other states on a variety of issues when world coffee
demand exceeds supply than it is when the coffee market
is glutted, other things being equal. More generally, a payments surplus puts a state in a stronger position in relations
with other states than a payments deficit. Thus, in the early
1960s, the shift from a U.S. surplus to a deficit undermined
the country's influence somewhat. Other factors loom larger,

however, than changing market conditions. No one would maintain that a deficit could make an America into a Colombia. The more decisive power capabilities are national size, industrial and technological development, and self-sufficiency or openness—the more nearly constant factors.

In summary, these cases have provided occasions for rethinking familiar international power analysis. The most useful approach is to use this perspective together with others. A market perspective that disregarded the power structure would be superficial. On the other hand, defining "power" so broadly as to encompass payments deficits, for example, would dull the distinction between market conditions and power structures, and thereby waste a promising analytical tool.

At the same time it has been possible to integrate the international and national levels of analysis when addressing questions of state behavior. Power hypotheses originally formulated in reference to properties of international systems have been reformulated to explain state behavior. The three American monetary cases then invited a comparison of these structural influences with others at the national or subnational level.

These recent events show that the "declining hegemony" thesis inspired by the case of Britain in the 1920s and 1930s has some validity beyond that period. The United States experienced some decline during the postwar period, and in some respects it eventually trimmed its foreign monetary policy to fit its evolving power position. But a careful look at the evidence also raises an unresolved problem with this thesis. The theory stipulates that a large disparity between a single dominant state and all other states is necessary for stability and the provision of collective goods. But how large a disparity is needed? Conversely, how much of a decline is necessary to cause the dominant state to abandon "leadership" policies? In the case of Britain, the decline was large. Britain's share of world trade, which reached 25 percent during the 1860s, had fallen to 14 percent by 1912.

Meanwhile the ratio of foreign trade to national product had become very high.[3] An hypothesis generated by the British case would presumably hold that a decline of this degree is necessary for policy change. By contrast, the American decline after 1945 was much smaller. Only by stretching the British-based hypothesis regarding the matter of degree can one infer from power considerations that the United States should have abandoned the multilateral initiative by the early 1970s. Both sets of evidence can be accounted for in a more compelling manner by preserving the original hegemony thesis, such that a gradual, partial decline would not be considered sufficient to produce dramatic policy change. The decisive lapse in the American monetary initiative after 1968 and the sudden effort at coercion which followed would then be explained by a cognitive perspective rather than on power grounds.

The U.S. share or world reserves declined to a much greater degree than did general U.S. capabilities, and the United States did abandon convertibility. But an issue-structure hypothesis applied in this manner to the monetary area can be misleading. International monetary policies are inherently macropolicies, cutting across sectors and issue-areas. On theoretical grounds, one would expect monetary policies to reflect states' general strengths and vulnerabilities more than policies in other realms. Empirically as well, Germany and Japan, the states whose putative "reserve power" was rising and surpassing that of the U.S., did not act so as to make more active use of their apparently increased monetary power. Real American monetary power was declining by less than the U.S. share of world reserves. The U.S. capacity to defend convertibility and to influence the monetary policies of other states rested on the U.S. military position, the global size of the American market, and U.S. borrowing capacity, all relative to those of the other states, as well as on its reserves. Neither a general

[3] Simon Kuznets, *Modern Economic Growth: Rate, Structure, and Spread* (New Haven: Yale University Press, 1966), Tables 6.3 and 6.4.

power hypothesis nor a narrowly monetary one is adequate to explain why the U.S. went off gold and turned to coercion for a time. Some of the limitations on an issue-structure hypothesis identified in these cases would not apply, however, in other issue areas, such as trade policy for particular sectors or telecommunications policy. In the broadest terms, we may conclude what has been concluded many times before: Power and "interest" analysis, as important as it is, leaves objectives insufficiently specified.[4]

IDEAS

Finally, the third powerful source of change in American foreign monetary policy was the circulation of policy ideas in Washington. Judging from these events, Keynes was correct in declaring that "the power of vested interests is vastly exaggerated compared with the gradual encroachment of ideas." The common assumption among analysts of foreign economic policies that attention can focus solely on "interests," that intellectual variables do not need to be conceptualized and investigated carefully, is called into serious question. A cognitive approach is particularly useful in explaining the content of new policy.

Taken alone the cognitive perspective, too, is inadequate. To rely entirely on the phenomenological postulate that behavior has meaning only in the terms in which actors themselves understand it, or that behavior depends only on perceptions, would vastly exaggerate the range of likely policy responses. Such an approach would be continually surprised by changes that appear more predictable when policy is viewed through other frameworks.

On the other hand, this perspective rests on the assumption that "interests" do not fully or always determine ideas. The latter have origins that cannot be reduced to material developments, and ideas can have substantial and

[4] Cf. *Contemporary Theory in International Relations*, ed. Stanley Hoffmann (Englewood Cliffs, N.J.: Prentice-Hall, 1960), pp. 31-32.

independent effects. Here ideas refer to innovations in economics and political science, the spread of ideologies, the circulation of schools of thought through government by means of personnel turnover, and changes in the perceptions of specific situations and the salience of particular variables. The approach is not restricted to, though it does include, the intellectual idiosyncrasies of individual leaders. The perspective illuminates the scope for choice permitted by systemic and domestic circumstances. Max Weber, thinking on a broader scale, wrote in his later years: "Not ideas, but material and ideal interests directly govern man's conduct. Yet very frequently the 'world images' that have been created by 'ideas' have, like switchmen, determined the tracks along which action has been pushed by the dynamic of interests."[5] In parallel fashion, ideas have here been shown to be particularly important for explaining the direction of new policy.

Several decisive elements of U.S. policy that were inexplicable or anomalous from other perspectives can be explained readily with this one. During the early 1960s, a Triffinite diagnosis of international monetary problems was encroaching in Washington. It reached the office of the Treasury Secretary in April 1965 and was the strongest influence producing the new direction in U.S. policy. Intellectual innovation produced the notion of creating a new international reserve asset; the associated diagnosis began to persuade many in Washington, and to a large extent for this reason, it became the basis of U.S. policy. The reigning school of thought was predisposed to preserve the Bretton Woods regime even at considerable cost, and so a strategy of multilateral bargaining was used rather than one of unilateralism. The United States responded to downward market pressure on the dollar by resisting the market through

---

[5] Max Weber, *Gesammelte Aufsaetze zur Religionssoziologie*, Vol. I, p. 252, quoted in *From Max Weber: Essays in Sociology*, translated, edited, and with an introduction by H. H. Gerth and C. Wright Mills (New York: Oxford University Press, 1946), pp. 63-64.

capital controls, rather than executing or promoting a depreciation, partly because Kennedy and Johnson administration leaders did not accept the diagnosis that pointed to devaluation or floating. They were more suspicious of unhindered free market forces—in general and especially in the foreign exchange market—than were the officials who followed them in the 1970s.

During the early Nixon administration, the silence of high-level officials regarding international adjustment reform was anomalous for a power perspective. A major reason initially was the idea of "benign neglect," the strategy whereby Washington would remain passive, waiting for market conditions to force surplus countries to revalue their currencies against the dollar, without the American President having to make unpleasant concessions and without destroying the Bretton Woods regime. This notion proved to be one of the two clearest American political miscalculations during this era. Major surplus states, most notably Japan, declined to play their parts in this scenario. The strategy had failed to take sufficient account of the power diffusion and of the determination of foreign political leaders to avoid the appearance of making painful decisions without a U.S. contribution to a compromise solution.

An international market analysis can account for the U.S. policy of active depreciation in 1971. In this respect a cognitive perspective is not called for. By 1971, the payments situation had become extreme, and there was little dissent over the need for exchange-rate change. In general, intellectual influences are likely to be least independent, and therefore a cognitive perspective is likely to be most clearly spurious, when market conditions or other situational features are extreme.

However, neither a market nor a power approach is adequate for explaining the American choice in 1971 between a bargaining initiative and overt coercion. An observer monitoring the inflow of ideas would have noted a key change with the appointment of a Peter Peterson and especially of a John Connally as Treasury Secretary and presidential adviser at the end of 1970. The previous predispositions in favor of multinational monetary compromise diplomacy gave way to perceptions emphasizing foreign causes of American economic problems and an unwillingness of surplus countries to respond to anything short of overt U.S. coercion. The global structure and the domestic situation permitted scope for choice in foreign economic policy, and the President accepted this diagnosis rather than the alternatives. If a more conventional American school of thought had been dominant, U.S. policy probably would have taken a different course.

This oscillation away from traditional alliance diplomacy after 1968 and then back again in 1972 is also much more readily understandable from a cognitive perspective. After a year, the unilateralist view itself had been displaced at the top. By this time economic fundamentals and foreign exchange markets were sending mixed and confusing signals. The United States responded with a second devaluation partly because of the intellectual predispositions through which the signals were interpreted. Nixon's personnel changes in the 1970s also elevated the Friedman theory of flexible foreign exchange markets to the pinnacle where Triffinism had once held sway. Although this theory was not applied in a direct manner, it did help shape the interpretation of the market situation and thus helps explain some features of U.S. behavior that seemed inconsistent with the campaign to reform the established par-value regime. In addition, the Treasury's earlier diagnosis that the dollar remained overvalued was still influential inside the government in 1973, though not universally outside it. The expectation that a second devaluation unaccompanied by an American pledge to defend the new rate would calm the currency storms proved to be the second major miscalculation. If the difficulty in 1969 lay in anticipating the reactions of other states, in 1973 it lay in knowing what the transnational private actors' response would be. The immediate result was the final collapse of the par-value regime.

Leaders' beliefs and expectations about domestic politics were not often salient in these decisions. When they were, they conflicted with each other. In 1970 and 1971, Nixon, Connally, and their political advisers knew that the electorate wanted more jobs. Yet they also expected that going off gold and depreciating the dollar, policies which would create more jobs, would entail domestic political costs as well. With respect to this policy option, as with other economic policy instruments, domestic political calculations partially or fully offset each other.

One consequence of considering a cognitive perspective jointly with other modes of analysis is that it forces a rethinking of these other approaches. In the area of military power analysis, Thomas Schelling and Albert Wohlstetter provoked such a reconceptualization in the late 1950s. Previously, it had been assumed that if country A built a larger and stronger weapons arsenal than country B, country B would probably not launch an attack on A. These theorists, by directly analyzing the *expectations* of B under different technologies, derived the opposite conclusion in some circumstances.

To a less dramatic extent here, separating intellectual variables from others permits a clearer view of the strengths of those others in the shaping of foreign economic policies. Commentators often attribute government policies to "politics" in an ad hoc manner, confounding variables that are not perfectly covariant and obscuring possible objective patterns. If instead the analyst distinguishes between, say, shifts in mass opinion outside the government and shifts in domestic political motives within, it becomes possible to see more clearly the links between domestic politics (as defined here) and policy. Similarly, once the spread of substantive ideas is considered a potential influence in its own right, then it can be seen more clearly that bureaucratic politics analysis has often confused organization with substantive ideas. The two can vary independently, with different practical consequences.

Conventional market analysis provides another example. Some economists may be tempted to find in objective conditions a convincing explanation for why a government was "forced" to take an action, since to act otherwise would have seemed irrational to these observers. But very often other economists, observing the same market conditions, draw different conclusions as to what would have been rational. Once it is emphasized that economists, too, have varying intellectual predispositions and values, and that policy may be sensitive to such differences, then one can begin to isolate better the degree to which objective market conditions themselves constrain policy probabilities.

Not all policy analysis will be based on detailed evidence about the thinking of senior officials. But any analysis will be improved if a cognitive perspective is employed at least as part of the conceptual formulation. Even interpretations not based on direct evidence about the thinking of senior officials are likely to be more persuasive if the hypothesis of changing ideas is at least entertained as a distinct alternative.

THE DYNAMICS OF POLICY LEARNING

A cognitive perspective can also have a dynamic component. These American monetary experiences add to our knowledge of how ideas change, of how policy learning takes place. By "policy learning" I mean the acquisition of new concepts, the accumulation of new information, changes in beliefs, and changes in attitudes toward a policy measure or other object. Use of the term "learning" is not meant to imply that afterward, knowledge is necessarily more valid or accurate than it was before. Clearly, one can learn new but invalid ideas. Also the concept refers to cognitive change rather than change in behavior. It may be applied to officials only or to wider publics as well.

Keynes has misled us in one respect. New ideas typically do not "encroach" gradually, but rather in a lumpy, jerky manner. In the first place, intellectual creativity or innovation is an unpredictable process, and one that does not always move at a steady pace. Furthermore, the spread of new concepts, beliefs, and attitudes from their originators to (other) policymakers is often resisted for months or years, until some dramatic public event leads first to a policy change. This change may be influenced by prior or new ideas, but it often is not the result of the adoption and deliberate application of a full-blown academic theory. Then, in this pattern, the combination of dramatic events and policy change subsequently crystallizes a previously available outlook in the minds of officials and a wider public. There are reasons for thinking that this pattern of resistance and change may be repeated in the future.

An alternative dynamic model of the policy learning process is what John Steinbruner calls "causal learning," a part of his rational or analytic theory of decision.

> Perhaps the central characteristic of the analytic decision maker is the construction of careful, explicit, disaggregated calculations of the possible results of his actions. By the assumptions of [this] paradigm, the analytic decision maker constructs a model of the causal forces controlling the environment in which he acts. As new information becomes available over time, it should be integrated into the working model and the critical causal assumptions of the model should be adjusted whenever the weight of evidence requires it.[6]

A causal learning process includes two forms of expansion of knowledge. As time passes after the policy maker forms an initial simple model, he successively adds to the model environmental phenomena that might affect the outcome in question but which had previously been excluded. He

[6] John Steinbruner, *The Cybernetic Theory of Decision: New Dimensions of Political Analysis* (Princeton: Princeton University Press, 1974), pp. 40-41.

focuses on previously ignored causes and unforeseen consequences. This process is labeled "lateral expansion." Causal learning also involves "upward expansion." As time passes and experience accumulates further, the policy maker takes into account an ever wider range of policy objectives or missions, some of which may conflict with each other. The analytic decision maker continually endeavors to reach a higher-order integration of the various objectives his government seeks. For example, a study in the early 1950s by the RAND Corporation was originally designed to address the question as to what overseas bases the U.S. Air Force should develop in order to solve logistical supply problems. But the study expanded upward from the aim of reducing the cost of delivered supplies to a broader focus on the cost of destroying a given Soviet target system. Higher-level value integration allowed the study to coordinate not only decisions on base procurement and location, but also other decisions including weapons procurement and force operations.[7]

Despite other examples that also fit this rational model, students of security policies have been more impressed with the evidence for a different model of policy learning. Steinbruner finds that U.S. leaders exhibited "constrained learning" rather than causal learning in the case of the NATO multilateral force in the early 1960s, and he maintains that this process is likely when policy makers face complex phenomena. A cognitive perspective assumes that any decision maker will approach a complex problem with pre-existing beliefs. The mind normally operates so as to incorporate new information in ways that will be consistent with prior conceptual categories and beliefs. To reconsider one's model of the environment with every turn of events requires an abnormal and costly effort. Given the ambiguity of the new, as well as the old, evidence, changing one's beliefs and policies at every stage could easily create self-defeating turmoil in the environment rather than an ever closer ap-

[7] Steinbruner, *Cybernetic Theory*, pp. 43-44.

proach to one's goals. Thus, the normal expectation would be learning in the sense only of selective bolstering of old ideas.

Evidence indicates that makers of security policy do learn new beliefs and do change attitudes in some circumstances, but that they tend to read history and their own experiences selectively. Statesmen pay more attention to more dramatic events than to less dramatic evidence. They are disproportionately impressed by the events of their own generation and personal experience. They glean lessons from history, but the process is not akin to the scientists' method. Instead, when thinking about a historical analogy,

> decision-makers usually fail to strip away from the past event those facets that depend on the ephemeral context. They often mistake things that are highly specific and situation-bound for more general characteristics because they assume that the most salient aspects of the results were caused by the most salient aspects of the preceding situation. . . . The search for causes is usually quick and oversimplified . . . and no careful attempts are made to make the comparisons that are necessary to render a judgment on the causal efficacy of the variables.[8]

In retrospect, learning has often been inappropriate, partly for reasons beyond the control of decision makers. Another reason, however, is that "people learn little from negative outcomes—aggression that does not occur, crises that are avoided, quiet compromises, and slow, peaceful transformations."[9]

Regarding foreign economic policy, learning has taken place, though through a jerky process in which policies and ideas influence each other in a complex manner that can be seen only dimly. One impetus to cognitive change by statesmen and broader publics is the creation of new in-

[8] Robert Jervis, *Perception and Misperception in International Politics* (Princeton: Princeton University Press, 1976), pp. 228-229.

[9] Jervis, *Perception and Misperception*, p. 235.

tellectual constructs as candidates ready to replace conventional wisdoms. Another might be the creation of organizations devoted to publicizing and promoting a new scheme, or a compaign conducted by individuals or the press. But in policy making, the weight of substantive predispositions is likely to discourage the learning of fundamentally new orientations. Anomalous evidence may appear but often it will not be taken as a compelling basis for modifying familiar ideas until market or political conditions become extreme, or some vivid event triggers a cognitive change. Thus, a third impetus to learning is, simply put, a major failure of past policy, or rather, extreme or accumulated evidence that can be readily interpreted as a consequence of past policy. A final impulse to attitude change, particularly for wider publics, may often be necessary—namely, the government's adoption of a new policy, which legitimates a new conventional wisdom.

This spasmodic process of policy learning is evident in the earlier, domestic case of deficit spending in the United States. The extremity of the Great Depression led the first Roosevelt administration to begin in late 1933 an urgent program of spending through the Civil Works Administration, intended to provide work relief to the jobless. The CWA program raised total spending sharply and created budget deficits. The extreme labor market imbalance led to policy changes, but not because Keynesian ideas had first been learned. Keynes had not yet published his path-breaking *General Theory of Employment, Interest, and Money* (1936). Roosevelt in 1933 fixed his own mind on the direct benefits of the program to the workers hired, and squelched arguments that spending would have indirect benefits for income and employment generally.

A fuller change in U.S. policy came in response to the sharp recession of 1937. From that disappointing experience many inferred that changes in the budget position had strong effects on the economy. Federal expenditures fell and revenues rose significantly, and thereafter the economy slumped sharply. The New Deal had tried a number of policies other than spending, and yet the country was sliding back into depression. The inadequacies of earlier policies pushed a reluctant Roosevelt toward accepting for the first time "spending for its own sake," or spending to generate purchasing power. This decision he made in the spring of 1938, when he proposed a major program of increased spending. Washington had a corps of "spenders" urging such programs, but their ideas were essentially pre-Keynesian. Keynes himself urged Roosevelt to increase spending, but the evidence indicates that this advice and the early efforts of Keynes's New World disciples had only marginal effects on policy in 1938. It was really only after the enormous spending of World War II that the U.S. government adopted the goal of maintaining full employment, and the American economics profession came to learn and accept Keynesian theory. It was still later that the wider public's attitude toward compensatory fiscal policy became more favorable.[10]

In the late 1950s and early 1960s, the revisionist Triffinite conception of the international monetary system spread in the United States. Many came to believe that there was an inherent contradiction between maintaining confidence in the U.S. dollar and continuing to rely on national currencies for increases in international liquidity. This instance of learning does not exactly fit the general pattern of resistance, dramatic failure, and change. Triffin's ideas began to spread fairly steadily after he published them, despite the lack of a sharp traumatic event. But the exception may prove the rule. The cause was weaker, and so was the effect. Prevailing policy began to stumble on small but significant signs of trouble, and the new idea spread but probably not as widely as acceptance of Keynesian fiscal policy had earlier nor as widely as the idea of floating did later. President de Gaulle's striding into the monetary arena in early 1965 and

[10] Herbert Stein, *The Fiscal Revolution in America* (Chicago: University of Chicago Press, 1969).

taking away U.S. gold helped to trigger acceptance of the new policy idea on the part of its most prominent erstwhile opponents.

In the 1970s, American policy makers learned to love floating, or at least to accept it as the best available policy. (There was still much criticism of the dollar's decline, but often the critics' fire was directed at domestic more than external policy.) The process of cognitive change bears an interesting resemblance to the case of Keynesian fiscal policy. Before the 1970s, U.S. presidents and monetary statesmen believed that a policy of floating was conducive to disorder in international finance and commerce. Many also believed that, in the context of the United Nations and the Bretton Woods institutions, a switch to floating was tantamount to a return to interwar American isolationism. It is easy to see how the catastrophes following Weimar Germany's float and American isolationism after World War I could have discredited the idea of floating, particularly for the generation that first became politically aware during those events. Whether this learning was appropriate or not, by the 1950s it was established. As a "constrained learning" model would then have anticipated, many interpreted the payments imbalances of the 1960s in a way that did not require abandoning the established ideas. Friedman's theory was available as an alternative well before the 1970s, but it was generally ignored or resisted. Less extreme versions of the fundamental notion that price change will equilibrate a market were also resisted.

But then ideas changed, and not gradually. In 1971, several sudden and dramatic events occurred in international political-economic relations. The U.S. imbalance became extreme, and President Nixon and Secretary Connally changed policy, doing so in an unusually colorful, startling manner. The change was partly shaped by new ideas, but, as in the case of Roosevelt, it was not the result of the prior adoption of a full-blown alternative theory. Evidence of payments imbalances and currency crises that had before been set aside as anomalies accumulated and became extreme in 1971, and it was sufficient to extinguish the belief that the dollar's prevailing exchange rate could be defended successfully. Prior to 15 August 1971, however, the evidence did not lead many Americans or others to conclude that all pegged exchange rates or multilateral bargaining were unworkable, nor were many convinced that American difficulties were mainly caused by foreigners. The fact that Washington suddenly adopted the policies that it chose, as opposed to alternatives, profoundly influenced subsequent thinking among U.S. officials and wider publics. The payments evidence, the dramatic new policy, and the associated rhetoric from Washington combined to encourage a widespread new view that the United States was weaker and victimized, that a "Marshall Plan mentality" was no longer justified, and that foreigners were the cause of problems.

Further dramatic events in 1972 and 1973 pointed toward a further cognitive change. The belief that a floating policy would cause market disorder was replaced by the belief that policies of pegging exchange rates could themselves exacerbate instability. During those years, several governments continued to try to peg their currencies and to accomplish adjustments without altogether withdrawing from par values, and during that time currency markets became more and more disorderly. While not accepting the alternative theory in full, many Americans became more favorable to floating in these conditions. As in the 1940s, events outside the international monetary system subsequently intervened to lead to a more permanent acceptance of the new policy.

Calling attention to psychological influences on a policy sometimes seems to cast a color of disapproval across it. This negative connotation is a reflection of the way the approach is typically deployed rather than an inherent implication of the approach itself. In practice, commentators rarely invoke psychological influences to explain a policy of which they approve. Normally they are readily convinced that favored policies were compelled by the objective market or power situation. But in principle, of course, there is no reason why "good" policies should be any more independent of ideas or cognitive processes than "bad" policies.

I have tried to show that cognitive analysis can be important in explaining a policy regardless of one's own attitude toward the policy in question. To say that perceptions were shaped by predispositions or that choices were based on miscalculations is not necessarily to argue that policy makers were guilty of avoidable incompetence. Of course, sloppy searches for understanding, failures to examine preconceptions carefully, and hasty decisions are common enough in history; incompetence at that level is avoidable. But a substantial degree of cognitive consistency is functional and unavoidable, for policy makers and for human beings in every situation. Facing a complex situation, the best a policy maker can hope to do is to choose an appropriate framework for diagnosing the situation, to find the needed information, and after reaching a conclusion to submit it to scrutiny from the perspective of different values and beliefs. In my view, the United States during the period of this study was served by many monetary policy makers who were as able as could be hoped and who succeeded in avoiding much of what was avoidable. Problems may be due as much to deficiencies in the frameworks themselves, and to the values guiding policy, as to leaders' incompetence. We simply lack the ideal political-economic theories that would command consensus and permit smooth problem-solving.

It has not been my purpose here to generate prescriptions for action. But one implication is clear enough, an implication more directly for analysts than for actors. Much better knowledge is needed about international economic relations and particularly about how political actors are likely to respond to given policy measures. Knowledge of that sort is still quite primitive, partly because of lack of effort. Another implication is equally clear. While striving for parsimonious explanations, we must not relax our skepticism about the elegant but overly simple analysis. The strategy of confronting such an approach with its rivals is the best precaution. Simple-minded scribblers can be as dangerous as hasty leaders.

INDEX

RELATED BOOKS WRITTEN UNDER THE AUSPICES
OF THE CENTER FOR INTERNATIONAL AFFAIRS,
HARVARD UNIVERSITY

United States Manufacturing Investment in Brazil, by Lincoln Gordon and Engelbert L. Grommers, 1962. Harvard Business School.

The Economy of Cyprus, by A. J. Meyer, with Simos Vassiliou (sponsored jointly with the Center for Middle Eastern Studies), 1962. Harvard University Press.

Entrepreneurs of Lebanon, by Yusif A. Sayigh (sponsored jointly with the Center for Middle Eastern Studies), 1962. Harvard University Press.

The Dilemma of Mexico's Development, by Raymond Vernon, 1963. Harvard University Press.

Foreign Aid and Foreign Policy, by Edward S. Mason (sponsored jointly with the Council on Foreign Relations), 1964. Harper & Row.

Public Policy and Private Enterprise in Mexico, edited by Raymond Vernon, 1964. Harvard University Press.

Export Instability and Economic Development, by Alasdair I. MacBean. 1966. Harvard University Press.

Europe's Postwar Growth, by Charles P. Kindleberger, 1967. Harvard University Press.

Aid, Influence, and Foreign Policy, by Joan M. Nelson, 1968. The Macmillan Company.

The Brazilian Capital Goods Industry, 1929-1964, by Nathaniel H. Leff (sponsored jointly with the Center for Studies in Education and Development), 1968. Harvard University Press.

Economic Policy-Making and Development in Brazil, 1947-1964, by Nathaniel H. Leff, 1968. John Wiley & Sons.

Taxation and Development: Lessons from Colombian Experience, by Richard M. Bird, 1970. Harvard University Press.

The Kennedy Round in American Trade Policy: The Twilight of the GATT? by John W. Evans, 1971. Harvard University Press.

Korean Development: The Interplay of Politics and Economics, by David C. Cole and Princeton N. Lyman, 1971. Harvard University Press.

Sovereignty at Bay: The Multinational Spread of U.S. Enterprise, by Raymond Vernon, 1971. Basic Books.

Organizing the Transnational: The Experience with Transnational Enterprise in Advanced Technology, by M. S. Hochmuth, 1974. Sijthoff (Leiden).

Multinational Corporations and the Politics of Dependence: Copper in Chile, by Theodore Moran, 1974. Princeton University Press.

The Andean Group: A Case Study in Economic Integration among Developing Countries, by David Morawetz, 1974. M.I.T. Press.

Big Business and the State: Changing Relations in Western Europe, edited by Raymond Vernon, 1974. Harvard University Press.

Economic Policymaking in a Conflict Society: The Argentine Case, by Richard D. Mallon and Juan V. Sourrouille, 1975. Harvard University Press.

The Politics of International Monetary Reform—The Exchange Crisis, by Michael J. Brenner, 1976. Cornell University Press.

The Oil Crisis, edited by Raymond Vernon, 1976. W. W. Norton & Co.

The Arabs, Israelis, and Kissinger: A Secret History of American Diplomacy in the Middle East, by Edward R. F. Sheehan, 1976. Reader's Digest Press.

Perception and Misperception in International Politics, by Robert Jervis, 1976. Princeton University Press.

Power and Interdependence, by Robert O. Keohane and Joseph S. Nye, Jr., 1977. Little, Brown & Co.

Soldiers in Politics: Military Coups and Governments, by Eric Nordlinger, 1977. Prentice-Hall.

The Military and Politics in Modern Times: On Professionals, Praetorians, and Revolutionary Soldiers, by Amos Perlmutter, 1977. Yale University Press.

Money and Power: Banks and the World Monetary System, by Jonathan David Aronson, 1977. Sage Publications.

Bankers and Borders: The Case of the American Banks in Britain, by Janet Kelly, 1977. Ballinger Publishing Co.

Shattered Peace: The Origins of the Cold War and the National Security State, by Daniel Yergin, 1977. Houghton Mifflin.

Storm Over the Multinationals: The Real Issues, by Raymond Vernon, 1977. Harvard University Press.

Political Generations and Political Development, ed. Richard J. Samuels, 1977. Lexington Books.

Cuba: Order and Revolution, by Jorge I. Domínguez, 1978. Harvard University Press.

Defending the National Interest: Raw Materials Investments and American Foreign Policy, by Stephen D. Krasner, 1978. Princeton University Press.

Commodity Conflict: The Political Economy of International Commodity Negotiations, by L. N. Rangarajan, 1978. Cornell University Press and Croom Helm (London).

Israel: Embattled Ally, by Nadav Safran, 1978. Harvard University Press.

Access to Power: Political Participation by the Urban Poor in Developing Nations, by Joan M. Nelson, 1979. Princeton University Press.

The Quest for Self-Determination, by Dov Ronen, 1979. Yale University Press.

The Rational Peasant: The Political Economy of Rural Society in Vietnam, by Samuel L. Popkin. University of California Press.

Congress and the Politics of U.S. Foreign Economic Policy 1929-1976, by Robert Pastor, 1980. University of California Press.

The Collapse of Welfare Reform: Political Institutions. Policy and the Poor in Canada and the United States, by Christopher Leman, 1980. M.I.T. Press.

Insurrection or Loyalty: The Breakdown of the Spanish American Empire, by Jorge I. Domínguez, 1980. Harvard University Press.

Palestinian Society and Politics, by Joel S. Migdal et al., 1980. Princeton University Press.

Weak States in the International System, by Michael Handel, 1980. Frank Cass, London.

On the Autonomy of the Democratic State, by Eric Nordlinger, 1981. Harvard University Press.

American Politics: The Promise of Disharmony, by Samuel P. Huntington, 1981. Harvard University Press.

Bureaucrats and Politicians in Western Democracies, by Joel D. Aberbach et al., 1981. Harvard University Press.

Library of Congress Cataloging in Publication Data

Odell, John S., 1945-
    U.S. international monetary policy.

    Revision of thesis (Ph.D.)—University of
Wisconsin, 1976.
    Includes bibliographical references and index.
    1. International finance.   2.   Monetary policy—
United States.   3.   Devaluation of currency—United
States.   4.   United States—Foreign economic relations.
I. Title.   II.   Title: U.S. international monetary policy.
HG3881.027   1982   332.4'5'0973   82-47607
ISBN 0-691-07642-1
ISBN 0-691-02212-7 (pbk.)

Milton Keynes UK
Ingram Content Group UK Ltd.
UKHW021840180823
427121UK00006B/667